POLAR IMPERATIVE

POLAR

A HISTORY *of* ARCTIC
SOVEREIGNTY *in* NORTH AMERICA

IMPERATIVE

SHELAGH D. GRANT

DOUGLAS & McINTYRE
D&M PUBLISHERS INC.
Vancouver/Toronto/Berkeley

Douglas & McIntyre
An imprint of D&M Publishers Inc.
2323 Quebec Street, Suite 201
Vancouver BC Canada V5T 4S7
www.douglas-mcintyre.com

Cataloguing data available from Library and Archives Canada
ISBN 978-1-55365-418-6 (cloth)
ISBN 978-1-55365-806-1 (pbk.)
ISBN 978-1-55365-618-0 (ebook)

Editing by Jean Wilson
Cover photograph: *Bergy Bits under Cloudy Sky* © Corbis
Text printed on acid-free paper
Printed in Canada by Friesens
Distributed in the U.S. by Publishers Group West

We gratefully acknowledge the financial support of the Canada Council
for the Arts, the British Columbia Arts Council, the Province of British
Columbia through the Book Publishing Tax Credit and the Government of
Canada through the Canada Book Fund for our publishing activities.

For Jon,
my children and grandchildren

CONTENTS

· · · ·

MAPS

. . . .

PREFACE AND
ACKNOWLEDGEMENTS

.　.　.　.

INSPIRATION COMES unexpectedly and often in the strangest places. I always knew I would write this book but never quite understood why, until a visit in the summer of 2006 to the abandoned RCMP detachment at Dundas Harbour not far from the eastern entrance to the Northwest Passage.

Jon and I, along with our fourteen-year-old grandson, had just debarked from a Zodiac and climbed up a rocky incline. It was warm and sunny, the skies a vibrant azure blue and not an animal to be seen. When we reached the top of the hill, the sight before us was breathtaking: three tiny boxes set slightly apart on a vast landscape of green tundra, pebble beach and glistening waters that stretched endlessly to the horizon. Behind lay towering cliffs and nestled on the side, a white picket fence that I knew enclosed the graves of two police officers. The compelling beauty of the scene slowly gave way to one of incomprehension. How could three young men assisted by two Greenlandic Inuit families possibly protect Canadian sovereignty in this remote and barren land, which had never been occupied by Inuit and rarely, if ever, been visited by hunting parties? Even the whalers had long departed. With a small wooden skiff and rifles used for hunting, how could they do anything of greater significance than raising a flag on Beechey Island? Was it just symbolic? Perhaps a deterrent?

The Canadian plan to maintain sovereignty in the High Arctic was predicated on the legal requirement to show "effective occupation." But why and to what purpose were they carrying out such "administrative tasks" as operating a post office, taking a census and making regular reports on wildlife resources and routine sled patrols? The Greenlanders had supplied the dog teams and sleds. And we all know that the young policemen could not have survived without them. Was it some sort of "paper sovereignty" designed to fulfill the legal requirements?

Admittedly, more southerly detachments like Pond Inlet, Pangnirtung and Lake Harbour served nearby Inuit camps. But unlike the Danes in Greenland, the Canadian government made no attempt to provide them with an education or medical services, at least until they were shamed into doing so thirty-odd years later following reports by American airmen who served in the Canadian Arctic during World War II. Why was the United States and Danish treatment of their Inuit so different?

The rationale behind the establishment of the High Arctic police posts continued to haunt me. Was it simply a matter of national pride? Perhaps inspired by another country wanting the land? Or was it just the least costly means to maintain sovereignty—like cats marking their territory? These were hard questions and the answers lay in British, Canadian, American and Danish history.

Global warming has once again brought the Arctic and related sovereignty questions to the forefront of public attention. Yet there is something unsettling in the current discourse that at times resembles a hodgepodge of facts and opinions, akin to pieces of a patchwork quilt waiting to be incorporated into the finished product. It was time to put the pieces together, fill in the gaps and provide the context to complete the story. I now knew why I was writing the book and it was time to think "outside the box."

For the most part, major Canadian studies on Arctic sovereignty have tended to focus on legal interpretations and potential challenges, but with only a cursory review of circumpolar history. *Polar Imperative* takes a much different approach, initially by narrowing the parameters of the study to exclude the Subarctic, then adopting a comparative platform to broaden the scope by encompassing all of the North American Arctic, including Alaska and Greenland, and finally by extending back over thousands of years to identify circumstances and events that influenced changes in occupation or authority. Where pertinent, the inquiry touches on parallel situations in the European and Russian Arctic to establish a global context for changes taking place. This book also explores the "human dimension" to show how the vision and commitment of various individuals had a major impact on government actions. Only through understanding the history of all three Arctic countries can we fully comprehend the implications of the current situation.

My personal attraction to the Arctic began further south, with an enduring childhood love of the northern wilderness experienced first-hand through camping and canoeing. Inevitably my vision of "north" moved further north until academic research led me to the Arctic, my own personal *ultima Thule*. Thus it was as a student of history, rather than of political science or law, that my curiosity raised questions about Arctic sovereignty: who? when? why and where? Interest naturally broadened with travels across Arctic Canada, to Greenland, the Svalbard Islands and central Siberia, even to a Saami reindeer farm in northern Finland. In Greenland, I visited remote west coast fishing villages, research stations at Meistervig and Station Nord, as well as the U.S. air base at Thule.

Researching this book dominated much of my time for the last thirty years, beginning with a graduate thesis on Canada's northern policies during and after World War II. Subsequent research in Washington and London broadened the inquiry and led to the publication of *Sovereignty or Security? Government Policy in the Canadian North, 1939–1950*. My archival research continued, backwards and forwards of the original timeline, but still focussing on sovereignty-related issues.

Teaching in the Canadian Studies Program at Trent University inspired a more interdisciplinary and comparative approach to my inquiries, leading to a number of papers on circumpolar relationships and presentations at international conferences in Russian Siberia,

Scotland and Iceland. I also had first-hand experience in writing comparative history as co-editor and contributor for a collection of essays, *Federalism in Canada and Australia: Historical Perspectives 1920–88*. Two projects required further study of Inuit cultural history. The first examined the motivation and implications of the 1953 Inuit relocations to the High Arctic; the second took the form of another book in 2002 on a sovereignty-related incident—*Arctic Justice: On Trial for Murder, Pond Inlet, 1923*. Once the Inuktitut translation of my more general history *Pond Inlet—Mittimatalik*—was published, it was time to set out on my lifelong ambition and begin writing a comparative history of Arctic sovereignty.

Over the years, I amassed a large collection of photocopied archival documents on Arctic sovereignty issues dating from the 1870s through the 1960s, filed in fifty-nine three-ring binders, each with its own annotated finding aid. While labour-intensive and costly, it permitted easy verification of precise details years later. Considering the volume of secondary sources available, selecting the best was a formidable task. Final choices required a rigid litmus test of accuracy and applicability. Did the work reflect first-hand knowledge of events and issues? Did it reflect attitudes of the time, or was it a retrospective view influenced by more current opinions? Not surprisingly, many excellent works in recent years lacked precise details critical to writing a comparative history. Hence several outstanding works may not appear in the notes, but are highly recommended and referenced in the selected bibliography. Articles in newspapers and magazines were equally important to assess public opinion and are readily available on website archives.

Compared to my previous books, *Polar Imperative* was written for a more general audience, educated but not necessarily well-informed. This required making the narrative interesting, yet as straightforward as possible without compromising academic integrity. Notes are included for colleagues and their students, because there are a number of revisions to previous histories that were written when key documents were not yet available. Some academics, particularly political scientists, experts in international law, military historians and anthropologists, may find sections related to their respective discipline lacking detailed explanations and theory.

Most histories of the Canadian Arctic start with the British Admiralty expeditions, creating essentially a British/Canadian history with perceived American challenges arising before and after the turn of the twentieth century. By comparison, *Polar Imperative* travels further back in time, beginning long before humans roamed the planet to show how climate change affected Arctic plant and animal life 20 million years ago, then forward to the present. There is also more emphasis on Inuit history, their arrival in North America, their life in the colonial period, then bringing the story full circle to their success in regaining greater control over their homelands. In timeline and focus, I was influenced by two notable exceptions to the usual Canadian-centric Arctic histories: *The Arctic: A History* by Richard Vaughan and *The Last Imaginary Place: A Human History of the Arctic World* by Robert McGhee, both very highly recommended.

Writing this book took far longer than anticipated. Hopefully the passage of time will have made it even more valuable in understanding the historical context and patterns of continuity that lie behind current sovereignty issues in the North American Arctic.

THIS WORK would not have been possible without the generous assistance of so many individuals. Over the past thirty years, I have been particularly grateful for the assistance of Doug Whyte, recently retired from Library and Archives of Canada (LAC), who more than once helped locate the proverbial "needle in the haystack" in the volumes of archival records dealing with Canada's northern affairs. My thanks also to individuals at various institutions for their assistance in locating key photographs, maps and/or information: Ilene McKenna at LAC, Vincent Lalonde at the Canadian Museum of Civilization, Sandra Johnson at the Alaska State Library, Trisha Carleton at the Arctic Institute of North America, Elisabeth Ward at the Vikingaheimar in Iceland, Janice Millard at Trent University Archives, Jamie Owens at the Royal Geographical Society in London, Lucy Martin at the Scott Polar Institute in Cambridge, Gudrun Muller at the National

Portrait Gallery in London and Kate Melo at the New Bedford Whaling Museum.

Appreciation also goes to Oran R. Young, Mark Nuttall, Franklyn Griffiths, Robert McGhee, David Morrison and Georges-Hébert Germain, who granted permission to use lengthy quotations from their works; to Michael Cullen, who helped restore old photographs; and to David R. Gray, Carsten Egevang, John England, Martin Lipman, Georg Nyegaard, Richard Olsenius, John P. Smol, Sheila Watt-Cloutier, Chris Windeyer and the Inuit Circumpolar Council (ICC) for Greenland, for permission to use their photographs.

Special mention goes to two of my colleagues in history and Canadian Studies, Dale Standen and Bruce Hodgins, now professors emeriti at Trent University, who read most chapters in their early stages and gave much-needed encouragement. Other colleagues such as archaeologists Robert McGhee and Peter Schledermann, historian Jack Granatstein, political scientist Franklyn Griffiths and medieval historian Ivana Elbl kindly read specific chapters and offered their sage advice. Bob McGhee, especially, added substantively to my knowledge of Inuit archaeology. I am particularly indebted to Mary Simon, president of the Inuit Tapiriit Kanatami, and Aqqaluk Lynge, president of the ICC (Greenland), for their helpful advice and comments on the chapter "Arctic Oil and Aboriginal Rights."

Special thanks go to Scott McIntyre for convincing me that the story was worth writing and his patience when I missed deadlines owing to unforeseen circumstances, to Jean Wilson whose talents were indispensable in masterfully copy-editing the manuscript, to Eric Leinberger for the excellent maps and to the editors and staff at Douglas & McIntyre for bringing the book to publication.

Above all, my heartfelt gratitude goes to Jon, my lifeline to survival for the past fifty years, along with my family and friends for their patience and support as I attempted to put thirty years of research into a single volume of history.

Shelagh D. Grant

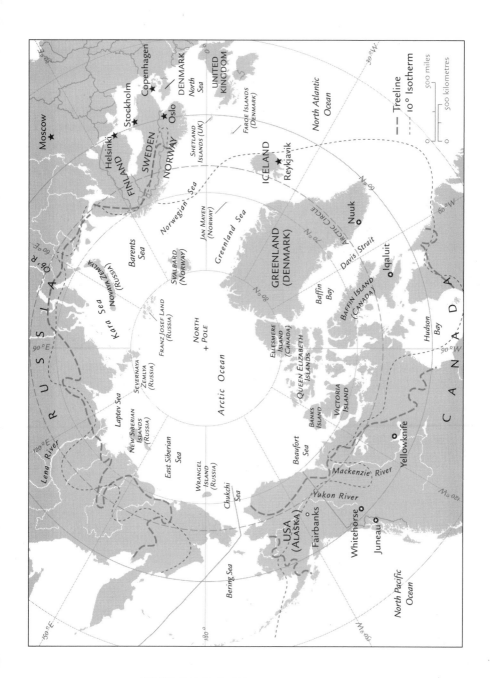

CIRCUMPOLAR VIEW OF THE ARCTIC, C2009

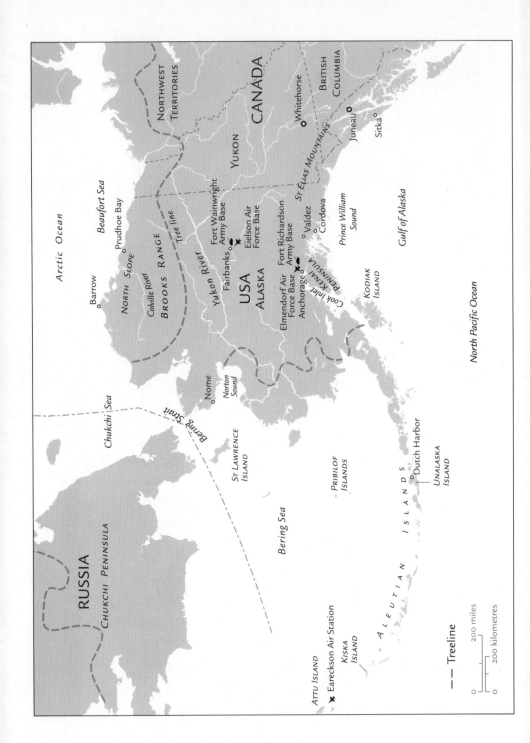

ALASKA, 2009

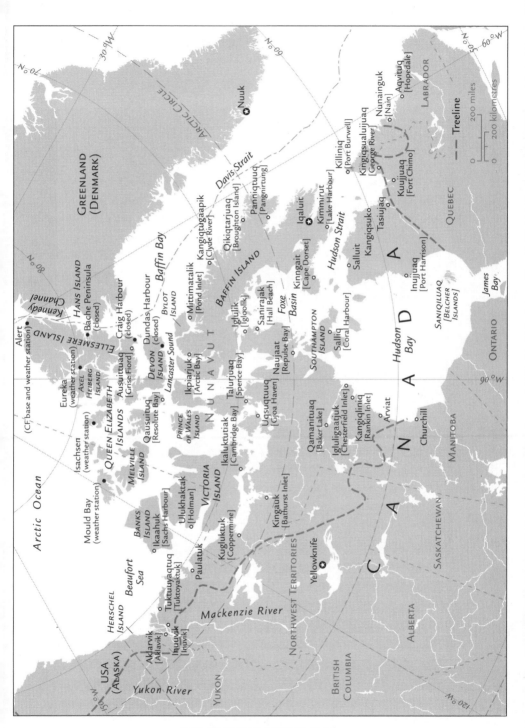

THE CANADIAN ARCTIC, 2009

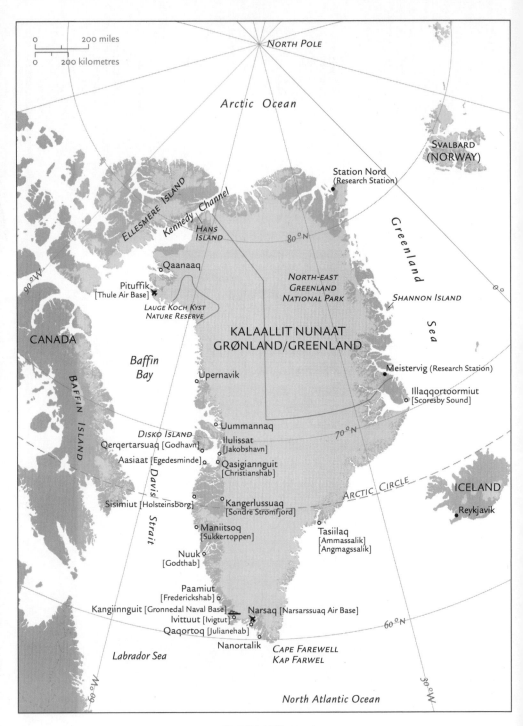

GREENLAND, 2009

PART I

SETTING THE STAGE

A COMPARATIVE history of this magnitude requires a road map to locate the geographical markers and define specific terms related to Arctic sovereignty. Equally important is the evolution of international law that established the guidelines for sovereign authority over land and seas.

With the first chapter having established the parameters of the inquiry, the second chapter begins with a brief look at climatic changes occurring long before humans roamed the planet, followed by a description of the first inhabitants of the North American Arctic: the Palaeo-Eskimos from Siberia. Then several millennia later, Norse families from Iceland settled in southern Greenland. This was followed by yet another eastward migration of indigenous people commonly referred to as Thule Culture, this time from Alaska and crossing the Canadian Arctic to reach Greenland around 1250 AD. Eventually the Palaeo-Eskimos and Viking settlers disappeared from North America, yet the Thule Inuit survived. The reasons why are still the subject of contentious debate.

The final chapter in this section deals with early explorations by Europeans and Russians, the exploitation of Arctic marine and fur resources and establishment of trading company monopolies by Denmark in western Greenland, by Britain in Hudson Bay and by Imperial Russia in Alaska. Initially only Russia and Denmark seemed interested in establishing permanent settlements that provided employment opportunities for the aboriginal people as well as religious and educational instruction—once again raising the question why.

(1)

DEFINING THE PARAMETERS

The Arctic is still a place that is seen primarily through the eyes
of outsiders, a territory known to the world from explorers' narratives
rather than from the writings, drawings and films of its own people.
To most southerners the Arctic remains what it was to their counterparts
centuries and perhaps even millennia ago: the ultimate other world.

ROBERT MCGHEE, 2005 [1]

.   .   .   .

HILE MOVIES, television and illustrated coffee-table books
have done much to bring more reality to southern knowledge
of the Arctic, many still cling to visions of a pristine, snow-
clad wilderness, sparsely inhabited by a race of people once known
as Eskimos. Yet the origins of that image can be traced back to a time
before Europeans had ever set foot in the polar regions of the New
World. Since the age of the classical Greek philosophers, the Arctic
has held a mysterious fascination for Western civilizations, which
often portrayed this mythical region with fanciful images that belied
reality. The word "Arctic" itself originated from the Greek word *arktos*
meaning "bear," and was used to describe the land and seas lying to
the north under the constellation Ursa Major, the Great Bear.

Although the term "Arctic" is circumpolar by definition, the focus
here is on the polar regions of North America—Alaska, the Canadian
Arctic and Greenland. The latter, as a former colony of Denmark, was
often omitted from discussions of North America but is included
here because its geographical location and history are closely tied to

Arctic Canada. On the other hand, because current sovereignty issues and those of the last century relate only to the Arctic, there are only minimal references to the Subarctic.

Scientists still debate the appropriate criteria to define the precise location of the Arctic. Initially the northern polar regions were described as the lands and seas above the Arctic Circle (66° 30´ N latitude), the most southerly point where the sun neither sets in summer nor rises in winter for at least twenty-four hours. In North America, however, this definition omits vast areas of treeless tundra located well south of the Arctic Circle, although having all the physical attributes of a polar landscape. Similar discrepancies arise when this definition is applied to Europe and Asia, where one finds forests and warmer climates north of the Arctic Circle.

Some scientists prefer to define the Arctic as the area north of 10°C July isotherm, or in lay terms, north of the region that has a mean July temperature of 10° centigrade. Geographers tend to favour boundaries set by the presence of continuous permafrost, as opposed to the discontinuous permafrost found in the Subarctic. If global warming continues, the boundaries set out in the last two definitions will change.

A more apt description of the Arctic would be those lands and waters lying north of the treeline—the boundary between the stunted coniferous forest and the northern tundra—to delineate the Arctic regions from the Subarctic taiga that lies between the treeline and the closed canopy forests to the south. Although also likely to be affected by climate change, the treeline definition is more appropriate to North America as it marks the boundary between Inuit traditional homelands and those occupied by northern Indians.[2]

At present, Arctic Canada comprises Nunavut and northerly portions of the Northwest Territories, Quebec and Labrador, as well as the northern coastal regions of the Yukon and Manitoba. The remainder of the North American Arctic stretches across the northern and northwestern shores of Alaska and includes the Aleutian Islands and all of Greenland.

The indigenous peoples of the North American Arctic are called by a variety of names. In Alaska, there are Aleuts, Yup'iks and Inupiat, the latter two having retained the original term "Eskimo" given by Europeans in the sixteenth century and thought to have derived from early explorers' interpretation of a Cree Indian name meaning "eaters of raw meat." In Arctic Canada they had rejected that name in preference to their own—i.e., Inuit, meaning simply "the people." In Greenland they were originally called Skraelings by early Norse settlers in 1000 AD, but today they are generally referred to as Greenlanders or Inuit, with those living in the far north calling themselves Inughuit.

THE MOST distinguishing characteristic of the Arctic is its climate— fiercely cold in the winter and surprisingly temperate during summer. On occasion the Subarctic is subject to even colder temperatures as it lacks the warming effect of the Arctic Ocean. Contrary to what one might expect, snowfall is heavier in the Subarctic, with depths decreasing as one moves northward to the windswept High Arctic, where the sun sits closest to the horizon, never setting in summer and never rising in winter. The long daylight hours in spring and summer have a profound effect on the environment, bringing the energy needed to sustain animal and plant life without melting the frozen ground. In this manner, ice and snow have shaped the northern landscape, with changes occurring only in times of dramatic temperature change.[3] The Great Ice Age and the Little Ice Age are two examples; the current warming trend is yet another.

The last major ice age was around 50,000 years ago, reaching its peak between 30,000 and 25,000 years ago, when most humans lived in more temperate zones. Scientists have shown that what is now Scandinavia and northern Canada were covered in sheets of ice that spread southward, burying parts of Europe and North America in roughly kilometre-deep ice. During the latter part of this period, it is thought that hunters from Asia may have crossed the land bridge created by the lower sea levels between Siberia and America to become the early ancestors of the Amerindians. Approximately

8,000 years ago, the land had returned to a state nearer the present and humans began moving slowly northward.[4]

The Little Ice Age, not to be confused with the Ice Age, is a term used for a cooling period known to have affected much of Europe between roughly 1250 and 1850 AD, but as Robert McGhee points out, "the environmental effects of climatic change varied greatly from one region to another, both in their extent and in the time period when they occurred."[5] In some parts of Arctic Canada, a cooling trend seems to have occurred in the fourteenth century, causing some Inuit to migrate to warmer climates. Polar explorers and whalers, on the other hand, experienced increasing difficulty advancing north through the icebound Davis Strait from the mid-seventeenth century to the beginning of the nineteenth century.

With the exception of the Danish colonization of Greenland in the 1700s, Europeans during the Victorian Age considered the Arctic unfit for year-round settlement by anyone other than indigenous peoples, fur traders and missionaries. Until the discovery of gold in the Klondike, the same held true for Americans, who had purchased Alaska in 1867, and the Russians who had controlled the territory before them.

While the new Dominion of Canada saw its Arctic as a natural extension of its boundaries, it too had no thoughts of establishing permanent settlements at any time in the near future. In the process of expansion, however, Canada by 1880 had become a large nation bounded by three oceans, but with scant population, no navy to protect adjacent waters and only a rudimentary infrastructure to govern the newly acquired lands.

There are two distinct images of the Arctic in the minds of most North Americans: one is largely imaginary, the other rooted in reality. Since the time of Pytheas the Greek's northern voyages around 320 BC, Europeans envisioned the polar regions as a freezing cold, pristine environment with snow-clad mountains, glaciers, frozen seas, majestic icebergs and polar bears. The Inuit and Eskimos of North America perceived—and still perceive—the Arctic as their homeland.

By the mid-nineteenth century the imaginary Arctic became even more magical thanks to romanticized literary and artistic renditions of British polar explorations. Eventually these images were absorbed into the psyche of Canadians, in particular anglophones, as an integral part of their heritage and identity. As a result, any perceived threat to Canada's Arctic sovereignty was met with public outrage. Danes and Americans also incorporated Arctic images into their identity, but more as part of a peripheral extension of their countries than as central to their national identities.

Although relatively few southern Canadians have travelled or lived in the Arctic, the romantic imagery is kept alive with the dramatic photographs in coffee-table books and spectacular settings for Arctic film documentaries. Recent representations have attempted to portray the realities of Inuit life, but the impression left in the minds of most southern Canadians is still one of "we and they." Yet partly because of the uniqueness of their culture and remoteness of the Arctic, Inuit in Canada have retained their separate identity in an increasingly multicultural nation, an identity that also enhances the image of the Arctic as a distinct entity from the rest of North America. Geography created a similar experience for Greenlanders.

With the region now more accessible, the general public is better informed, largely a result of recent publicity about the effect of global warming on Inuit culture and the environment. Although the secrecy that once surrounded the Arctic world is no longer, the mystique of imagined images lingers, as does confusion over various interpretations of international law pertaining to Arctic sovereignty.

THE CONCEPT of "sovereignty" is an underlying, yet integral, factor in the recent discourse by scholars of international law.[6] Although this historical overview of Arctic sovereignty does not pretend to explore inherent legal complexities, references throughout explain its evolution. The definitions used here have been simplified to emphasize basic concepts as they apply to various declarations of sovereign rights over Arctic lands and adjacent waters.

Many definitions of "sovereignty" have appeared over the last century, but only a few are relevant to the history of Arctic sovereignty. A generic definition of sovereignty as it relates to a nation-state would be having supreme and independent political authority over the land and its people. In ancient history, this was most often achieved by invasion and subjugation, with or without conflict. Such actions were considered an aspect of imperialism or empire-building—a quest for power—as in the case of Roman or Persian acquisition of new territories. In most cases the common underlying motive was the desire to acquire valuable resources, an objective that has persisted.

Descriptions by Pytheas the Greek, Irish monks and the Vikings contributed to early perceptions of the Arctic, with ancient maps revealing the transition from mythical images to slightly more accurate depictions. The existence of eleventh-century Norse settlements in Greenland appears to have been common knowledge among traders, but the information was not widely shared for fear of competition.

As trading and fishing in the North Atlantic increased, sovereignty questions initially arose over control of the high seas and only later over lands that might be used to build permanent whaling stations or fur-trading posts. Not until publication of Gerardus Mercator's map of the world in 1569 was there any indication that there might be northern sea routes connecting Europe to Asia, a concept that inspired northern European countries to search east and west for entrances to the passages.

In the nineteenth century, the most valuable resources found in the Arctic were whales, fish, furs and the ivory tusks of narwhals and walrus. Over the next century that list grew substantially to include coal, iron, lead, zinc and, in Greenland, cryolite that would eventually be used in the manufacture of aluminum. By the 1960s, the discovery of oil and gas added further value to the Arctic, as did the more recent discovery of diamonds and other minerals.

In the twenty-first century, rapidly melting sea ice in the Northwest Passage and the Northern Sea Route offers northern nations the potential for a faster, safer and more economical shipping route to Asia. Yet from the fifteenth century to the present, there is only one constant with regard to Arctic resources. Whether furs or ivory, oil or diamonds, for southerners it was—and still is—all about profits. For the Inuit, whose environment was inextricably tied to their cultural traditions, their resources now offer new hope for economic prosperity.

Some Old World explorers were drawn to the Arctic by curiosity and the thrill of adventure, but they still required financial support. To achieve their goals, they turned to the monarchs and merchants of the time, in much the same manner as today's lobbyists pressure governments and large corporations for subsidies. Both royalty and commercial enterprises expected a return on their investment, either a route through the Arctic to the Orient or, failing that, discovery of valuable resources. Only if there was the potential for considerable wealth to offset the cost of colonization was there any interest in acquiring title to the land.

By the nineteenth century, however, Arctic exploration had become a matter of national prestige, with the ultimate prize going to the United States in 1909 when Robert Peary allegedly planted the Stars and Stripes at the North Pole. No one at the time believed there was any monetary value attached to the feat. Yet this was not the case in 2007, when Russia claimed rights to the North Pole because of its potential for seabed mining on the undersea ridges adjacent to the Pole.

With one exception, the Arctic lands presently claimed by the U.S., Canada and Denmark are considered secure. Still outstanding is the dispute over ownership of Hans Island in Kennedy Channel, lying midway between Ellesmere Island and Greenland. A mere 1.3 square kilometres in size, it was once considered no more than a large pile of barren rocks. Today it offers a cheaper and safer location for oil-drilling rigs than the offshore waters.

More critical sovereignty disputes relate to foreign rights of transit in adjacent waters, particularly the Northwest Passage. Other issues under debate include the offshore boundary in the Beaufort Sea, submarine activity under the sea ice and rights to seabed mining beyond a nation's territorial waters and continental shelf.

In recent years the word "sovereignty" has taken on a variety of meanings. For purposes here, there are two basic definitions: *de jure* and *de facto*. The first—*de jure* sovereignty—is defined as supreme power or title over a specific territory by political or legal right recognized by other nations. Political scientist Franklyn Griffiths defines sovereignty as "the ability of the state to exercise recognized rights of exclusive jurisdiction within a territorially delimited space."[7]

According to international law as interpreted by Oppenheim in 1905, sovereign title might be claimed by various means: discovery, cession, accretion, subjugation, prescription or contiguity. If title was based on discovery alone it was considered "inchoate" (undeveloped or temporary) and could lapse if not followed within a reasonable time by "effective occupation." Other than permanent settlement, effective occupation could be achieved through acts by government such as the provision of basic services, administrative structures for governance and enforcement of a nation's laws and regulations.

In an attempt to lay claim to unexplored or uncharted lands, Canada introduced the Sector Principle in 1907, sometimes referred to as the Sector Theory, by declaring its western marine boundary as the extension of its mainland boundary, running along the longitudinal meridian to the North Pole. The boundary on the east was drawn midway between Greenland and the Arctic Islands. Although the Sector Theory was rejected by the U.S. and never officially proclaimed, Canadian maps published after 1910 used it to define the outer limits of the nation's boundaries. Russia and later the Soviet Union agreed with the concept of the Sector Theory, but other Arctic countries—Norway, Finland and Denmark—for the most part remained noncommittal. Current interpretation of international law by respected jurist Malcolm Shaw from the University of Leicester suggests that the Sector Principle is more a "political proposition" than a legal right, particularly with regard to the pack ice and permanent ice cover surrounding the North Pole.[8]

International law, like British common law, is not static but rather continually evolving as a result of court decisions and other forms of public consensus.[9] Basic knowledge of its application to Arctic sovereignty is critical to understanding the options available to governments in the past and how the criteria may change in the future.

As explained by political scientist Michael Byers, "The evolution of international law is a subject that has absorbed international lawyers for centuries, for, among other things, the way in which law develops and changes clearly determines the rules that are applicable today."[10]

In 1921 the Permanent International Court of Justice (PICJ) was set up in The Hague; it was succeeded in 1946 by the International Court of Justice (ICJ) with the same statute and jurisdiction. The purpose was to consolidate the international legal system and provide a means to settle disputes between states.[11] As specified in the statute, "a general practice accepted as law" is necessary to establish a principle of international customary law and must be accepted by a majority of states to be legally binding.[12]

The fact that international law is based on precedent and tacit agreement may explain modern nations' preference for negotiated bilateral or multilateral agreements rather than submission of a sovereignty dispute to the ICJ. A unilateral declaration of sovereignty must be followed by treaties or tacit recognition to become credible. Otherwise, it is considered ahead of the law. Negotiation and compromise are considered a major advancement in the modern world, compared to ancient and medieval times when countries resorted to wars to settle contested claims over lands or seas.

The term *"de facto* sovereignty" normally refers to having power "in fact" or in real terms, but usually without the political or legal right inherent in *de jure* sovereignty. This term is usually applied in the negative, as in the case of a loss of economic, political or military control over a specific area by a sovereign nation. The colloquial term "paper sovereignty" refers to a situation where two nations have signed an agreement officially recognizing one nation's sovereign rights over an area, even though the other nation may have *de facto* power that diminishes the sovereign nation's ability to exert full control. This situation occurred in northern Canada during World War II, when American military and civilians governed by U.S. laws outnumbered the Canadian population of the Yukon and Northwest Territories combined.

Another example occurred in the 1960s when foreign companies appeared to hold the majority of exploratory licences and leases for oil and gas fields in the Canadian Arctic. To affirm overall sovereign control over transportation and development, Canada unilaterally claimed the right of authority over the internal waters of the Archipelago, as well as its airspace, landfast ice and seabed. This and other claims were later validated by the United Nations Convention on the Law of the Sea (UNCLOS) upon ratification by a majority of states.[13]

The term "sovereignty" has been used in other instances, such as when applied to governance within a nation-state, as in the case of aboriginal rights to self-government or Quebec sovereignty within the Canadian nation. In both cases, the powers are specified and not a supreme power. Historian Kenneth Coates offered two additional definitions: "symbolic" and "developmental" sovereignty. The first refers to government actions designed to publicly assert a nation's claim, such as raising the flag and making a public declaration, whereas developmental sovereignty involves executing plans for settlement or government services.[14] These terms are helpful in describing the nature of various government actions used to support a nation's claims of sovereignty, but neither is recognized in official legal terminology. There are numerous other interpretations of the word "sovereignty" such as might be applied to culture or the environment, but only indirectly relevant here.[15]

ONE SIGNIFICANT term in discussion of the history of Arctic sovereignty is *terra nullius*, meaning uninhabited or "nobody's lands." At the time of discovery, Europeans referred to the lands of the New World as *terra nullius* in spite of sizable aboriginal populations, based on the argument that indigenous peoples were uncivilized because they were pagans and without a structured form of government, thus could not be considered rightful owners of their lands. This opinion was first advanced by Pope Alexander VI as head of the Roman Catholic Church, supported by the King of Spain, and readily accepted by other European countries laying claim to portions of the Americas. Yet the rationale differed in each country. Spain and, to a lesser degree, France believed that the object of advancing Christianity and "civilizing the savages" was sufficient justification for appropriation of indigenous lands. Initially the British used the Indians for their own benefit—to trap furs and help fight their wars—and only later considered how to acquire Indian lands without unnecessary bloodshed.[16]

The belief that Natives were savages and pagans who had no rights to their lands stemmed from the 1493 Papal Bulls of the Catholic Church following Spanish and Portuguese discoveries in the New World and were incorporated into subsequent interpretations of international law by Protestant countries which otherwise rejected the validity of Catholic decrees. Pope Paul III in 1537 attempted to moderate the abuses of European occupation in the New World when he decreed that Amerindians should not be treated as "dumb brutes" and should not "be deprived of their liberty or the possession of their property." Although repeated by Pope Urban VIII a century later, these instructions were never acknowledged by most monarchs. Hence, when European explorers in the 1500s and even the Russians in the 1700s left gifts for Native leaders signifying promises of protection, it was not an act of kindness but an indication of ownership to deter other nations which might challenge their claims of possession.[17]

For Catholic countries such as Spain and France, conversion of the "savages" to Christianity was central to their plans for colonization. English monarchs placed no such requirement in the monopoly charters granted to the Hudson's Bay Company, which covered most of the Arctic mainland of North America, a fact that gave rise to the fur traders' claim that the initials HBC stood for "Here Before Christ."

After the Reformation, Protestant countries ignored papal instructions and considered it acceptable to acquire newly discovered territories as long as they had not been previously claimed by another Christian monarch. At no time was any thought given by either Protestant or Catholic states to securing the consent of indigenous peoples to legitimatize discovery claims. Moreover, force was considered acceptable if they resisted subjugation.

In spite of intellectual discourse to the contrary, the English still held to the belief that New World indigenous peoples had not cultivated or made appropriate use of the land, so could not claim ownership to it. As explained by Olive Dickason, proprietary rights were set out in the laws of an organized state, whereas "the land of prestate people without such law was therefore legally vacant," or *vacuum domicilium*.[18]

In the Age of Discovery, European declarations of sovereignty over lands of the New World were usually accomplished by raising a flag and erecting a cross bearing an inscription or the nation's coat of arms, leaving behind buried tokens of possession such as coins, beads or metal objects, and returning home with objects such as sod, rocks and unusual animals from the new lands as evidence of their discovery. In 1576, for example, Martin Frobisher employed the usual form of symbolic possession in the Arctic by erecting stone cairns on top of high hills, sometimes accompanied by a flag, and clearly visible from the water. In addition to rocks and earth, Frobisher also returned home with an Inuk as further evidence of Queen Elizabeth's new possession.[19]

England, and later Great Britain, gave little thought to the matter of Inuit rights to their lands. Experiencing no resistance after claiming possession, it used land whenever it was needed and made no attempt to gain approval or provide compensation. Unfortunately this practice continued far too long, in spite of the Crown's recognition of limited Indian rights to their lands in the Royal Proclamation of 1763, which recognized their right to inhabit lands in unsettled British territory even though they possessed neither sovereignty over them nor the right to sell them to anyone but the Crown. This concept of limited or "usufructuary" title later became the basis of aboriginal land claims settlements in Canada.[20]

To encourage Indians to cede their lands to the Crown, treaties were negotiated that provided a cash payment upon signing, an annual annuity, fishing and hunting privileges, and reserved lands set aside for their sole use. Following Confederation, the Canadian government continued the practice by negotiating a series of numbered treaties under the jurisdiction of the 1869 Indian Act and its various extensions.

The policy of usufructuary rights to compensation was not supported by nineteenth-century jurists' interpretations of international law. Even in 1905, renowned English authority L.F.L. Oppenheim declared in his *Treatise* that a territory may be acquired through occupation "if inhabited by natives whose community is not considered as a State" even though "natives may live on a territory under a tribal organization." He argued that any agreement with indigenous peoples to cede their perceived rights "is usually neither understood nor appreciated by them" and that even if they did understand, "such agreements had only "a moral value."[21]

As a consequence Canadian Inuit were never asked to sign a treaty and were never represented under the Indian Act, in spite of a Supreme Court decision in April 1939 that "Eskimos were Indians" and thus should be considered wards of the federal government.[22] This decision was never followed up with legislation, with the result that another forty years passed before the Canadian government recognized Inuit rights to their homelands.

In fact, Canada was never in the forefront in recognizing Inuit rights to their lands. While the rights of Alaskan Eskimos were also ignored during the same period, in 1971 the Alaska Native Claims Settlement Act was passed to allow development of oil reserves on their lands. In Greenland pressure came from the Inuit themselves, who likely developed a broader view of the world after living under U.S. protection during World War II. Thus in 1978 Denmark granted "home rule" to Greenland, with the Inuit constituting 80 percent of the population. Twenty years later, the territory of Nunavut was finally carved out of Canada's Northwest Territories to give the majority Inuit population control over local issues such as education, health care and the environment.

LEGAL INTERPRETATIONS as they apply to Arctic sovereignty are still evolving and still based on accepted principles set down in international law. The law of nations, or international law as we know it today, is rooted in Roman law—the Laws of the Twelve Tables—dating back to 415 BC. Yet for those Teutonic and Nordic countries beyond Roman influence, "oral tribal rules" prevailed. After Christianity spread throughout Europe, the Catholic Church became accepted as the legitimate voice of knowledge and justice until the Reformation. According to Olive Dickason in *The Law of Nations and the New World*, international law in Europe evolved into a more secular form during the Age of Discovery, a period which also saw the rise of Protestantism and a shift of power from the Catholic Church to the monarchies.[23]

Closely paralleling evolution of the law of nations were the laws of the sea. Here the basic concepts of Roman law also prevailed, with *mare liberum* referring to high seas open to all nations and *mare clausum* or "a closed sea" under the authority of adjacent nations. In ancient Norway, royal sovereignty also applied to coastal waters, with the "median line" principle applied to marine boundaries between two countries. As a result, sea routes between Greenland, Norway and Russia were considered to be a *mare nostrum,* meaning "our seas," and under the protection of Norway and Russia, a concept similar to the Roman *mare clausum* applied to the Mediterranean.

Claiming a monopoly over the North Atlantic by the mid-thirteenth century, Norwegian kings banned foreign ships from trading north of Bergen, Norway's main port.[24] At that time, trade in Arctic goods such as furs and ivory was flourishing as a result of Greenland being incorporated into the Kingdom of Norway's "tax lands" or Crown lands. As demand for these items increased, ships from other European countries appeared on the scene and the Norwegian monarchy found it increasingly difficult to maintain its authority against major maritime powers like England and the Netherlands. As a result they negotiated special treaties in the late 1400s and early 1500s. Still tensions remained. In 1599, when the Danish/Norwegian Crown decided to uphold its claims by seizing several English ships, Queen Elizabeth I protested vigorously and invoked the law of nations in support of *mare liberum*.[25]

The law of nations was rudimentary in ancient times, as there was no means to enforce the principle of *mare liberum* without resorting to war. By the sixteenth century, economic and political factors forced transitional changes in laws applying to both land and seas. After gaining international support for the principle of "freedom on the high seas," countries like the Netherlands, France and Britain focussed on the "rights of innocent passage" through straits once claimed as territorial seas by adjacent nations.

Eventually, the laws of the sea collided with the law of nations as competition intensified to lay claim to lands in the New World. As explained by B.J. Theutenberg, a Swedish expert on international law, "Modern international law—the rules of law regulating behaviour between sovereign states, consisting of both international customs and treaties or agreements between states—took its present shape during the early seventeenth century [and] was closely connected to the law of the sea."[26]

When England launched its campaign to assert supremacy on the high seas to ensure free access to trade and fishing, other nations resisted and the rules invoked became more rigid. As a result, when foreign ships refused to salute a sovereign ship in its waters, they were attacked, captured and/or sunk, suggesting early on that a nation's "rights" were directly proportionate to its ability to enforce them.

European monarchs increasingly sought to establish permanent colonies to secure title to lands initially claimed by discovery. In the New World, however, these were inevitably influenced by the laws of the seas. Actions by English monarchs, in particular, followed a course of pragmatic self-interest rather than natural rights espoused by theologians and intellectuals of the time. Thus it was not surprising that King James I of England had asked jurist John Selden to codify international laws on the territorial seas, then later banned the work's publication for fear of provoking a dispute with Denmark.[27]

Selden's interpretation was based on English customary practice, rather than on "natural law" espoused by scholar Hugo Grotius of the Netherlands. And so began a series of treatises written by scholars defending the principles of either customary or natural laws. In time, customary law emerged as the more universally accepted theory in international law and would be tested against public acceptance, treaties and court decisions.[28]

Likely for pragmatic reasons, the requirement of a permanent settlement to protect a discovery claim did not appear in a written document until the 1884–85 Berlin Conference on Africa, which decreed that a discovery claim to lands on that continent would be valid only if followed in reasonable time by "effective occupation." Otherwise, such a claim would be "inchoate" or temporary, and thus vulnerable to challenges by other nations. This statement is significant as it provided the basis for future interpretations of Arctic sovereignty.

The decision whether to establish permanent settlements was also governed by pragmatism. If colonization was feasible, newly claimed lands were settled as soon as possible, as occurred throughout central and southern areas of North America. With the exception of the Danes and Norwegians, Europeans viewed the Arctic as inhospitable and unfit for agricultural settlement.

Considering such regions of value only for commercial trade, England and Russia established fur-trade posts to secure their discovery claims. The Netherlands, however, failed in its attempt to assert a trade monopoly over portions of Greenland when challenged by Denmark, largely because the Dutch traded from their ships and made no effort to establish onshore stations.

The 1800s witnessed a major shift in sovereign authority in the North American Arctic, beginning with the U.S. purchase of Alaska from Russia, followed by Canada's purchase of land rights held by the Hudson's Bay Company and finally Britain's transfer to Canada of its discovery claims to the Arctic Islands. At the end of the Napoleonic Wars, Denmark was no longer tied to Norway, but retained control of its Greenland colonies.

At the turn of the twentieth century, William Edward Hall (1835–94) was considered to be the leading expert in England after publication in 1880 of his *Treatise on International Law*.[29] His sudden death in 1894 left a temporary vacuum in British legal expertise on the subject, one soon filled by Lassa Francis Lawrence Oppenheim (1858–1919), a German-born, British legal scholar and professor of international law. His two-volume *International Law: A Treatise* published in 1905–6 gained immediate acclaim and was recognized for more than seven decades as the standard reference on international law.[30] A comparison of the interpretations by Hall and those by Oppenheim partly explains the change in Canada's policy on Arctic sovereignty after the Great War.

Hall's interpretation described how formal annexation or acts of possession could protect a discovery claim or inchoate title from lapsing: "An inchoate title acts as a temporary bar to occupation by another state, but it must either be converted within a reasonable time by planting settlements or military posts, or it must at least be kept alive by repeated local acts showing an intention of continual claim."[31] Thus repeated "acts of possession" such as raising the flag and making proclamations, as occurred with Canadian government expeditions from 1897 to 1911, seemed adequate to keep alive British discovery claims until physical settlements or other administrative acts were established.

Oppenheim's interpretation, however, did not accept this option, causing Canadian officials to consider other actions to protect their title to the Arctic Islands. Both Oppenheim and Hall argued that discovery claims alone were not sufficient to maintain title to uninhabited lands and must be followed within reasonable time by some form of effective occupation. But Oppenheim went further, arguing that this could be accomplished only by actual settlement accompanied by administrative acts. Otherwise acts of possession by themselves constituted "fictitious occupation only, unless there is left on the territory a settlement which is able to keep up the authority of the flag."

> After having, in the aforementioned way, taken possession of a territory, the possessor must establish some kind of administration thereon which shows that the territory is really governed by the new possessor. If within a reasonable time after the act of taking possession, the possessor does not establish some responsible authority which exercised governing functions, there is then no effective occupation, since in fact no sovereignty of a State is exercised over the territory.[32]

Oppenheim was firm on the question of "effective" versus "fictitious" occupation. In addition, he argued that "occupation may only be accomplished by an act of a state, or performed in the service of a state, or subsequently acknowledged by a state."[33]

Increasingly, governments began to rely more on "prescription," as in treaties or bilateral agreements, to resolve various disputes, rather than submitting a case to the Permanent International Court of Justice. Since then, there have been other interpretations by legal scholars, some agreeing with Oppenheim, others more critical of his interpretations depending on their bias. Yet his treatise has withstood the passage of time, as evident in subsequent treaties and decisions of the international courts.

In Canada, public knowledge of government actions and their rationale was obscured by an unofficial policy of secrecy. Strict confidentiality was first practised by British authorities in 1880, when they failed to alert the Canadian government of prior American claims to parts of the Archipelago that had prevented them from defining the boundaries in any official transfer document. Almost forty years passed before Canadian authorities became aware of the inherent weakness in British discovery claims. Meanwhile in 1913 the British Colonial Office had issued a warning to Canada's governor-general that any information suggesting that sovereign claims to the Arctic might be weak "should not be published but permanently recorded."[34] The fact that Department of the Interior officials actually followed the advice of maintaining a "permanent record" has made it possible for historians today to explain what transpired behind closed doors.[35]

In the early 1900s, the Canadian government adopted a similar policy of confidentiality, allegedly until such time as its title to the Arctic Islands was fully protected against a possible challenge. After public outrage erupted over the outcome of the Alaska boundary dispute, press releases and government reports on sovereignty issues were now carefully worded to avoid raising alarm. Similarly, special meetings and memos on "sovereignty-sensitive" issues were restricted to certain ministers and senior officials involved in Arctic activities, largely on a need-to-know basis. On the political side, full disclosure was limited to the prime minister and cabinet unless actions required legislation or budget approval by parliament. Confidentiality on Arctic sovereignty matters continued during World War II and the Cold War because of the need for military secrecy—but it also avoided rousing public concern and possible criticism of government actions.

The degree to which this policy of confidentiality is still practised is not known, although one suspects that with current global communications and proactive journalism, a rigid policy would be impossible to enforce. Unfortunately in a democracy there is a downside to restrictions on full disclosure. If the public is assured that the nation's Arctic sovereignty is secure, the government in power has great difficulty justifying major expenditures required to ensure it remains protected.

In the first half of the twentieth century, interpretations of international law continued to evolve. United States title to Alaska was never challenged, but Canada's Arctic sovereignty was perceived as vulnerable and Denmark's authority over East Greenland was directly challenged by Norway. Ironically it was only after Canada had successfully enacted a number of measures to protect its title to the Arctic Islands that a new precedent supporting its claims was established in the 1933 judgment handed down in the case of *Norway vs Denmark* over title to northeast Greenland. On this occasion, the Permanent International Court of Justice gave a more lenient interpretation of the criteria and time required to enact "effective occupation." As a result, Denmark was awarded sovereign authority over the entire island.

Interpretations of laws of the sea have also evolved since the mid-twentieth century, particularly with regard to territorial waters, open seas, international straits and the continental shelf. Most changes were incorporated into the 1982 United Nations Convention on the Law of the Sea (UNCLOS). Exercising its inherent right as a major world power, the U.S. refused to ratify the convention without amendments that were still under consideration by the Senate under the George W. Bush administration.

AS WE face new challenges resulting from global warming, historical definitions may become less relevant. Of greater importance are the patterns of cause and effect that attended changes in Arctic sovereignty and the characteristic response by each Arctic country to potential threats.

(2)

FIRST INHABITANTS,
3000 BC—1500 AD

They must have been hungry people, used to cold and
hardship and a way of life that demanded constant movement from
one place to another just to wring a living from a sparse land.

DAVID MORRISON and G.-H.GERMAIN [1]

. . . .

THE PREDOMINANT world view of the Arctic may be a romanticized one, but Inuit see it as their ancestral homeland, with
their oral histories suggesting it has been so since the beginning
of memory. Most consider themselves part of their environment,
rather than a distinct entity as perceived by Western societies. These
two very different perceptions exist alongside two different interpretations of history. For centuries, Inuit retained their history in
the oral tradition through stories and songs handed down by their
elders. Western civilizations depended largely on written accounts
by learned scholars and more recently on archaeological research as
sources for their historical knowledge. This chapter is based primarily on written sources, with reference to archaeological studies and
Inuit oral history to fill in the gaps.

In recent years, scientists have made a number of exciting discoveries based on radiocarbon dating, DNA analyses and new
methodologies to shed light not only on the origins of the Arctic's first
inhabitants, but also on the nature of the polar environment millions
of years before the arrival of humans. The science has added greatly to

our knowledge of how climate change caused adaptations of ancient flora and fauna and, in some instances, their extinction. These new discoveries appear to confirm the theory that such changes are part of a cyclical pattern of warming and cooling periods that eventually led to the arrival, adaptation and later demise of the first humans to inhabit the Arctic.

According to a recent article in the *New York Times,* studies involving microbes, fossils and rock extracted from the seabed about 150 miles from the North Pole indicate that the Arctic Ocean was much hotter than thought at the peak of a warming trend 55 million years ago. Research by the Arctic Coring Expedition (ACEX), an international scientific team sponsored by the Integrated Ocean Drilling Program, provides further information on the effects of this unusually warm climate and theories as to probable causes. As an example, the presence of a deep freshwater layer above the heavier salt-laden Arctic Ocean was thought to have been caused by closure of the straits between the Arctic waters and the Atlantic and Pacific Oceans. As a consequence, the enclosed seas became the habitat of a number of freshwater plants and animate species until the land forms shifted and opened the straits to allow the warmer, salt water to flow north. Sediment cores taken from the sea floor at a depth of 4,260 feet on the underwater Lomonosov Ridge also contained tiny algae fossils thought to be around 55 million years old. These cores also confirmed a gradual cooling, followed by cyclical warming and cooling periods. Even then, it was only approximately 450,000 years ago that temperatures fell low enough to create the ice cover that exists today.[2]

In Canada, research on this once subtropical Arctic began with a report by the Geological Survey of Canada in 1985 that claimed to have discovered fossilized remains of large trees on Axel Heiberg Island in the High Arctic. A subsequent scientific expedition sponsored in part by the Royal Canadian Geographic Society filmed the remnants of tree trunks and conducted further tests on these and other fossils to verify the degree and timeline of this unusually warm climate. Some trees were found to be similar to redwoods, the size of their stumps indicating that they had grown to a great height, possibly 35 metres.[3] More recent studies of ice core samples from the interior icecap of south-central Greenland revealed vestiges of moths, butterflies, beetles and spiders, as well as the pollen and needles of spruce, pine and a species of yew, dating between 800,000 and 450,000 years ago when temperatures likely ranged from 10°C in the summer to −17°C in winter. These samples were compared with similar ice cores drilled at Kap Kobenhavn in northern Greenland and the John Evans Glacier on Ellesmere Island to confirm that the plants were indigenous to the region. Further analyses indicated that temperatures had dropped suddenly around 450,000 years ago, covering the forests and insect life in sheets of ice and effectively freezing them. The same studies indicated that this ice cover remained during the last major warming period around 125,000 years ago, when the temperature was estimated to be only 5°C warmer than at present.[4]

Other research expeditions focussed on prehistoric marine animals, such as in 1998 when scientists uncovered fossilized bones in the High Arctic of a cold-blooded crocodile-like reptile called a champsosaur. This was followed by another discovery in 2004 on Ellesmere Island of several perfectly preserved *tiktaaliks*, an intermediate form between fish and amphibian estimated to be around 35 million years old.[5] Then in 2006, John Tarduna, a professor of geophysics at the University of Rochester, and his team discovered a 90-million-year-old, perfectly preserved fossil of a freshwater Asian turtle on Axel Heiberg Island. The fact that it was found on top of a basalt deposit and indications of oxygen deprivation in adjacent core samples gave rise to suspicions that warming of the Arctic may have been caused by extensive volcanic eruptions along an underwater mountain range known as the Alpha Ridge. A few suggested that worldwide volcanic activity at the time may have pumped huge amounts of carbon dioxide into the atmosphere, essentially creating a massive greenhouse gas effect. While expressing keen interest in the recent discoveries of life forms, most scientists warn that more studies are needed to establish the potential causes and timeline for the high carbon dioxide levels. Others still subscribe to the theory that a subtropical Arctic existed prior to the earth's collision with a huge meteorite, causing a shift in the earth's axis. A recent report based on Oregon State University research using multi-year ice core samples suggests that major cooling periods were triggered by less than a 2° shift in the earth's axis, which reduced the solar radiation absorbed by the earth and ocean.[6] What we do know for certain is that a sub-tropical climate existed many millions of years ago in what we now know as a very cold and partially frozen Arctic.

In 2007, fossilized bones of a semi-aquatic, freshwater carnivore known as a *Puijila darwini* were discovered in the post-impact lake deposits of a large crater on Devon Island in Nunavut. The research team was led by Natalia Rybczynski, a palaeobiologist with the Canadian Museum of Nature. Returning in 2008 and 2009, the team was able to collect almost the entire skeleton, including its four, likely webbed feet, to confirm that this was indeed a new genus in the evolution of seal lineage, a transitional form between the flippered seal and a terrestrial ancestor. Previous studies indicated a cool temperate climate with the area surrounding the meteor-created lake forested with transitional boreal and conifer trees.[7]

Homo erectus, the apparent genesis of the human race, appears to have evolved about a million years ago, possibly in central Africa. What have been described as "fully modern humans" appeared some-time around 50,000 years ago and quickly spread toward more temperate regions, adapting their tools, clothing and accommodation to the increasing cold as they followed the herds of grazing animals that had gravitated to the treeless plains of the earth's mid-latitudes. A period of intense cold between 80,000 and 20,000 years ago, commonly referred to as the Great Ice Age, expanded across North America, destroying existing vegetation and animal life and leaving a thick covering of glacial ice across much of what is now known as Canada and the northern U.S. Because of the glaciers, the sea level was significantly lower than now and exposed a vast ice-free plain known as the Bering Land Bridge connecting what is now Siberia to the land form we know as Alaska.

Human remains found near the Siberian coast date to around 25,000 or 30,000 years ago, suggesting that hunters likely crossed

Palaeobiologist Natalia Rybczynski of the Canadian Museum
of Nature inspects a three-dimensional model of a *Puijila darwini*,
a virtual reconstruction of a seal-like amphibian from fossil
bones discovered on Devon Island and believed to be over 20 million
years old. The model was generated from 3D surface scans, CT scans
and 3D surface reconstruction of the few missing bones.
Photo courtesy Martin Lipman, 2009

from here over the wide land bridge to the shores of Alaska. Evidence of their presence was found in the recent discovery of animal bones cut by humans at the Bluefish Cave site in the northern Yukon and dated over 20,000 years ago. The cave is located in the interior, where herds of muskox, mammoths, horses and caribou were thought to have passed through during their annual migrations. Around 15,000 years ago, these first immigrants to the western hemisphere were thought to have travelled southward as the glaciers began to melt and opened up an ice-free corridor just east of the Rockies. Current thinking suggests that they may also have followed a coastal route that would have been available several millennia earlier. Always in search of grazing animals for food and clothing, they appeared to have continued on until some reached Central and South America. These migrant hunters are thought to be the ancient ancestors of the aboriginal peoples who resided in the temperate zones of the New World prior to the arrival of Europeans.[8]

Around 11,000 years ago, the ice cover in North America had melted enough to create large inland lakes at the glacier edge. Forest and grassy plains gradually replaced the polar tundra as the treeline moved northward. Along the former beaches of the Great Lakes, archaeologists have discovered remnants of ancient Indian camps, indicating that some early migrants returned north as the climate continued to warm. Although these Amerindians may have made occasional hunting forays into the Subarctic tundra during the summer months, the location of ancient camps suggests that they preferred the warmth and protection of the advancing forest. As a result, the Arctic regions of the New World remained unoccupied by humans until around 5,000 years ago.[9]

Using a combination of carbon dating and DNA to analyze skeletal and camp remains, archaeologists have pieced together a remarkable story about the origins, characteristics, migration paths and cultural adaptations of the Palaeo-Eskimos, who are believed to be the first inhabitants of the North American Arctic. We know, for instance, that they possessed markedly different characteristics than later migrations and that neither was related to the much earlier immigration of big-game hunters from central Siberia.[10]

These first migrants to inhabit the Arctic regions of the western hemisphere date back to around 3000 BC, after the glaciers had receded to almost their present state. Confirming their origins, remains found at campsites along the northern coasts of Alaska were found to be similar to people of the Chukchi Peninsula at the eastern tip of Siberia. Unlike the earlier Amerindian migrants crossing on the land bridge, the Palaeo-Eskimos would have crossed the Bering Strait on the ice or in small boats, then moved slowly eastward on foot across the land and frozen ice of the Canadian Arctic. Some migrants eventually reached Greenland and Labrador. Why they made this trek is not known, although David Morrison, a curator at the Canadian Museum of Civilization, suggests that "they must have been hungry people, used to cold and hardship and a way of life that demanded constant movement from one place to another" just to survive.[11]

Travelling in small groups, they appeared over the years to have adapted their hunting techniques to the environment and the availability of wildlife that provided both their food and clothing. With a note of admiration, Robert McGhee, curator of Arctic archaeology at the Canadian Museum of Civilization, explains,

> By approximately 2000 BC, most regions of the New World Arctic were home to small and scattered bands of Palaeo-Eskimos. During the previous centuries, these people had accomplished the last major land-taking of an unoccupied region of the earth. They had explored countries that had been beyond the bounds of human knowledge and experience, had learned their secrets, and with a simple technology but a great deal of knowledge and adaptability, had learned to live and flourish in the new lands.[12]

They also earned the distinction of being the first to traverse the North American Arctic from west to east, on a route roughly paralleling the Northwest Passage. Unlike the Vikings thousands of years later, who travelled from east to west in search of a place to settle and carry on trade with Norway, the Palaeo-Eskimos sought no more than was necessary for their food, clothing and tools.

Although most archaeologists refer to the first migrants as Palaeo-Eskimos, meaning "old Eskimos," McGhee argues that this is misleading as they were clearly of different cultural and racial origins than the Inuit and Alaskan Eskimos now living in the Arctic regions of North America. Canadian Inuit refer to the first migrants as Sivullirmiut, meaning "the first people." Referring to them generally as belonging to the "Arctic Small Tool tradition" (ASTt), archaeologists assigned specific names according to the first discovery of their remains, such as the Denbigh people, whose bones were first discovered at Cape Denbigh near the western coastal plain of what is now

Alaska. Similarly, the Independence I and II cultures refer to those who had crossed the ice of Nares Strait to settle in northern Greenland, in the vicinity of Independence Bay. Finally the pre-Dorset and Dorset designations are used to identify the temporal periods of occupation by those whose remains were first discovered at Cape Dorset on Baffin Island. The latter appear to have inhabited the Arctic from roughly 500 BC until 1400 AD, and in a few locations even later. Today, Canadian Inuit refer to the Dorset culture as Tuniit, a people who still figure prominently in their oral history.

Climate change and availability of wildlife were the key factors causing these travellers to disperse over time and settle in small groups at different locations. According to Robert McGhee, none of these distinct cultural groups appear to have displaced one another; rather they evolved through diverse adaptations to changing climate, physical environment and/or availability of marine and land-based resources. As a consequence, he prefers using the Inuit name Tuniit for all early migrants to differentiate them from later arrivals who are considered the ancient ancestors of today's Inuit.[13] Not all archaeologists agree.

Possessing neither dog teams nor umiaks (large skin boats), the Palaeo-Eskimos apparently travelled on foot in small family groups, pulling their small sleds by hand. Initially they lived in oval-shaped skin tents supported by driftwood poles and anchored by a ring of boulders. For fuel and light, they burned bog moss, bits of driftwood, dwarf willow branches and animal bones in their stone hearths. They also used drill bits, micro-blades and bows and arrows of Old World Asiatic design. Those settling near Igloolik possessed harpoons similar in design to those once used in Siberia. Archaeologists suggest that they readily adapted to the climate and food resources in each locality. In the Igloolik area, for example, their garbage pits indicated that they had subsisted on fish and caribou, as well as seal, walrus, beluga and narwhal, which were easily caught in small pools and open leads in the ice. In other locations, they appear to have relied more on caribou. Generally they lived in small units of perhaps only two or more families, but as in the case of Igloolik they might gather annually in

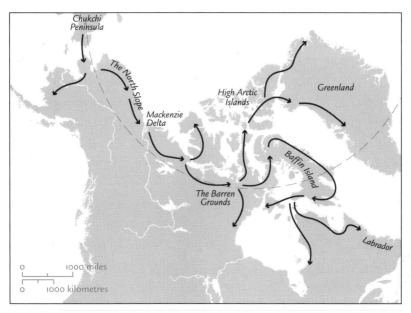

MIGRATION ROUTES OF THE PALAEO-ESKIMOS, 3000 BC–1000 AD

larger groups. Nonetheless, by adapting to the environment they survived for thousands of years.[14]

Between 1500 and 1000 BC, however, the climate began to cool but with each region of the Arctic affected differently. Many Palaeo-Eskimos migrated southward to more protected locations, adapting their equipment and survival techniques to defend against the cold. Archaeological remains show that some moved as far south as Newfoundland. In some locations, they built more permanent stone and sod houses, heating them with sea-mammal oil in small soapstone lamps. At some point before 500 BC, the cumulative effect of these cultural adaptations produced a way of life known as the Dorset culture, so named because of Diamond Jenness's discovery in 1925 of their distinctive artifacts near Cape Dorset on Baffin Island. The core area of the Dorset settlements appeared to be "in the northern Foxe Basin, in the Pond Inlet region of northern Baffin Island, on both sides of Hudson Strait, and on the islands of northern Hudson Bay." Migrations over the next millennium saw some return to the High Arctic and Greenland. The presence of native copper and meteoric iron in their tools and weapons suggests that they had either developed trading links to more distant sources or had themselves extracted the minerals from deposits near the Coppermine River or near Cape York in northern Greenland.[15]

Carbon-dated animal remains and artifacts have helped reconstruct Dorset hunting patterns, suggesting that they spent spring and summer on the coast hunting walrus and seal, then later gathered at fishing sites to spear char or trekked inland to hunt caribou. New tools appeared at later Dorset sites, including snow knives and harpoons capable of capturing walrus, perhaps even belugas and narwhals. The absence of any evidence of a sizable dog population implies that the small Tuniit sleds were pulled by hand. Also absent at these sites were the distinctive bows and the drill bits used by the earlier Palaeo-Eskimos. Changes were also evident in their winter accommodation to adapt to the cooler climate. These dwellings were partially dug into the ground, rectangular in shape, large enough to sleep two to four small families, with walls built of sod and insulated by snow blocks giving them the appearance of igloos. The roof was usually covered with skins but there was no evidence of whalebone supports. Instead they may have used driftwood, which was readily available. Igloos made from blocks of hard snow were used for spring hunting expeditions. Some archaeologists believe that deprivations encountered during the cooling period in the first millennium BC may account for the loss of certain skills and new adaptations, especially if driftwood was needed for fuel.[16]

On the west coast of Greenland, early Palaeo-Eskimos were referred to by archaeologists as Saqqaq; apparently they gave way to or perhaps were assimilated by the Dorset people around 800 BC. The latter appeared to have vanished from northern Ellesmere Island and Greenland by the tenth century AD. Inuit elders from Arctic Bay (Ikpiarjuk) on northern Baffin described the Tuniit as being stronger and larger than their ancestors, but a gentle people who were easily frightened. They were especially noted for their skill in carving miniature objects from ivory and bone. Those depicting animal spirits and shaman masks provide clues about their spiritual life and belief in shamanism. The increased number of amulets and other shamanistic objects found at later campsites suggests growing stress or fear, perhaps a result of the cooling climate, disappearance of wildlife or the arrival of strangers to their lands.[17]

Beginning around 1100 AD, a much different group of hunters travelled eastward along the shores of northern Alaska to the central Arctic, then northward toward Ellesmere Island and Greenland. These people belonged to an established maritime culture—hunters of whales, seals and walrus—who once lived along the Pacific Rim, perhaps for thousands of years before moving to the west coast of Alaska. Those who ventured east across the Canadian Arctic to Greenland are referred to as the Thule Culture, after the Danish scientist Therkel Mathiassen verified that artifacts found in campsites throughout the Arctic were similar to those first discovered near Thule, Greenland. These newcomers called themselves Inuit, meaning "the people," shared a common language called Inuktitut and are believed to be the distant ancestors of present-day Inuit.

Recent studies suggest that the Thule people originally came from the eastern coast of Siberia on the Bering Sea. Known as the Old Bering Sea culture, they lived in large permanent villages constructed of driftwood and sod, which were lit and heated by seal oil lamps. Also found among the village remains were kayaks and large umiaks, sleds, unique harpoons, cutting blades made of iron, ceramic pots and a sophisticated artistic tradition. The presence of iron tools reflected the influence of the vast Han Empire that had introduced iron tools into central Asia and Japan during the second century BC. Shortly after, similar tools began to appear in the Eskimo villages along the Bering Strait. While the Thule benefited from the abundant resources of the Bering Sea, the metal trade with Siberians was likely a fundamental underpinning in their economy. The location of their villages on the eastern tip of the Chukchi Peninsula in Siberia and the St. Lawrence Islands in the Bering Sea suggests that they may have assumed control of the iron trade between Asia and North America. Their superior weapons and aggressive behaviour also suggests that they may have been called upon to defend their middleman role against other groups attempting to take control of this lucrative trade.[18] More studies are needed to determine whether competition in trade or decline of marine life prompted them to move even further east. Likely it was a combination of both.

Skilled in hunting bowhead whales, the Thule people established villages near the sea mammals' migration routes. Their advanced weaponry and armour made of bone and ivory suggest frequent inter-tribal skirmishes. The Asian influence was also evident in their use of a recurved bow similar to those used by the Mongols. Their winter homes were distinctive, utilizing whalebones for the roof supports. Similar remains are found throughout the High Arctic. Some anthropologists believe that the summer migration of the bowhead and other large whales to the Beaufort Sea may have been the initial incentive attracting these people eastward, with other species in the Amundsen Gulf encouraging them to travel northward as far as Greenland. Robert McGhee questions this theory and suggests that the Thule migration to the High Arctic and Greenland was more likely driven by their search for the iron used by the Dorset people. In support of this idea, some of the earliest Thule sites were found near the meteorite deposits at Cape York in northern Greenland. It is also thought that their initial contact with the Tuniit may have alerted them to the presence of blue-eyed strangers in southern Greenland who possessed metal tools and might be interested in trading for furs and ivory tusks.[19]

Based on studies of early Thule sites found on the west side of Smith Sound, archaeologists Peter Schledermann and Karen McCullough estimated their first arrival at sometime around 1200 AD. Robert McGhee suggests a slightly later date based on newly revised carbon-dating methodology and modelling. Yet he agrees with Schledermann and McCullough that the Thule migration was not a leisurely affair, but instead a purposeful trek across 4,000 kilometres of unoccupied territory within several decades, likely facilitated by their large skin boats (umiaks) and long sleds pulled by dog teams. Confirming the rapid pace of their migration, McCullough discovered

Frame of a Thule house with its whalebone supports was reconstructed
from remains by a team from the Canadian Museum of Civilization, at a
winter campsite near Resolute Bay on Cornwallis Island, Nunavut.
Photo courtesy John P. Smol, Queen's University

clay pottery fragments with decorative etching on Skraeling Island
off Ellesmere that subsequent tests indicated had been made in northern Alaska. Thule-style stone winter houses framed with whalebone
were also found on the west side of Greenland, where the Thule had
crossed over Nares Strait and slowly gravitated southward along the
coast.[20]

Because the Thule were aggressive and possessed more sophisticated transport, tools and weapons, it was not surprising that within
a few hundred years they had driven most of the Tuniit from the
lands their ancestors had occupied for thousands of years. Although
the concept of land ownership was unknown to either the Tuniit or
the Inuit, from a historical perspective this event marked the first loss
of homelands in the North American Arctic as a result of new technologies and competition for its resources. Significantly, the timing
of their disappearance coincided with the onset of the Little Ice Age,
suggesting that climate change was also a factor. Over the following

centuries, all three factors—new technologies, competition for resources and climate change—contributed to changes in authority over the Arctic lands and waters of North America.

Explanations for the disappearance of the Tuniit are largely conjecture. Had they wished to resist being driven from their lands, they likely would have found themselves unable to defend against the Thule's advanced weaponry and aggressive behaviour. Inuit oral history describes the Tuniit as strong but lacking weapons and a fighting spirit, suggesting that they either were killed or simply retreated to poorer hunting grounds and succumbed to starvation.[21] The Little Ice Age beginning around 1200 AD would have placed even greater pressure on the area's wildlife resources and on the ability of the Tuniit to survive. Finding new hunting grounds would be equally difficult, if not impossible, particularly if Inuit oral history is correct in suggesting they had travelled north and northeast in search of seals and caribou. The degree of contact between the Thule and the Tuniit is also unclear, but some Inuit stories refer to times when they lived side by side. Artifacts and other remains discovered at abandoned campsites on Eclipse Sound in northern Baffin Island seemed to verify these stories.[22]

Yet given the competition for resources, their dislocation seems inevitable. Kuppaq, formerly of Arctic Bay but now deceased, described the Tuniit reaction on leaving. "There used to be a camp called Sannirut, near Pond Inlet. The people who lived there were known as Tuniit by the Inuit. The Inuit took their land and the Tuniit had to leave. As they were leaving their camp they cried, because the seal hunting was so good there all year round."[23] With a few exceptions, most had disappeared from the Arctic by the fourteenth century. The last to survive was a small group living on Southampton Island in Hudson Bay at the turn of the twentieth century, until finally succumbing to disease introduced by Scottish whalers.[24]

Although many Inuit also abandoned their traditional sites to move southward during the Little Ice Age, others remained in certain protected areas. Father Guy Mary-Rousselière, a Catholic priest and amateur archaeologist, discovered during his excavations around Eclipse Sound on northern Baffin Island that some campsites had been occupied continuously by a succession of cultures dating back to 2000 BC. The Thule may have remained in the area during the Little Ice Age, but they also developed new hunting practices that depended less on tracking whales in open waters. Eclipse Sound and the Igloolik regions, in particular, provided an optimum Arctic environment with their abundance of animal and marine resources, availability of fresh water, protection from harsh weather and the presence of quartz, flint, soapstone, copper pyrite and iron ore.[25] A similar environment was located in northern Greenland around Wolstenholme Bay, which was warmed by the open water of Baffin Bay and where a group of Thule Inuit, often referred to as Polar Eskimos or Ross's Highlanders, lived for several hundred years in relative isolation.[26]

For those who moved further south seeking warmer temperatures, their cultural practices underwent changes as they sought refuge inland along the deep fjords and bays of the Archipelago, the Canadian mainland and Greenland. No longer able to cache large supplies of whale meat and oil for the winter, they relied more on caribou, fish and seals. Seal oil, in particular, was critical to supply heat and light during the dark winter months. As soon as the sun reappeared on the horizon in locations north of the Arctic Circle, they headed out on the frozen ice to resume hunting seal and replenish their supplies. Summer months were spent travelling overland to fish and hunt caribou, which were stored for winter use. Changes in seasonal movements also required new forms of accommodation: snow-covered *qarmaqs* in winter; igloos or snow houses while travelling in the spring or late fall; skin tents during summer and early fall.[27] As with the Tuniit, the Thule design and use of materials depended upon the locality and availability of resources. Their migrations and cultural adaptations reflected their determination to survive.

Displacement of the Tuniit after the arrival of the Inuit represents the first known challenge in the western hemisphere to the modern concept of Arctic sovereignty. Whether the Tuniit were killed,

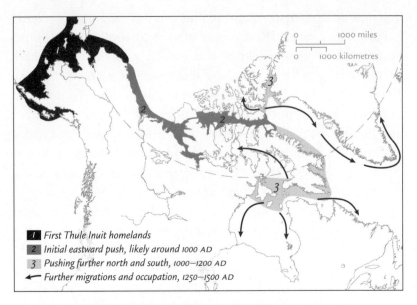

First Thule Inuit homelands
Initial eastward push, likely around 1000 AD
Pushing further north and south, 1000–1200 AD
Further migrations and occupation, 1250–1500 AD

MIGRATION ROUTES OF THE THULE INUIT, 1000–1500 AD

intimidated or threatened or simply left on their own accord, the fact remains that there was likely insufficient wildlife to feed both the newcomers and the Palaeo-Eskimos who had inhabited the Arctic for thousands of years. In this instance, the Thule Inuit considered the region's resources of sufficient value to take control of occupied lands. Their oral history suggests their conquest was not contested.

BEFORE THE Thule began their migration from the west, other newcomers were approaching from the east. The first European explorer to reach the Arctic was thought to be Pytheas the Greek, who had sailed north around 320 BC in search of tin. Six days north of the British Isles he reported reaching another land, one inhabited by barbarians with nearby frozen seas which he called Thule, meaning "farthest north." Likely he only reached northern Norway and possibly met ancestors of today's Saami people before being stopped by pack ice, but his observations of the stars, sea mammals, midnight sun and other phenomena confirm that he had indeed reached Arctic latitudes. Although many regarded his story as pure fantasy, the descriptions of icebergs and northern lights instilled a mystical image of the Arctic in the minds of learned men. As Robert McGhee explains, "The legend of the Arctic as a distant paradise has been with us since the time of Homer, and a myth of such antiquity will not fade away merely because of the ephemeral reports of a few Arctic explorers." [28]

The next reported voyage to the North Atlantic occurred around 565 AD, by the Irish priest Saint Brendan accompanied by fourteen monks. In a crude wooden boat rigged with a square sail, they ventured west from Ireland in search of a remote location to establish a solitary retreat. Descriptions of an island covered in slag, where "flaming rocks are hurled into the sea and fall spitting into waters, which start to steam," suggest a volcanic eruption such as frequently occurred in Iceland. The monks' stories were fanciful, filled with statements of divine purpose and faith, but provided little in the way of physical or scientific data. Bede, writing from England in the early eighth century, called the island Thule and referred to their making frequent voyages to the island. In 835 AD, the Irish cleric Dicuil referred to the Irish monks as *papar,* meaning "little fathers," and described their stay on Thule as seasonal. He also wrote that they left when the Vikings arrived, as they were not prepared to live among heathens. The island was later named Iceland because of the drift ice seen in the fjords during the winter. The first permanent settlement was established at Reykjavik by Norwegian Vikings accompanied by slaves and serfs they had acquired during raids on Scotland and Ireland. [29]

The first Europeans to actually settle in the North American Arctic were a group of Norse farmers led by Eirik the Red, who had been exiled from Iceland for his involvement in a blood feud. After spending three years searching for arable lands to the west, he returned to Iceland in 985 and convinced a number of families to join him in establishing a new settlement. The following year, sailing in a flotilla of twenty-five ships of which only fourteen arrived, the Norse families settled near the southern tip of Greenland to become the first European colonists of the New World. While Eirik likely named the island Greenland to attract potential settlers, the protected valleys where they built their farms must have appeared green and lush compared to Iceland's lava fields and barren landscape. For the most part, however, Greenland was a frozen desert with over three-quarters of the land covered in glacial ice.

The Norse settled in two separate locations. The first was called the Eastern Settlement, located at the southern tip of Greenland, whereas the less populated Western Settlement was 650 kilometres to the northwest, along the fjords that lay inland from the present-day capital of Nuuk. Additional families arrived in succeeding summers until all the fertile lands were occupied. By the end of the thirteenth century the Norse population in Greenland was estimated by some sources to be around 3,000. Kirsten Seaver claims a much larger number, citing between 4,000 and 5,000 in the Eastern Settlement and 1,000 to 1,500 in the smaller Western Settlement.[30] Either figure by New World standards was a sizable colony, yet at some time in the fifteenth century, the settlers disappeared without a trace.

Our knowledge of the early Norse settlements was originally derived from the *Icelandic Sagas,* in particular the *Groenlendinga Saga* written in the late 1100s and *Eirik's Saga* written around 1270. Occasional references are also found in history texts and a few in Inuit oral histories. The sagas' accuracy is often questioned, particularly in regard to dates, because they were based on verbal accounts and written many years after the fact. Similar problems of chronology arise with Inuit stories. Scholars such as Magnus Magnusson, Kirsten Seaver and Finn Gad have described the discrepancies and contradictions in great detail, citing the importance of archaeological evidence for verification. With discoveries of more Norse farm sites reported in 2009, it appears that there is still much to learn about these early settlements.

As recorded in *Eirik's Saga* it was his son, Leif Eriksson, who around 1000 AD sailed further west and south in search of new lands to claim in the name of King Olaf of Norway. His travels took him to southern Baffin Island, which he named Helluland ("slab land"), further south likely to Labrador and Newfoundland, which he called

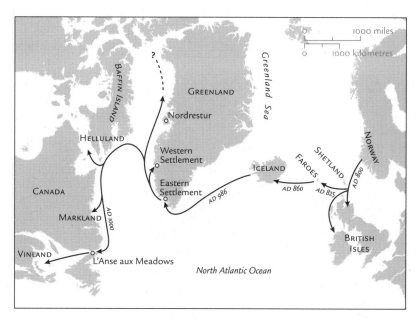

VIKING EXPLORATIONS AND SETTLEMENTS IN NORTH AMERICA, C1000 AD
Norse farm settlements on Greenland provided the base for
their voyages to Helluland, Markland and Vinland. After 1350 AD,
the advance of the Little Ice Age made their survival increasingly
difficult and eventually they simply disappeared.

Markland ("forest land"), and on to Vinland, where grapes were found
growing wild. The exact location of Vinland is still a matter of dispute, although it was likely located in the vicinity of the Gulf of St.
Lawrence. According to Icelandic researchers, the ruins of Norse
buildings discovered at L'Anse aux Meadows on the northernmost tip
of Newfoundland were likely a staging post for Leif Eriksson's explorations. A later attempt to establish a permanent settlement at the site
was unsuccessful after repeated attacks by raiders the Norse called
Skraelings, a term meaning "wretches" or "savages" used by the Norse
for all Native peoples. In this case, the Skraelings were probably distant ancestors of Beothuk or Montagnais Indians.

Archaeologists also identified the type of ships used by the Norwegian Vikings, largely based on recycled pieces of wood and toy

The reconstructed longship *Islendingur* was built by Gunnar
Eggertsson, modelled on the well-preserved remains of a vessel dating
around 850 AD discovered in a burial mound at Gokstad, Norway.
Courtesy Vikingaheimar, Iceland

models found in ruins of the early farm houses. Although varying in size, they were modelled on the classic Viking ship with its sharply pointed bow and stern, single mast and square-rigged sail, sets of oars and a rudder—similar in design to the reconstructed Gokstad ship shown on the facing page. Their size, measured as a ratio of length, width and depth, varied according to their use. The larger Norwegian-built *knaar* used by merchant traders to carry goods or settlers with their livestock was broader across the beam, deeper and usually built of oak with iron nails and tar as a sealant. Ships built in Greenland were smaller, generally for local use, but some were sufficiently large to sail to Iceland or to Markland to carry timber back to the settlements. Greenlandic construction differed in that their ships were held together with wooden pegs, baleen or sinew lashings and covered in seal oil.

Buildings at the Greenland settlements were similar to those in Iceland, with thick walls of turf and stone, built on a foundation of large rocks and topped with a sloping sod roof supported with beams and branches of scrub. Inside, wooden poles held up the roof supports. Although driftwood and white birch were found locally, analysis of the wood found in the ruins indicated that most of the lumber was indigenous to Labrador, not Norway. Aside from its importance in shipbuilding, the "Markland" timber was also used for doors, wood panels, window frames, benches, tables, bed frames and weaving looms.

The first farm buildings were small, sufficient to house a family and their few domestic animals. The size and design of the structures changed over the years, initially to a longhouse style or a passage design with rooms opening onto a long hallway that ended with storehouses and animal barns. Larger farms later adopted a more centralized layout, with a large dwelling area that was not necessarily connected to their barns. Many were equipped with bathhouses similar to a Scandinavian sauna and at some sites there were stone-faced channels that carried spring water to the homes. Those with churches were by far the most prosperous. Archaeologists suggest there was a hierarchical economic system at play, with the owners of the larger farms trading services and dairy products in return for caribou from the smaller inland farms or for fish and seals from the even smaller coastal farms.

As expected, the settlers' diet was similar to that of Iceland as the colonists had brought a variety of farm animals and seeds with them. From all appearances, the Norse also emulated the farming methods and cultural traditions of the Scandinavian countries, with most of the farm implements and utensils made locally from driftwood and smelted iron ore. Larger farms seemed remarkably self-sufficient, having an assortment of cows, sheep, pigs, goats, horses and dogs. Excavations have also revealed fences and grazing pastures. At one site, a barn had stalls for 104 cows. While meat and dairy products were central to their diet, they were supplemented by caribou, fish and seal. Sheep, on the other hand, were essential to provide wool cloth for domestic use and export. Examination of the bodies found in adjacent cemeteries revealed that clothing styles of both men and women were similar to those worn in Iceland and northern Europe.

Social order was established on the Icelandic model, with hereditary chieftains from each district and a lawspeaker exercising their power through regular meetings of the *Alping*, a legislative and judicial assembly. By 1350, the lawspeakers were replaced by two lawmen appointed by the King of Norway as he attempted to assert tighter control over the remote colony. Norwegian-born Kirsten Seaver believes the farmers likely resisted the King's demands for strict allegiance and increased taxes, as they were now building their own ships and thus were capable of trading with English and other foreign ships fishing in Greenland waters.

Greenlandic records indicate that by 1300 AD, there were over 150 farms listed in the Eastern Settlement and 90 in the Western Settlement. Although the total population figures vary according to the sources consulted, in terms of New World settlements, these were substantial colonies. Furthermore, they preceded other European settlements in North America by half a millennium and had survived for over 300 years—a major accomplishment in medieval times. Then what occurred to cause their demise?

Ruins of the Hvalsey Fjord Church built by the Norsemen
around 1300 AD are located on the shores of Qaqortuk Fjord in South
Greenland. Site of the last recorded wedding in Greenland, the
church was reported to accommodate thirty to thirty-five worshippers.
Photo courtesy Georg Nyegaard, archaeologist with National Museum of Greenland

Some scholars point to the role of the Catholic Church. In the
early years, religion appeared to dominate the lives of the Norse farmers, with Leif Eriksson being credited with building the first church
for his widowed mother after the death of his father. In total, remains
of seventeen churches have been identified in the Eastern Settlement,
with likely two or three more in the Western Settlement. Bishops
were appointed to Greenland as early as 1124, but the first to live on
the island did not arrive until around 1210, at which time he made his
home at Gardar, by then the largest farm in the Eastern Settlement.
The Gardar Cathedral, built around 1200 in anticipation of the bishop's arrival, was unique in its size and construction. The walls were
made of local red sandstone, with a separate bell tower, moulded
soapstone for trim, and windows of opaque greenish glass of southern European origin. In addition to the churches, there was also an
Augustine monastery and a Benedictine convent.

Only one church survived the ravages of the hostile environment.
Unlike the others, which used clay to hold the stones in place, the

church built at Hvalsey in the Eastern Settlement used lime mortar, which held firm, even after the sod roof disintegrated and exposed the inner walls to rain and snow. Built around 1300, with a dwelling house and outbuildings nearby, the Hvalsey church earned the distinction of being the site of the last recorded wedding in Greenland—sometime in the autumn of 1408.

The first bishop of Gardar was described as a powerful man in the community and had little difficulty collecting tithes in the form of trade goods, which were taken by ship back to Norway and sold to Bergen merchants. As religious leaders acquired more power, they also became more secular and their demands increased. As a result, the religious fervour that once dominated the lives of the settlers declined in the fourteenth century—as did the prosperity of their settlements.

Because of the mystery surrounding the disappearance of the Norse farmers, the nature of their contact with the Skraelings has been the subject of intensive study by scholars in North America and Scandinavia. The first written record of contact, apart from the attacks at L'Anse aux Meadows, appeared in a Norwegian history text written in the fifteenth century, *Historia Norwegiae*, which recounted how Viking hunters had come across a group of Skraelings "beyond Greenland, still farther to the north." When they were stabbed, their wounds were said to have turned white, but when dealt a mortal blow, they bled profusely. The site of the encounter was thought to have been north of Nordrestur (or Nordresta), an area around Disko Island where the Norsemen hunted for furs and ivory. The Skraelings, in this case, were likely Thule Inuit migrating from camps on Smith Sound. There is no written record of the Norse ever trading with the Skraelings, even though recent studies indicate an active trade with the Tuniit in Helluland.[31] This may be simply a matter of pride, since the name itself reflects disdain.

At present, there is no archaeological evidence of direct contact with the Thule Inuit before the mid-thirteenth century, at which time the Norse likely encountered families advancing south. A few Inuit stories tell of clashes with strangers, but without supporting archaeological evidence it is impossible to establish a date and location. In the sagas, there are vague references to northern voyages. On this count, archaeologists have found undisputable evidence that the Norse indeed sailed north, likely in search of walrus and narwhal. Excavations at abandoned Inuit sites on both sides of Smith Sound uncovered numerous Norse objects dating around 1270 AD—chess pieces, iron ship nails, woven woollen cloth, a carpenter's plane and fragments of chain mail—which Danish sources suggest would not have been traded willingly. Based on his own field studies on Skraeling Island and nearby Ellesmere, Peter Schledermann tends to agree. The abundance of artifacts and their nature might suggest a shipwreck or an Inuit attack on a small Viking ship.[32]

Around 1350, a priest named Ivar Bårdsson was sent to the Western Settlement to investigate rumours of difficulties with the Skraelings. He reported finding only cattle and sheep roaming free in the fields, and suggested that "the Skraelings now have the entire West Settlement." Later, in the Icelandic annal for the year 1379, it was reported that "the Skraelings assaulted the [Norsemen], killing 18 men, and captured two boys and a bondswoman and made them slaves." Subsequently the pope was informed that heathens had attacked, destroying most of the churches and taking many inhabitants prisoners. Some Danish historians cast doubts on the authenticity of the papal brief, while others suggest the "heathens" from "neighbouring coasts" may have been pirates from Europe.[33] Most Inuit stories suggest close friendships with the Norse. Only a very few tell of violent clashes.[34]

Apart from the energy and determination of the settlers themselves, at least partial credit for the colonies' success was attributed to the ongoing trade with Norway during the first 150 years. Although hunting parties frequently travelled to Nordrestur around Disko Bay, the resources here were not unlimited and maintaining the farms would have been a priority. Trade with the Skraelings seemed a likely alternative, yet there were no Tuniit or Thule in Greenland during this period. Similarly, there is no evidence that the Norse had sailed north at the time, even though strands of Viking wool were found at abandoned Tuniit campsites in northern Baffin Island.[35]

Pat Sutherland of the Canadian Museum of Civilization appears to have solved the conundrum. With a team of international experts and thousands of artifacts collected from abandoned Dorset sites on Hudson Strait, she has assembled convincing evidence that the Norse regularly traded with the Tuniit here, possibly within twenty years of settling in Greenland. Remnants of woollen cloth were found at all sites she investigated, but the most telling sign was the discovery at Avayalik in northern Labrador of over fifty walrus skulls, all of them crushed to remove their ivory tusks. At the Nanook site, not far from Kimmerut on the southern shore of Baffin Island, Sutherland also unearthed what appeared to be the ruins of a Norse-style sod and stone structure, likely used for shelter. For the Tuniit, who were adept at hunting fur-bearing animals and walrus, trade for scraps of iron would be welcomed.[36] For the Norse, these rather timid Skraelings who lived in small groups on the open tundra would have been ideal trading partners. The eventual disappearance of the Tuniit from the area around 1250 AD may also explain Norse attempts to sail north to Smith Sound, in search of either sea mammals with ivory tusks or Skraelings who might trade with them.

There were other circumstances that would adversely affect the farm settlements in the mid-thirteenth century. The once powerful Kingdom of Norway began to crumble and the King sold his trading privileges to a Bergen firm. Soon there was a glut of Arctic produce and fewer ships sailed westward after a ban had been issued on trading with Iceland and Greenland. The situation worsened after 1300 AD as the climate became significantly colder. The first to experience problems was the more northerly Western Settlement, possibly aggravated by the arrival of Thule Inuit in the area. While some farmers may have joined their countrymen in the Eastern Settlement, they no longer had easy access to ivory after the disappearance of the Tuniit from Helluland. Then in 1349, the Black Death struck Norway, bringing shipping in the North Atlantic to a standstill. Although trade gradually resumed, the ship sent annually by the Norwegian government was not replaced when it sank in the 1360s. The epidemic ravaged Iceland in 1402, but there is no evidence that it ever reached Greenland. On the other hand, the Little Ice Age was relentless, with additional cold spells in the 1380s and early 1400s.[37]

At some point in the fifteenth century, the farmers in the Eastern Settlement also disappeared. Robert McGhee suggests that without any evidence of mass graves or unburied bodies, it was possible that the families may have made their way back to Iceland. Pulitzer Prize-winning author Jared Diamond believes they starved to death because of overgrazed lands, their inability to adapt and their reluctance to seek assistance from the Inuit. Richard Vaughan puts part of the blame on the church and the king, describing the Norse farmers as "victims of climate change and human avarice and elitism." Kirsten Seaver believes they simply changed their trading partners and survived for several more decades by trading fish and whale oil with English ships, until they departed on their own volition.[38]

A much different story was told by the Inuit and recorded in 1750 by Niels Egede, son of missionary Hans Egede:

Then three schooners came here from the southwest and attacked the Norse, plundering and murdering. But the Norse defeated them and two of the ships fled to sea, while they captured the third. At that time my people still had no permanent dwellings, they were struck with fear and fled far inland. The next year a fleet of ships attacked them [the Norse] and killed many people and stole their livestock and all the valuables they could find, then sailed away. Most of those who survived this battle launched their boats, loading them with the remaining valuables, and sailed south along the coast, but some stayed behind and my people promised to assist them if such events occurred again. And the next year these evil-doers came yet again, and when my people recognized the ships they fled to the head of the fjord and several women and children with them. In the autumn when my people hoped to meet the Norse again they were shocked to find everything had been pillaged, houses burnt to ashes and the farms destroyed with no stone left unturned. When my people saw this state of affairs they took the women and children with them

and moved to more remote places where they remained undis-
turbed for a long time, while the women, five in all, married my
kinsmen.[39]

His story seems plausible in light of similar reports by Icelandic settlers during the same period that described how their own villages
were attacked by English fishermen and the men captured to be sold
as slaves. We also know that in the early 1400s, King Erik VII of Denmark, Norway and Sweden made repeated requests to King Henry V
of England to stop illegal contact with the Norwegian colonies in the
North Atlantic.

Archaeologist Peter Schledermann suggests there were many con-
tributory factors to the decline of the colonies' prosperity, ranging
from the cooling climate, soil erosion, greedy church officials and
Norwegian kings, to the increasing presence of Inuit and possible
pirate attacks—but he argues that "no single reason can explain the
final collapse of Europe's most westerly outpost." [40] Yet Hans Egede,
the Norwegian missionary responsible for the Danish recolonization of Greenland in 1721, remained convinced that at least some of
the Norse settlers would have survived. His grandson, Hans Egede
Saabye, was also certain, believing that they must have migrated further east. According to stories he heard from the Inuit, "they had seen
tall, bearded men, who were terrible, and, doubtless, man-eaters" far
to the east. He also relates the story recorded in *Historia Gronlandica*
about an Icelandic bishop who had been driven by a storm to the
coast of East Greenland around 1540 and saw "people driving their
sheep and lambs on the meadows." [41] If true, it would support Kirsten
Seaver's belief that some Norse had survived well into the sixteenth
century.

What we do know for certain is that two groups of immigrants
arrived at Greenland around a thousand years ago—first the Norse
and later the Thule Inuit. In the end only one group survived. As the
British author Magnus Magnusson wryly observed, "Despised Skraelings, so much better adapted to the climate than the Vikings, had won

Young Inuit family look out on Eclipse Sound, the homeland
of their distant ancestors.   Photo courtesy Richard Olsenius, 2004

out at last." [42] As long as the mystery remains unsolved, the Norse
farmers will not be forgotten but will remain alive as a vibrant episode in the history of the Arctic.

VIEWING THIS period of time in the broader context, there are only
vague similarities to the present, but they are nonetheless significant.
The most obvious factor that altered the demography of Greenland
and the Canadian Arctic was climate change. Translated into the
modern definition of sovereignty, the Vikings gained access to build
their farms on Greenland during a warming period but like the Tuniit
disappeared at some time during the Little Ice Age. Perhaps of greater
significance were factors that differentiated those who survived from
those who did not—the tenacity of the Thule Inuit and their uncanny
ability to adapt. Their descendants now residing in Greenland seem
to possess similar traits, as reflected in their drive to regain control over their lives through independence from Denmark and their
eagerness to take advantage of the recent warming trend to exploit

their oil and mineral resources. As explained in pragmatic but no uncertain terms in 2007 by Aleqa Hammond, the foreign minister in Greenland's Home Rule Government, "We are an Arctic people—but our way of life is changing and we have to change with it."[43]

There is another, more subtle comparison. The difficulties of administering a remote colony were complicated in Norway's case by a declining economy, internal unrest and difficulty in maintaining an active mercantile trade. Once the Greenland settlements were no longer valued as a major source of revenue, they were neglected and then abandoned. Centuries later, when Russian settlements in Alaska were no longer profitable, they were sold. Should a similar situation arise today, would the Arctic countries still have sufficient incentive to support and protect their northern hinterlands? Times have changed, but have motivations driving government action changed with them?

(3)

MERCHANTS AND MONARCHS,
1500—1814

I know it is my bounden duetie to manifest this secret unto
your Grace, which hitherto, as I suppose, hath beene hid: which is,
that [with] a small number of ships there may be discovered divers
New lands and kingdomes, in the which without doubt your grace
shall winne personal glory, and your subjects infinite profite.

MERCHANT ROBERT THORNE to KING HENRY VIII, 1527[1]

·   ·   ·   ·

IN THE years following discovery of the New World, merchants and monarchs of northern Europe combined forces to explore the Arctic, each driven by slightly different objectives. Both were empire builders with worldly ambitions. The merchants envisioned a monopoly that would guarantee huge profits and revenue growth. Monarchs dreamed of vast domains supported by military might and mercantile trade. The relevance of these years to the present status of sovereignty in the Arctic rests in understanding the motivations of rival nations, their strengths and weaknesses, and how they were affected by changes in climate technologies and demand for Arctic resources. Too often the distant past becomes contracted in one's mind, perceptually diminishing the importance of previous centuries compared to the present. A distant past, in particular, is often too remote and obscure to trigger a sense of déjà vu that so often accompanies memories of the recent past.

Admittedly each event is important to its own generation, yet there are a number of similarities between then and now. Consider, for instance, whether the ambitions of the merchants and monarchs of yesteryear are comparable to those of today's large multinational corporations and political leaders. Or how the acquisition of lands might depend upon the personal bias or whims of the current monarch or political leader. Or how susceptible either might be to pressures by commercial interests. One might even consider whether indigenous peoples are still ignored in present sovereignty disputes. Some will point out similarities; others will emphasize the differences. Both views are equally important if accompanied by the question "Why?"

The history of Arctic sovereignty in North America belongs to more than just the Inuit, Britain, Canada, the United States and Denmark. For over 300 years, it also involved the Dutch, Russians, Portuguese, French and Spanish Basques, all vying for control over the Arctic seas of the Old and New Worlds. Success or failure depended on a number of factors: the effect of European wars and internal conflicts, adoption of new technologies, accessibility of resources and market demand; the Protestant Reformation; as well as changes in economic and political power within the global community. Overriding all else during the late seventeenth and eighteenth centuries was an event beyond anyone's control—the cumulative effect of the Little Ice Age—when cooler temperatures increased the area and depth of Arctic sea ice, temporarily halting exploration. By the time a warming trend reopened the northern waters of Davis Strait, shifts in economic and military power had changed the world map. Not only were different nations competing for control of the Arctic, but their objectives and priorities had also changed.

For European nations, the search for a northern sea route through the Arctic involved sailing in the North Atlantic, which was fraught with dangers and uncertainties for wooden sailing ships. The ability to manoeuvre around drifting icebergs and pack ice in heavy fog or stormy weather required expert navigation skills, an experienced crew, a sound ship and a measure of good luck. An experienced navigator was invaluable and timing was critical. The summer months offered periods of clear skies and calm seas, but delay in departing for home could spell disaster. Shipwrecks were frequent, resulting in major losses of investment, knowledge and expertise.

In the fifteenth century, Portuguese ships dominated the search for new lands, initiated by the legendary Prince Henry the Navigator, the third son of King João (John) of Portugal. A devout Catholic, Henry was a paradox, a visionary but also an uncanny businessman. Stories about his school for navigators, mapmakers and shipbuilders are apparently unfounded, but he did personally finance numerous expeditions in search of unknown lands. Henry also actively encouraged the slave trade and reportedly donated his share of profits to the Order of Christ. His expeditions were almost always successful, making Portuguese navigators a force to be reckoned with long after his death. By the early 1500s, the design of their ships had evolved, with the *caravela reconda* combining the former lateen-rigged style with full rigging, a forerunner of the much larger galleons built in the next century.

By the end of the fifteenth century, the Portuguese had discovered and established settlements on Madeira, the Canary Islands, the Cape Verde Islands and the Azores. The latter became the base for Portuguese ships that fished off Newfoundland and Labrador, in competition with the English and the Basques. In the second half of the century, the Portuguese were thought to have reached Iceland and possibly Greenland. On occasion they captured Natives and sold them as slaves.[2] The Portuguese were not alone. According to the chronicler William Worcestre, English fishermen frequently sailed to Iceland and possibly Greenland in the 1400s, where they traded European goods for dried cod. Denmark, which claimed a monopoly over trade in the northern seas, accused the English of unlicensed fishing, trading and even kidnapping Icelanders. The existence of new lands to the northwest was said to be common knowledge among some merchant traders, but none were eager to share knowledge of their routes or destinations with competitors. Intense rivalry encouraged secrecy and at times deception. Pointing to the distortions and errors on early maps as an example, anthropologist Saladin d'Anglure suggests that these rivalries encouraged fanciful illusions and false rumours to mask the commercial objective of their explorations.[3]

In medieval times, the Pope played a central role in deciding which nations had the right to explore and acquire lands in the New World. In the eleventh century, the Catholic Church split into Roman and Orthodox, with the Eastern Orthodox Church becoming even more isolated after the Ottoman conquest of the Byzantine Empire in 1453. Throughout this period, the Church in Rome claimed to maintain its authority by "divine right," derived from the belief that the world belonged to the Christian God, who granted authority over the world to the Pope. In turn, European kings derived from him their authority to acquire new lands in return for their professed loyalty and support.

After Columbus's "discovery" of the New World in 1492, the Pope issued a decree in the form of two papal bulls that recognized the right of Spanish interests in the west and Portugal in the east. This in turn led to the Treaty of Tordesillas between Spain and Portugal, which divided the undiscovered lands of the world into east and west. The line passed through the Atlantic Ocean at approximately 46° W longitude some 370 leagues west of the Cape Verde Islands. Spain was granted the right to explore and claim lands west of the line, with Portugal acquiring similar rights to the east. This line gave Portugal rights to not only Africa, but also slices of what are now Newfoundland and Brazil. Within a few decades Spain assumed control over the sea route around South America through the Magellan Straits or by Cape Horn, whereas Portugal claimed authority over the passage around Africa's Cape of Good Hope. With control over the only sea routes to the Orient, Spain and Portugal became wealthy trading nations, leaving the northern seafaring nations and their merchants at a serious disadvantage.

Without water access to the lucrative trade with China and the East Indies, English and Dutch merchants had two options, either to find an alternative route around the New World, or to convince their monarchs to declare war on Spain and Portugal. In essence, they pursued both options. The English search for a northern sea route through the Arctic began first to the northeast in 1496 and then in 1553 to the northwest. The inhospitable region had suddenly acquired unexpected strategic value—not as a place to colonize, but merely as a place to sail through as quickly as possible. Then 1585 through to 1807 saw England and Spain on opposing sides in a prolonged series of wars that ended with the defeat of Napoleon in 1815, leaving the British Empire a formidable world power. Spain, France and even the Netherlands fell far behind.

During the fifteenth century, the port of Bristol in England became a major trade centre, at times rivalling the city of London. John Cabot, a seasoned navigator born in Italy, arrived in Bristol to convince the English merchants of the importance of finding a route to Cathay. In 1496, he set out with letters of instruction from King Henry VII to sail north, east and west and lay claim to lands in the name of the Crown. His first voyage was a failure, but the next year he reportedly reached the northernmost tip of Newfoundland and possibly the coast of Labrador before the expedition was beset by storms. One ship returned, but Cabot and his crew were never seen again. Sebastian Cabot assumed his father's role in England and led a number of expeditions between 1500 and 1510. Of greater significance was his part in helping the Bristol merchants set up the first English syndicate for overseas trade, called the Company of Adventurers for New Found Land. By 1504 their ships were already providing their investors with profits from cod caught off Newfoundland and Labrador.

The Cabots were not the only navigators hired by English merchants. In 1499, João Fernandes, called "Lavrador," meaning farmer (because he had acquired lands in the Azores), had sailed under orders from King Manuel of Portugal to explore and govern lands to the northwest. Maps of the period suggest that he likely "rediscovered" Greenland, which he named Land of the Labrador, a name later applied to the nearby mainland coast. Perhaps persuaded of greater rewards offered by the Bristol merchants, he returned to England rather than Portugal and in 1501 joined Sebastian Cabot as a member of the company established by the Bristol merchants. This time the company's ships arrived at an island they named New Found

Land, returning again over the next several years to fish. They always returned with a variety of presents for the King, including animals, birds, bows and arrows and, on occasion, Natives captured as slaves. Fernandes appears to have disappeared on the 1501 voyage, but on a later map there is an inscription stating that the Land of Labrador "was discovered by the English of the town of Bristol. They gave it that name because he who gave them directions was a lavrador from the Azores."[4]

The same year Fernandes was rediscovering Greenland, another Portuguese navigator named Corte-Real led an expedition for the King of Portugal, arriving at what he described as a "a cool land with large trees." By its location, it appears that he too had landed in what is now Newfoundland. The next year Corte-Real conducted a slave raid and sent a ship back to Portugal with fifty-seven men and women, likely Beothuk, who were described as the "best slaves that have hitherto been obtained."[5] Corte-Real remained on the island to conduct further explorations, but was never heard of again. Either he was lost at sea or the Natives had successfully exacted their revenge.

King Henry VIII's split with the Roman Catholic Church had unexpected advantages for the merchant traders. By 1534, with Parliament rejecting any further payments to Rome, English ships were no longer bound by papal laws to respect the rights of Portuguese or Spanish ships. Although the King had other priorities that occupied his time—internal uprisings, war with France and six wives—the records suggest he sponsored at least one expedition to the New World in 1527, but with no notable results. Essentially, English merchants were left to their own devices to expand their trade.

Equally frustrated by Spain and Portugal's control over the New World, the King of France took a different approach. In 1534 Francis I convinced Pope Clement VII to modify the papal bulls so that other nations might seek lands in the New World not already claimed by Spain or Portugal. That same year the King commissioned Jacques Cartier to enter the Strait of Belle Isle and search for lands containing precious metals or a sea route to Asia. Cartier dutifully entered the Gulf of St. Lawrence and erected a cross on the shores of the Bay of Gaspé, taking possession of the land in the name of the King of France. The following year he sailed further up the river, reaching Indian villages located near the present sites of Quebec City and Montreal. Here he laid claim to both sides of the river, and then returned home with hopes of convincing the King of the potential for great mineral wealth.

Challenging the Spanish monopoly, King Francis declared that possession, not discovery alone, was necessary to secure title to new lands. Putting words into action, he sent Cartier back in 1541 to establish a colony on the St. Lawrence as evidence of France's permanent occupation. Forts and buildings were erected, but after two hard winters the settlers were returned home and colonization plans deferred. Although commercial fur trading and fishing continued, it was not documented. A half century later and with the state impoverished by wars, King Henry IV of France was credited with the plan to use profits from the fur trade to pay for the colonization of New France.[6] The originator of the idea that only colonization could protect discovery claims is unclear, but almost 200 years would pass before the King of Denmark and Norway applied that same principle to Greenland. By comparison, the Royal Charter granted to the Hudson's Bay Company in 1670 did not include any specific instructions for colonization beyond the trading posts required to collect furs from the Indians.

With the death of King Henry VIII in 1553 and Queen Mary's accession to the throne, Catholicism was temporarily restored as England's official religion. That same year, a consortium of London merchants established the Muscovy Company, which sent three ships in search of a northeastern passage through the Asian Arctic. The ships became separated, the two under the command of Sir Hugh Willoughby reaching Novaya Zemlya before becoming icebound on a remote island. There were no survivors. The ship commanded by Richard Chancellor also came to grief and drifted south toward the Dvina River. Abandoning the vessel and accompanied by a handful of men, Chancellor trekked overland to Moscow where he successfully negotiated a trading agreement with Ivan the Terrible. Other attempts to sail further east ended in failure, causing the English merchants to abandon their search. Meantime, the Muscovy Company was able to control the White Sea route to Moscow for over a decade.[7]

When Queen Elizabeth I ascended the throne in 1558, she restored the Church of England as the state religion and unofficially allowed English privateers to interrupt Spanish trade in the Caribbean. Open war with Spain followed, beginning what is referred to as the Eighty Years War. With navy ships prowling the waters between Spain and the Caribbean, English merchants once again looked to the northwest to expand their trade, either by setting up colonies on the North American coast or by finding a sea route through the Arctic to the Orient. Such was the case in 1574, when Martin Frobisher approached Michael Lok, an agent for the Muscovy Company, about funding an expedition to search for a northwest passage.[8]

The Frobisher story is well known in the English-speaking world, but significant to the history of Arctic sovereignty for a number of reasons. Not only was Frobisher the first European to officially lay claim to lands in the North American Arctic, but the course of events illustrates the interrelationship between the rising merchant class, the monarchy and public opinion, as well as difficulties encountered in navigation, attitudes toward the indigenous people and, finally, the secrecy invoked by the Privy Council with regard to the records and charts from the expeditions. All established precedents for British actions in later years.

During his twenty years at sea, Frobisher had acquired a somewhat dubious reputation as a privateer engaged in nefarious enterprises that included piracy and conspiracy. Lok, however, was sufficiently impressed by Frobisher's conviction that a passage existed and that he was capable of finding it. The two men obtained a licence from the Muscovy Company and began preparations. Lok was responsible for garnering financial support, whereas Frobisher organized outfitting of the expedition. Christopher Hall was hired as navigator, with the scholar John Dee responsible for obtaining maps drawn by Flemish cartographers as well as advice on the latest navigation techniques and use of instruments. To gain public support for the venture, Sir Humphrey Gilbert published a tract that described potential riches to

Map by the Flemish cartographer Gerhardus Mercator (1595–1602)
shows the circumpolar world as understood by navigators of the
time. Note particularly the existence of a passage north of the
New World and a similar route north of Europe and Russia. The North
Pole appears as a large rock structure, surrounded by open seas.
Library and Archives Canada (LAC) C-101874

be found in undiscovered lands of the New World, the potential for new markets for English goods and the possibility that these lands could be settled by "such needie people of our Countre which now trouble the common welth."[9] Although more delusionary than practical, the intent likely found a receptive audience among the gentry of sixteenth-century England. Only merchant seamen would understand the unlikelihood of establishing a permanent settlement in the Arctic.

With two small ships and a tiny pinnace for shore landings, the expedition left London in June 1576, with Queen Elizabeth waving farewell from her palace window at Greenwich. Storms off Greenland separated the fleet. One ship turned back and the pinnace was lost at sea, but Frobisher continued until reaching a small island off the shore of Baffin Island which he named Queen Elizabeth's Foreland. He then entered a strait he thought would lead to the Pacific and promptly named it after himself. Approximately 150 kilometres along the narrow channel, the ship came upon a group of Inuit approaching in kayaks. Initial contact seemed friendly, with the Inuit trading their sealskin coats, meat and fish for trinkets and later competing with the sailors in a display of acrobatic stunts on the ship's rigging. The goodwill ended abruptly when five of the ship's crew disappeared after going ashore. Believing they had been kidnapped, Frobisher captured an Inuk and took him aboard as a hostage. His men still had not returned when a snowfall signalled it was time to depart. Three centuries later, Inuit explained to the American explorer C.F. Hall what had happened, describing how five white men had been abandoned by their ship and after spending the winter with the Inuit had built a small boat and were lost at sea trying to sail home.

On returning to England, Frobisher showed off his hostage as evidence that he had visited the New World. He had also brought back a number of material objects, including a black stone that was claimed to contain flecks of gold. Rumours spread quickly about an island with rocks full of gold just lying on the ground. This time a new company was formed called the Company of Cathay, in which Queen Elizabeth herself invested £1,000. The next spring, Frobisher

Model of Martin Frobisher's mine on Countess of Warwick Island
(Kodlunarn Island), showing his ships being loaded as in the summer of 1578.
Canadian Museum of Civilization, s2000-4600, photographer Steven Darby

again set sail with two small ships, and a large naval vessel with 120
sailors, soldiers and miners and even an assayer. His instructions
were to bring back a cargo of gold ore and, if he had time, to continue the search for a route to the Pacific. Reaching Baffin Island, then
called Meta Incognita, a party landed and erected a stone cairn on a
height of land, declaring possession in the name of Queen Elizabeth.
Frobisher's attempt to obtain news of the lost men, however, ended
in a skirmish leaving a half-dozen Inuit dead and one of his men seriously injured. This time in retaliation he kidnapped a man, woman
and child. The captives, like the Inuk two years earlier, all died within
a month of reaching England.

Selecting a potential mine site on Countess of Warwick Island,
now known as Kodlunarn or "white man's island," the shore party
landed and immediately set to mining the ore. Over 200 tons of
rocks were brought back to England, where samples were tested and
declared to be rich in gold. Plans were immediately made for a third
expedition in 1578, to include colonists to protect their equipment
and property over the winter against vandalism by the Inuit. The plan,

if it had succeeded, would have created the first English settlement in the Arctic and in North America. This time, however, Frobisher was given specific instructions to treat the Inuit kindly to encourage friendship and prevent any "offence or myslikings [sic]." [10] The third expedition set out with fifteen ships and 400 men. The intention was to leave three ships and 100 men at the settlement with provisions for eighteen months should they become icebound. The fleet first made a stop somewhere along the coast of southwest Greenland, which Frobisher mistakenly thought was Friesland, a non-existent island that appeared on a number of sixteenth-century maps. Here a landing party discovered an iron trivet and nails at an abandoned Inuit camp. Frobisher renamed the island West England and formally claimed it for the Queen.

While crossing Baffin Bay, the fleet encountered a severe storm that sank the ship carrying most of the building supplies for the winter settlement, leaving no alternative but to abandon plans to remain for the winter. Instead, the men built a stone house and a workshop for their equipment to test whether they could withstand the weather and possible attacks by the Inuit. They also planted seeds and peas. The last ships left Kodlunarn Island around the first of September, unaware that no white man would return for another 300 years. This time the assay results found the 1,300 tons of rock to be totally worthless. Even Michael Lok's enthusiastic report describing an enchanted country with sea unicorns and "monstrous great ilands of ise" failed to moderate public anger. Accusations abounded, with Lok and Frobisher casting blame on each other. The first gold rush in North America had ended in scandal, with Frobisher's reputation in shambles, the Company of Cathay bankrupt and Lok in debtor's prison. Long before the term "lobbyist" was coined to describe the role played by friends of government to garner support, the merchants in sixteenth-century England were fully cognizant that an expedition's success depended on the blessing and financial support of their monarch. They also learned how quickly that support would disappear in the event of scandal or deception.

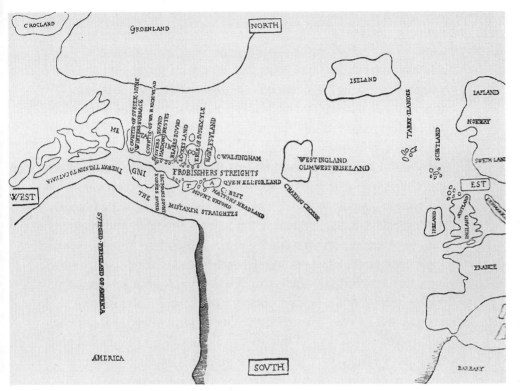

Sketch map of "Meta Incognita" in George Best's booklet on the
Frobisher Expeditions published in 1578, reportedly drawn by the
expedition's principal surveyor James Beare. The map mistakenly
identifies Baffin Island as Greenland and presumably southern Greenland
as an island referred to as "West England" or Friesland. As a
result, Friesland appeared on a number of subsequent maps until
finally disappearing by the mid-seventeenth century.

Stefansson and McCaskill (1938), Special Collections, Trent University Archives

In spite of public accusations, Frobisher was allowed back in the
English navy. In 1585 he was made a vice-admiral under Sir Francis Drake and three years later knighted for his part in defeating the
Spanish Armada. In 1594, however, he was seriously wounded while
leading an attack on a Spanish fort and died shortly after his return
home. Ironically, Martin Frobisher would be immortalized in history
for his participation in a fraudulent gold scheme, rather than for his
achievements. The Privy Council Office impounded all the records

and charts from his three Arctic voyages, with the result that only two maps showing the location of the discoveries exist today, both of them with distortions that made it impossible to locate the mine sites. Subsequent maps tended to show Frobisher Strait either as dissecting the southern portion of Greenland or simply as a bay on the southeast coast.[11] The principle of confidentiality concerning naval records and charts would be invoked again by British officials centuries later, this time to support the illusion of secure claims to the Arctic Islands.

Regardless of his weaknesses and failures, Frobisher had inspired visions of a vast northern empire in the mind of his queen. Apparently undeterred, Elizabeth seemed determined to turn disaster into opportunity when she asked John Dee to prepare an argument proving ownership of the lands Frobisher had claimed in her name. Dee obliged and in 1580 presented the Queen with a large parchment document, with a map of the world on one side and a detailed justification for her claims on the other. Citing a number of historical precedents, ranging from King Arthur's mythical voyages to Frobisher's recent discoveries, the document declared that these events gave Queen Elizabeth the right—"by the force of Law"—to claim sovereignty over northern portions of North America and the islands lying to the north.[12] Unfortunately it would take far more than a piece of parchment to achieve Elizabeth's dream of empire. There was much more work to be done, more money to be spent, more ships and lives to be lost.

After Sir Humphrey Gilbert's failed attempt to establish a settlement on Newfoundland in 1583, Queen Elizabeth threw her support behind Sir Walter Raleigh and his plan to establish a colony much further south on Roanoke Island in present-day Virginia, leaving the London merchants on their own to carry on the search for the Northwest Passage. Their primary object was profit, either from new markets for English goods, or from resources extracted from the Arctic lands and seas. To achieve their goal, they hired John Davis to lead a series of expeditions. A proficient navigator with a penchant for detailed charts and navigation notes, Davis compiled valuable information for future expeditions.

On his first voyage in 1584, Davis followed the west coast of Greenland, where he met a party of Natives eager to trade. Crossing the strait that now bears his name, he entered Cumberland Sound, which he thought would lead to the Pacific. Curiously, he made no attempt to locate or enter Frobisher Bay. His second voyage the following year took a similar route, but this time he encountered Greenland Inuit, who attempted to steal anything made of iron. Upon reaching Baffin Island, he followed the coast southward to Labrador, missing the entrance to Hudson Strait and returning home after two of his men were killed by hostile Natives. His last expedition in 1587 was more successful. This time, Davis convinced his merchant backers that he would return with enough cod to pay for the expedition. As a result, two barques were sent on a fishing expedition while Davis sailed north along the Greenland coast to 72° 12´ N latitude, the farthest north attained in the North American Arctic to date. Returning along the Baffin coast, he again explored and charted Cumberland Sound, noted the entrance to Frobisher Bay, which he renamed Lord Lumley's Inlet, then located and charted the entrance to Hudson Strait before returning home. He was now convinced that the passage to China lay north of Baffin Bay, where he had seen open seas.[13]

Davis had intended to return, but was seconded to sail against the Spanish Armada. Still convinced a passage existed, he later joined a private expedition planning to circumnavigate the world, with the provision that once through the Magellan Straits he would be allowed to sail north along the coast of America in search of a western entrance to the elusive sea route. The voyage ended in disaster before reaching the Pacific Ocean, but he did discover the Falkland Islands.

Meanwhile the Basque fishery off Labrador had suffered a major decline after its ships were diverted to serve in the Spanish wars against England and France. Other factors contributed to their eventual departure: a decreasing whale population, Spain's diminished sea power after wars with France, the Netherlands and England, and a more than ample supply of whale oil from Dutch operations in the northeastern Arctic.[14] The Spanish Basques made no attempt to develop a trading relationship with the Inuit, but reported several instances when they plundered and vandalized their shore stations during the off season. Anthropologist William Fitzhugh of the Smithsonian Institution described the Labrador Inuit at that time as being inordinately aggressive and at times hostile.[15] Such behaviour might be explained by the fact that the self-sufficient Basques had no need of their assistance, thus little incentive to establish friendly relations. Yet considering the murders of John Davis's men along the same shores, one cannot help wonder if the migrating Inuit had heard stories of those who had died or been kidnapped by the Frobisher expeditions.

The success of the English navy during the wars with Spain was eclipsed by the rise of the Netherlands as a sea power during the sixteenth and seventeenth centuries, partly a result of its hard-won independence from Spain in 1581. Under the authority of the States General of the United Netherlands, Dutch merchants sent two expeditions in 1594 and 1595 in search of a passage to the northeast. On the first voyage, one ship reached open water in the Kara Sea, but attempts to push further east the following year failed because of heavy ice. Discouraged, the States General withdrew its financial support, but offered a reward of 25,000 guilders to anyone finding the northern sea route. While not directly related to the North American Arctic, activities in the northeast show the close interrelationship of influences and events throughout the circumpolar regions.

In 1597 the Amsterdam merchants financed a search of their own. This time the ships sailed past Novaya Zemlya, discovered Bear Island, and eventually reached Spitzbergen. Mistaking it for part of Greenland, they erected a coat of arms in a small bay and claimed the land for the Netherlands. On its return, the ship commanded by Willem Barents was icebound for the winter near the northern tip of Novaya Zemlya. Unable to release the ship the following summer, the captain and crew made their way south in two small boats. Unfortunately, Barents died on the journey home, but he gained worldwide fame because of the detailed narratives of his three voyages, which were eventually published in seven languages.[16] This was only the beginning of a literary tradition in which stories of polar exploration recited tales of high adventure in a mystical landscape, strange sights and equally strange animals, and emphasized narrow escapes from certain death. All were written and illustrated to create fanciful and much-exaggerated images of the Arctic.

The seventeenth century brought a new face, new visions of empire, and empty pockets to the English monarchy. After Queen Elizabeth's death in 1603, King James found himself too pressed for cash after the war with Spain to fund further searches for the Northwest Passage. Priorities had also changed. After the failure of Sir Walter Raleigh's colony on Roanoke Island, new plans were afoot to establish a settlement further south on the east coast of North America. While receiving some support from lesser members of the royal family, the expeditions sent to explore and map Hudson Bay in the early 1600s were funded almost entirely by commercial interests. In 1610, London merchants formed the Company for Discovery of the North-West Passage, later shortened to the Northwest Passage Company. Among the investors were individuals whose names still appear on modern maps, such as Thomas Smith, Dudley Digges, John Wolstenholme and Francis Jones.[17] While "naming" was considered just reward for financial support, their appearance on published maps was also a means of identifying the extent of a nation's discovery claims.

Subsequent expeditions were surprisingly numerous, perhaps on account of instructions to trade for furs and ivory during the course of their explorations. The most notable was led by Henry Hudson in 1610–11, likely remembered more for the manner of his demise than for his extensive exploration of the bay and strait that now bear his name. Fearful of being icebound for a second winter without food or supplies, a mutinous crew set Hudson adrift in a small boat with his son and a few crew members. They were never seen again. The mutineers, however, ran aground on Digges Island, where hostile Inuit killed four of the men. Robert Bylot, who had joined the mutiny after Hudson had stripped him of his rank as mate, was credited with sailing the ship safely back to England and subsequently pardoned for his part in the revolt. He returned to Hudson Bay the following year with an expedition led by Sir Thomas Button, this time sponsored in part by the Prince of Wales.

In 1615, the Northwest Passage Company sent Robert Bylot back to Hudson Bay as captain of his own ship with William Baffin as his pilot. Both were seasoned Arctic explorers. After a thorough search of the Bay as far north as Foxe Channel, they concluded there was no possibility of an ice-free outlet to the north or west. Again in 1616 Bylot and Baffin set out on behalf of the company on what might be described as the most successful Arctic exploration of its time. Using Bylot's navigation expertise and Baffin's mapping skills, they charted the west coast of Greenland as far as Smith Sound and returned south along the coast of Baffin Island, locating the entrances to Jones and Lancaster Sounds, and mapping the shores of Bylot and Baffin Islands. Based on their observations, they came to the same conclusion as John Davis, that any passage leading through the islands to the Arctic Ocean was permanently blocked with ice.

Robert Bylot was the first European navigator to reach 77° 45′ N latitude, a record that stood for over two centuries. The expedition also claimed the distinction of being the first to locate and name Lancaster Sound, which eventually proved to be the entrance to the Northwest Passage. A number of other important features named by Bylot still appear on modern maps, like Smith and Jones Sound named for his patrons, and Lancaster Sound out of respect for King James, who held the title of Duke of Lancaster. Yet because Bylot had named the largest island of the Archipelago after his pilot, William Baffin is often mistaken as the leader of the expedition. The only tragedy occurred after they returned home. The expedition's reports and charts were so exceptional that they were discredited by British naval experts and refused publication. By the time Captain John Ross of the British Admiralty confirmed the findings 200 years later, most of the original documents had been either lost or destroyed.

English merchants funded three more expeditions to Hudson Bay, one in 1625 and two in 1631. Both were unsuccessful in finding an exit to the west. The monarchy would soon be embroiled in civil war, leaving the merchants to their own devices to defend against rival whalers and traders. By then, they faced stiff competition and the distortions dating back to the Frobisher expeditions remained on maps. Five maps in particular—by Mercator (1595), Wytfliet (1597), Gerritsz (1612), De Wit (1667) and Blaue (1638)—all show Frobisher Strait on the southeast shore of Greenland, with Cumberland Sound marked as the only major inlet on Baffin Island. The De Wit and Blaue maps both show Baffin Bay emptying into Hudson Bay with no outlet to the Pacific Ocean. All are grossly distorted in spite of the excellent charting by John Davis, Robert Bylot, Henry Hudson and others, reflecting the tight secrecy maintained by English merchants to gain competitive advantage.

The Dutch and English were not the only ones intent on laying claim to Arctic lands. In 1605, King Christian IV of Denmark attempted to reclaim Greenland for the United Kingdoms of Norway and Denmark. The expedition found no traces of the former Viking colony, but landed on the west coast and took possession of Greenland in the name of their king. Perhaps believing the renewed claim would hold after two more uncontested voyages, King Christian then turned to the northeast in hopes of securing Danish control over the northern sea routes originally controlled by Norway. In 1609 he sent an expedition led by Jens Munk to find a passage eastward through the Asian Arctic. Munk failed in his mission, but nevertheless was made a captain in the Royal Danish Navy. Ten years later he was sent to search for an alternative route to the northwest. With two ships belonging to the Danish navy, Munk entered Hudson Bay in 1619 and wintered near the mouth of what is now called the Churchill River. Unable to find any Natives to assist in obtaining food, the crew slowly died of scurvy and starvation. Only Munk and three others survived to return home. The disastrous voyage ended Danish interest in exploring Hudson Bay. Another century would pass before the Danish kings again attempted to secure control over the northern seas and Greenland.

Meanwhile Dutch merchant traders were already looking westward for new resources. In 1614, the States General of the United Parliament of the Netherlands granted the Noordsche Compagnie a monopoly over trading and fishing extending as far west as

Davis Strait. That same year, the company sent Joris Carolus on an expedition to investigate the waters off Greenland. Carolus sailed north along the island's western coast until he was halted by ice at 73° N latitude, just short of the record Bylot would reach two years later. Whether by coincidence or design, in 1616, the same year as Bylot's voyage, Dutch skippers claimed to have taken possession of West Greenland from 60° to 66° N latitude, which they named Statenland. The next year, Carolus sighted Greenland's east coast, which he named New Holland. His map published in 1634 included a number of Dutch names on the harbours frequented by their whaling ships. Soon Dutch whalers combined their fishing with a lucrative trade in furs and ivory with the Greenland Inuit. On several occasions King Frederick II of Denmark-Norway sent ships to assess the situation, but he still made no attempt to reclaim Greenland.[18]

By the early seventeenth century, the whaling industry was flourishing because of increasing demand for whale oil and baleen. Competition intensified, but none was as fierce as in the waters off the Svalbard Islands, also known as Spitzbergen. Although these islands were not geographically part of North America, the rivalry that began here continued in Davis Strait, with new countries now vying for control of the Arctic waters.

The British Muscovy Company, which for over fifty years held a monopoly over fishing and trade along Russia's northern coast, sent two ships to Spitzbergen in 1611—both sank. Although the sailors were humiliated at being rescued by a rival English ship, reports of seas teeming with huge whales and rocky shores covered with walrus could not be ignored. The next year, the company sent more ships only to discover Dutch and Basque whalers hard at work. In 1613, now armed with a new charter from King James I, the Muscovy Company sent a fleet of seven vessels, its flagship carrying twenty-one guns. Seventeen foreign ships were warned off that year and either had their cargoes confiscated or handed over a portion to ensure immediate departure.[19]

In retaliation, the Dutch Noordsche Compagnie with a charter provided by the States General sent its whalers to Spitzbergen in

1614 with a fleet of eleven armed ships, accompanied by three war-ships to ensure that they could hunt unmolested. The following year King Christian IV of Denmark-Norway also sent a fleet from his Royal Navy to assert his country's rights. In the end, neither the Netherlands, England nor Denmark could maintain control over the Svalbard Islands and surrounding waters. Instead there were periodic agreements between the whalers to share the many bays and har-bours of the island, but not without frequent skirmishes over rights and privileges. The events of 1613 marked the beginning of a century-long struggle between the Dutch and the English for supremacy on the seas. By mid-century, the Dutch whaling fleet dominated the industry, in both the number of ships and their productivity.

The success of the Dutch whalers and the relative decline of the English were partly attributable to the former's ability to adapt their techniques to the open seas. The large bowheads, or Greenland whales as they were called at the time, initially required land-based stations on Spitzbergen in order for their blubber to be rendered into whale oil. The Dutch station at Smeerenburg rapidly grew into a small town during the summer, but there were no volunteers to remain in the off season. English whalers attempted to establish year-round settlements by employing prisoners from the London Gaol, with the promise of amnesty if they remained over the winter. After one summer, the convicts agreed that jail was preferable to spending the winter on Spitzbergen. The failure to establish permanent Arctic set-tlements would become the single most common reason for a lapse of discovery claims and attempted possession by another nation.

The seventeenth century also witnessed the beginning of an intense debate over whether *mare clausum* (closed seas) or *mare liberum* should apply to the waters surrounding continental Europe. John Selden, scholar, jurist, legal historian and sometime parliamentar-ian, wrote a treatise titled *Mare Clausum*, c1618, in which he defended England's right of control over the "British Sea" lying between Britain and Europe, based on customary practice and English law. Although remaining unpublished until 1635 and dedicated to King Charles I, the treatise was essentially a response to *Mare Liberum*

(1609) by the Netherlands jurist and philosopher Hugo Grotius, who argued in defence of the freedom of the seas, based on abstract theory and natural law.[20] Opposing theories of customary versus natural law re-emerged in the twentieth century during negotiations at the United Nations Law of the Sea Conference.

The Protestant Reformation led to almost continual European wars between Protestant and Catholic states, ending with the signing of the Peace of Westphalia in 1648, which essentially gave equal rights to both religions. The situation in England was further complicated by a series of civil wars beginning in 1642 and resulting in the beheading of Charles I in 1649 for treason. During this period of unrest, English merchants had little hope of financial support from Parliament for further Arctic explorations. Not until 1660, when King Charles II was restored to the throne, did thoughts return of looking to the Arctic regions for new trading opportunities. Unexpectedly, a proposal came from two unlicensed fur traders from New France.

Angered that both the French trading company and the Governor of New France had refused to consider an expedition to Hudson Bay, in 1668 Pierre-Esprit Radisson and Médard Chouart Des Groseilliers arrived in London seeking support from the English merchants. After two exploratory voyages to the bay, the second returning with a valuable cargo of furs, the merchants were convinced that trading posts on Hudson Bay would allow access to the northwest and at the same time bypass the St. Lawrence River controlled by the French. The sudden demand for beaver hats added even further incentive.[21] Prince Rupert, a favourite cousin of the King, was the driving force behind the Company of Adventurers of England Trading into Hudson's Bay, which was granted a charter by Charles II in 1670, covering a vast territory that encompassed all the lands that drained into Hudson Bay, popularly known as Rupert's Land. The Royal Charter was the most generous ever granted by a monarch, in terms of the size of territory, but more importantly because of the powers it granted to the "true and absolute Lordes and Proprietors" over largely unexplored lands, an area roughly equivalent to 40 percent of modern Canada. In spite

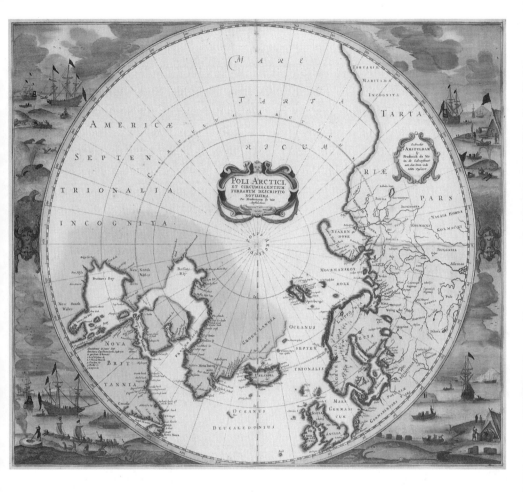

Map of the Arctic Regions, c1680, by Flemish cartographer Frederick De
Wit, based on information obtained from explorers and whaling captains.
Note that the American northwest is still largely uncharted.

RH-002, Robert Hunter Map Collection, Trent University Archives

of vigorous protests by merchants excluded from the company, an act confirming the charter was passed by the English Parliament twenty years later.[22]

Eventually named the Hudson's Bay Company, the syndicate appointed Prince Rupert as the first London-based governor, followed by the Duke of York and later John Churchill, Duke of Marlborough. Its main source of furs would be inland in the Subarctic, but large warehouses for furs and trade goods were built along the coast of Hudson Bay. The impressive Fort Prince of Wales was built near the mouth of the Churchill River to defend the major centre at York Factory from attack by French rivals. Other posts included Rupert House, Fort Charles, Fort Albany and Moose Factory at the bottom of James Bay. The company's ships arrived annually at Hudson Bay, creating a continual English presence in the area. They were not, however, without competition.

The first serious threat came from La Compagnie du Nord of France formed by Radisson and Des Groseilliers, who had been lured by a Jesuit priest to work for France. In 1682, they set out for Hudson Bay in two ships and stole a year's trade in pelts stored at York Factory. On their arrival at Quebec, however, officials confiscated their ships and charged them duty on their furs. Disgusted with the turn of events, Des Groseilliers retired but Radisson returned to London and negotiated a deal to work for the Hudson's Bay Company. Tensions between British and French fur traders escalated elsewhere in North America, spreading to Hudson Bay in 1686, when the Governor of New France authorized overland raids to James Bay by Chevalier de Troyes and Pierre Le Moyne d'Iberville. Moose Factory was captured, then Rupert House and Fort Albany, but these were soon reoccupied by the English. For a number of years, the French seemed to win the small skirmishes. These ended in 1697, when d'Iberville in the forty-four-gun *Pélican* faced two armed HBC freighters and the Royal Navy frigate *Hampshire* in a four-hour battle. Against all odds, the *Hampshire* was sunk, the HBC ships surrendered and France had won the battle for Hudson Bay. The Treaty of Ryswick signed that September gave France possession of all English posts on the bay with the exception of Fort Albany. Then in 1713, the Treaty of Utrecht returned the posts to Britain.[23]

In 1734, the HBC began construction of a large stone fort located at the mouth of the Churchill River to protect York Factory from attack. On completion, it was said to rival the French fortress at Louisbourg. York Factory, meanwhile, was continually expanding as the distribution centre for Hudson Bay, supplying trade goods to the other posts and receiving their furs for transport to London. Trade continued to flourish in spite of fierce competition with the French and free traders. Then tensions between France and Britain again intensified after the French provided assistance to the Thirteen Colonies during the American War of Independence.

After 1776, hostilities continued between the two European countries, coming to a head in the West Indies. In 1782, three ships of the scattered French navy sailed north with the intent of destroying British trading posts on Hudson Bay and stealing the furs. Both Fort Prince of Wales and York Factory were destroyed, but the French ships came away empty-handed. While the fort was under attack, the HBC supply ship sailed away undetected with the annual fur proceeds. The damage inflicted on the company was severe, but victory was short-lived. The following year, the Treaty of Paris (1783) ended the war, and Hudson Bay was once more firmly under Britain's control.

Although HBC trading posts on Hudson Bay were located in the Arctic, the majority of its trade was conducted with Indians living in the Subarctic. With beaver the fur most in demand, Inuit were initially excluded from regular trade. Even then, HBC ships were often met in Hudson Strait by Inuit in kayaks seeking trinkets for their ivory and sealskins. Following the 1707 Act of Union that united England and Scotland, the trading company increasingly employed Scots to manage its posts. Dependent on the outside world for staples, clothing, trade goods, guns and ammunition, they learned to live in the Arctic to make their fortune but retired to their homeland to enjoy their rewards. In this sense, Richard Vaughan, in his history of the Arctic, argues that they were not "real settlers" compared to the Danish colonizers of Greenland.

Fort Prince of Wales has been restored and is now a National
Historic Site. The fort was originally built in the mid-1700s at the mouth
of the Churchill River to protect the Hudson's Bay Company's cargo ships
from French rivals. Construction took forty years beginning in 1731 and
forty cannons were placed along the outer walls, which were over 40 feet
wide and 16 feet high. It was believed to be the largest stone fort on the
continent when it fell to the French in 1783, without a single shot being fired.
Parks Canada, H.07.72.02.06 (27), photographer R.E. Bill

During the first century of operation, the Hudson's Bay Company financed only two attempts to search for the Northwest Passage.
The first was by James Knight, a former overseas governor. Based
on Indian stories about a river with copper along its banks, he was
convinced that there must be a passage to the west. In England, he
convinced the company of his plan and was loaned two ships, with
instructions "to find the Streights of Anian [Bering Strait], and to
make what Discoveries you possibly can, and to obtain all sorts of
Trade and Commerce... Especially to find out the Gold and Copper
Mines if possible."[24] In 1719, Knight set out with two ships and thirty-
five men, presumably heading north toward Roes Welcome Sound,
where he believed he would find an outlet to the Arctic Ocean. Neither he nor his ships and his men were ever seen again.

Under pressure by merchants who believed the HBC had not fully explored the territory under its charter, in 1745 the British Parliament offered a reward of £20,000 for the discovery of a northwest passage. More interested in expanding inland trade, the company initially made no effort to conduct such a search that might benefit other traders. Finally in 1771, it sponsored an overland trek by Samuel Hearne to investigate stories about copper deposits along a large river emptying into the Arctic Ocean. Hearne took eighteen months to reach the outflow of the Coppermine River. His reports on the mineral potential in the area were respectfully received, but the HBC made no attempt to turn the knowledge into practical purpose. Its sole aim was to acquire as many furs as possible from the Indians and to auction them at the highest price in London. According to its interpretation of the charter, its governance responsibilities did not include educating the Natives, looking after their medical needs or converting them to Christianity. From the outset, this was a business proposition, with Britain retaining sovereignty over a vast territory without investing a cent.

For northern Europeans, it was more economical for their whalers to return to Davis Strait than to travel south. Still considered dangerous because of the icebergs and pack ice, the only safe waters were along the shores of southwest Greenland, where the Gulf Stream warmed the water until blocked by cold Arctic currents from the north. Attempts to sail north to Melville Bay or across to Baffin Island in search of more whales resulted in major losses of men and ships. Eventually, trade with the Inuit along the shores of west Greenland became common practice to compensate for declining whale stocks. Dutch whalers had a distinct advantage because of new techniques they had adopted, as well as maps and navigational data supplied by Carolus. With their larger ships, they were able to use the "tryworks" method of rendering oil on board, thus eliminating the need to build onshore stations. Their trading operations were efficient, with a ship anchored offshore acting as a floating trading post.

By the early 1700s, Dutch whalers dominated the trade off the western coast of Greenland, a status that was soon challenged by the British. In an attempt to rebuild their fleet, in 1733 the British government offered to pay 20 shillings per ton for every whale weighing over 200 tons. When the amount doubled twenty-five years later, the whaling fleet experienced a sudden regrowth, with hundreds of ships now sailing from a variety of ports, including London, Hull, Whitby, Aberdeen, Dundee and Peterhead.[25] By the end of the Napoleonic Wars, the British whaling fleet had surpassed all others and the Dutch had all but disappeared.

Since trade with the Greenland Inuit was sporadic during this period, they were still largely dependent on wildlife resources for their survival. According to Danish historian Finn Gad, "Greenland Eskimo society was not really one society but a group of small communities living along miles of coastline without any centralized governing authority. The dominant force was inertia which governed as long as life continued and new life was born. Consequently tradition grew to be of vital importance as it guaranteed that life would go on." Most scholars attribute their survival to their sophisticated hunting techniques and ability to adapt.[26]

When the Little Ice Age advanced, the Greenland Inuit migrated southward, except for those living in a protected area around Wolstenholme Bay. Isolated, the Inughuit or Polar Eskimos, as they are called, retained their distinctive cultural traditions, as did a few families who had remained on the east coast in the vicinity of Angmagssalik (or Ammassalik). Otherwise, the majority were living along the southwestern seacoast, in small pear-shaped houses built of turf and stone. Likely because of the cooler weather and sporadic trade with English and Dutch whalers, they seemed to have abandoned the use of bows and arrows. Eventually, individual dwellings were replaced by communal longhouses.[27]

The Danish kings were fully aware of Dutch activities in Greenland. Although ships had been sent to observe on several occasions, no action was taken. Then in 1719, King Frederick IV of Denmark-Norway received a petition from Hans Egede, a young Lutheran minister from Norway, who set out a plan to reclaim Greenland. The project required the support of the Bergen merchants, the King's navy and the Lutheran Church. Granted a royal charter, Egede set sail in 1721 with his wife and children, plus twenty-five men and three women. The objective was to create a number of permanent settlements along the western coast of Greenland, supported by trade in fish and furs. In Egede's mind, however, the main purpose was "the propagation of the pure and true doctrine of God."[28] On arrival, he found the Greenlandic Inuit shy but willing to assist in unloading the ship. He also discovered that they had no goods to trade as they had already been visited by the Dutch. The first settlement was in Godthab Fjord, but was moved in 1728 to Godthab, now the site of Nuuk, capital of Greenland.

To further protect their sovereignty claims against the Dutch, in 1723 King Frederick granted a royal charter to the newly formed Bergen Company, covering "the whole of Greenland with all its lands, coasts, harbours and islands from Cape Farewell as far as it stretched in all directions." Foreign ships were forbidden to trade within four miles of the coast and permission was granted to build forts to protect their interests. The King retained the right to name the commander of the trade expeditions and the clergymen assigned to the new settlements. Of particular note were the instructions that the Inuit were to be treated kindly and not taken as slaves.[29]

In 1726, Egede reported persistent intrusion by Dutch and English ships, including instances where they raided Inuit communities and stole their whale blubber and skins. Viewing these episodes as a major encroachment on Danish sovereign rights, King Frederick consulted his council. Maintenance of Danish sovereignty in Greenland now became a state affair and a naval expedition was sent in 1727 to construct and man a fort near Godthab to give further evidence of "effective occupation." In a manner similar to that employed in New France, those who were to man the fort were volunteers or soldiers who had been imprisoned for military offences. As well, the new colonists were men and women collected from houses of correction and married before departure "with a view to people the country." A governor was appointed to administer the colony with the help of his council, again with explicit instructions that the Inuit were to be treated kindly to facilitate good relations with the new settlers.

This ancient cemetery with over fifty-six graves—only three of them with
white crosses—is located on Kitsissunnguit Island in the southern part of
Disko Bay, a reminder of the devastating effect of infectious diseases during
the early years of the mission settlements. The smallpox scourge in 1733–34,
for example, nearly decimated the Inuit population in western Greenland.
CE-5997, photographer Carsten Egevang, ARC-PIC, Greenland

In 1730, reports from Godthab suggested that the Danish colony
had failed. Not only was the garrison unable to control Dutch traders,
but internal revolt had erupted between the governor, the military
and the settlers. In Copenhagen, a commission reviewed the problems and suggested recall of the governor and that new settlers be
brought from Iceland where conditions were similar to those in
Greenland. That year, building supplies and provisions were sent to
Godthab in anticipation of the arrival of the new immigrants, but it
all came to naught when King Frederick died that winter and his successor Christian VI ordered all Danes to return home.

Egede, his family and a few loyal followers elected to remain,
sending the King a lengthy report requesting continued support
of the colony and the mission. After lengthy discussions with the
merchants, King Christian VI renewed efforts to put the colony
on a sound footing. He first approved a new trade agreement with

merchant Jakob Severin and granted him a seven-year monopoly on the Greenland trade. To give further support, all goods to and from Greenland were exempted from taxes and customs duties. The King also sent three Moravian missionaries to assist the Lutherans, resulting in three new mission stations at Jakobshavn, Christianshaab and Frederikshaab. The Brethren were self-sufficient artisans and built their own buildings, tended the gardens and took care of the sick and elderly. In 1750, the trading monopoly passed to the General Trading Company. The Moravians remained until 1900, at which time their missions were taken over by the Danish Church.[30]

In 1782, the Danish government took direct control of the colony's trade with establishment of the Royal Greenland Trading Company, which held a monopoly over all trade on the island and effectively closed the country to foreigners. For administration purposes, the island was divided into North and South Greenland, each with a governor or inspector who reported directly to the managing director in Copenhagen. The headquarters for the southern district was located at Godthab and for the northern district at Godhavn on Disko Island. Settlement costs were to be sustained by exports, with the governors given control over activities in each settlement and reporting directly to the managing director of the Greenland Department, a division of the Department of Interior in Copenhagen. "Instructions" were issued which were described as similar to a "bill of rights" or benevolent paternalism, with the intent of protecting Greenlanders from exploitation and the abuse of European civilization. Foreign ships were banned from ports and heavy penalties were assigned for anyone providing liquor to the Inuit. It was left to the missionaries to teach their children to read and write.

Although the trade monopoly was lifted in 1967, the Royal Greenland trading company (Den Kongelige Grøndlandsk Handel, or KGH as it is commonly called) has survived in each community. Unlike the Hudson's Bay Company, which was run as a private business, the trading company was a government-controlled entity designed to affirm Danish sovereignty over Greenland through administration of its settlements. Danish trading stations and missions were set up in existing Inuit communities, which provided the company with a variety of products including furs, seal blubber and fish. The objective was not profit-oriented, but aimed at breaking even by adjusting the price of imports and exports to cover transportation and administration costs. Denmark, however, earned revenue and profits from various mining operations which were not channelled through the Royal Greenland Trading Company. The Moravians and Lutherans were responsible for the education and medical needs of Greenlanders, but were also under the direction of the Danish government.[31]

In the opinion of Diamond Jenness, the isolation policies and cost controls created "a purely artificial community" that failed to achieve its objectives. In the short term, the Danes were unable to enforce the four-mile territorial waters limit to prevent foreign traders from plying Greenlanders with liquor. Over the longer term, the isolation policy denied them the opportunity to adapt gradually to the modern world. As well, the Danes shared the European belief in the superiority of the white man, creating an entrenched two-class social structure.[32]

Meanwhile, events taking place on the other side of the world eventually put Russia in competition with the Hudson's Bay Company. Until the mid-1500s, the Arctic region of Siberia had remained remote and the Native peoples relatively unaffected by intruders until Ivan the Terrible sent his Cossacks to subdue and conquer the lands east of the Urals. The small indigenous communities had no guns and no means to defend themselves when the Cossacks arrived, demanding they turn over their furs. In just over a hundred years the Russians advanced across Siberia and overland to Kamchatka. Their sole purpose was to expand their fur-trading empire by exacting a tax, or *yasak,* from Native peoples. Only the Chukchi and the Chukotka Eskimos remained free of Russian rule, but they too succumbed in 1789 after several hard-fought battles.

Arctic Siberia is a narrow strip along the northern Russian coast, stretching from Yamal to Chukotka and including a number of offshore islands. The fur most prized in Moscow was sable, found only in the Subarctic region, whereas walrus, valued for their ivory tusks, were found only along the coast. Cossack traders travelled from one river mouth to the next along the Arctic shores, in a small sailing ship called a *koch,* which had a shallow draft and rounded sides that enabled it to manoeuvre easily through the ice. Square-rigged with a single mast, the ship was easily handled by half a dozen crew members and could carry thirty passengers and up to 30 tons of cargo. Using wooden dowels instead of iron nails, the ships could be constructed out of the forest using reindeer skins for sails instead of canvas. Although Vitus Bering has been credited as the first person to explore the Bering Sea, in 1648 a Cossack trader by the name of Simon Dezhner sailing in a *koch* was actually the first to reach the islands in what is now known as Bering Strait. A fur trader rather than an explorer, he made no official claims of discovery.[33]

Anthropologists believe that Cossack traders had conducted a thriving trade with indigenous peoples along the coast of the Bering Sea in the late 1600s and possibly as far east as Alaska. As occurred with the English traders, their routes and contacts were kept secret to protect their sources from competitors, especially Russian traders in Moscow. The final stage of Russian expansion across northern Siberia took place at the direction of Czar Peter the Great. As part of the Great Northern Expedition, Vitus Bering, a Danish-born captain in the Imperial Navy, was sent to Siberia in 1728, where he built two ships out of the forest and continued eastward along the coast. His instructions were to explore the eastern coast of Siberia and determine whether it was joined to America. After sailing through the strait and into the sea that both now bear his name, he continued until sighting the Diomede Islands before being forced back by ice. He was close, but failed to sight the American coast. On his return, Bering wrote a report recommending continued mapping of the Siberian coast and an additional expedition to explore the coast of America. Peter the Great had died during his absence, but the Great Northern Expedition continued as commanders and surveyors of the Imperial Navy mapped the Arctic coast. By 1742 they had completed all but the Chukchi Peninsula—a remarkable achievement.

Meanwhile, Bering again built two ships, this time at Okhotsk in Kamchatka, and in 1741 set sail for America. The two ships became separated, but Bering managed to map the strait before sailing south to the Aleutian Islands, which he claimed for Russia. Both ships reached America before turning back. Sadly, Bering and several crew members died of scurvy when their ship was wrecked on a small island now bearing his name. The survivors, however, made their way home with an assortment of furs and ivory, which caught the attention of Russian merchants. Drawn by the prospect of huge profits, Russian traders risked stormy weather and hostile Natives in their insatiable quest for furs and ivory. In the process they explored and mapped the islands and coast of Russian America, naming the latter Alaska after an Aleutian name meaning "mainland." Subduing the Aleuts involved skirmishes and in 1773, a fierce battle that lasted three years.

Reports of Russian activities in the North Pacific brought the British explorer James Cook to investigate. In 1776, his explorations in the Bering Sea and Strait were extensive but he was blocked by ice when attempting to push further east. He fully expected to return the following summer to make another attempt to locate the western entrance to the Northwest Passage, but was murdered by Hawaiian Natives. His crew tried again the following summer but they too were forced back by heavy ice. Not one to be intimidated by the British, in 1785 Catherine the Great sent the Imperial Navy to Alaska to reaffirm title to the lands claimed by Bering. However, when the naval ships attempted to assert authority on Vancouver Island, they were defeated by the British and Spanish, and Britain laid claim to the British Columbia coast.

In the interim, a Russian merchant by the name of Gregori Shlikov had equipped three vessels in 1783 and set out with plans to build an empire, with settlers, schools, churches—a self-supporting community that would even build its own ships. He first claimed the American coast and offshore islands north of 55° 21′ N latitude for Russia, then established a settlement on Kodiak Island, with outposts on nearby islands. The first school was built on the island in 1786 and clergy arrived from the Russian Orthodox Church. Count

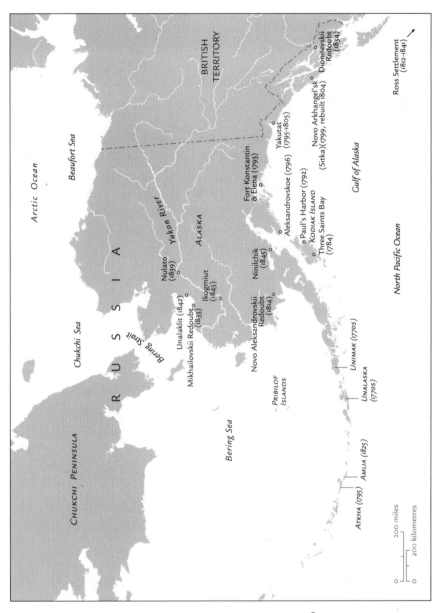

RUSSIAN SETTLEMENTS IN ALASKA, C1800

In spite of support from the czars and the Eastern Orthodox
Church, the Russian trading settlements suffered
repeated attacks by hostile Natives and rival traders.

Sketch of the Russian fur-trading settlement at Novo Arkhangel'sk,
by Captain Lisiansky of the Russian navy, 1805. The wooden
fort shown on the hill was burned to the ground at least once.
PCA 20-143, Alaska State Library, Alaska Purchase Centennial Photograph Collection

Aleksandre Baranov was placed in charge of the settlement and literally controlled the entire Alaskan trade. A second settlement called
Novo Arkhangel'sk was established on Sitka Island in Tlingit territory.
The priests' attempts to protect the Natives from Baranov's brutality
resulted in lasting loyalty to the Orthodox Church long after the Russians departed.

As an increasing number of British and Spanish ships began to
trade in Russian America, the Russians sought the protection of the
Imperial Navy. Eventually in 1799 the Russian government established the Russian-American Trading Company, with a royal charter,
similar to that of the Hudson's Bay Company, that granted a monopoly over hunting and mining on the Alaskan mainland and offshore
islands north of 55° N latitude and the right to make new discoveries. Like the Hudson's Bay Company, the Russian-American Company
became a vehicle for the Russian government to gain control over the
North Pacific.

Over a period of twenty years, additional colonies were established, bringing the total number of permanent settlements to fifteen
with a combined population of roughly 600 Russians and mixed-
bloods. The largest was Novo Arkhangel'sk. An attempt to find an

agricultural base to provision the northern posts led to a colony near what is now San Francisco. Established in 1812, Fort Ross actually survived for three decades before being sold to American interests shortly before Mexico ceded California to the United States.[34]

Throughout the Renaissance, the concept of a chartered company had become a popular means of promoting trade, but only if such companies were supported by a strong navy could they avoid attack by foreign ships. Monopolies that began as a means of protecting trading interests soon expanded to the whaling industry, as in the case of the English Muscovy Company, the Dutch East India Company and the Noordsche Compagnie. Similarly, Russia and Britain adapted the monopoly charter specifically to the fur trade, with both the Russian-American Company and the HBC granted governance of the areas specified under their charters. Unlike Russia, however, Britain used its fur-trading monopoly to maintain sovereignty over a vast territory without spending a penny on colonization.[35] Establishment of the Royal Greenland Trading Company in 1774 was different again, as it was directly controlled by the Danish government, a difference that would translate into policies that provided protection for Greenlanders compared to the tendency to exploit the Inuit of Alaska and British North America.

As happened elsewhere in the Arctic, the Little Ice Age prevented Russian exploration and settlement along the northern Alaskan coast. But it also prevented foreign ships from sailing along the Northern Sea Route and denied American whalers access to the Beaufort Sea. As long as the ice was a formidable barrier, Russia's claim to its Arctic mainland and islands was secure. At the turn of the nineteenth century, the lands most vulnerable to challenge by foreigners were the Alaskan coast, the western and central Arctic mainland, the Arctic Islands and to a lesser extent Greenland. Vast areas of Greenland and the Arctic Archipelago were still unclaimed and unexplored because of the ice. In the eyes of the Russians and Europeans, the Inuit, who had adapted and survived in the colder climate, still had no rights to their lands, as they were still not recognized as a civilized people.

PART II

THE NINETEENTH CENTURY

MAJOR CHANGES took place on the nineteenth-century map of the North American Arctic, initially as a result of the British Admiralty's discovery claims in the Arctic Islands, followed later by the United States purchase of Alaska, the Hudson's Bay Company's sale of its land rights in Rupert's Land and the North-Western Territory in 1870, then in 1880, Britain's transfer of the Arctic Islands to Canada. Aside from affecting governance of the region, these changes also represented a new way of acquiring sovereign authority other than discovery, war or subjugation.

Boundaries elsewhere in North America had also changed as a wave of American expansionism extended the nation westward to the Pacific Ocean. In terms of size, the new Dominion of Canada experienced even greater growth, with its land mass multiplying over tenfold within thirteen years of its creation in 1867. Meanwhile, the Industrial Revolution had altered the character of the world economically and socially, creating a powerful middle class and an increasingly discontented labour class. Also changing were interpretations of international law and motivations for polar exploration. Once driven for economic reasons, new discoveries were now a matter of national honour and prestige, initially for Britain and later for the United States.

(**4**)

THE BRITISH ADMIRALTY
AND THE ARCTIC, 1818—53

The physical power of the navy of England has long been duly
appreciated at home, also by most foreign nations, and is a matter
of public record; its moral influence, though less the object of publicity,
requires only to be more extensively known to be equally felt and esteemed;
and nothing can be more conducive to this end than the results to be
derived from voyages of discovery whose great aim has been the acquisition
of knowledge, not for England alone, but for the general benefit of mankind.

SIR JOHN BARROW, Second Secretary of the British Admiralty, ND [1]

. . . .

T HE BALANCE of world powers had changed significantly as a
result of the Napoleonic Wars, with Britain emerging as the major
force among European nations. Not only was its navy considered
invincible, but the Industrial Revolution had fuelled a robust mercantile economy. The other two nations with vested interests in the
North American Arctic—Russia and Denmark—experienced severe
economic reverses after the wars and were reduced to being lesser
players on the world stage. In their absence, the British Admiralty
seized the opportunity to play a dominant role in Arctic exploration.

Denmark, in spite of attempts to remain neutral during the Napoleonic Wars, saw the destruction of its Royal Navy, during Britain's
second attack on Copenhagen in an attempt to blockade European
trade. With links to Norway tenuous, the Danes sought refuge from
further attacks by allying with France. In retaliation at the end of

the wars, the Peace of Kiel placed Norway under Swedish rule, thus adding to Denmark's economic hardship and endangering the future of the fledgling Greenland colony. Although Russia was somewhat better off and its Imperial Navy less affected, the state faced enormous costs in rebuilding the army and repairing the damage to Moscow wrought by Napoleon's invasion. The Netherlands, once a major sea power but with no claims in the Arctic at the turn of the century, was humbled after Napoleon's invasion and takeover of the Dutch fleet, which was subsequently destroyed during the Battle of Trafalgar. With its maritime strength already in decline as a result of competition with British and New England whalers, the Netherlands had little hope of returning to its former status as a predominant seafaring nation.

The three major trading companies operating in the Arctic and Subarctic in the early 1800s—the Hudson's Bay Company, the Russian-American Company and the Royal Greenland Trading Company—also experienced hardships in varying degrees during the wars. The Royal Greenland Trading Company, in particular, suffered severe financial losses as a result of the English blockade and loss of Danish ships. Unable to export its products between 1807 and 1817, the company was forced to purchase bare necessities from English ships at inflated prices. The effect on Greenlanders was disastrous, made worse by a general exodus of Danes. The Inuit were reported to be ill-nourished, impoverished and still living in stone and sod houses. Diseases were responsible for a decline in population. As economic conditions improved by 1825, Denmark initiated plans to restore the Greenland trade and colonies to their pre-war state. New instructions were issued, but conditions in the settlements were slow to change.[2]

Initially the Russian-American Trading Company appeared to benefit from the Napoleonic Wars because of the relative absence of the British and Spanish navies in the North Pacific, which allowed expansion of Russian settlements southward along the Alaskan coast. The Ross Colony, set up in 1812 some 90 miles north of San Francisco, had initially survived because Spanish forces were too thinly dispersed to oust the intruders. Yet the settlement never prospered and in 1841 was sold to Spanish interests. At the end of the Napoleonic Wars the administration of the Russian-American Company was assigned to the Imperial Navy. Although company management was replaced by a succession of naval officers, the high cost of supplies and trade goods made it difficult to remain competitive with its British and American counterparts. Furthermore, the sea otter, upon which Russian traders had depended for most of their profits, was now almost extinct, forcing the company to rely more on inland furs that brought it into direct competition with the Hudson's Bay Company.[3]

The HBC supply ships may have derived some benefit from British navy protection during the Napoleonic Wars, but traders now experienced fierce competition from the North West Company, which had amalgamated the Montreal fur trade after the fall of New France. By 1811 the "Norwesters," as they were called, had moved into the Liard Valley and three of their traders—Alexander Mackenzie, Simon Fraser and David Thompson—had reached the Pacific coast. Additional competition came from American free traders and a company owned by John Jacob Astor, who had set up a permanent post on the Columbia River. After years of exceptional profits, the HBC was suddenly unable to pay dividends from 1809 to 1820. The most expedient remedy was to combine the two British companies.

Although promoted as a merger, the agreement had all the characteristics of a takeover. By an 1821 act of Parliament the new company retained the name of the Hudson's Bay Company and continued to operate under its charter, which now legally supported and geographically expanded exclusive trading privileges in both Rupert's Land and the North-Western Territory. While the amalgamation substantially increased the number of shareholders, the senior officials and administrative structure remained intact. New terms were added to the charter, however, to include responsibility for the care of Aboriginals, promotion of settlement and general mapping of an area now roughly 3 million square miles in size. With competition reduced, the company again prospered and resumed its expansion westward. Only one new post was established in the eastern Arctic, at Fort

Chimo on the Koksoak River flowing north into Hudson Strait. By comparison, numerous posts were added in the northwest, including Fort Youcon (Yukon) well within Russian territory. With the beaver still the primary fur in demand, there was no incentive for the HBC to open posts in the central Arctic mainland or the islands. Nor was there any interest in assisting the search for the Northwest Passage. Governor George Simpson, responsible for the company's North American operations, believed that discovery of the passage would bring new competition, encourage settlement and eventually lead to loss of the company's monopoly.[4] As with all commercial enterprises in the Arctic, sovereignty issues were only of concern if they affected the profits of the venerable trading company.

The whaling industry was also affected by the Napoleonic Wars. Scottish and English whalers avoided enemy ships in the Atlantic by confining their activities to the Greenland Sea, the lower Davis Strait and a narrow stretch of open water along the coast of western Greenland. Slow and unarmed, the American ships were easy prey for British and French warships and some owners simply retired their vessels to await better times.[5] After 1814, however, American whalers resumed their activities in the North Pacific, supplemented by trading for furs and ivory with Native communities along the Alaskan shores. With the assistance of auxiliary steam engines, by mid-century they began to follow the path of the bowhead whales through the Bering Sea and Bering Strait as far as the Arctic Ocean. In support of their activities, the port of San Francisco replaced Hawaii as the main centre for reprovisioning and ship repairs. Once the transcontinental railway reached the port, the whalers were able to remain on the west coast and send their oil and baleen overland by rail to industrial cities in the east, thus avoiding the twice-yearly voyage around Cape Horn.[6]

The United States government had shown little interest in the Arctic during the first half of the nineteenth century, as it was pre-occupied with continental expansion by way of natural growth, purchase and even invasion. The 1803 Louisiana Purchase from France cost $15 million, but more than doubled the size of the new nation. Not all invasion attempts were successful. The attack on Upper Canada in 1812, for instance, failed to find local support and ended in failure, with the 1814 Treaty of Ghent returning boundaries to their pre-war status. Adopting a more amicable approach to settle the western boundary between British North America and the United States, bilateral negotiations resulted in the Convention of 1818, which established the 49th parallel west of the territories claimed by the United States and Britain, with a ten-year agreement for joint occupancy of the disputed Oregon Territory. At the time, there were marked differences in the goals and ambitions of Canadian and American citizens. While Americans were expanding their country westward, Upper and Lower Canadians were pressing for political reforms and devolution of their colonial government. The only factor in common was the absence of interest in the Arctic.

For Great Britain, however, it was quite another matter. Of all the European countries, Britain had emerged from the Napoleonic Wars relatively unscathed, creating a serious logistics problem for the Admiralty. At the height of the wars, the British navy had grown to an enormous size, with a fleet of 773 ships commanded by 4,000 officers and crewed by 140,000 sailors.[7] At the wars' end, crew members were sent home and most ships laid up. Officers, however, were not so easily retired, with the result that their numbers actually increased, creating a ratio of one officer for every four sailors and little hope of advancement. Although First Lord of the Admiralty Viscount Melville retained ultimate power for decisions affecting the activities of the Royal Navy, it was primarily his nephew Second Secretary John Barrow who had the most influence on his decisions.[8]

To keep his officers gainfully employed, Barrow directed the navy's peacetime activities toward exploration, scientific research and mapping of unknown territory. One report that piqued his interest was by whaling captain William S. Scoresby, who claimed that the rapidly melting Arctic pack ice would enable discovery of new northern sea routes. When asked why whalers had not made a greater effort to find the Northwest Passage after Parliament's offer of sizable cash rewards—£5,000 for the first to reach 110° W longitude and £20,000

Sir John Barrow as second secretary of the British Admiralty.
D-23404, National Portrait Gallery, London, England

to reach the Pacific—Scoresby explained that the potential cost of losing ships, men and whales far exceeded the value of the award. For that reason, he believed that the publicly financed Admiralty had a far better chance of success, even if it took a number of expeditions over an extended period of time to achieve its goal.[9]

After the Admiralty's failed expedition to the Congo in 1816, Barrow revisited Scoresby's recommendations, particularly the idea of traversing the Northwest Passage or being first to reach the North Pole. The Second Secretary was convinced that a navigable Northwest Passage existed and that the North Pole was a rock or pile of rocks surrounded by open water. Given the southerly flow of ice to the Atlantic and Pacific, he reasoned that it must be driven by a body of temperate water circling the Pole. Barrow was confident in his officers' ability and believed that the Royal Navy would achieve both objectives.

Thus, in 1818 the British Admiralty launched two expeditions to the Arctic: one led by Captain David Buchan and Lieutenant John Franklin to the North Pole by way of Spitzbergen, the other led by Captain John Ross and Lieutenant William Edward Parry to locate and chart the Northwest Passage. The plan was for the two expeditions to meet in the Pacific before returning home. Although both expeditions failed, it was a credit to their competence that no ships or lives were lost, as none of the officers and crew had previous Arctic experience. Yet Barrow's personal pride was at stake, with the result that John Ross would be severely reprimanded for his failure to proceed further along Lancaster Sound and was never again employed by the British navy. Buchan, who also failed to achieve the goal set by the ambitious second secretary, was relegated to administrative duties.

The following year Parry, now promoted to captain, was sent back to Lancaster Sound in command of a second expedition to find the Northwest Passage. Almost effortlessly he led his two ships through Lancaster Sound to Barrow Strait and Viscount Melville Sound, dutifully naming the latter two bodies of water after the Second Secretary and the First Lord of the Admiralty. Unable to proceed further because of ice, the ships wintered over in a protected cove on the southern shore of Melville Island that now bears the name Winter Harbour. Returning home the next summer without undue hardship, Parry reported that he was certain that the Arctic Ocean lay beyond.

Parry's published journal of the voyage, along with John Ross's a year earlier, set the tone for the many exploration narratives that followed. While these tomes had the practical purpose of ensuring financial support for future expeditions, they also fuelled the aspirations of future Arctic explorers the world over. Amply illustrated with sketches of the polar landscape and wildlife, these works inspired journalists and authors to write countless Arctic adventure stories accompanied by exaggerated images of stormy seas, sheer cliffs or grotesque icebergs and fierce polar bears, many appearing as serials in periodicals and reviews. Oil paintings soon followed, creating full-coloured majestic images of what we now call the "Arctic Sublime."

The Admiralty expeditions launched the era of the venerated polar explorer, the epitome of manliness and virtue, usually victorious in overcoming seemingly insurmountable challenges, and bestowing honour and prestige on his country. Yet even in their surreal portrayal, there was order. Janice Cavell in *Tracing the Connected Narratives* describes how "the Navy or the Admiralty made decisions and took actions; the press described the explorers' deeds in glowing terms; and the British public, jingoist yet docile, believed whatever it was told."[10]

Motivation to find the Northwest Passage had changed dramatically since the seventeenth century. Instead of potential commercial benefit, for the Admiralty it was now a matter of national glory and honour. For John Barrow, the motivation was personal. For expedition leaders it was even more so, as success or failure directly affected their careers. After John Ross's experience, they also realized that they had to take risks to avoid chastisement by the Second Secretary. In less than two years after the Admiralty's first announcement of its plans for Arctic exploration, the original purpose of charting and expanding scientific knowledge was now incidental to being the first to sail through the Northwest Passage or reach the North Pole.

The Admiralty's position on taking possession of the Arctic Islands was unclear from the beginning. In Barrow's view the islands were worthless and discovery claims of little importance, as seemed evident in his comments about John Ross raising the flag at the entrance of Lancaster Sound. Claiming the ceremony was "silly," Barrow went on to argue that it was even "more silly, when the object is worthless, as is the present case—a barren, uninhabited country, covered in ice and snow, the only subjects of His Majesty in this portion of his newly-acquired dominion, consisting of half-starved bears, deer, foxes, white hares, and such other creatures as are commonly met with in these regions of the globe."[11] The irony, of course, rests in the contrast between the public's romantic images of the Arctic and the worthlessness of the region in the mind of the man who was the driving force behind the discoveries that had caught the British imagination.

"Boats in a Swell amongst Ice" by George Back, RN, 24 August 1826, appeared
in John Franklin's *Narrative of a Second Expedition to the Shores of the Polar Sea,*
1828. The illustration is representative of the "Arctic Sublime" found in many
British and American publications in the mid-nineteenth century.

N-1585, Scott Polar Research Institute, Cambridge University, UK

Regardless of Barrow's views, the Admiralty's Map Division dutifully charted every claim of possession made by its explorers and later
added discovery claims made by foreign expeditions. At the time,
there was no indication what the British government intended to do
with these claims and certainly no suggestion of creating permanent
settlements. One might even argue that the discovery claims were
less an act of imperialism than the inadvertent acquisition of sovereign rights over lands considered of little value through the diligent
efforts of those responsible for Admiralty charts.

Although the Admiralty did not intend for them to follow Ross
and Parry's route to Lancaster Sound, English and Scottish whalers took the same course—north along the west coast of Greenland,
across Baffin Bay, then south along the shores of Baffin Island—followed by Robert Bylot 200 years earlier. On Parry's return south in
1820, he met two whaling ships off the coast of Baffin Island, which
reported an abundance of whales near Bylot Island. Dozens more

whalers followed the next year and even more in subsequent years, each carefully charting and naming inlets and other features after their ships and owners, or cities and rivers back home. For the whalers, the value in the Admiralty's explorations was in the Arctic waters and not the lands claimed by Britain.

Over the next decade, roughly 750 ships were reported fishing along the Baffin coast with an average catch of ten whales each. The whalers also probed deeper into Lancaster and Jones Sounds, Prince Regent Sound, Admiralty Inlet, Eclipse Sound and the inlets along the east coast of Baffin Island. In some years, many lives and ships were lost when caught in the ice of Melville Bay or in the middle of Davis Strait, but the potential of commercial gains invariably outweighed risks. So intense were whaling activities that by mid-century whale stocks were nearly depleted.[12] Support for the whaling industry was never part of the Admiralty's mandate. While it occasionally acknowledged the experience of certain whaling captains, they were never recognized as equals to Royal Navy officers.

After a second unsuccessful African expedition, the Admiralty again concentrated its efforts on the Arctic. In 1821 Captain Parry and Lieutenant George Lyon set out again in search of the Northwest Passage, this time with instructions to seek an entrance through Hudson Bay and Foxe Basin. If successful, Parry was to go directly to the Arctic coast and meet John Franklin, who had not been heard from for two years after setting out on an overland expedition to the Arctic coast by way of the Coppermine River. Similarly, if Parry located a route free of ice, he was not to waste time charting the coastline but to head directly to the open sea. Success, however, remained beyond his reach. After spending two winters near Igloolik in an attempt to penetrate the ice in Hecla and Fury Strait, Parry returned to report his failure to locate a navigable passage to the west. In the interim, Franklin had returned from his overland trek to report the loss of half his men to starvation.

Still intent on achieving success, Barrow sent out four more expeditions. In 1824, Lyon was put in command of a single ship, HMS

Captain John Franklin in 1823, after completion of his overland trip to the Arctic Ocean by way of the Coppermine River. Later knighted, he became legendary in Arctic history after he disappeared along with his ships and men during the 1846 expedition in search of the Northwest Passage.

LAC, e002139966, Peter Winkworth Collection, engraver William T. Fry, artist T. Wageman

Griper, and sent to Repulse Bay with instructions to trek overland to Boothia Bay. That same year, Parry was placed in command of two ships and sent back to Lancaster Sound to resume his search for the passage, whereas Franklin and Sir John Richardson were sent down the Mackenzie River to map the Arctic coast. In 1825 Frederick Beechey was to sail around Cape Horn and head for Bering Strait to meet Franklin and possibly Parry and Lyon. The grandiose scheme, had it succeeded, would have been an extraordinary achievement, but fate decreed otherwise. Franklin and Richardson succeeded in mapping a combined total of over 1,000 miles of shoreline and both were awarded knighthoods for their accomplishments. Beechey successfully passed through Bering Strait and reached a point some 200 miles short of Franklin's furthest point west. Lyon, however, experienced horrendous storms, nearly lost his ship and returned with *Griper* badly damaged and missing both anchors. Another victim of Barrow's displeasure, Lyon did not receive another command and died in 1832, blind and wasted by disease. Parry successfully wintered at Port Bowen, but he too fell victim to storms in Prince Regent Sound and left the wrecked *Fury* behind. Somehow Parry managed to remain a hero in the eyes of the Second Secretary and was rewarded with yet another expedition.

In 1827, still determined to achieve high honours for the Admiralty, Barrow sent Captain Parry with Lieutenant James Ross to the North Pole. The plan was to anchor their ship at Spitzbergen and proceed across the ice in 20-foot-long boats fitted with bamboo masts, steel runners and detachable wheels and drawn by teams of reindeer. In the belief that the North Pole was a large rock surrounded by open seas, Parry and Ross were to launch the boats when they reached open water and sail on to the North Pole. A trial run near Spitzbergen revealed the idiocy of the plan. Not only were the reindeer unable to pull the heavy loads, but the wheels sank down to their axles on the snow-covered ice. The only alternative was to rely on the steel runners and haul the boats by hand across the ice. After a month of slow trekking, Parry realized that they were unable to make headway because the ice was drifting steadily south. He finally called a halt 500 miles from the North Pole at 82° 45′ N latitude, a record that stood for almost a half century. It was Parry's last naval command. By the time the officers had returned, budget cutbacks had left the Admiralty short of funds, forcing Barrow to put further expeditions on hold. Instead he began writing *The Eventful History of the Mutiny and Piratical Seizure of H.M.S. Bounty: Its Cause and Consequences* (1831), about one of his naval officers, Captain Bligh. Unlike the Admiralty expeditions, his book was an outstanding success.[13]

Having been refused a command by the Admiralty, John Ross talked his nephew James Ross (now Captain) to join him in a private venture aboard the steam-assisted *Victory*. After hearing no word for four years, Captain George Back set out overland but failed to find them. Held in the ice for three winters, Ross finally gave orders to abandon the ship and with his men headed for Lancaster Sound in two small boats. Their rescue by a whaling ship was considered miraculous and they were treated as heroes on their return home. In spite of being knighted on his return, John Ross continued to criticize the Admiralty, Barrow in particular, for refusing to acknowledge the accuracy of his maps and scientific data. In Ross's opinion, the Admiralty's only achievement was its charting, which he believed was about as useful as sketching "the anatomy of a fly." [14] Perhaps to show that the Admiralty could succeed where Ross had failed, Barrow sent Captain George Back in command of an expedition to Wager Bay in 1836, with instructions to cross overland to the Northwest Passage. Back also failed to complete his mission and left his badly damaged ship beached on the shores of Ireland.

Although the British people were clamouring for more, there was a pause of more than fifteen years in the Royal Navy's explorations. By 1844, Barrow was almost eighty years old and still had not achieved his lifelong dream of having the Admiralty's ships sail through the Northwest Passage. Asking for one more chance, Barrow lobbied the First Secretary and even the Prime Minister for support. His only problem was finding a suitable commander. Senior officers, such as James Ross, Parry, Back and Beechey, all refused to apply. This left only Sir John Franklin, who had returned from Van Diemen's Land, known today as Tasmania, where as governor he had been subjected to intense criticism and ridicule for his alleged ineptitude. To everyone's astonishment, Franklin applied for the command, urged on by his ambitious wife, who sought to redeem his reputation after the debacle in Australia. Franklin was fifty-nine and considered by his fellow officers mentally and physically unfit. Yet Lady Jane lobbied shamelessly on her husband's behalf and gained acceptance of his application. Thus in May 1845, Franklin departed for Lancaster Sound with two ships, *Terror* and *Erebus*, fitted with small auxiliary steam engines and enough food to last for three years. Neither Franklin nor his ships were ever seen again.

British enthusiasm for polar exploration had been at its peak when Franklin set sail; then anticipation slowly turned to concern. By tradition, Admiralty captains always returned from the Arctic, although occasionally without their ships. Finally, after no word for three years, the Admiralty sent three expeditions in 1848 to search for Franklin and his men. Only months after their departure, John Barrow died at the age of eighty-three without knowing that even the rescue mission had failed.[15] Sharing disbelief with their readers, the British press continued to excite hopes that their heroes would return. By mid-century the influence of the periodicals and dailies had reached a zenith, and they were more powerful than government leaders or royalty in influencing public opinion.

Ironically, it was Lady Jane Franklin who first focussed American attention on the Arctic when she wrote President Zachary Taylor in April 1849 requesting assistance in the search for her husband. She specifically referred to the importance of becoming involved in a "noble" cause and the honour that it would bring to the United States should its ships find him. After several months of consideration, Taylor asked Congress for funds to fit out an expedition. Henry Grinnell, a wealthy shipowner, offered to supply two ships, whereas the U.S. Navy would be responsible for the men, provisions and loan of scientific instruments. Following rigorous debate, a joint resolution of the House and Senate approved the project. Among Whig supporters was Senator William Seward, who argued that the U.S. should participate in the search on the grounds of humanity, friendship with Britain and the great honour that would be bestowed on the Americans should they find Franklin and his men alive.[16]

National prestige would be earned in the search itself rather than by successful completion of the mission. In *The Coldest Crucible*, Michael Robinson writes that Congress had learned from the British experience "that many of the greatest benefits of exploration were symbolic, that they accrued to national reputation rather than

Painting titled "The Arctic Council Discussing a Plan of Search for Sir John Franklin in 1847" depicts an imaginary gathering based on previous portraits by Stephen Pearce, commissioned to commemorate the Admiralty's searches for the lost Franklin expedition. Completed in 1851, the painting is considered important as it shows the key Admiralty explorers and now hangs in the National Portrait Gallery in London.

Those represented L–R are Sir George Back; Rear-Admiral Sir William Edward Parry; Admiral Edward Joseph Bird; Rear-Admiral Sir James Clark Ross; seated front centre, Admiral and Hydrographer Sir Francis Beaufort; Archivist Col. John Barrow; Sir Edward Sabine; Admiral William Alexander Baillie Hamilton; Sir John Richardson; and seated on the far right, Rear-Admiral Frederick William Beechey. Note also the portraits on the wall of Sir John Franklin and Sir John Barrow in their later years.

LAC, C-023538, after Stephen Pearce

to commerce or territorial gain, and that however effervescent its objects, expeditions for glory were valuable enough to stake money and lives on their prosecution." [17] The U.S. also had a zealous press that incited readers' interest in the expeditions and in a polar region that in terms of geography was more North American than British.

Thus on 22 May 1850, USS *Advance* and *Rescue* under the command of Lieutenant Edwin Jesse De Haven set sail from New York for Lancaster Sound. Commonly known as the First U.S. Grinnell Expedition, it was joined that same year by no fewer than six British expeditions— four under direction of the Admiralty and two privately sponsored by Lady Franklin. De Haven's expedition, however, had a dual purpose. As part of his instructions, he was to sail north of Lancaster Sound in hopes of proving the existence of an open polar sea near the North Pole. Turned back by ice in Barrow Strait, De Haven sought anchorage for the winter in the protected harbour of Beechey Island, where he was joined by the six British ships. Shortly after dropping anchor, the American captain learned that the British had already discovered evidence of Franklin's winter quarters, along with three graves, two of them dated 1846. The articles left behind indicated a quick departure to take advantage of a break in the ice. Additional evidence suggested that Franklin's ships then sailed south to King William's Island, where they again became icebound.[18]

Over the next several years, the Admiralty continued its search— north and south of Lancaster Sound, from the west by sea and overland along the coast of the Arctic mainland. Aside from the American vessels, ships from other seafaring nations joined in the search, from Norway, Germany and Italy, all without success. Crisscrossing the islands by sleds and scouring the shores, Admiralty searchers learned much about the lands they had discovered, but little about Franklin and his ships. Initially the multiple searches created an atmosphere of anticipation among the British people, a combination of excitement and pathos as imaginations ran wild. By 1853, hopes of finding anyone alive had faded and the Admiralty ships were recalled to help fight in the Crimean War.

The following year, while exploring the Arctic coast for the Hudson's Bay Company, John Rae came upon a group of Inuit who reported having met forty white men several years earlier who were weak and hungry, dragging their boats toward the mainland. Later he met another group who reported finding thirty corpses west of the Back River and gave Rae relics they had gathered. There was also disquieting evidence that the starving men had resorted to cannibalism. When Rae's report reached London that summer, the reference to reports of cannibalism was met with a storm of protest. Believing men of the Royal Navy incapable of such barbarian acts, the Admiralty and the press denounced Rae and suggested that the sailors were likely killed by the Inuit. As a result, it would be Rae, not the navy, who bore the brunt of public condemnation.

Lady Franklin still refused to give up and raised funds for yet another private expedition, this one led by young Captain Francis Leopold McClintock, RN. When he returned in 1856, he reported finding two bodies, a small boat left abandoned in the snow and an assortment of scattered belongings. Of greater importance, he found a note left in a cairn that recorded the death of Sir John Franklin on 11 June 1847 along with other officers and men. As the reality of the suffering and futility of their heroic efforts set in, the British people's enthusiasm for Arctic exploration soon faded. The fact that it was a private expedition that solved the mystery and closed the book on the tragic story also cast a shadow on the Royal Navy and its officers. The heyday of Admiralty polar explorations had come to an end, without honour and without glory.

Arctic explorations continued in the second half of the nineteenth century, but for the most part they were carried out by zealous Americans who also sought national prestige and personal honours. More importantly, they were also seeking unclaimed lands. For these adventurers—notably Dr. Elisha Kent Kane leading the Second Grinnell Expedition in 1853, Dr. Isaac Israel Hayes in 1860 and Charles Francis Hall in 1860, 1864 and 1871—the object of their search had shifted from Franklin to the open "Polar Sea" and discovery of new

This illustration titled "Graves on Beechey Island" appeared in
Dr. Elisha Kane's narrative of the First Grinnell Expedition, reflecting the
sombre mood of the Western world after learning of Franklin's fate.
s0020062, Royal Geographical Society Picture Gallery, London

lands. In spite of British claims of discovery, the U.S. maintained that
the Arctic was *terra nullius*—a "no man's land"—where explorers and
scientists were free to roam without interference by national interests.

The expansion-minded Americans had found a "new frontier." As
a result, by the end of the nineteenth century the United States had
replaced Britain as the leader in Arctic exploration. Moreover, Britain's apparent apathy toward the newly claimed possessions and
lack of interest in settlement would create an opportunity for other
nations to challenge British title based on discovery claims alone.

(5)

PURCHASE OF ALASKA,
1818—67

Open up a highway through your country from New York
to San Francisco. Put your domain under cultivation, and your
ten thousand wheels of manufacture in motion. Multiply your ships, and send
them forth to the East. The nation that draws most materials and provisions from
the earth, and fabricates the most, and sells the most of productions and
fabrics to foreign nations, must be and will be, the great power of the earth.

SENATOR WILLIAM HENRY SEWARD, 1853[1]

. . . . .

IN THE first half of the nineteenth century, American politicians
were preoccupied with westward expansion and gave little thought
to the Arctic regions of North America. Nonetheless, they had
grand ambitions for their country. A belief in the nation's "manifest
destiny" fuelled a dream that someday the United States would cover
all of North America, with the immediate objective to acquire lands
contiguous to existing American states. Indeed, since the Declaration
of Independence, growth of the new nation had been phenomenal.
The 1803 Louisiana Purchase from France and the 1819 purchase of
Florida from Spain were followed in rapid succession by the annexation of Texas in 1845, acquisition of the southern portion of Oregon
ceded by Britain in 1846, the defeat of Mexico in 1848 and subsequent
purchase of lands west of Texas to the California coast for $15 million.
In 1853, payment of an additional $10 million for a portion south
of the original Texas cession completed expansion plans, at least

temporarily. More ambitious politicians were convinced that the U.S. would also become a great commercial power through growth of its merchant marine and export of its industrial products to the Orient.

The term "manifest destiny" was coined in 1845 by John O'Sullivan, owner of *The Democratic Review,* to justify this westward expansion. With Texas as his prototype, O'Sullivan believed that "pioneers would acquire the entire continent for the United States peacefully, by settling in remote areas, forming their own autonomous governments, then seeking annexation to the United States."[2] While President Andrew Jackson and his Democrats are credited with popularizing the idea, the phrase was also adopted by a number of Republicans following the Civil War, many of whom shared Benjamin Franklin's earlier view that the division of North America was unnatural and peace impossible as long as the northern portion remained under British influence.[3] As a consequence, the inherent concept of Manifest Destiny was seen as a direct threat by descendants of British Loyalists who had resettled north of the border after the American War of Independence.

Adding to the perceived threat was the frequency with which reference to Manifest Destiny appeared in speeches alongside the Monroe Doctrine, a policy introduced 1823 by President James Monroe warning that the U.S. would not tolerate further European colonization or interference in North America. Over time the latter evolved into a tenet of U.S. foreign policy, whereas Manifest Destiny was an ideology or euphemism used to support expansion and annexation initiatives, and only indirectly to justify the Monroe Doctrine. As noted by American historians, it was not until the turn of the century that the U.S. had the military and economic power to physically enforce the Monroe Doctrine, which likely explains the lack of official protest over British explorations and discovery claims in the Arctic Islands.

According to historian Anders Stephanson, the idea of Manifest Destiny appears to have originated in the biblical context of the "chosen people" and the "promised land." He argues that the ideology was "of singular importance in the way the United States came

"American Progress," lithograph from an oil painting
by John Gast, exemplifying the era of American expansionism
and the nation's belief in its "manifest destiny."
Library of Congress, PGA LC-USZ62-737, lithograph by George A. Crofut

to understand itself in the world and still does; and that this understanding had determinate effects" such as Woodrow Wilson's belief
in the "providentially assigned role of the United States to lead the
world to new and better things."[4] Stephanson also points to a similar theme in a number of Ronald Reagan's speeches that referred
to America's "rendezvous with destiny" and how the U.S. had been
chosen by a higher authority as "a beacon of hope to the rest of the
world."[5] Another American historian, Thomas R. Hietala, provides a
slightly different interpretation, suggesting that Manifest Destiny is
"one of the many euphemisms that have allowed several generations
of Americans to maintain an unwarranted complacency in regard
to their nation's past, that has contributed to the quandary faced by
the United States when attempting to define a realistic role for itself

in a world that seldom acts according to American precepts."[6] Whatever the consequences, real or surmised, the idea of Manifest Destiny was a powerful argument used to defend the U.S. purchase of Russian America in 1867 and later to support explorations of the High Arctic.

Americans initially thought they might acquire all of British North America by force as attempted in the War of Independence and again in the War of 1812. While the latter defeat deterred further thoughts of military action, American politicians still believed that the British territory would eventually be absorbed into the U.S. through peaceful annexation. It was only a matter of time. As a commercial incentive, President Franklin Pierce signed the 1854 Reciprocity Treaty that allowed freer trade between the two countries and shared maritime fishing rights on the east coast. Once the proposed new Dominion of Canada seemed imminent, however, the treaty was abrogated with no plans for renewal. Even then, the idea of annexing Canada continued to percolate under the surface of official U.S. foreign policy.[7]

While the youthful U.S. was undergoing a major growth spurt, events in the North Pacific were evolving in a manner that would provide an unexpected opportunity for further American expansion. Although placed under the supervision of the Russian Imperial Navy following the Napoleonic Wars, the Russian-American Trading Company was still struggling to compete against British fur traders and American whalers. In an attempt to secure Russian title to the territory and halt illicit trade, Czar Alexander I issued an ukase, or edict, in 1821 that claimed the coast of America for Russia—from the Bering Strait south to 51° N latitude to include the Alaska Panhandle. The edict also declared all waters up to 100 verst (a verst is approximately two-thirds of a mile) from the coast off limits to foreign ships. A second ukase renewed the Russian-American Company's charter and extended its authority over the entire territory now claimed by Russia. Emulating the British Admiralty's exploration of the Arctic Islands, Russia sent naval officers in 1821 and 1822 to survey the coast of northern Alaska but they failed to reach even the mouth of the Yukon River.[8]

The 1821 edicts raised the ire of both the Hudson's Bay Company, which had planned to move northward into the land now claimed by Russia, and American traders, who had been supplying food to Sitka Island and transporting the company's furs to China and Asia. By alienating Britain and the U.S., the Russian government had essentially opened a double front with both countries registering official protests. Moreover, the edicts had a particularly harmful effect on the Russian-American Company, causing severe food shortages at Novo Arkhangel'sk as a result of denying American traders access to the island. To repair the damage, the Russian foreign minister negotiated a settlement with the U.S., known as the Russian-American Convention of 1824, that set the southern boundary at 54° 10´ N latitude and allowed the Americans to trade with both the Indians and Russians north of the boundary. Britain negotiated a similar treaty in 1825 that included the Alaska Panhandle and inland territory along a line of demarcation that followed the summit of the mountains that parallelled the coast. Once the line intersected with 141° W longitude, the boundary would follow that meridian to the Arctic Ocean.[9] Although this limited the Hudson's Bay Company's westward expansion, their traders soon realized that they could get Indians in the interior to trade with them rather than take their furs to the Russians on the coast.

Relations between Britain and Russia steadily deteriorated after the 1820s as a result of clashes in the Middle East, the Mediterranean, Persia, Afghanistan, Central Asia and the Far East. During the search for the lost Franklin expedition, a number of British naval vessels arrived at Alaskan ports, raising fears among company officials that the humanitarian purpose was simply a guise for reconnaissance of Russian territory. Mistrust and increasing resentment over British interference on the high seas made rapprochement with the U.S. virtually inevitable. At first glance, the two countries appeared to have little in common—a new democratic republic versus an entrenched monarchy—but both had suffered continual obstruction and harassment by British ships. As noted by American historian Thomas Bailey, "misery and common enemies make strange bedfellows."[10]

Russian investment in the settlements was considerable. At the beginning of the nineteenth century, Novo Arkhangel'sk on Sitka Island was the Russian-American Company's administrative centre and shipbuilding port inhabited by 300 workers, mostly Aleutians. The fort was located at the foot of a mountain, with the upper part on a rocky plateau that had two hexagonal towers fitted with cannons and was surrounded by a nine-foot-high wooden fence. Within the fortress lay the two-storey manager's house, barracks, workshops and a hospital. The lower fort contained an Eastern Orthodox Church, windmill and twelve houses for employees.[11] By mid-century, the settlement had expanded substantially to include new administration buildings and living quarters, a sawmill and flour mill, a Lutheran church, a laundry, ice houses, new piers and a tannery. The 1863 census for Novo Arkhangel'sk and the immediate area listed 480 Russian and Finnish employees, plus 50 women, 510 persons of mixed blood and 67 Aleuts and Kuriles.[12]

After the Napoleonic Wars there was a concerted effort to improve the conditions of the settlements and diversify the Russian-American Company's operations. In 1821 its charter was renegotiated, adding new responsibilities for improvement of working conditions, maintenance of churches, better school programs and medical care for Natives. The latter were to be protected as imperial citizens, a status similar to that of free peasants in Russia. A new middle class emerged, largely made up of educated mixed-bloods, who increasingly assumed administrative jobs once held by Russians. Provided with living quarters and other company benefits, they were known as "colonial citizens."[13] Indians, on the other hand, were employed to travel inland to trade for furs with tribes in the interior. The charter was renegotiated in 1842, further expanding responsibilities for Native education, with specific instructions that skills such as construction of kayaks and use of bows and arrows were to be included.[14]

Meanwhile the activities of the American whalers continued to put pressure on the Russian-American company's profits. In 1849, for instance, the company complained that American whalers far outnumbered their own ships in the North Pacific and that they were now visiting Native communities to trade for furs and ivory. Yet in spite of frequent petitions for assistance to stop the illegal trade, the Russian government refused to take action lest it adversely affect its relations with the United States. A history of the company compiled in the 1860s and recently translated by historians Richard A. Pierce and Alton S. Donnelly shows that the operations after 1821 were closely supervised by the board of directors, appeared to be well-organized and continued to dedicate a good portion of company revenue to maintenance and development of settlements.[15]

Of particular significance was the influence of the Eastern Orthodox Church and the dedication of its priests to advancing Natives' education and their conversion to Christianity. By 1860, there were over 12,000 Christians reported living in the colonies, of whom fewer than 800 were Russian. On average the company paid 12,000 rubles a year to the church in addition to supplying numerous ancillary services. Each settlement had a church that was used as a base for missionary work in the surrounding area. As the settlements grew in size and number, so did the church's influence.[16] For instance, Fort St. Michael, established on Norton Sound near the mouth of the Yukon River in 1833, had grown within a decade to become an important trading centre, made up of six buildings, a church and a blacksmith shop, surrounded by a stockade with two lookout towers and six cannons. Eskimos from nearby villages were employed to trade with Indians along the Yukon River, by sled in winter and umiak in summer.[17]

In an attempt to diversify, the Russian-American Company began exporting other products such as timber, coal, ice and fish. To compete with American whalers, the Russian-Finnish Whaling Company was established in 1850 as a subsidiary of the Russian-American Company. Although initially meeting with some success, the company failed to recover from losses incurred during the Crimean War and was liquidated after only a decade in operation. In 1851 a contract was signed with the Union Ice Company to export ice to California. Three years later a twenty-year agreement was signed with an American businessman to trade coal, timber and fish. But it was all too little and too late.[18]

In March 1854, Britain entered the Crimean War, siding with Turkey against Russia. To protect their interests, the Hudson's Bay Company and the Russian-American Company concluded a convention of neutrality approved by both governments, but Britain insisted the agreement did not extend to the high seas and that it had the right to seize the Russian-American Company's ships and blockade Russian ports. Senior naval officers had warned Czar Nicholas I that Russian America would be absorbed by Britain or the U.S. if left undefended. As a result Russian troops were sent to guard the trading centre. Already the thought had entered some minds that Russian America had become too costly to support, causing a representative of the Russian government to approach California Senator William Gwin in the midst of the Crimean War to see if the U.S. might be interested in acquiring Alaska. President Pierce replied in the affirmative, but Czar Alexander II was not yet convinced it was necessary.[19]

For a variety of reasons, the Crimean War was considered a watershed in European and Russian history. The stature of France was inflated, that of the Ottoman Empire deflated; Germany was aligned with Italy and Britain was now officially Russia's adversary. The war also revealed Russia's incompetent leadership, an outdated political and social system, an inferior navy and obsolete weapons, all of which forced the imperial government to seek peace through a series of treaties while attempting to mollify internal discontent with promises of "great reforms."

The Russian-American Company's losses during the war were largely due to disruption of trade, but were offset in part by government subsidies. But the Russian government had financial problems of its own, and operation of the company and provision for its defence were proving far too costly. When its charter came up for renewal in 1862, the company was in debt to the tune of 1,000 rubles, despite an annual government subsidy of nearly 2,000 rubles.[20] Renegotiation of the charter was put on hold, while the subject of disengagement was debated. Company officials and shareholders argued strongly against the sale of its assets, claiming that the financial situation was improving and that trade was stabilizing with diversification. Others countered that Russian America would be absorbed by either the U.S. or Britain if left undefended, so it was better to sell the territory now than get nothing for it later. Moreover, in light of the U.S.'s commitment to expansion and its previous payments of large sums to acquire lands, as in the case of Louisiana and Florida, the Russians believed it would be willing to pay a fair price. Again, tentative inquiries were made to see if there was any interest in the purchase, but serious discussions were put on hold until after the American Civil War.[21]

By 1866, the die was cast. The terms demanded by the Russian-American Company for renewal of its charter were too costly and Russia could not afford to take over its administration. Geologists' reports of finding gold in the interior only added to arguments supporting the sale. Having witnessed the thousands of unruly miners descending on British Columbia in 1858 when gold was discovered on the Fraser River, company officials were convinced that they would lose control should a similar situation occur in Russian territory and that it would fall into U.S. hands.

As a consequence, the Russians' discovery of gold was kept a secret. There were other arguments supporting sale of the territory, including the need to cultivate a friendly relationship with the U.S. as a makeweight against ongoing tensions with Great Britain. Another major factor related to the difficulties in maintaining colonies not contiguous with the Russian mainland. Furthermore, Russian America was no longer needed as a base for Pacific trade after the recent acquisition of lands in the Amur region. With an eye to the future, advisers to the Czar argued that it would be prudent to earn money from the sale of Alaska now, rather than allow it to fall into U.S. hands, or worse, British. Finally on 30 December 1866, Czar Alexander II agreed to the sale. Baron Edouard de Stoekl, Russian minister to the U.S., was assigned to negotiate a transaction with instructions that the price should not be less than $5 million.[22]

Lady Franklin may have opened the door to American polar exploration, but it was Senator William Henry Seward who set the stage for U.S. territorial expansion into the Arctic. A staunch supporter of expansionism, Seward along with other radical Republicans

William Henry Seward, former senator for New York and U.S.
secretary of state under Abraham Lincoln and Andrew Johnson, 1861–69.

Alaska State Library P20-023, Alaska Purchase Centennial Photograph Collection

believed in Benjamin Franklin's precept that the division of North
America was unnatural and that there would never be peace on the
continent as long as Canada remained under British influence.[23] As
might be expected, his speeches also reiterated the familiar "theme
of imperial manifest destiny ordained by Providence for the American People."[24] Yet unlike his mentor, John Quincy Adams, Seward
believed that expansion must be tied to an open-door commercial
policy to ensure future prosperity. He was first elected a senator for
the Whig Party in 1849 and was a strong advocate for naval support
of the First Grinnell Expedition to the Arctic. When the Whig Party
dissolved in 1855, he joined the Republican Party and in 1861 was
appointed secretary of state in President Abraham Lincoln's Union
Government. After Lincoln's assassination, Vice-President Andrew

Johnson assumed the presidency, but as a former Democratic senator from Tennessee he was continually at odds with the Republican-dominated Congress. Seward remained secretary of state but was only moderately successful in establishing policies that supported his vision of America's new empire.

The timing could not have been better when Stoekl arrived in the U.S. in February 1867 to discuss the proposed sale of Russian America. By then, expectations of peaceful annexation of the Canadian provinces had faded as plans progressed to unite the Canadian provinces in the new Dominion of Canada, despite strong protest from Congress that creation of a new British state would violate the Monroe Doctrine. By then, the only prospect for possible annexation lay with British Columbia, which had so far resisted pressure to join Confederation.[25]

Stoekl played his hand cautiously by initially remaining in New York while a mutual friend called on the Secretary of State with news that Russia might consider sale of its American territory. Three weeks later Stoekl met with Seward and tentatively broached the subject of a possible purchase. Over the next few days, discussion quickly advanced to procedure and price, with Seward insisting on maintaining secrecy until the terms had been agreed upon. Seward's initial offer was reportedly $5 million, but additional bargaining by Stoekl brought the figure to $7 million. On 15 March the Secretary of State presented a draft of the purchase agreement to cabinet, whereupon members insisted on revisions allowing more time for payment and denying Stoekl's request for certain rights accorded to the Russian-American Trading Company. Seward assured him that payment would be made within a year of ratification, but that the purchase was to be free of "any reservations, privileges, franchises, grants, or possession by any such company." To mollify Stoekl, however, he added another $200,000 to the purchase price.[26]

According to his son Frederick Seward, the process was expedited quickly. Once cabinet gave its tentative approval, Stoekl reported to his government by telegraph. When the Russian minister arrived at the secretary of state's residence on the evening of 29 March to report that the Czar had just wired his approval, Seward insisted that the formal documents be prepared that night. As a result, the Treaty with Russia was signed by both Stoekl and Seward at four AM the next morning. The regular session of Congress ended at noon that day, but President Johnson declared that "an extraordinary occasion" required the Senate to reconvene the following Monday. In the interim, the treaty was presented to the Senate executive and a copy sent to the Committee on Foreign Relations.[27]

Some observers assumed that the hasty conclusion of negotiations was prompted by Seward's fear that Stoekl might change his mind. Certainly the purchase price of $7.2 million suggests that the buyer was more eager than the seller, but it seems more logical that Seward anticipated strong opposition to the purchase and hoped to present the treaty more or less as a "done deal," thus giving dissenters little time to mount an organized campaign before Senate ratification. Perhaps it was only a coincidence, but Seward and Stoekl had signed the treaty document only a few hours after Queen Victoria signed the British North America Act establishing the new Dominion of Canada. The initial reaction in the press was more negative than Seward anticipated, dubbing the sale "Seward's Folly" and the territory "Seward's Icebox." In response the Secretary of State launched a vigorous campaign in support of the treaty and with the help of Senator Charles Sumner, chairman of the Committee on Foreign Relations, the Senate ratified the agreement on 9 April by a vote of 37 to 2, only ten days after the signing. In a sense it was a phenomenal exercise in expediting the political process. Later a group of friends commissioned Emanuel Leutze to do the now famous painting depicting the treaty signing.

The winning argument appeared to be Sumner's assertion that like previous acquisitions the purchase would eliminate yet another foreign nation from North America, "all giving way to that absorbing Unity which is declared in the national motto, *E pluribus unum.*" Sumner's speech in the Senate reportedly went on for four hours, during which he described in exhaustive detail Alaska's many resources, its history and inhabitants, potential benefits for the United States, the

A painting commissioned to represent signing the Treaty with Russia for the United States purchase of Alaska, 30 March 1867. The document was signed by Secretary of State William Seward and Russian Minister to the United States Baron de Stoekl. Those involved in the negotiations are shown here L-R: Robert S. Chew, William H. Seward, William Hunter, Mr. Bodisco, Edouard de Stoekl, Senator Charles Sumner and Frederick W. Seward (son of William Seward). A Russian document known as the Treaty of Cession was later signed by Czar Alexander II to formally conclude the agreement.

Alaska State Library P20-181, Alaska Purchase Centennial Photography Collection

importance of maintaining friendly Russian-American relations and a warning that Britain would be an eager buyer should the Senate refuse to ratify the treaty. Sumner even provided the details of a Russian engineer's report on the discovery of a "considerable" presence of gold in three different locations, a pronouncement that was ignored in the press. Significantly, the only mention of the Arctic was in reference to providing more convenient ports for American whalers.[28]

Others argued that the "deal would sandwich British Columbia between American territory and make inevitable its annexation."[29] The *New York Herald* expanded the argument further, suggesting that it was the nation's "fiat of inevitable destiny, which, in time, must give us the whole of the North American continent." [30] Yet dissidents in the House stood their ground. A minority report by the Committee on Foreign Relations concluded that the territory was of no value, and "that the right to govern a nation... of savages in a climate unfit for the habitation of civilized men was not worthy of purchase." [31] The sale was also vigorously opposed by at least one Russian journalist, who decried his government's need to sell valuable real estate to pay off its debts.

In the end, the ratified copies were exchanged and the cession of Alaska officially proclaimed on 20 June 1867, only eleven days before the Dominion of Canada officially came into being. From an American perspective, the timing was likely a fortuitous coincidence, but the implications were unsettling to British officials. The United Kingdom's ambassador to Washington, Sir Frederick Bruce, when writing to Lord Stanley, expressed his concerns that "the Russian-American rapprochement would serve to humiliate Great Britain by neutralizing their efforts in the Near East and enabling the United States to claim British Columbia." It was his opinion that "a step had been taken toward the absorption of the entire continent." His fears seemed justified when he later claimed to have overheard Seward urging an American capitalist to form a company to buy out the rights of the Hudson's Bay Company. [32] Certainly if American takeover of Rupert's Land or annexation of British Columbia had occurred, Seward would have been accorded much higher regard in the annals of American history, and enormous disdain among the advocates of Canada as a nation stretching from "sea to sea."

Formal transfer occurred on 18 October that same year. In an official ceremony held at Novo Arkhangel'sk, the flag of the Russian-American Company was lowered and the Stars and Stripes raised in its place. American officials immediately renamed the settlement Sitka, whereas "Alaska," originating from an Aleutian word for "the land beyond the sea" and previously used in reference to the panhandle, became the official name for the new U.S. territory on the recommendation of Senator Sumner. [33] There was only the question of the appropriation bill to pay for the purchase, which still required approval by the divisive House of Representatives. This exercise proved more difficult than even Seward anticipated, as it coincided with the failure of impeachment proceedings against President Johnson. As the House appeared determined to defeat the bill to humiliate Seward and Johnson for having bypassed that body during the ratification process, the fine art of "lobbying" went into high gear. At Seward's suggestion, Stoekl hired former senator Robert J. Walker to lobby members of the House, while friends of the Secretary of State pressured the Democrats. Newspapers were encouraged to carry articles lauding potential mineral deposits, the fisheries and commercial opportunities. Aside from the argument that the U.S. was morally obligated to pay for Alaska now that the transfer had taken place and that Russia would have an iron-clad claim against America for payment of $7.2 million plus interest, many newspapers were again suggesting that the purchase was a first step toward acquisition of the entire continent. Finally on 24 July 1868 the House approved the appropriation bill by a vote of 113 to 43, with 44 abstaining.[34]

American payment for Alaska took place far later than the terms of the agreement demanded and Russia received only $7 million. The remaining $200,000 was spent on "unitemized expenditures." According to his biographer, Seward later admitted that Stoekl "had greased palms liberally," paying newspapers and lobbyists and at least two Congressmen to ensure the vote, a statement that was verified in part when Walker later confirmed that he was paid $21,000 in gold and $2,300 in dollars for his services. But when brought before a House committee investigating charges of bribery, Seward claimed he knew nothing of how the Russian minister had used the money. The Russian legation refused to testify and the charges were dropped for lack of evidence.[35]

The Russian presence in North America ended in 1867 and the United States now had direct access to the northern Pacific Rim. Yet the lack of enthusiasm was overwhelming. For its first seventeen years Alaska had no form of government or appropriation of federal funds. Views changed after the discovery of gold, but even then most Americans considered Alaska unsuitable for permanent settlement.

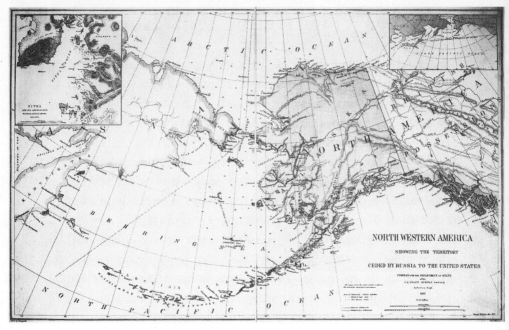

Map of the Russian territory purchased by the U.S. and prepared
by the State Department in 1867 suggests that Seward knew
precisely what the U.S. was purchasing from Russia.
Alaska State Library P20-216, Alaska Purchase Centennial Photograph Collection

According to Article 1 of the Treaty with Russia, the boundaries
of the newly acquired territory were defined by the Anglo-Russian
Convention of 1825. The second article gave all property and buildings not privately owned to the United States, with the sole exception
of the buildings and contents of the Orthodox churches. The third
article related to existing inhabitants, allowing them to either return
to Russia or remain to enjoy "the rights, advantages, and immunities
of citizens of the United States," but there was a significant exception.
"Uncivilized native tribes" were specifically excluded from rights of
U.S. citizenship and instead would be "subject to such laws and regulations the United States may from time to time adopt in regard to
aboriginal tribes of that country." [36] Suddenly Alaskan Natives found
themselves unemployed and in some case homeless when the U.S.
closed down the Russian-American Company's operations and left
inhabitants to fend for themselves. Moreover, the mixed-bloods, who

had acquired respect and middle-class status during Russian rule, were now treated with contempt. The only institution left untouched was the Russian Orthodox Church, which remained the religion of choice among the Alaskan Natives.[37]

Some historians saw Seward's primary motive in purchasing Alaska as a means of expanding commerce to Asia. While this was partly true, he also saw the Arctic as a natural extension of the American frontier, waiting to be developed in accordance with the nation's "manifest destiny." Seward maintained that the purchase of Alaska was justified under the Monroe Doctrine as a means of eliminating foreign ownership in North America, and the longer-term strategy ran deeper. Enunciating sentiments shared by other Republicans, Seward and his supporters in Congress boldly argued that with Alaska in the north and the United States in the south, British Columbia "would be caught in a vice and forced into a union with America." Seward had intended to take the idea even further when he had a report drawn up recommending the purchase of Iceland and Greenland, purportedly to facilitate the defence of North America. If the purchase had occurred, it would have created a solid American flank on the northeast to bring further pressure for Canadian annexation to the U.S.[38] The proposal was withdrawn after Congress defeated the Danish West Indies Treaty that Seward had negotiated, but hopes of expanding American claims in the Arctic lingered in the minds of many Republicans.

Sadly, the major achievement of Seward's career was destined to stay under a cloud of confusion and circumspection owing to the divisive nature of the House and its animosity toward the president and his secretary of state. His aim had been to turn the United States into a world power, based on worldwide trade for American products. Yet with the exception of officially claiming possession of the Midway Islands in August 1867, Seward's other expansion projects were rejected by a Congress that turned its energy toward domestic concerns such as reconstruction, reducing the national debt and building the transcontinental railway. When Ulysses S. Grant took over the

White House in 1869, Seward retired from political life and died within two years, at the age of seventy-one. Yet his vision of America had never faltered. Even if his ambitions were high, his motives were honourable. Seward may have dreamed of a continent united under one flag, but he rejected the use of force to achieve that objective. Nor was there any evidence of his support for subterfuge or instigation of revolt against British authority. Seward was convinced that his dream was inevitable and that it would be achieved peacefully. Characterizing the man and his influence on America, his biographer Glyndon Van Deusen writes:

> But despite the disappointments and frustrations of his expansionist drive, Seward was right in thinking that he built for the oncoming generations. He was a follower in the footsteps of John Quincy Adams and like him dreamed of those places "where the strange roads go down." Adams had a vision of American expansion to the Pacific and helped pave the way to that goal. He foresaw the dominance of the United States on this continent. Seward's vision, larger than that of Adams, was of an expansion of American power and place that meant world leadership.[39]

Although many of his dreams came true, Seward was mistaken in his belief that the annexation of Canada was inevitable. He, like other pro-expansionists of the time, had miscalculated the strength of Loyalist support and the depth of anti-American sentiment.

IN ANCIENT and medieval times, countries went to war to settle sovereignty disputes. In the North Pacific, Britain appeared at first to be winning the battle with its mercantile trade and sea power, but ultimately lost in the end by alienating Russia through decisive defeat in the Crimean War. Instead, a peaceful transfer of sovereignty resulted from converging political forces in Washington and St. Petersburg, with Britain excluded from the discussions. Over the longer term, the U.S. was clearly the winner. Discovery of gold on the Klondike River may have ended complaints that the land was worthless, but its true value lay in the fact that it allowed the U.S. to become a bona fide "Arctic nation," enabling direct participation in critical circumpolar negotiations with regard to security measures, laws of the sea, sovereignty, economic development and environmental concerns. Historians may debate whether it was Russia or Britain which precipitated the sale of Alaska to the U.S., but the fact remains—it happened.

(6)

SALE OF RUPERT'S LAND, 1870

I would be quite willing, personally, to leave that
whole country a wilderness for the next half century,
but I fear if Englishmen do not go there, Yankees will.

JOHN A. MACDONALD, March 1865 [1]

. . . .

WITHIN THREE years of the United States purchase of Alaska, sovereign authority again changed in the North American Arctic when Canada purchased Rupert's Land and the North-Western Territory from the Hudson's Bay Company. The suggestion by U.S. Secretary of State William Seward and Senator Charles Sumner that the purchase of Alaska would accelerate annexation of British North America backfired. Instead, fears of possible annexation encouraged the expansion of its northern neighbour to a size greater than the continental United States, a good portion lying within the Arctic. In 1870, however, neither Britain nor Canada nor the United States considered Arctic lands to be of any particular value. Even the Subarctic was thought to offer only limited opportunities for settlement, primarily related to the fur trade and potential mineral exploitation. The southern portion of Rupert's Land and the North-Western Territory was valued for its potential as an area of agricultural settlement within a fertile belt near the southern border, a potential also recognized by the United States.

The Dominion of Canada as a member of the British Empire officially came into being on 1 July 1867, composed of four provinces: Nova Scotia, New Brunswick, Ontario and Quebec, the latter two formed from Canada East and Canada West, once parts of the former Province of Canada. Other provinces were added later—the postage-stamp-sized Manitoba in 1870, British Columbia in 1871 and Prince Edward Island in 1873. In 1870, the former Hudson's Bay Company lands were added to the Dominion as the North-West Territories. Although the country was commonly referred to as the Confederation of Canada, the British North America Act of 1867 (later renamed the Constitution Act, 1867) had created a federation with specific division of powers between the provincial and federal governments. The provincial governments retained authority over local issues such as education, health and transportation, with the federal government having authority over national interests and the right to assume powers not previously assigned. The federal government also retained the right to act on behalf of "peace, order and good government." Following the British bicameral system of government, members of the House were elected whereas senators were appointed for life. The leader of the party receiving the majority of votes assumed the position of prime minister, who in turn selected his cabinet from elected members of Parliament. An appointed governor-general retained overall control in the name of the king or queen of Great Britain, who in 1867 was Queen Victoria. Sir John A. Macdonald was knighted for his part in bringing about the union and became Canada's first prime minister.[2]

Compared to the United States' hasty purchase of Alaska, the process of acquiring the lands controlled by the Hudson's Bay Company was a prolonged exercise requiring patience and determination. Motives also differed. The acquisition of Alaska was perceived as a step toward unification of the entire continent. Canada's purchase of the Hudson's Bay Company's lands was considered a means to protect the new Dominion from future annexation to the United States. Even then, the purchase weighed heavily on the minds of Canadian political leaders, who were concerned whether they had the resources to govern such a vast territory. Macdonald, writing in 1865, two years before Confederation, stated, "I would be quite willing, personally, to leave that whole [HBC] country a wilderness for the next half century,

Seen here c1853, York Factory was the Hudson's Bay Company's primary
storage depot for furs and supplies and likely the largest British settlement
in the Arctic. Located not far from Fort Prince of Wales, the compound was
said to have had over fifty buildings, including a doctor's house, Anglican
church, school, hospital, library, cooperage and blacksmith shop.

HBCA P-114, Hudson's Bay Company Archives,
Archives of Manitoba, Lithographers Ford & West, artist unknown

but I fear if Englishmen do not go there, the Yankees will." [3] "Fear" was
a common factor in both purchases. Whereas the U.S. justified the
purchase of Alaska to prevent it from falling into the hands of Britain, both Canada and Britain feared that, unless Rupert's Land and
the North-Western Territory were annexed to the new Dominion, the
U.S. would acquire a major portion of the lands through purchase of
the company's assets and/or local support for annexation.

The years leading up to Confederation witnessed political unrest
and dissatisfaction with British colonial rule, complicated further by
the American Civil War. Periodic bursts of annexation sentiment gave
American politicians confidence that their dream of North America
united under one flag would soon become reality. In 1849, for instance,
an "annexation manifesto" was signed by over 1,000 disgruntled citizens from Montreal, which in turn prompted a strong anti-American
protest, largely from Québécois and Loyalists. Pride in their own

accomplishments and confidence in the superiority of their government may have blinded American leaders to the reality of the situation, as they misunderstood or perhaps simply miscalculated the degree of Canadian loyalty to Britain and animosity toward the United States. The French-speaking residents of Canada East also feared loss of their special privileges if they were annexed to the United States. Reports in the American press suggesting peaceful annexation was inevitable only strengthened Canadians' resolve to prevent such an occurrence. Richard Gwyn, in his recent biography of John A. Macdonald, suggests that in the end it was the Canadian attitudes of superiority that prevented annexation movements from taking hold.[4]

Long before serious discussions of unifying the British colonies, an expansionist movement was slowly emerging in Canada. Unlike its American counterpart, which was led by political leaders, the Canadian organization began with a small group of intellectuals who were convinced that the survival of British North America depended upon settlement of the west through acquisition of Hudson's Bay Company lands. Among them were Alexander Morris, Charles Mair and R.G. Haliburton, who effectively deployed their literary talents to tell their story. Their vision of Canada as described in pamphlets and speeches was accompanied by fanciful rhetoric reminiscent of the American manifest destiny theme, but with a distinct difference. In their view, Canada's future prosperity and identity would be derived from the northwest, rather than due west, and achieved without relinquishing ties to Great Britain.

Alexander Morris in his *Nova Britannia,* for example, wrote about "our *manifest destiny*" to possess the northwest, whereas R.G. Haliburton proposed that the new Dominion "must ever be ... a Northern country inhabited by the descendants of Northern races."[5] The original group of intellectuals later expanded to form the Canada First Movement that promoted Canadian nationalism in much the same manner as proponents of the American frontier, but untarnished by the violence toward Native Indians or the oppression of slavery. In contrast to adventure stories of cowboys and Indians, Canadian writers promoted the northern wilderness as a distinctive attribute of their national identity. Often referred to as the "myth of the north," their Canada was a land of quiet lakes, pine trees, granite rocks, winter snows and summer breezes, a land inhabited by wild animals and primitive Indians.[6] Significantly, there is no mention of the Arctic landscape and the Inuit in their literature. In the Victorian era, images of the Arctic still belonged to the British Admiralty and their polar narratives—a remote and alien land—unrelated to the mid-nineteenth-century vision of Canada.

With its charter coming up for renewal in 1859, the Hudson's Bay Company faced increasing criticism, both in Britain and among settlers in the Red River Valley. Up until then, company officials had been singularly successful in convincing Parliament that their lands were unfertile and of value only to the fur trade. In response to mounting criticism, a select committee of the House of Commons was set up to review the HBC's operations and consider whether at least a portion of their lands should be opened for settlement. At the hearings, Governor George Simpson reiterated his argument that the land was unsuitable for settlement but other testimony raised doubts as to the veracity of his statements.

To gain more information, Captain John Palliser was asked to conduct a three-year study of the area and report back to Parliament. At the same time, a Canadian expedition led by Henry Youle Hind would deliver its findings to the Province of Canada. Both reports confirmed the presence of a large area unsuitable for agriculture, commonly known as the Palliser Triangle, but they also identified a large fertile belt to the north that offered ample opportunities for future settlement. The Palliser report also emphasized the need to establish a new Crown colony as quickly as possible, before the territory was taken over by the United States. When the American Civil War broke out in 1861, the urgency to take immediate action subsided. Although the charter was not renewed, the HBC was permitted to continue its operations pending future disposition of the lands formerly held under its authority.[7]

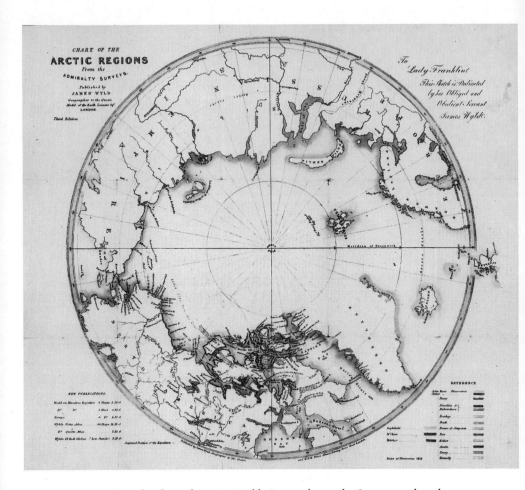

Map dated 1853 by James Wyld, Geographer to the Queen, was based
on Admiralty Surveys to show the extent of mapping achieved by the
British navy during its Arctic explorations and search for the lost Franklin
Expedition. Presumably the same Admiralty charts were the basis of
Britain's initial discovery claims to the Arctic Islands.   LAC, NMC-197197

As described in the company's original charter, Rupert's Land included all lands surrounding the streams and rivers that drained into Hudson Bay and Hudson Strait, stretching from Labrador westward to the southern prairies. The North-Western Territory, sometimes referred to as Indian territory, was added to the company's licence after its merger with the North West Company. Although never officially defined, this area was considered to include all remaining British lands west of Hudson Bay up to, but not including, British Columbia or the Arctic Islands.

When the Colonial Secretary received the Palliser report in 1860, he approached the company's governor to discuss future disposition of its lands and was told that it would be quite willing to surrender the lands for £1 million—roughly $4.5 million—a sum neither Canada nor Britain was willing to pay. Two years later in 1862, the asking price was raised to £1.5 million. This time a group of London bankers formed what today would be called an investment capital firm called the International Financial Society. In what Peter Newman describes as a "share flip," the original proprietors were paid £300 for each share—less than a third of the worth—the company was then recapitalized and new management put in place. Sir Edmund Walker Head was installed as governor and new shares worth £20 each were sold to 1,700 investors. The International Financial Society pocketed a clear profit of £300,000 then quietly removed itself from further involvement.[8]

After the end of the American Civil War, discussions began in earnest about unifying the British colonies into one nation under a single flag, with potential for expansion to the northwest. The situation was watched closely by the United States government, which had sent special agents to Canada to promote American interest in potential transportation and trade links. One agent, James Wilkes Taylor, had been hired by the U.S. Treasury Department in 1859 to observe the situation at the British Red River settlement near the Wisconsin border. His report in 1866 described the potential value of the Hudson's Bay Company lands and suggested that payment of $10 million might be sufficient to secure the lands and other assets. The report prompted the introduction of legislation in the House that provided for admission of the British provinces and the western lands to the United States of America. After two readings, the bill was sent to committee for review, where it died.[9]

By then, plans for a new Dominion of Canada were progressing toward completion. John A. Macdonald and other political leaders were now convinced that the only means to ward off annexation to the U.S. was to unify the provinces under a single government. In November 1866, delegates from the provinces met with British officials in London to negotiate the final terms of the British North America Act. Remaining overseas to ensure passage of the act through Westminster, Alexander Galt of the Canadian delegation wrote to his wife in January about his growing concern over British indifference, saying, "I am more than ever disappointed at the tone of feeling here as to the colonies. I cannot shut my eyes to the fact that they want to get rid of us ... and would rather give us up than defend us, or incur the risk of war with that country"—the United States. His concerns were warranted.[10]

That spring, Lord Stanley as secretary of the Colonial Office wrote the British ambassador to Washington, expressing his concern that Confederation would increase the risk of confrontation with the United States, noting that "the Colonies will remain Colonies, only confederated for the sake of convenience. If they choose to separate, we on this side will not object; it is they who would protest against the idea. In England, separation would be generally popular." The editorial in the London *Times* was more direct, stating that "we look to Confederation as the means of relieving this country from much expense and much embarrassment."[11] As Gwyn reminds us in his biography of John A. Macdonald, the concept of the British Empire under the Gladstone government was unfocussed, "an agglomeration of territories acquired or conquered or bought or swapped or stolen," certainly not the vision of empire expounded by the Disraeli government in the mid-1870s. Gwyn argues that it was only after Confederation that the "British really embraced their empire and so embraced Canada."[12]

Amidst British indifference toward Canadian interests and concerns over potential conflict with the United States, the British North America Act was passed by Westminister and signed by Queen Victoria on 29 March 1867, only hours before U.S. Secretary of State Seward signed the Treaty with Russia for the purchase of Alaska. Seward's dream of annexing Canada had not ended; only the time line was altered. As he stated to a Boston audience on the eve of Confederation, "I know that nature designs that this whole continent, not merely the thirty-six states, shall be, sooner or later, within the magic circle of the American Union." A similar response to Confederation appeared in the New York *Tribune*, claiming that "when the experiment of the 'dominion' shall have failed, as fail it must, a process of peaceful absorption will give Canada her proper place in the great North American republic."[13]

Ever conscious of opportunities to advance American interests, in early 1869 the State Department sent James Taylor once again on a mission to the Red River district to observe the disturbances and attitudes toward the United States. This time his report resulted in a resolution by the Senate to offer $6 million for the Hudson's Bay Company's land rights, but this too was shelved.[14] With the departure of Seward as secretary of state after the election of Ulysses S. Grant as president, there were no further offers of purchase. Instead, all eyes were directed on annexation sentiments expressed in British Columbia.

The British North America Act contained a clause to allow entrance of Rupert's Land into the Dominion of Canada, but Canada and Britain remained at odds over the cost and who would pay for the acquisition. Impatient with the impasse, the colonial secretary under the new Gladstone government, the second Earl of Granville, ordered representatives of the Hudson's Bay Company and the Canadian government to meet in London in March 1869, where he delivered a twelve-page ultimatum. The fur-trading company was to surrender authority over the lands in return for £300,000 (almost $1.5 million) to be paid by Canada with Britain guaranteeing the loan. The deal was reluctantly approved by both parties. Finally on 19 November 1869, the company surrendered to Britain "all or any of the lands, territories, rights, privileges, liberties, franchises, powers, and authorities whatsoever granted or purported to be granted by certain Letters of Patent..." The date of official transfer was slated for 1 December 1869, but delayed until political unrest in the Red River district was resolved—a feat accomplished through passage of the Manitoba Act of 1870, which created a postage-stamp-sized province to satisfy settlers' demands. On 23 June 1870, Queen Victoria signed an order-in-council, to take effect on 15 July, that officially admitted Rupert's Land and the North-Western Territory to the Dominion of Canada. The new acquisition, which amounted to an area ten times the size of the existing nation, would be called the North-West Territories and governed by an appointed lieutenant-governor and council.[15]

HBC shareholders protested vigorously but, as Peter Newman pointed out, over time they gained considerable benefit from the terms that included the right to continue trading operations without special taxes or tariffs, a grant of approximately 45,000 acres of land adjacent to the existing trading posts and the right to claim up to 20 percent of the fertile belt, amounting to roughly 7 million acres of the best agricultural land in the west.[16] In the years ahead, the venerable fur-trading company was essentially transformed into a major real estate company in competition with the government of Canada and the Canadian Pacific Railway. The boundaries of the new territory were well established on the south and west, but the northern limits were left undefined as the Arctic regions were not yet considered of any value to the Canadian government and of only minor importance to the HBC, which had retained but a few posts on the coasts of Hudson Bay and Hudson Strait.

Once the matter of the HBC lands was resolved, the British government was faced with the question of what to do with the Arctic Islands. The death of Sir John Franklin and his crew had stifled both public and Admiralty interest in further Arctic exploration. Nor did the British government attempt to secure the title of the various discovery claims by way of settlement or administrative acts. Only British whalers showed any serious interest in the Arctic and

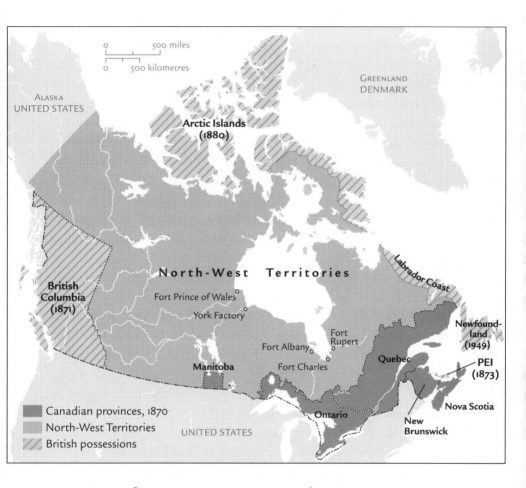

CANADA IN 1870 AFTER PURCHASE OF HUDSON'S BAY COMPANY LANDS

With the purchase of Rupert's Land and acquisition of the
North-Western Territory, the fledging Dominion of Canada suddenly
became one of the largest countries in the world but with a
relatively small population and economic base.

its inhabitants. Citing Denmark's success with its Greenland colonies, several whaling captains petitioned Queen Victoria to provide education and medical assistance for the Inuit of Baffin Island. Their submissions were ignored.[17] In contrast to British colonies elsewhere in the world, investment in the Arctic offered no foreseeable financial return.

Meanwhile the whalers fishing off the Baffin coast steadily increased in number. Unlike whaling activities in more southerly climates, this operation was strictly seasonal and often required a hasty departure to avoid being caught in the ice. The method they employed was referred to as "rock nose" whaling, with each ship anchoring off a rocky shore and sending its crew members out in small boats to harpoon the whales. Once caught, the whale was brought to the side of the ship, where it was flensed and the whale blubber and baleen stored for the voyage home. Contact with the Inuit was limited to sporadic trade for furs and ivory. Toward mid-century, stocks had drastically declined and other locations were sought, first in Cumberland Gulf, then along Hudson Strait and into the bay. The Scottish whalers had once dominated the Davis Strait fishery but were now joined by American ships that initiated the practice of wintering over in Cumberland Gulf. In order to compete, some Scottish whalers also adopted the practice. As a result, a number of shore stations were built in the gulf by both nationalities.[18]

The practice of wintering over dramatically changed the method of whaling. Inuit were hired to supply food and fur clothing, as well as to man the whale boats and help to render the blubber. Income was supplemented through trade in furs and ivory. Later the American whalers also began wintering over at Lake Harbour on the southern coast of Baffin Island and along the western shores of Hudson Bay. While Inuit gained benefit from access to trade goods, they also suffered from disease introduced by the whalers and eventually from diminished food and fur resources through overhunting. Reports of trade in alcohol and other abuse reached London, but provoked no concern. On one occasion, Captain William Penny, a veteran Scottish whaler, brought along a missionary who professed no interest in remaining among the Inuit.

The situation improved marginally when two Anglican missionaries arrived at Blacklead Island in 1894, but by then the whaling industry in Davis Strait was near an end. The new steam-assisted ships allowed the whalers to probe deeper into Lancaster Sound, Prince Regent Sound and Admiralty Inlet, but stocks continued to decline until the large Greenland whales, or bowheads, had virtually disappeared from the west coast of Davis Strait. At the end of the nineteenth century a few Scottish ships continued to fish in north Baffin waters, as did American whalers in Hudson Bay, but for only a few years.

Similar problems of declining resources were also encountered on the other side of the continent. The number of American whaling ships in the North Pacific and the Bering Sea had declined dramatically as a result of the first oil well drilled in 1859, which in turn led to a number of refined products that further decreased the need for whale oil. Eventually whalebone, used in the manufacture of women's corsets, overtook the oil as the major source of profit for the industry, still supplemented by trade in ivory and furs. Reports of outbreaks of disease among villages suffering from food shortages became prevalent. As whale stocks declined from overfishing in southern waters, the remaining ships cruised further north through the Bering Strait in search of new grounds. After several disastrous seasons marked by major losses of ships and lives, new steamships were built and two U.S. revenue cutters were sent to patrol the waters to assist whalers in trouble and prevent the trade of guns and alcohol with the Natives.[19]

Meanwhile, after the sale of Alaska, Russia's Pacific trade prospered from its base at Pravaosk in the Amur delta. As in past centuries, Russia's possessions on the Arctic rim remained protected from foreign ships by the ice blocking the Northern Sea Route. This did not deter Norwegian whalers and sealers from fishing in the Kara Sea, with their small, shallow-draft ships that were easily manoeuvred through the ice-strewn waters. Not surprisingly, the first ship to sail through the

Northeast Passage was the 300-ton *Vega* under the command of Nils Nordenskiold, a Swede born in Russian Finland. With the support of Russian and Swedish merchants and the King of Sweden, Nordenskiold had the vessel equipped with an auxiliary steam engine and strengthened hull. He set out from Tromso, Norway, in the spring of 1878, accompanied by two cargo ships bound for the Yeniesei and Lena Rivers. They reached the river mouths without difficulty but after the *Vega* headed alone for the Bering Strait it became icebound off the northern coast of Chukotka. With no loss of life or equipment the ship sailed on through the Bering Strait the next summer. The Northern Sea Route, sometimes referred to as the Northeast Passage, had been traversed but it would be another half century before the route was used for commercial shipping and then only with the assistance of Soviet icebreakers.[20] In retrospect, Russia's decision to sell Alaska when pressed for funds after the Crimean War was likely the only option available at the time. In addition, it also removed a continual source of friction with both Britain and the United States.

Another event in Russian history was made significant by the fact that it established a precedent elsewhere in the Arctic. Although Novaya Zemlya was considered under Russia's sphere of influence, an increasing number of Norwegians began to hunt and fish there and reportedly destroyed huts and crosses belonging to Russian hunters. To establish control, in 1894 the czarist government sent ten aboriginal Nentsy families to the island to create a permanent settlement. They were joined two years later by eight more families. By the end of the century, the population of the island was divided between three separate communities, for a total of 102 Nentsy, a few Russians, a priest and a medical assistant. Although the Russian government attempted a similar experiment of settling Yakuts in the Kamchatka region, the Native settlements on Novaya Zemlya were the first to succeed on a long-term basis.[21]

Throughout this period little was known about the Danish colonization of Greenland, largely because settlers' problems were internal and unrelated to the Franklin search or the quest for the North Pole. After 1825, without government subsidies but under new management, the Royal Greenland Trading Company gradually returned to its former level of prosperity in spite of pressure to open the trade to private interests. The Royal Commission set up in 1835 to consider ending the monopoly agreed in principle, but deferred plans—allegedly until such time as the Greenlanders were better able to adjust to a competitive environment. In the interim, all profits from the company were to be directed toward bettering the education and welfare of the Greenlanders to enable them to integrate into the modern world. Progress, however, was negligible.

While most Inuit children had learned to read and write, the adults were abandoning their social and cultural traditions, yet still lived in conditions of near poverty. Municipal councils were created to allow Greenlanders the opportunity to discuss and direct their own social affairs. A local chief or *forstander* was elected from each district and met annually with other chiefs and representatives from the missions and trading company. In spite of these efforts, the population actually declined in the 1860s. By the end of the century, most Greenlanders were still living in primitive sod huts, even though they now had glass windows and interior wood walls instead of animal skins.[22]

Rules established to discourage mixed marriages had failed, with the result that there were ever more children of mixed blood who were not brought up to be skilled hunters and accordingly not fully accepted into Inuit society. This in turn had an adverse effect on the RGT company, which required a steady supply of furs, whale oil and ivory. Eventually measures were introduced to protect offspring of mixed marriages, who were often rejected by Inuit society. As the young men had no training to become successful hunters, they were generally hired by the missions or the trading company. Over time, they formed the nucleus of West Greenland society.

Class distinctions became even more evident. Those born in Greenland were now called Greenlanders, as opposed to Danes, who were born in Denmark. Seeds of discrimination were also inherent in practices intended to "protect" the Inuit, such as denying them access to tea, coffee, beans, flour and bread to encourage them to retain a more traditional diet. Attempts to restrict tobacco utterly failed. Sale

Reconstruction of a typical Greenlander sod house shown
here represents Inuit accommodation in the nineteenth and early
twentieth centuries. Improvements on the original structure included
a wood door, a stove pipe, wooden roof and eventually glass windows.
By 1920, sod houses were often lined with wood and in a few cases
had a second floor constructed of timbers and wood siding.
CE-2778, photographer Carsten Egevang, 2009, ARC-PIC Greenland

of alcohol to the Greenlanders was banned, except for those working
in the whaling industry where it was considered a "necessity."

By mid-century, reports to the commission concluded that the
island's resources were insufficient to support a sustainable economy.
New measures were introduced, including prefabricated wooden
homes for the Greenlanders and coal-burning stoves. Local boards
were established, composed of appointed representatives of the clergy
and the trading company, as well as a Greenlander elected from each
community. The Boards of Guardians, as they were called, provided
a means of communicating problems, but their official function was
to act as a court of law, settle minor disputes and administer public
relief. In 1894, Denmark assumed responsibility for the Inuit in the
Angmagssalik area of East Greenland. Their presence was discovered

Godhavn, Greenland, seen here in 1881, had a variety of
wooden buildings used by the Royal Greenland Trading Company,
church missions and their employees, a stark contrast to the Inuit
sod houses. ss *Proteus,* which carried the Greely expedition
and supplies to Lady Franklin Bay, is seen anchored in the harbour.
Library of Congress, LC-USZ62-136193, photographer G. Rice

ten years earlier but at the time the Danish government made no
effort to expand its jurisdiction eastward or, for that matter, northward to the region inhabited by the Inughuit, sometimes referred to
as the Polar Eskimos.

A serious problem persisted with attempts to educate the Greenlanders as there were few teachers conversant in both the Danish
and Inuit languages. A number of initiatives under the direction of
Dr. Henrk Rink as governor of South Greenland included the establishment of two seminaries to instruct students in both languages, a
monthly newspaper with public notices and articles on Greenland
and its people, a Danish-Eskimo dictionary, the introduction of paper
money, a savings bank at Godthab and an apprentice training program for young Greenlanders. Not all were an immediate success.

More restrictive measures enacted by Rink's successor included attempts to deter mixed marriages, with surprising consequences. Instead of the intended outcome, fewer Danes applied for Greenland service, allowing more employment opportunities for Greenlanders. Danish policy toward the Inuit has often been criticized for being too altruistic and paternalistic, but at the time it was vastly superior to American, British or Canadian treatment of their Arctic peoples.[23]

Danish geologists conducted numerous surveys of Greenland in hopes of discovering valuable minerals but with only modest results. The most important find was a large deposit of cryolite located near Ivigtut (Ivittuut) in southern Greenland. Although the discovery of the mineral was first described in 1806, the mine did not come into operation until almost fifty years later. At the time, little was known about cryolite, except that it could be used in the manufacture of alum, mirrors and enamels. The first shipments from the mine arrived in Denmark in 1854. The Danish company which owned and operated the mine also ran a refinery in Copenhagen to process the mineral. The mine employed only workers brought from Denmark with the result that all profits went directly to the Danish company and were not included in the revenue of the Royal Greenland Trading Company.

Then in 1886, two scientists, an American and Frenchman, discovered a process of making aluminum with cryolite as the essential component. In 1902 the Øresunds Chemiske Fabriker company was established to operate the mine and market the product, but not until World War I was there a major demand for the mineral. By World War II, however, it had become a key component in airplane manufacturing.

Although the mine operated for well over a century, the Greenland colony received no direct benefit from the export sales.[24] On the other hand, Danish historian Finn Gad argues that the Greenland Inuit benefited indirectly, since state revenues from royalties and later partnership were added to the "Greenland Account." Nevertheless, employment at the mine remained closed to all Greenlanders until after World War II.[25]

Ships loading cryolite at Ivigtut (Ivittuut), Greenland, in 1898.
The mine was in operation from 1854 to 1987 and originally owned
by a private Danish company which hired only Danes to work the mine
and load ships. Revenue went directly to the company and was not
shared with the Royal Greenland Trading Company, denying
the Inuit direct benefit from use of their natural resources.
#00483, Danish Arctic Institute (Arktisk), Copenhagen, photographer R. Bentzen

In the interim, a number of exploration activities took place in
Greenland, primarily American expeditions using Inughuit from the
Etah area in northern Greenland as guides. For the most part, Denmark's exploration activities in Greenland were modest and primarily
scientific in nature, such as the meteorological research at Godthab
for the First International Polar Year, 1882–83, or the *Galathea* expeditions in 1884 and 1886.

Although other countries showed a greater interest in polar science and exploration after world attention was brought to bear on the
Franklin search, British expeditions to the Arctic regions had come
to an abrupt halt. A few Admiralty officers attempted to rouse public
support for further exploration, such as Captain Sherard Osborne,
who gave a paper before the Royal Geographical Society on 23 January 1865, in which he stated:

The Admiralty will, as good servants of the public, do whatever the public calls upon them to do; and it is by the action of public opinion, directed by the men of science of this country, that I hope to see a Polar expedition sent forth in this generation under official auspices. The navy needs some action to wake it from the sloth of routine, and save it from the canker of peace... The navy of England cares not for mere war to gratify its desire for honourable employment or fame. There are other achievements it knows well, as glorious as a victorious battle, and a wise people should be careful to satisfy a craving which is the life blood of a profession.[26]

Initially the message fell on deaf ears, but the Royal Navy did launch one more expedition in 1875 in an attempt to reach the North Pole and map the coasts of northern Greenland and Ellesmere Island. It failed to attain its primary objective and the men were severely afflicted with scurvy. This would be the navy's last polar expedition. Both the Admiralty and the British public had lost their enthusiasm for Arctic adventures.

Countries that claimed sovereignty in the Arctic regions during the late nineteenth century had different motives and objectives, hence different priorities and attitudes toward responsibilities. Denmark, the United States and Russia viewed their Arctic possessions as a place for settlement and exploitation of resources, which in varying degrees meant some form of responsibility for the education and welfare of the indigenous peoples. In direct contrast, Britain accepted no direct responsibility for the Inuit—nor did Canada until well into the twentieth century.

BRITISH TRANSFER OF THE
ARCTIC ISLANDS, 1870–1900

The object of annexing these unexplored territories to Canada is,
I apprehend, to prevent the United States from claiming them,
and not from the likelihood of their proving of any value to Canada.
British Colonial Office memo, 1879 [1]

. . . .

WITH THE Admiralty no longer interested in polar exploration, the British government took no further action on discovery claims in the Arctic Islands. Then seemingly out of the blue, an inquiry was received in January 1874 from a Mr. A.W. Harvey of St. John's, Newfoundland, concerning ownership of Cumberland Gulf, where he hoped to purchase land to build a whaling station. This was followed in March by another request for a land grant in the same area, this time from Lieutenant William A. Mintzer, formerly of the United States Engineering Corps. His purpose, according to an application made to the British consul in Philadelphia, was to prospect for minerals in an area he described as "not inhabited except by a few wandering Esquimaux and does not appear to be claimed by anyone." [2] The dilemma facing the Colonial Office was whether Britain intended to secure its discovery claims, in which case the sale of any portion of the territory would be considered an administrative act toward "effective occupation."

Uncertain as to who owned the properties in question, the Colonial Office sought advice from the Hudson's Bay Company, which affirmed that the Cumberland "Gulf" had never been part of its lands. Lord Carnarvon as secretary for the colonies then asked the British Admiralty if Britain had ever claimed possession to the area. The hydrographer in charge of the maps reported that while the English navigator John Davis had explored the gulf in 1585 and 1587, the only official acts of possession had taken place to the south by Martin Frobisher in 1576, and to the north at Agnes Monument by Captain John Ross in 1818. Otherwise, the hydrographer admitted that the Admiralty's knowledge of the area was "very imperfect," although it had been reported that English and American whalers "occasionally" visited the area and had established summer fishing stations.[3] Had anyone thought to ask their own Scottish whalers, they would have learned that whaling ships had been wintering over in Cumberland Gulf for over twenty years, including American whalers. Apparently forgotten was a memo in 1854 from the Foreign Office to the British ambassador in Washington, suggesting that the United States government should be warned that American whalers established on "Cumberland Island [sic]" were trespassing on British territory.[4]

Already on record for wishing to avoid confrontation with the United States—and concerned that officially declaring title to the Arctic Islands might be considered in contravention of the Monroe Doctrine—Britain proposed a rather creative solution. In a secret despatch dated 30 April 1874 to Lord Dufferin as the governor-general of Canada, Lord Carnarvon recommended transfer of the Arctic Islands to Canada, with the caveat that the gift would come with added responsibilities. Carnarvon went on to explain that the Colonial Office had received inquiries about the purchase of property on Cumberland Sound, but did not feel it "appropriate" to authorize such a sale unless Canada was "prepared to assume the responsibility of exercising surveillance over it as may be necessary to prevent the occurrence of lawless acts or other abuses." Carnarvon also requested that the information be communicated "confidentially to your Ministers" and that he be informed if the Canadian government was in favour of such a transfer.[5]

Lord Carnarvon, Secretary
of State for the Colonies
from 1874 to 1878, inherited
the title of fourth Earl
of Carnarvon and was
appointed to the position
of secretary for the colonies
in 1874 by Prime Minister
Benjamin Disraeli. One of
his first acts in office was to
recommend the transfer of
the Arctic Islands to Canada.
LAC, C-018523

The proposal seems to have taken Canadian politicians by surprise, as many assumed the Arctic Islands were part of the Hudson's Bay Company territory they had acquired four years earlier. A reply was not immediately forthcoming due to a change in government in late 1873 following the defeat of John A. Macdonald and his Conservative Party. Yet apparently Prime Minister Alexander Mackenzie and the Liberals also had dreams of nation. Attaching a report of the Canadian Committee of the Privy Council, Dufferin informed Carnarvon in November 1874 that the Government of Canada was "desirous" of including the aforementioned Arctic Islands within the Dominion, but requested more information regarding the precise boundaries of the new lands.[6] Given that Canada had neither a navy nor a coast guard, that the country was in economic depression and the government in debt, one might have thought there would have

Lord Dufferin served as governor-general of Canada from 1872 to 1878, a period of rapid change which saw the entry of Prince Edward Island into Confederation, establishment of the Supreme Court of Canada and building of the Intercolonial Railway. Dufferin took a keen interest in promoting Canadian unity and was the liaison with the Colonial Office in negotiations for Britain's transfer of the Arctic Islands to Canada.

LAC, PA-028628, photo Notman & Fraser

been a serious debate on how it intended to conduct adequate surveillance of the newly acquired lands. Yet due to the secrecy attached to the despatch, there is no record of discussion or opinions of those involved in the decision.

The Colonial Office requested more information from the Admiralty regarding the boundaries. A few weeks later, a reply was received with the new information that evidently Scottish and American whalers had wintered in Cumberland Gulf and had employed Inuit to assist them. Registering some disbelief that the lands in question might include "the inhospitable regions chiefly visited by British Arctic explorers," the hydrographer instead provided details about the Labrador coast and southern Baffin Island. He also suggested that the Newfoundland government might have more information about the area's resources as "very little known in this country."[7] Carnarvon sent the Admiralty report on to Dufferin for review with the Committee of the Privy Council, along with a minute from the Colonial Office reporting that "the northern boundary of Canada has never been defined and it was impossible to say what British Territory had already been annexed to Canada." On 30 April 1875, a second report from the Canadian Committee of the Privy Council expressed concerns over the boundary definitions and manner of transfer, suggesting that resolutions be prepared for approval by the Canadian Parliament since the acquisition would likely involve expenditures.[8] This was the first indication that the Canadian politicians had considered the costs of providing surveillance for the area.

What does not appear in this exchange of correspondence was the fact that the Admiralty charts showed prior American claims to portions of Ellesmere Island in the vicinity of Lady Franklin Bay, well north of any point reached by the British navy. With the stated purpose of reaching the North Pole, the Admiralty sent an expedition that summer, consisting of two ships, HMS *Alert* and *Discovery*, under the command of Captain George S. Nares. There was nothing in his instructions about checking on activities in Cumberland Gulf on his return voyage. Although failing to reach the Pole, the *Alert* anchored and wintered over at Floeberg Beach near the northernmost tip of Ellesmere Island. A sled party set out and reached a record 83° 20′26″ N latitude, but the achievement was marred by the loss of three men. The larger *Discovery* anchored for the winter in a bay off Lady Franklin Inlet, now called Discovery Harbour. Sled patrols then explored the general area where American expeditions reportedly had visited on three previous occasions. In spite of the extensive scientific work, the expedition was considered a failure because of the loss of men and inability to reach the North Pole. Twenty-five years would pass before the Admiralty despatched another polar expedition and this time it would be to the Antarctic.[9]

While the Nares expedition was returning from Ellesmere Island, Lieutenant Mintzer was busy extracting minerals from Cumberland Gulf, or so Edward Blake, Canada's minister of justice, had reported to the Colonial Office. A clipping from the 12 July 1876 *British Colonist* described the purpose and history behind the American expedition:

An expedition is now being fitted out in which several famous investigators of the polar seas will participate, which is likely to open up a new branch of commerce between that section of the world and the more civilized quarters. It appears that during the search for the ill-fated Polaris over a year ago, rich veins of graphite were discovered in Cumberland Inlet. On the return to St. John's, Lieut. W.A. Mintzer, United States Naval Engineer, chartered a small steamer, and went back and continued his mineral survey... The topsail schooner Era has been recently fitted at New London, and will sail next Monday under Mintzer's command and under government auspices, to get a cargo of these minerals... [The *Era*] is well provided with mining tools and labourers for quarrying, and as deposits are situated some distance up the mountain side, they will take 3.000 feet of tramway in order to more easily load the vessel, and a quantity of lumber to erect tool houses and buildings...[10]

Carnarvon responded by suggesting that before the British government considered the matter, they would appreciate knowing whether Canada had made any steps to present the proposal to Parliament. Blake, who was currently in England, replied that he could not speak for the Government of Canada, but would inquire when he returned home. In the interim, Carnarvon informed Dufferin that his government did not plan to take any action unless "expressly asked to do so" by Canada.[11] By November the Mintzer expedition had safely returned to Philadelphia with 150 tons of mica said to be worth five to ten dollars a pound. The *New York Times* reported that this was a private venture funded by Philadelphia capitalists and that the three veins had been exhausted with no evidence of further deposits. The newspaper also reported that "Eskimo Joe," who previously worked for explorer Charles Hall, had accompanied the expedition and that a few Inuit had helped out for a short time before leaving to hunt caribou.[12]

There was no further correspondence on the subject until a year later. As the Committee of the Privy Council later explained, "There did not seem to be any pressing necessity for taking action." Finally on 2 October 1877, a second report of the Canadian Committee was

HMS *Alert*, one of the two ships taking part in the Admiralty expedition of
1875 led by Captain George S. Nares, is seen here anchored for the winter
off Floeberg Beach on the northern coast of Ellesmere Island, less than 10
kilometres east of the present site of Canadian Forces Base Alert. Although
failing to reach the North Pole, a sled party from *Alert* achieved the record for
travelling the farthest north, but not without the loss of men.   LAC, C-026564

presented to the Governor-General, which repeated the request that
the boundaries be specifically defined and that the transfer take place
by an imperial act of Parliament. Carnarvon relayed the request to
the Admiralty and instructed it to prepare maps and additional information for consideration by the Canadian ministers. It did so, with a
memo to the Colonial Office that it was complying with the request
"as far as the Admiralty are in a position to do so" in the form of thirteen "published" maps and notes from the last British expedition.
Carnarvon's covering letter to Lord Dufferin on 23 October referred
to the enclosed maps and notes, but gave no information regarding
any unpublished maps which showed American claims to northern
Ellesmere Island.[13]

In a separate communication to the Governor-General, however,
Carnarvon reflected his impatience and frustration, warning that
because of the newspaper reports, American citizens were aware that

"private expeditions have been sent out to explore certain portions of the territories, and that if it should be the wish of the Canadian people that they should be included in the Dominion, great difficulty in effecting this may easily arise, unless steps are speedily taken to place the title of Canada to those Territories on a clean and unmistakable footing." This time, Carnarvon firmly requested that he be informed "with as little delay as may be possible, of the steps which you propose to take in the matter." Finally the Canadian Committee concurred that the issue was now "urgent," and agreed to bring up the question at the next session of Parliament.[14] By implying that the Mintzer expedition of 1876 might be the basis of his concerns, Carnarvon avoided mention of a more serious issue.

In February 1877, Captain Henry W. Howgate, formerly with the United States Navy and now posted to the United States Army Signals Corps, presented to Congress a detailed proposal for polar exploration, which subsequently was sent for consideration to both the Committee on Appropriations and the Committee of Naval Affairs. The plan involved establishment of a "colony" at Lady Franklin Bay on Ellesmere Island, which would serve as a base for at least three years of extensive exploration and scientific studies. Included would be an attempt to reach the North Pole. Over the next few months, Howgate lobbied senior politicians and naval officers for support. As he had expected approval of the requested $50,000 and participation of military officers, he outfitted an advance party with munitions, scientific equipment and charts provided by various military departments. Thus on 2 August 1877, Captain George E. Tyson and the advance party departed on the *Florence* from New London, arriving six weeks later at Cumberland Gulf, where the ship anchored for the winter. Here, Tyson set about collecting fur clothing, food supplies, dogs and Inuit families. According to plans, the *Florence* would join the main expedition the following summer at Disko Island (Greenland), then the two ships would head north through Kennedy Channel and Kane Basin to their destination.[15]

If the British Foreign Office was only vaguely aware of Howgate's proposal before Congress, it certainly was forewarned by an

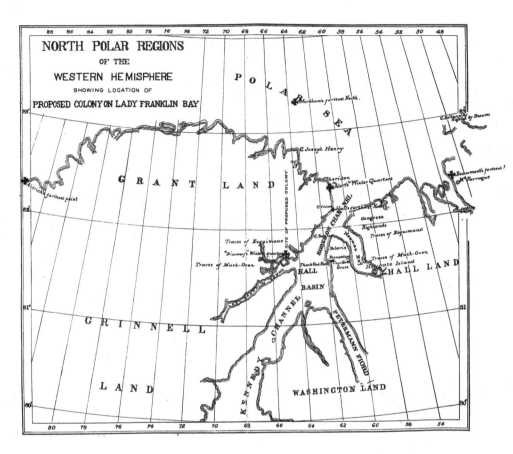

"North Polar Regions of the Western Hemisphere Showing Location
of Proposed Colony on Lady Franklin Bay" accompanied U.S.
Army Captain Henry W. Howgate's proposal to Congress of a "polar
colonization" project on northern Ellesmere Island. Note the
naming of various land forms after prominent Americans: Grant
Land after U.S. President Ulysses S. Grant, Washington Land, Hall
Land after the American explorer, and Grinnell Land, after the
newspaper magnate who had funded previous polar expeditions.

Captain Henry W. Howgate, *Polar Colonization: Memorial to Congress and Action of
Scientific and Commercial Associations* (Washington, DC: Beresford Printer, 1878), frontispiece

article appearing in the London *Standard*. The author of the article was identified as a former member of the 1876 British polar expedition, who had visited the *Florence* before departure, interviewed crew members and met both Howgate and Captain Tyson. Although there were no specific details about the purpose of the American expedition, other than that they intended to do some whaling in Baffin's Bay, the Colonial Office was now on the alert.[16] The timing also explains the "urgency" Carnarvon referred to in his request for an immediate response about the Canadian government's intentions, although he had been careful to refer only to "private expeditions" in his despatch to Dufferin. At this point, secrecy was critical to prevent American knowledge of the proposed transfer before its completion. The two unknowns were whether the U.S. Congress would approve Howgate's plan and on what terms the Canadian government would accept the transfer.

Whether on his own initiative or at the suggestion of the Colonial Office, Lord Dufferin decided to investigate further. On 31 January 1878, he gave a speech at a meeting of the American Geographical Society in New York, attended by an estimated 500 or 600 members and guests—a meeting that had been convened expressly for the purpose of hearing Captain Howgate's plan for "polar colonization." Apparently well known among the society's members, Dufferin was warmly welcomed as the governor-general of Canada, referred to "as the best of neighbors." For reasons unstated, Howgate failed to attend the meeting, but instead sent Lieutenant Adolphus Greely to read a prepared address that described the proposal in detail, including its purpose, location, expected climate conditions, participants, preparation and safety measures. Greely also read off an impressive list of supporters that included William Cullen Bryant, Chief Justice Daly and veteran Arctic explorers Dr. Isaac Hayes and Dr. John Rae. Participants were expected to remain at the colony for at least three years, supplied annually by support ships. The address also explained that Howgate intended to learn from the mistakes of the Nares expedition by using Inuit guides and their dogs and would utilize the coal deposit the British expedition had discovered while wintering in Discovery

Bay.[17] Perhaps a coincidence, but Lord Carnarvon was replaced as secretary four days later by Sir Michael Hicks-Beach, a barrister with considerable experience in the government.

Not waiting for a reply from the Canadian government, the Colonial Office asked the Crown's legal advisers to review the circumstances of the transfer. As before, they concurred that an imperial act of Parliament was unnecessary. Finally on 3 May 1878, the documents outlining the proposal were tabled in the Canadian House of Commons. David Mills as minister of the interior introduced the resolutions, which were strongly supported by both parties, with only one dissenter—Peter Mitchell, a Conservative member from New Brunswick, who argued that it was too costly and it would be better if the imperial government continued its responsibility until Canada was better able to take on such a commitment. Opposition leader John A. Macdonald refuted Mitchell's concern, claiming there would be no cost until the region was settled, at which time revenue would offset expenses. He also argued that if Canada refused, Britain might abandon her claims, allowing the United States to occupy the region unopposed.[18]

Without further delay, the resolutions passed and a joint address to the Queen was passed by the Canadian Senate and House of Commons acknowledging their acceptance of the transfer. An attachment, however, reiterated their view that the transfer should be executed by an imperial act of Parliament with precise definition of the boundaries.[19] Before these questions were addressed to the satisfaction of both Canada and Great Britain, a number of other events had intervened. First, the U.S. Congress refused funding for Howgate's proposed colonization scheme. Captain Tyson returned home with his ship and crew after failing to connect with the "main expedition." Then, apparently at the urging of Prime Minister Disraeli, Lord Dufferin was replaced in late October by the Marquis of Lorne, Queen Victoria's son-in-law.

Not pleased with the Canadian government's insistence about an imperial act of Parliament, Hicks-Beach had written Dufferin the previous July to say he would defer presenting the proposed transfer to the Queen to allow the Canadian government time to consider whether letters patent would be sufficient and leave "the question of Imperial legislation for future consideration." The Dominion's response in October came in the form of yet another order-in-council from the Canadian Committee of the Privy Council, this time with an attached report by Canada's minister of justice, Rodolphe Laflamme, who again argued in favour of an imperial act. This time the Admiralty reacted when presented with a draft copy of the proposed legislation. In its view, it did not matter whether the instrument was an order-in-council or an imperial act of Parliament; it could only define boundaries as far as 78°N latitude because of the American discoveries to the north. To prove the point, a chart was attached marking British and American discoveries with flags of different colours. The Admiralty's letter was dated 28 January 1879 and addressed to the Under-Secretary of State for the Colonies. Not surprisingly, the letter and attached chart were not forwarded to Canada. After further consultation, Hicks-Beach informed the Marquis of Lorne on 18 April 1879 that imperial legislation was not advisable. A longer letter the same day explained what he had termed "obvious reasons," namely that "questions might be raised in the discussion of such a measure which might, in the great press of business, not improbably lead to the abandonment of the project."[20]

A reply arrived six months later on 5 November 1879, with the Marquis of Lorne now advising that the Canadian government would agree to the transfer by an order-in-council. There is nothing recorded as to why Macdonald and his cabinet changed their minds or what influence was brought to bear. After British law officers were once again consulted, the final document was drawn up and on 24 July 1880 shown to Prime Minister Macdonald, who happened to be in London. Within a week, on 31 July 1880, in the presence of Queen Victoria, the Lord President, the Lord Steward and the Lord Chamberlain, the imperial order-in-council was signed, declaring:

From and after September 1, 1880, all British territories and possessions and all islands adjacent to any of such territories or possession, shall (with the exception of the Colony of Newfoundland and its dependencies) become and be annexed to and form part of the said Dominion of Canada; and become and be subject to the laws for the time being in force in the said Dominion, in so far as such laws may be applicable thereto.[21]

As Alan Cooke of McGill University observed, with a stroke of the pen "Canada had become the second-largest nation in the world."[22] The oft-quoted line that "the Imperial Government did not know what they were transferring, and on the other hand the Canadian government had no idea what they were receiving" was only partly correct.[23] Documents retained by the Colonial Office showed that Britain knew exactly the limitations of the title it was transferring. The Canadian government, on the other hand, was kept in the dark for another forty years, at which time copies of the documents were finally forwarded to the Ministry of the Interior.[24]

What seems extraordinary about the transfer was the autonomy of the Colonial Office in suggesting the idea, then implementing the transaction as recommended by the Admiralty, but without any record of consultation or prior approval by members of the British Parliament. Although discussions must have taken place during the process, there is no mention of them in official documents or informal diaries. The size of the lands transferred was enormous, perhaps explaining the secrecy attached to open discussion of the matter. One internal memo suggests the Colonial Office considered the land worthless and was interested only in keeping it out of the hands of the United States, so perhaps it was a matter of honour and prestige. But the question also arises whether the idea of the transfer originated in the Colonial Office or the Admiralty. Certainly the latter had reason to relieve itself of the expense and responsibility of maintaining surveillance of the discovery claims and avoid further risk of losing men and ships. Yet if the Admiralty felt unable to carry on the responsibility, then how would Canada manage without a navy, a coast guard or the financial means to acquire them? The Secretary's reference to possible abandonment of the transfer if it was brought before the British Parliament suggests not everyone was in agreement. Underlying the transfer were the same concerns expressed at the time of Confederation—that some elements within Great Britain wished to reinforce a friendly relationship with the United States and would go to great lengths to avoid potential conflicts. Nevertheless, the rationale and motivation directing the terms and process of the transfer remain an enigma for historians, who have failed to find substantiated evidence to prove their suspicions and speculations.

The sudden haste to complete the transfer that summer was likely prompted by Howgate's resubmission of his "polar colonization" proposal to Congress in 1880, this time as part of a scientific research project for the International Polar Year. A revised plan submitted by the Naval Committee of the House was approved in May, then withheld for further review. Finally in March 1881, a further revised plan, this time by the U.S. War Department, was approved with Lieutenant Adolphus W. Greely of the Fifth Cavalry appointed commander of the expedition. Now under the auspices of the United States Army Signal Corps, the project called for the party to remain at Lady Franklin Bay for at least three years but to be visited annually by supply ships. Howgate's proposal had suggested only a "temporary colony," but internal documents of the revised plan specifically refer to a "permanent party" and a "permanent colony."[25] How permanent will never be known as the project ended abruptly with the tragic loss of twenty-two lives. In the interim, Howgate resigned from the military in December 1880 and two years later was indicted for embezzling funds from the Signal Corps. He escaped but was finally captured in 1894 and spent six years in Albion Penitentiary for his misdeeds.[26]

The concept of an International Polar Year (IPY) was initiated by Austrian scientist Karl Weyprecht, who successfully lobbied the geographical societies of interested nations to gain support for meteorological and magnetic research projects throughout the circumpolar region. Scientists from many countries had become interested in Arctic research as a result of the Franklin search and saw the IPY as an opportunity to share collected data. Although most countries considered the Arctic a largely unknown region that offered opportunities to advance scientific research, Great Britain and the United States continued to view Arctic exploration as a means to attain national glory. As Professor Trevor Levere of the University of Toronto explains, there were "two models of polar science in play, one based on international cooperation, the other based on national colonization." The countries agreeing to participate in the first International Polar Year (1882–83) included Germany, Austria, Denmark, Norway, Finland, the Netherlands, Russia and the United States, with France and Sweden planning projects for the Antarctic. The IPY also created the precedent that scientists of any country had the right to conduct research in lands claimed by other states. Initially disagreeing with the concept, Great Britain belatedly agreed to send four men to conduct magnetic studies from a base near Fort Rae in Canada's North-West Territories. At Britain's request, the Canadian government's contribution would be a modest $4,000 to offset transportation costs for the British scientists, an embarrassingly insignificant form of participation considering three of the twelve IPY projects were conducted on Canadian soil by other nations.[27]

As Trevor Levere has suggested, coordinating the American proposal with the International Polar Year conferred "on America's scheme for polar colonization the dignity of contributing to an international scientific enterprise."[28] Initially, everything ran smoothly. The ship landed the Greely party at Lady Franklin Bay on schedule without incurring any serious problems with ice. Greely was accompanied by two other officers, a physician, eight non-commissioned officers, eleven enlisted men and two Inuit from Greenland. A permanent dwelling was built on the site, which they called Fort Conger after the Michigan senator who had so strongly argued on behalf of the expedition. Most of their surveys and scientific experiments were concluded within the first year. All told, their explorations covered over 2,500 square miles, including one party's survey of the northern Greenland coast, which established the record for reaching the farthest north at 83° 24′ N latitude at 40° longitude, some 350 miles from the North Pole. Other parties surveyed the interior of northern

Fort Conger on Lady Franklin Bay under construction in 1881.
The U.S. contribution to the International Polar Year involved building
a permanent winter camp on northern Ellesmere Island for a
three-year-long project that would include extensive mapping, scientific
studies and an attempt to reach the North Pole. Under the leadership
of Army Lieutenant Adolphus Greely (see inset), a party of twenty-
three assisted by two Inuit believed they would succeed where the
Nares expedition had failed, by using dog teams to pull their sleds and
establishing a large, permanent and fully equipped facility which would be
supplied annually with fresh food and supplies. Nature defeated their
plans, resulting in the death by starvation of all but six of the men. Greely
was promoted to captain in 1886 and the following year to brigadier
general. In 1906, two years before retirement, he was promoted
again, to the rank of major general.   LAC, C-5660

(*inset*) Lieutenant Adolphus Greely.
LAC, C-5557. Courtesy National Archives, Washington, U.S. Signal Corps, 93536a

Ellesmere Island as far as the western coast. Although they had sufficient supplies to last two years, Greely had specific orders to abandon
the site if no ship appeared by the summer of 1883, and head south
in small boats to Littleton Island, where it was expected they would
meet the supply ship.[29]

Not only did the first supply ship fail to reach Fort Conger, but
the second ship sent in 1883 was crushed in the ice south of Littleton Island and sank along with the supplies destined for the colony.
When the supply ship failed to appear, Greely followed orders and
moved his men in small boats as far south as the ice would allow,
losing one of the Inuit guides when his kayak capsized. With still no
sign of their supply ship, they erected a crude hut out of stone at Cape
Sabine across from Littleton Island and waited to be rescued. With
only forty days of food, the men soon succumbed to starvation. Ches-
ter Arthur, who had assumed the presidency after the assassination
of President Garfield, was reluctant to take any action until pressured
by public outrage reported by the major newspapers. Finally Arthur
approved a rescue mission and offered an additional $25,000 to any
whaler that might happen to reach the party first.

With the U.S. Army's handling of the project under severe criticism, the rescue mission was handed over to the navy, which
equipped two ships in readiness to depart that spring. The British
Admiralty provided a third, the steamship *Alert*, which had been used
in the Nares expedition a few years earlier. This gesture was viewed
by the U.S. Navy as a humane offer of assistance, but it also indicated
that Britain had accepted the responsibility on behalf of Canada for
an expedition stranded in a territory now owned by the new Dominion. In essence, yet another precedent was established in terms of
responsibilities of a sovereign nation, this time with regard to search
and rescue operations. The U.S. Navy's ships, *Bear* and *Thetis*, were
first on the scene and spotted the crude stone shelter on Cape Sabine.
By that time there were only seven men still alive, all in advanced
stages of starvation and unable to walk. Another died before returning home.

The Greely tragedy had a slightly different effect on the American public, compared to the reaction in Britain to the loss of Sir John Franklin and his ships. Initially treated as a hero on his return home, Greely escaped criticism, which was directed at the War Department for failing to adequately supply the party. The daily newspapers were filled with the stories and the survivors were well compensated for personal interviews. Within months, however, Greely found himself accused of cannibalism after families of the dead had insisted on exhumation. Shortly after, Secretary of War Robert Todd Lincoln managed to divert criticism of his department with the release of the deceaseds' diaries, which portrayed a complete breakdown of command, drunkenness, insubordination and even the execution of a party member for stealing food. Hints of "scandal" sold even more newspapers and the stories continued, many of them exaggerated. As expected, Congress reacted by announcing it would no longer fund any Arctic expeditions, thus ending whatever further plans the U.S. War Department might have had for the "colony" on Lady Franklin Bay.

There were two unexpected consequences. Although deprived of government funding, potential polar expeditions had no problem finding support from newspaper magnates and other wealthy patrons, such as Grinnell, James Gordon Bennett of the *New York Herald* and Morris Jessup of the American Museum of Natural History. The American public, however, was less enamoured with scientific achievements than it was eager to see who would be "the first" to reach the North Pole, to traverse the Northwest Passage, or simply to reach the "farthest north," as in the case of the Greely expedition. In the United States, personal glory was accompanied not by promotion, as with the British Admiralty, but by lucrative publications and lecture tours. The "Arctic Fever" that caused American explorers to return north again and again was described by Michael Robinson in *The Coldest Crucible* as "a condition that affected the heart against the better judgement of the mind." That infection also spread to the "armchair explorers" thanks to the overzealous press. As a result, the scientific value of such expeditions became secondary to achievement of heroic feats. Increasingly, Arctic exploration was promoted to the American public as representing manliness and character-building, as a contrast to the alleged decadence of urban life. In terms of commercial value, scandal and tragedy simply added spice to sensational journalism. Stories of cannibalism and starvation may have ended further government funding for polar explorations, but they appeared to have increased support from the private sector. In spite of increasing anti-commercial sentiment toward the end of the century, polar expeditions provided additional monetary benefits not only to the explorers, but also to the newspapers and media who exploited tales of Arctic adventures for their own gain.[30] The quest for rich resources and lucrative trade routes had been replaced by another source of wealth—newsworthy tales of the Arctic.

A second consequence of the success in rescuing the remaining members of the Greely expedition was a concerted effort to rejuvenate the U.S. Navy. The administrative structure was overhauled; a Naval War College was created and a Naval Intelligence Office established. More importantly, the antiquated ships left over from the Civil War were replaced over the next fifteen years by new battleships and cruisers, to create what is commonly referred to by American historians as "the New Navy."[31] By the turn of the century, the U.S. finally had the naval power to enforce the action implied in the Monroe Doctrine.

Although there were no official changes to the Monroe Doctrine before the turn of the century, the policy was often seen as part of a scheme to diminish the overall power of European countries. Concerns were voiced in British journals over the growing number of American exports around the world, where "the markets are flooded with all description of American manufactures." In this context, American commercial expansion was perceived as a consequence of the Monroe Doctrine, with the *British Trade Journal* observing that "it is all very well to ignore and ridicule America's Monroe Doctrine in its purely political aspects," but there is "an unwritten Monroe-ism working like yeast in the commercial world of America."[32] Yet as occurred at the time of Confederation, the British government continued to avoid situations that might result in direct conflict with the

U.S., perhaps in recognition that Britain's influence as a world power was gradually declining as America's was rising. Canada, meanwhile, soon discovered that there would be little support forthcoming from Britain to protect its Arctic sovereignty if threatened by American interests.

Initially the Canadian government had difficulty obtaining information on the Arctic Islands it had acquired. In 1882, the Minister of Justice contacted the Hudson's Bay Company, requesting information about the Arctic's resources and its inhabitants. When company officials replied that they were unable to provide the information, the minister recommended that no steps be taken to legislate for the region until circumstances or a sizable influx of settlers warranted them. This was followed by a Dominion order-in-council informing the Colonial Office of the government's decision. Thus it was not until 1895, fifteen years after the transfer, that Canada passed an order-in-council which formally acknowledged acceptance of the transfer and incorporated the Arctic Islands into the newly created Provisional District of Franklin. Other provisional districts created at that time were the Yukon, Mackenzie and Ungava. Some historians have suggested that Canada was unable to deal with the territories prior to the Imperial Colonial Boundaries Act of 1895, an opinion disputed by Arctic sovereignty expert Gordon W. Smith, who argued that the 1871 revision of the British North America Act had given Canada the necessary authority and that the imperial act was legislated on behalf of other British colonies.[33]

After the Greely disaster, surveillance might have seemed unnecessary had it not been for reports that American whalers were wintering over in Hudson Bay and Cumberland Gulf, now known as Cumberland Sound. Yet Prime Minister Macdonald seemed less concerned about American whalers than about the opportunities for resource development with the proposed construction of a railway to Hudson Bay. On 23 February 1883 he announced to Parliament that discussions were under way with the Admiralty to survey Hudson Strait. The Admiralty, however, was not interested, leaving the government to fund its own three-year study to evaluate use of the strait for commercial navigation and potential development of the area's resources. A whaling ship, *Diana*, was chartered for the expedition under the command of Lieutenant Andrew Gordon, whose report advised a limited navigation season of only three months. Gordon also recommended a closed season on whaling, the licensing of foreign ships and initiation of a regular patrol to collect customs duties.[34]

Two years later, when asked whether the government intended to prevent foreign whalers from fishing in Hudson Bay, issue licences or collect customs duties, a spokesman for the Conservative government stated that "it is not the intention of the government to take any steps in that direction at present." The issue was again raised in 1892 based on a report from the Lieutenant-Governor of Keewatin, John Schultz. The response this time came from the Minister of Justice, who stated that "the present was not the opportune time to announce any action." Liberal opposition member David Mills, formerly the minister of the interior who had promoted acceptance of the transfer and at the time a professor of international and constitutional law at the University of Toronto, retorted that "the whole of Hudson Bay is in Canadian waters." Yet another two years passed before the question of sovereign authority in Hudson Bay was again raised in the House, this time by David Mills, who spoke to a motion for retrieval of all correspondence between Canada and Great Britain over "Her Majesty's exclusive sovereignty over Hudson Bay." Mills gave a long pedantic speech that argued the need for police surveillance in the bay and raised concern that Canada's sovereign rights might be lost through negligence.[35] The motion passed, but there appears to be no record that any copies of the correspondence were received.

Although the Conservative governments from 1878 through to 1896 appeared reluctant to take any overt measures to assert Canada's authority in the Arctic, the Geological Survey of Canada continued to conduct small-scale geological and other scientific investigations in the vicinity of Hudson Bay and James Bay. One member, Albert Peter Low, reported finding a large deposit of mica on the southern shores of Baffin Island. In his view, the mineral resources and the whaling activities were sufficient reason to assert Canada's sovereignty in the area. As historian Trevor Levere suggests, these scientists saw their work as a form of "effective occupation" and may have cited potential sovereignty issues as a lobbying tool to assure continued government funding for their research.

While Andrew Gordon, A.P. Low and Robert Bell were concentrating their efforts on Hudson Bay, privately funded scientific studies were also taking place in northern Greenland and Ellesmere Island, primarily by the American Robert Peary and Norwegians Fridtjof Nansen, Otto Sverdrup and Roald Amundsen without a word of protest from Denmark or Canada. During this same period, the Smithsonian Institution and other museums were collecting artifacts throughout the Arctic, as if it was a *terra nullius*, belonging to no one. Yet Canadian parliamentarians voiced no concerns.

Hudson Bay was another matter, as American whalers had dominated fishing there since the 1860s, without regulation or supervision.[36] From the beginning, the Canadian government's sovereignty concerns were predicated on resource potential and costs, rather than national honour and prestige. After the British Admiralty had made it clear that it was not interested in surveillance or conducting scientific research, any decision on further action was predicated on costs, as Canada would be required to charter vessels and hire a captain and crew to supervise the American activities. From the perspective of the Conservative government, such costs could be justified only if there were valuable minerals or other resources worth protecting.

The Canadian government's apparent apathy toward Arctic sovereignty questions changed abruptly in 1896 with the election of a Liberal majority led by Prime Minister Wilfrid Laurier. Ably supported by lawyers Clifford Sifton as minister of the interior and David Mills as minister of justice, the Laurier government took the first step toward asserting Canadian authority by chartering a vessel in 1897 and sending an expedition led by Commander William Wakeham, to Hudson Bay and Cumberland Gulf. Unable to enter Hudson Bay proper because of the ice, ss *Diana* continued on to the Scottish whaling station on Kekerton Island in Cumberland Sound, where Wakeham raised the Union Jack and claimed Baffin Island and all

U.S. Revenue Cutter *Thetis*, shown here off Alaska c1900, was still in the service of the U.S. Navy in 1889, when it followed two American whalers to Herschel Island and sent a party ashore to survey the island and sound the harbour. ss *Thetis* and ss *Bear* were originally purchased by the U.S. Navy to rescue the Greely expedition from Lady Franklin Bay. Both ships were later assigned as revenue cutters to patrol the Alaskan coast.

#27, U.S. Coastguard Cutter History, photographer Bulger

adjacent lands as "under the exclusive sovereignty of Great Britain." The reference to Great Britain rather than Canada seems inconsistent with the British transfer of title, but indicative of the perception that Canada was still a British nation. Wakeham reported a rapid decline in whale stocks and the abandonment of two American stations in the area. Although admitting that American whalers were still wintering over in the upper reaches of Hudson Bay, he did not suggest taking any action as he believed that whaling would soon disappear entirely from the region.[37]

Meanwhile, an earlier report from Lieutenant-Governor Schultz indicated that American whaling was on the increase in the western Arctic north of the Mackenzie River Delta. He recounted how in 1889 the United States naval ship *Thetis* had followed two whalers to Herschel Island, approximately a mile off the mainland and some

100 miles west of the Mackenzie Delta, where the party surveyed and mapped the island, then sounded the harbour. American whaling ships arrived yearly thereafter, many of them remaining for the winter. Schultz also reported that the crew were trading with the Inuit and supplying them with alcohol and firearms, "thus violating the laws of Canada and defrauding her of revenue. I am aware, of course, of the great difficulty which will be found in endeavouring to enforce Canadian rights on this distant sea, and that the Government have had this subject under consideration; but if the rich whaling grounds near the estuary and off the mouth of the Mackenzie and as far east as Cape Bathurst are to be preserved for Canadian use, some restrictive measures must be adopted to prevent the wholesale destruction of the valuable species of that region . . ."[38]

As expected, there was no response forthcoming from the Conservative government. The report in 1896 to the Liberal government from Schultz's successor made no mention of conditions in the western Arctic, but referred to problems of American whalers wintering over and conducting illicit trade with the Inuit in the upper reaches of Hudson Bay—perhaps explaining why the Liberal government had approved the Wakeham expedition prior to dealing with problems in the western Arctic.

Whaling historian John Bockstoce confirmed the story of U.S. Navy involvement in surveying Herschel Island when he described how USS *Thetis* had been sent north to assist the American revenue cutters in "looking out for the commercial and whaling interests in the Beaufort Sea and Arctic Ocean." The naval party who surveyed the island also added new names to the charts. News spread rapidly to the San Francisco whaling centre, bringing more ships to Herschel Island and adding more buildings until it took on the appearance of a small village. In 1894–95, there were fifteen ships wintering in Pauline Cove, this time accompanied by a number of captains' wives and their children. Inuit were hired from both Alaska and Canada to assist in the whale hunt and provide food for the whalers, adding another fifty or more winter residents.

July 4th celebrations at Herschel Island, 1896. After the party from
USS *Thetis* had surveyed the island in 1889, news spread rapidly to San
Francisco, bringing more whaling ships to Herschel Island and adding
more buildings until it took on the appearance of a small American village.
In 1894–95, there were a total of fifteen ships wintering in Pauline Cove.
NBWM 2000.1000.202.216, New Bedford Whaling Museum, photographer unknown

Bockstoce also described how young Inuit women were sold by
their fathers or husbands to serve as mistresses for the crew members
and how the sailors had introduced smallpox and other infectious
diseases, which spread throughout the Native communities and decimated the area's population. Aside from the Yukon and Mackenzie
Valley Inuit, who were likely not aware they were "Canadians" or did
not understood what it meant, the only non-American presence was
Reverend Isaac O. Stringer and his wife from Fort McPherson, who
first visited the island in 1892. They were welcomed by the whaling
captains, who felt they had a "mollifying influence on the tensions"
that arose among men living in isolation. In 1897 the Stringers
established a mission at Pauline Cove, where the husband-and-wife
team continued their services of worship and campaign against the
whisky trade.[39]

Canadian Minister of the Interior Clifford Sifton and his party are seen here
en route to the Yukon in 1897 to investigate rumours of gold discoveries in
the Yukon. Sifton is in the front row, third from the left, with Dr. W.F. King
in charge of the boundary survey, next on the right and J.M. Walsh,
newly appointed commissioner of the Yukon, second from the left.
VPL WO 7220, Historical Photos/Special Collections, Vancouver Public Library

An 1896 report from the North-West Mounted Police (NWMP)
detachment in the Yukon raised multiple alarm bells. Inspector Con-
stantine reported the unlawful activities and abuse of young Inuit
women by the whalers on Herschel Island, as well as the frequent
desertions by their crew members, who headed across to Rampart
House on the Porcupine River in an attempt to reach the Yukon
River. He recommended that an "armed government vessel, with a
strong and disciplined crew" could put an end to the liquor traffic and
help protect the resources of the area. His major concern, however,
was the sudden influx of American miners from Alaska into Canadian territory, after gold had been found on small tributaries of the
Yukon River and a major discovery on Bonanza Creek. He urgently
requested the appointment of a gold commissioner and registry

office to handle the claims, a steamer to enable the police to travel easily among the prospectors' camps and two more police posts to bring the total number of policemen in the area to seventy-five.[40] The list of additional equipment and building materials might have been mind-boggling in 1896, but nothing compared to the demands over the next two years.

Clifford Sifton as Canada's minister of the interior arrived at the gold fields the following year to assess the situation first-hand, accompanied by Dr. W.F. King, who had been in charge of survey-ing the boundary between Alaska and the Yukon, William Ogilvie of the Geological Survey and J.M. Walsh, the newly appointed com-missioner of the Yukon. The party also included an additional ten police officers, nine dog drivers, six government officials, as well as four months' rations for sixty men, seventy-eight dogs, twenty-five dogsleds, a revolver for everyone and two machine guns. While the main party prepared the outfit for transport, Sifton, Ogilvie and Walsh proceeded by horseback up the Chilkoot Pass to confer with Inspector Strickland and his men, who were building police barracks near the customs post at Tagish. A quick assessment of the situation brought swift action. Not only did Sifton order additional reinforce-ments, he imposed strict police and customs controls at the summit of the passes, just within Canadian territory.[41]

When police officers suggested a location further inland to avoid confrontation, Sifton refused: "Boundary is at the summit or farther seaward. Instruct your officers that provisionally the boundary is at the summit & to act accordingly." Believing the lack of an official pro-test over American settlements in Dyea and Skagway had weakened Canada's claims to the area, he later explained his actions. "In another ten days, they would have been in possession of the territory down to Lake Bennett and it would have taken twenty years of negotiating to get them out, in fact I doubt if we would ever have got them out . . . It is a case of possession being ten points in the law, and we intend to hold possession."[42] Sifton's biographer, D.J. Hall, argued that had it not been for the minister's decisive action the region between the two passes would have been lost to the Americans.

Sifton was an advocate of strong measures to protect the integrity of the Canadian border, but he also recognized that the future prosperity of the Yukon, and indirectly Canada, would depend on gaining unrestricted access to the interior for Canadian trade goods. As a consequence, he promoted the construction of a railway along an "all Canadian Route" to the Klondike by way of the Stikine River. Unfortunately, the process of negotiations and approvals came to a standstill due to unreasonable demands by the contractors and strong protests by the Conservative opposition. Before Sifton could get an agreement acceptable to Parliament, the Americans had begun building a rail line from Skagway through the White Pass.[43]

Sifton also recognized the need for effective local government. As a result, the Yukon was elevated from its status as a provisional district and made a separate territory with its own executive, legislative and judicial institutions, and governed by an appointed commissioner and council. By then, the police force had increased to 239 with additional support provided by 200 militia men. The ability of the NWMP to maintain law and order in what otherwise might have been chaos has been immortalized in Yukon history and lionized elsewhere in Canada. Even Queen Victoria acknowledged their importance by allowing the force to be renamed the Royal North-West Mounted Police. As might be expected, they were soon mandated to play a similar role as protectors of sovereignty in the Arctic.[44]

Although the NWMP are usually credited with having retained control over the Yukon for Canada, it was Sifton who gave the orders for changes in governance structures, added further police and militia to man the summit posts and brought Police Superintendent Sam Steele from Fort McLeod to take charge—all in advance of the 1898 massive rush of newcomers to the gold fields. Stories of the virtual population explosion at Dawson City became legendary. Although the police were above reproach in the eyes of the Canadian public, the Conservative opposition continued to voice fierce criticism of the Liberal government. Indirectly, partisan politics weakened the Liberal government's ability to negotiate a peaceful settlement of the boundary dispute. Laurier, who always tried to balance the need for public support of his policies against the potential alienation of Britain and/or the United States, learned a lesson from the Yukon experience. Where possible, the prime minister began to treat any planned actions or negotiations on sovereignty issues as highly confidential until the matter was resolved. Eventually, secrecy and occasionally censorship would become accepted practice for any party in power when dealing with questions concerning Arctic sovereignty.

The discovery of gold had an equally dramatic impact on Alaska. After its purchase, the U.S. had provided no financial support or form of government for sixteen years, a period defined by Alaskan historians as one of total neglect. Initially, the territory had been placed under the direction of the U.S. Army based at Sitka. Yet, as historian Stephen Haycox notes, Congress did send a number of fact-finding missions to assess the potential of resource development. Sadly, one report argued conclusively that the region had no immediate economic potential and was best left to the fur trade. In spite of objections, the negative view prevailed and plans to provide an infrastructure for civil government were deferred indefinitely.

Those who had come to Sitka in hopes of finding adventure and opportunity soon departed. By 1877 the army garrison had also been withdrawn, leaving the responsibility for policing the area to two U.S. revenue cutters. On occasion, when drunk and disorderly conduct was reported to be threatening the lives of white residents, the U.S. Navy was ordered in to maintain law and order. The major stabilizing factor was the influence of a Presbyterian preacher, Dr. Sheldon Jackson, who established missionary programs to "civilize" the Natives by replacing their traditional cultures with "mainstream, white, Protestant, American culture," a program found acceptable by the United States Congress.[45] Otherwise, the U.S., like Britain and later Canada, saw little value in expending effort or money on governing their respective Arctic regions unless there was a justifiable economic reason to do so.

For the U.S. government, "justifiable reasons" surfaced with the discovery of gold within Alaska in the late 1870s, near what is now called Juneau. By 1880 several thousand prospectors and entrepreneurs had arrived, creating a number of small settlements whose residents demanded some form of civil government. In response, Congress passed the Alaska Act in 1884, which provided the area with minimal government and designated Alaska as a civil district with a governor and judicial infrastructure. The laws of Oregon were applied, as were general U.S. mining laws. At Dr. Jackson's urging, the act also provided for the establishment of schools for all races. In 1891, the U.S. Congress added provisions for Alaska in the new Western Lands Act that allowed orderly disposal of land through a General Land Office authorized to identify town sites, survey lots and sell land to citizens. This all happened in advance of the major gold finds in the Yukon, which ended in a virtual invasion of gold seekers after the news reached San Francisco in 1896. Almost instantly, Alaska acquired the characteristics of a new frontier similar to the Wild West of yesteryear. The gold rush also brought a major infusion of government funding, initially for policing and surveillance, then for court and treasury officials, and improved lines of communications. Additional legislation provided the necessary infrastructure for transportation, construction and governance of the new settlements.[46]

The Klondike gold rush primarily affected the Subarctic regions, but its significance to Arctic sovereignty lay in the subsequent boundary dispute and its manner of resolution. Although there was a long-standing difference of opinion as to the location of the boundary in the Alaskan Panhandle, previously neither Britain nor the United States considered it an urgent matter. Finally in 1892, the U.S. Secretary of State called for a joint survey of the contested boundary to provide data for consideration by a joint committee. With Dr. W.F. King, chief astronomer of the Department of the Interior, acting as the commissioner for Canada and T.C. Mendenhall for the U.S., eleven American parties and four Canadian completed the survey within four years. Their report was submitted on 31 December 1896, but no action was taken as news of the discovery of gold in the Yukon had taken priority.

Sitka, Alaska, in 1896 shows the absence of the Russian fort which once
stood on the island and a major expansion of buildings along the shore
resulting from arrival of prospectors on their way to the Alaskan gold fields.
Alaska State Library P87-1499, Winter and Pond Photograph Collection

Finally in 1898, a Joint High Commission was set up to deal with
a number of issues between Canada and the U.S., the Alaskan boundary being one of them. Laurier had wanted a compromise settlement,
but Sifton refused to give in to what he described as "the condescend-
ing willingness of the American people to take everything Canada
has got and give nothing in return." The meetings of the high commission ended in 1899 without an agreement, but both parties
concurred that a provisional boundary should be surveyed in order
to maintain law and order in the panhandle. Influenced by biased
press coverage, the Canadian public enthusiastically supported its
government's refusal to "give in" to the U.S., thus ensuring the Liberal
party's popularity through to the next election. On the diplomatic

front, however, Canadian-American relations were at an all-time low, with the British Colonial Office expressing increasing concern that the unresolved boundary dispute would adversely affect Anglo-American relations.[47]

The role of the Canadian press in exerting political pressure should not be minimized. Yet unlike the U.S. and Britain, Canada had no Arctic explorers or even government ships capable of sailing in the ice-infested waters of the Arctic Islands. Thus knowledge of the Arctic was generally acquired second-hand from British and American sources. Inevitably, Canada's polar regions were lumped together as part of the "great Canadian North," and the indigenous people generalized as "Natives." The media made no attempt to educate their readers on the difference between the Subarctic and the Arctic. At the turn of the century, the most exciting stories that absorbed the attention of the Canadian media were about the police and prospectors in the Yukon. Otherwise, their focus was generally on political leaders, government activities and settlement of the west. The francophone press in Quebec was even more parochial. The one issue, however, that was guaranteed to spark the interest of anglophone readers was any hint that the U.S. might seek to acquire lands that were rightfully theirs. In this respect, the media of the three countries were alike, forever seeking stories that would sell their wares. Arctic sovereignty, as we know it today, was soon to appear on the public's radar screen.

WITH THE exception of Greenland, the map of the North American Arctic underwent a major change in the last half of the nineteenth century. At the time, transfers of sovereign authority were never contested, likely because no other country considered the lands to be of any particular value. Purchase of a territory was acceptable under existing international law but the transfer of a title to lands that had not been perfected by "effective occupation" had no prior precedent upon which to measure its legality. Fortunately for the Canadian government, no other country appeared willing to bear the expense of administering and policing such a vast region. Furthermore, the vague terms defining exactly what lands had been transferred to

Canada required clarification before full assertion of authority could take place. In accepting the gift of the Arctic Islands, government officials recognized they had accepted responsibility for maintaining sovereignty over the entire Archipelago, but were still unaware that the title was not yet secure.

At the turn of the twentieth century, the new Dominion of Canada—large in area but small in population—found itself in the unenviable position of becoming commercially dependent on the United States and equally dependent upon Britain for support against aggressive American actions. The question yet unanswered was whether Canadian politicians and officials had learned anything from the Yukon experience that could be applied to protect Canada's claims of sovereignty over the Arctic Islands.

PART III

THE TWENTIETH CENTURY

THE ARCTIC experienced many changes during the twentieth century as a result of scientific research, discovery of new resources and technological advances, particularly in offshore drilling, aviation and submarine travel. Yet there were no major changes in boundaries because of measures Canada and Denmark had taken to protect their respective claims to the Arctic Islands and Greenland. Potential conflicts were settled peacefully, either through negotiation and bilateral agreements, by tacit recognition or, as in the case of Norway's challenge to Denmark's authority in northeast Greenland, by the Permanent International Court of Justice. The Arctic also gained new significance in terms of continental security, initially during World War II and then the Cold War, resulting in a major influx of American troops and civilians to Alaska, the Canadian Arctic and Greenland. During the latter half of the century, oil and gas discoveries added a new dimension to sovereignty issues in terms of adjacent waters, sea ice and the seabed, leading to negotiation of the United Nations Convention on the Law of the Sea. Offshore drilling also raised questions concerning the environment and ownership, resulting in a unified protest by Inuit living in the North American Arctic that in turn led to global recognition of inherent aboriginal rights to their lands.

(8)

PERFECTING SOVEREIGN
TITLES, 1900—38

The nineteenth century belonged to the United States;
the twentieth century belongs to Canada.

PRIME MINISTER WILFRID LAURIER, May 1902[1]

. . . .

PRIME MINISTER Laurier's oft-quoted statement was little more than a promise in 1902, but it reflected Canadians' optimism and the determination of Liberal politicians to stand their ground in a world of imperial ambitions. The quotation is even more apt when applied to Arctic Canada, which had been under continual threat in the nineteenth century, either by American explorers searching for unmapped islands, by whalers establishing permanent stations in Canadian territory or by wild political schemes of encircling Canada through the purchase of Greenland. Yet within thirty-odd years, Canada not only secured sovereign title to the Arctic Islands but in the process appeared to have developed a strategy to deal with future conflicts.

During the same period, Denmark faced an official challenge by Norway over rights to East Greenland. The issue was eventually settled by the Permanent International Court of Justice, but not before Canada and Denmark had agreed to support each other's claims to Arctic sovereignty, setting a precedent that later evolved into cooperation between circumpolar countries to defend their rights against more powerful nations. With the exception of the

Svalbard Islands, the Soviet Union by decree in 1926 claimed sovereignty over all islands between its mainland and the North Pole, in the sector bounded by meridians 168° 49′ 30″ W and 32° 49′ 30″ E, in accordance with the policy set out in 1916 by the imperial Russian government, a claim that has never been officially challenged in the courts.[2]

At the turn of the century, Canadian claims to portions of the Arctic still appeared vulnerable, partly because of the vague terms describing the lands Britain had transferred in 1880, but also because of the tension between Canada and the United States over the Alaska Boundary Dispute, the collapse of the Joint High Commission in 1899 and in 1901 the rise of Theodore Roosevelt to the presidency following the assassination of President McKinley. A less tangible factor, but nonetheless a concern, was Britain's tendency to prioritize friendly Anglo-American relations ahead of Canadian interests. Yet the character of the Canadian government had changed considerably from earlier years. Following the Liberal victory in 1896, Prime Minister Laurier filled the cabinet with men of talent and experience, many of them lawyers. Moreover, his first term in office coincided with a return of economic prosperity which, when coupled with the government's apparent success in managing the Yukon gold rush, inspired a sense of confidence among Canadians in the future of their country. Strong sentiments of Canadian nationalism were emerging, but as Robert Craig Brown and Ramsay Cook have argued, it was still driven by a "fear of the real or imagined potential of the United States to absorb Canada."[3]

Laurier's appointment of Clifford Sifton—a lawyer and former attorney general of Manitoba— as minister of the interior guaranteed Canada a strong defence of its boundary rights and appropriate governance for the new territories. Also important was the appointment as minister of justice of Senator David Mills, a seasoned parliamentarian with professional expertise in constitutional and international law. Along with others such as W.S. Fielding, A.G. Blair, J.I. Tarte and Sir L.H. Davies, Laurier's cabinet provided the support and advice necessary for the government to devise a clear plan of action to defend

Sir Wilfrid Laurier, prime minister of Canada, 1896–1911. Laurier's first term in office coincided with a return of economic prosperity, which inspired a sense of confidence among Canadians in the future of their country. Laurier may have had suspicions of American motives in Alaska and doubts about British support, but he voiced them with diplomatic caution.
LAC, C-000688

Canadian claims to Arctic sovereignty without provoking official protest from the U.S. Laurier also had the backing of most Canadians, who supported a firm stand against overt or implied threats to Canada's sovereign authority.

Laurier and Sifton may have been of one mind in their objectives, but the two men sometimes differed as to appropriate action. Laurier suspected American motives in Alaska and had doubts about British support, but he voiced them with diplomatic caution. Sifton was younger, often outspoken in his anti-American views and distrust of the British, but, like Laurier, he believed it best to protect Canadian rights by preventive action before a problem arose. Not surprisingly, Sifton was already laying plans to assert Canada's authority in the Arctic long before the Alaska boundary dispute had been settled. Nor was he alone in his concerns. In the North-West Mounted Police's Annual Report of 1901, Commissioner A. Bowen Perry repeated the warnings of his predecessors and called for police supervision in the eastern and western Arctic. Referring to reports of lawlessness, he argued that "the cost of carrying law and order into the Arctic regions may cause hesitation, but when our territory is being violated and our

Clifford Sifton, minister of the interior, 1896–1905. Unlike Laurier, Sifton tended to be outspoken and impetuous, a characteristic that was largely responsible for the Canadian government's swift action to protect its sovereign authority in the Yukon and the Arctic.

LAC, PA-027942, Topley Studios

people oppressed, cost should be the last consideration."[4] Plans to build a police post on the Mackenzie River the following year were deferred because of a rumoured miners' revolt in the Yukon, but not abandoned.

Meantime, several foreign explorations had taken place in the Arctic Islands. In 1902, Robert Peary, a former U.S. naval officer, returned from yet another expedition, this time involving mapping northern Ellesmere Island, still referred to as Grant Land on American maps. That same year, news reached Ottawa about a four-year expedition led by Norwegian Otto Sverdrup that centred on Ellesmere Island. Further west, he discovered three new islands, which he named Ellef Ringnes, Amund Ringnes and Axel Heiberg after the beer companies that had funded his explorations. Unknown to the Canadian government, Sverdrup's submission to the Swedish king requesting that his work be accepted as a national claim was ignored, as was a second request to the Norwegian government following separation of the two Scandinavian countries. Yet in the Canadian view, there always remained the possibility that Norway might attempt to claim the three islands. Rumours also reached Ottawa that yet

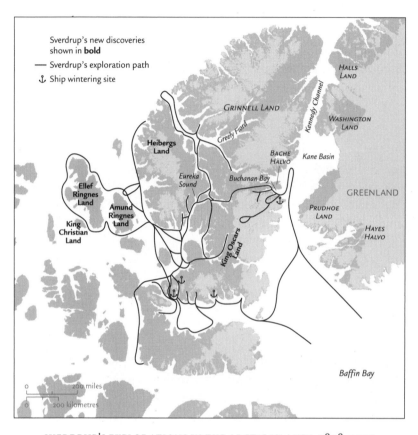

SVERDRUP'S EXPLORATIONS IN THE ARCTIC ISLANDS, 1898–1902
Explorations by Norwegian Otto Sverdrup and his party
covered areas which much later were found to have major oil and gas fields.
At the time, the King of Norway expressed little interest in claiming title
to the lands by right of discovery because of their remote location
and the assumption that they were of little value.

another Norwegian explorer, Roald Amundsen, was planning to traverse the Northwest Passage.[5]

Then in the fall of 1902, Sifton received a report co-authored by Comptroller Fred White of the NWMP, Commissioner McDougald of the Customs Department and Robert Bell of the Geological Survey, calling for the government to take immediate steps to assert its authority in the Arctic. In response, Sifton authorized two expeditions under the auspices of the Department of Marine and Fisheries, with the intent of establishing police posts in the western and eastern Arctic.[6]

By then, Laurier had realized that it would be necessary to settle the Alaska boundary dispute before trade agreements and other matters could be resolved with Britain and the U.S. Thus, with the consent of the Canadian government, the Hay-Herbert Treaty creating the Alaska Boundary Tribunal was signed on 24 January 1903 by the U.S. secretary of state and the British ambassador in Washington. The tribunal was to be held in London and made up of six "impartial" judges, three appointed by the U.S. president and three by "His Britannic Majesty." Although two of the latter were Canadian, the process reflected the lack of control Canada had over the situation and its foreign affairs. Sifton was irate. In a personal letter he claimed that the British government had decided "to sacrifice our interests at any cost for the sake of pleasing the United States." Reflecting genuine despair, he suggested that "whatever the United States demands from England will be conceded in the long run, and the Canadian people might as well make up their minds to that now."[7] Yet with revitalized tenacity, Sifton continued to defend Canadian sovereign rights, against friend and foe, real or imagined.

Norman Penlington, in *Canada and Imperialism*, argues that English Canadians had difficulty understanding, much less accepting, that Britain would support Canadian interests only if they did not adversely affect Anglo-American relations. Nor did they realize that "Britain's very existence in the twentieth century was to depend on the benevolent neutrality and friendly assistance of the United States." Yet Canada was also dependent on the United States—initially

Members and advisers of the Alaska Boundary Tribunal,
held at the Foreign Office in London, October 1903. The six judges
(unnamed)—two from Canada, three from the U.S. and one from Britain—
are sitting on a raised podium at the rear of the photograph, with delegates
and legal advisers in front. The British judge sided with the Americans
against the Canadian claim, sparking angry protests in
Canadian newspapers against both Britain and the United States.

LAC, C-021425

economically and later militarily—a factor that Penlington believed contributed to the country's ambiguity and weakened Canadian nationalism.[8] At the turn of the century, however, the triangle relationship had not yet matured. Instead an acute sensitivity emerged, particularly among anglophone Canadians, to any perceived threat to the nation's sovereign rights, a sensitivity that flourished with growing recognition of Canada's unique identity as a northern nation. In time, the Arctic became the *ultima Thule* of the Canadian North and would be celebrated in Canadian art and literature.[9]

Although Canada's claims in the Alaska boundary dispute were tenuous at best, the popular press stirred up strong anti-American sentiment in advance of the tribunal, charging that the U.S. was trying to steal land that rightfully belonged to Canada. American newspapers were equally persuasive in portraying "British" Canadians as villains. To make matters worse, President Theodore Roosevelt ignored the impartial criteria and appointed his secretary of war and two senators as judges, all with vested interests in an advancing American claims. As Laurier anticipated, Britain did not protest the appointments. To ensure that the Canadian argument was presented in the best possible light, Laurier appointed Sifton to head the legal delegation, which included Joseph Pope, who later became Canada's first under-secretary of state for external affairs, and chief astronomer Dr. W.F. King, by then a respected authority on sovereignty issues. Should Canada lose the case, Laurier was determined that no blame would fall on the legal team or his government. En route to London, however, Sifton became increasingly concerned about Canada's claims elsewhere in the Arctic after discussion with King and requested that he prepare a "thorough and complete" report on Canada's title to the Arctic Islands.[10]

Before leaving for London, Sifton had left precise instructions for his deputy minister to obtain prior approval from opposition members to ensure the appropriation bill for the new police detachments was passed by Parliament as quickly and quietly as possible. He also prepared an innocuous press release to avoid embarrassing questions concerning the purpose of the two expeditions. As planned, funding for them was expedited through Parliament in his absence, with the result that they departed without fanfare, each accompanied by six mounted policemen. As a result, two NWMP detachments were established and staffed in the summer of 1903, one at Fort McPherson on the Mackenzie River and the other at Fullerton Harbour on Hudson Bay. Police from the Fort MacPherson detachment would visit Herschel Island that summer to ensure that American whalers knew they were in Canadian territory and were required to comply with the country's laws and customs regulations.[11] After their success in the Yukon, the NWMP were thought to be the most effective means to maintain sovereignty in areas occupied by Americans. They were also responsible for a variety of administrative tasks such as postal service, issuing of licences and collecting customs duties, which provided evidence of "effective occupation."

The expedition to the eastern Arctic had an additional mandate. Albert Peter Low of Canada's Geological Survey commanded the party aboard the chartered SS *Neptune,* with the full knowledge and assent of Lord Minto, Canada's governor-general, and presumably that of Britain's Colonial Office.[12] Instructions to Superintendent J.D. Moodie, in charge of the new detachment, indicated that the government's plan had been carefully designed with a view to expanding the Canadian presence even further. "The Government of Canada having decided that the time has arrived when some system of supervision and control should be established over the coast and islands in the northern part of the Dominion, a vessel has been selected and is now being equipped for the purpose of patrolling, exploring, and establishing the authority of the Government of Canada in the waters and islands of Hudson Bay, and north thereof."[13]

The expedition first sailed to Cumberland Sound to observe whaling activities, then proceeded to Fullerton Harbour, where the party spent the winter and assisted the police in building the detachment. Moodie had also been given clear instructions to avoid "harsh enforcement of the laws" and instead was to give captains of foreign ships fair warning that in the future "laws will be enforced as in other parts of Canada."[14] That winter only one American whaler—*Era*—was anchored in Hudson Bay. The next spring, the *Neptune* dropped Moodie off at Port Burwell; he then made his way south to report to Ottawa.

From Port Burwell, the expedition sailed north along the Greenland coast until reaching Ellesmere Island and the site of Robert Peary's former camp at Cape Sabine. After a thorough investigation, Low built a cairn at nearby Cape Herschel, raised the flag and took formal possession of Ellesmere Island "in the name of King Edward VII for the Dominion."[15] The ship then sailed south and westward along Lancaster Sound, stopping at Beechey Island where the crew found recent evidence of a visit by Roald Amundsen, reportedly on his way through the Northwest Passage in his tiny ship *Gjoa*. Once again the flag was raised, possession declared and a photograph taken of the event. Heading toward Port Leopold on North Somerset Island, Low stopped to investigate what appeared to be a building. On closer examination, a large stash of supplies left for Amundsen was discovered, leaning against a ship's steam boiler and marked with a Norwegian flag. Low again raised the Union Jack, but this time deposited a proclamation and a copy of Canadian customs regulations in the abandoned boiler.

Returning south, the ship stopped to visit whalers anchored in Eclipse Sound and Cumberland Sound, carried on to Port Burwell for supplies, then headed back to Fullerton Harbour before returning home. Low's published report, over 300 pages long, finally provided the Canadian government with detailed information about the Arctic Islands, the geology and wildlife, whaling and trading activities, descriptions of Inuit communities and a complete history of previous explorations. As a first priority, Low recommended that a police post be built at Port Burwell near the entrance to Hudson Strait, even though his statistics on American whaling activities indicated a drastic decline. From the government's perspective, the latter information tempered the urgency to construct more police posts in the area.

Meanwhile, news that the Alaska Boundary Tribunal had rejected Canadian claims spread throughout southern cities and towns. Angry protests in the daily newspapers again fuelled public outrage

Raising the flag at Port Leopold as a symbol of Canada's sovereign authority. When the expedition led by A.P. Low arrived at Port Leopold on North Somerset Island, they discovered a Norwegian flag flying above an abandoned ship's boiler and a cache of supplies left by explorer Roald Amundsen, who was attempting to traverse the Northwest Passage by ship.

LAC, PA-050922, Geological Survey of Canada

that helped solidify anti-American sentiment and ended any lingering support for annexation to the U.S. This time, however, anger was also directed toward Britain, as the British judge had sided with the Americans in rejecting Canadian claims. In the House of Commons on 23 October 1903, Laurier attempted to explain the problem by stating that "as long as Canada remains a dependency of the British Crown, the present powers we have are not sufficient for the maintenance of our rights." [16] As he had hoped, no blame for the decision would be attached to the Canadian judges, the Canadian legal delegation or his government.

After receiving Moodie's initial report recommending seven new police posts and twenty-seven police officers to staff them, Sifton waited for reports from King and Low before making a firm

commitment.[17] Prime Minister Laurier was moving in a similar direction but cautiously. In the fall of 1903, he explained to Senator W.C.
Edwards that his plan was to "quietly assume jurisdiction in all directions," with police posts along with "a cruiser to patrol the waters
and plant our flag at every point." Only when "we have covered the
whole ground and have men stationed everywhere" would he consider a proclamation declaring sovereignty over the entire region.
Laurier also believed it important to conduct thorough surveillance
in advance of any public declaration, lest there were existing American settlements unknown to the government.[18]

King's confidential report in January 1904 prompted immediate
action, with Laurier submitting a request for a sum of $200,000 for
polar exploration, of which $70,000 would be spent on purchase of
a German ship, *Gauss*, previously used for Antarctic expeditions. The
ship was renamed CGS *Arctic* with Joseph Elzéar Bernier appointed
as its captain, the only Canadian to have expressed a keen interest in
Arctic exploration. In 1904, under the authority of the Department of
Marine and Fisheries, the new government ship returned Moodie and
replacement officers to the Fullerton detachment and remained for
the winter. The next spring, during a brief reconnaissance of Hudson
Bay, the ship's propeller was damaged by ice, forcing Bernier to return
home for repairs and await further instructions. Like Low, Bernier
also recommended that a police post be established at Port Burwell, a
proposal that first required clarification of the boundary between the
Northwest Territories and Labrador/Newfoundland, the latter still
held by Britain.[19]

By now, Sifton and Laurier had had sufficient time to digest King's
final report together with the earlier reports from Moodie and Low.
With whaling in both the eastern and western Arctic in decline, concern now centred on foreign explorations taking place in the remote
uninhabited islands. On this issue, King's report was not reassuring.
With lengthy explanations concerning the vague boundary definitions and the method of transfer, the chief astronomer blamed Britain
directly for apparent weaknesses in the title, arguing that while British claims rested on acts of discovery and possession, they "were

never, prior to the transfer to Canada, ratified by state authority, or confirmed by exercise of jurisdiction." As a result, King argued, "Canada's assumption of authority in 1895 may not have full international force." In summary, he suggested that "Canada's title to some at least of the northern islands is imperfect" but "may possibly be perfected by exercise of jurisdiction where any settlements exist." [20]

A supplementary memo dated 7 May 1904 was somewhat more optimistic, suggesting that British discoveries might have greater legal force because Admiralty explorers were under specific instructions to take possession in the name of the Crown, whereas recent foreign explorations did not have official sanction nor were their claims followed by government ratification. Hence King advised that initial action should centre on locations where Americans were occupying sites in Canadian territory without the authority of their government, in which case Canadian authority could and should be firmly asserted. Otherwise, he believed that Canada had been fortunate that there had been no attempt by foreigners to establish officially sanctioned settlements in Canadian territory, as "occupation" was the most effective means of "perfecting" an inchoate or temporary title claimed through discovery. [21]

Some of King's opinions were open to debate, such as the statement that until the passage of the Colonial Boundaries Act in 1895 the Canadian government may not have had the legal authority to deal with the Arctic Islands. This assertion was later refuted by Dominion Archivist Henry Holmden, who based his report in 1921 on recently acquired documents and maps dating back to the transfer. Noting that King did not have access to this material at the time of writing, Holmden acknowledged that the error was understandable. [22] Even then, analysis based on existing knowledge of international law was only tentative as legal interpretations varied and generally required a court case to test their validity. Nonetheless, King's report confirmed that immediate action had to be taken to avoid a challenge to Canada's title.

Of particular significance was King's assertion that under "accepted principles of international law, the waters of the northern

Joint British-U.S. survey team mark the Yukon-Alaska
boundary at the Arctic Ocean. The surveyor on the left waving a pennant
from Princeton University is Thomas Riggs Jr., who later became
governor of Alaska Territory (1918–21). On the right is John Davidson
Craig, waving a Queen's University pennant, who was appointed
the first commander of Canada's Eastern Arctic Patrol in 1922 and later
Canadian chair of the International Boundary Commission.
Alaska State Library P297-280, Early Prints of Alaska Photograph Collection

archipelago and of Hudson Bay and Strait are considered territorial."
Based on that assumption, the Canadian government took the first
official action in asserting its authority in Hudson Bay by passing an
amendment to the Fisheries Act that imposed a licence fee of fifty dollars for all whalers fishing in Hudson Bay, including Canadian vessels,
and in all waters north of 55° N latitude. Upon receiving notice of the
new legislation, British authorities expressed concern that it would
cause an official protest from the U.S. After reading a detailed report

on the Canadian position, Lord Crewe as secretary of state for the colonies wrote to Canada's governor-general, suggesting that Canada might wish to avoid any action that might lead to tribunal arbitration, which he warned might result in denial of its claims. While Canada claimed Hudson Bay as *mare clausum*, Crewe suggested that tribunal jurists might narrowly restrict the limits of territorial waters which, he reminded the governor-general, was "an inclination which His Majesty's Government share on grounds probably well known to your ministers."[23] Once again, it appeared that Canada was expected to defer to the interests of the mother country. In the end the Colonial Office did not advise disallowance of the legislation, as Crewe had intimated it might, and there was no formal protest from the U.S. government. Instead, licence fees were collected and customs duties paid without difficulty, in spite of a U.S. notice to American whalers to disregard demands for licences.[24]

Following the decision to defer construction of additional police posts, Captain Bernier was placed in command of three expeditions that took place in 1906–7, 1908–9 and 1910–11, with precise instructions from the Minister of Marine and Fisheries on how and where to take possession of lands by "raising the flag" and leaving a written proclamation in stone cairns. On each voyage, he wintered over on the ship: the first year near present-day Pond Inlet, the second at Winter Harbour on Melville Island and the third in Arctic Bay off Admiralty Inlet. Since Bernier's expeditions were not accompanied by the police, he was granted permission to perform a variety of administrative functions, such as issuing the new licences and collecting customs duties from foreign whalers. Yet he, too, was warned to be "most careful in all your actions not to take any course which might result in international complications with any foreign country."[25] On his first expedition in 1906–7, Bernier made fifteen claims of possession, on the second a total of eleven and on his last voyage only eight.[26] In each case he took possession for "the Dominion of Canada" with no reference to a British monarch, as was the case in A.P. Low's proclamations, likely because the instructions had come from Canadian sources without consultation with the British Colonial Office.

Norwegian explorer Roald Amundsen and his crew aboard
the *Gjoa* arrive at Nome, Alaska, in August 1906, after successfully
traversing the Northwest Passage from east to west and
allegedly discovering the magnetic pole.
Alaska State Library P 48-104, Frank H. Nowell Photograph Collection

News that Amundsen had successfully traversed the Northwest Passage raised new concerns about its possible designation as an international strait. Equally disconcerting was the fact that the Norwegian claimed to have charted and named several newly discovered islands. In an attempt to resolve the status of the Northwest Passage and protect Canadian lands against encirclement by foreign claims, in 1907 Senator Pascal Poirier proposed adoption of the Sector Theory to lay claim to all lands north of its mainland.[27] Laurier rejected the idea, arguing that the exercise of authority was the only reliable means of protecting title in remote areas. Yet in spite of political implications, boundaries defined by the Sector Theory, or Sector Principle as it is sometimes called, began to appear on Canadian maps and even on the plaque Bernier erected in 1909 on Melville Island. A glance at any circumpolar map shows why the U.S. consistently rejected the principle and why Russia and later the Soviet Union supported it. There were no islands north of Alaska but hundreds north of mainland Canada and Russia.

For the time being, Bernier's "sovereignty patrols" were considered sufficient evidence of "effective occupation" as long as no foreign country attempted to establish a colony in the area. King's report had relied on the writings of jurist William Edward Hall for his interpretation of international law, noting in particular Hall's statement that if "duly annexed and the fact published, or ... recorded by monuments or inscription on the spot," such action was sufficient to maintain title, "allowing for accidental circumstances or moderate negligence," before settlements or "military posts" were established to gain full rights of possession. If no action occurred within a reasonable time, then a temporary or inchoate title claimed by reason of discovery would lapse.[28] Although criticized later as inadequate, Bernier's acts of possession were commensurate with King's understanding of international law.

To provide further evidence of administrative acts, Bernier had recommended that Parliament pass a game law to protect against indiscriminate hunting, thus providing him with additional government regulations to administer. Laurier agreed but it was too late to secure legislation during that session. Of particular importance at the time had been the proposal to create a separate department to deal with foreign affairs. After intense debate, the bill creating the Department of External Affairs finally passed both houses, received royal assent and took effect on 1 June 1909, with Sir Joseph Pope appointed as the department's first under-secretary of state. Even then, another three years passed before the new department gained significant power, by way of legislation allowing it to report directly to the prime minister.[29] The public appeared to support the idea of gaining more independence from Britain, but only to a degree. Laurier's plans to build a Canadian navy met with intense ridicule from both the Conservative opposition and the press, which sarcastically labelled it "a tin can navy." No one will ever know if the prime minister's plan was simply to deploy a few ships to patrol the eastern Arctic, since the

Liberal government went down to defeat in October 1911, abruptly ending Laurier and Sifton's plans to protect Canada's Arctic sovereignty. Upon his return home late that month, Bernier tendered his resignation in the knowledge that the new government would likely have other ideas on how Arctic sovereignty should be maintained. Some have suggested that he was asked to resign for having misappropriated government funds for private trade with the Inuit.[30]

Although Bernier received considerable publicity for his "sovereignty patrols," it was Sifton and Laurier who proposed them and made them possible. Admittedly Sifton is better known for his promotion of western settlement, but as his biographer D.J. Hall argues, he "can be credited nevertheless with making some of the earliest attempts to establish a credible, continuous Canadian presence in the far north." Hall also contends that he took a much stronger anti-American stand than the prime minister and that while "Laurier appeared cowed by American bluster and threats, Sifton stood firm in asserting Canadian rights." Even in later years when chairing the Conservation Commission, Sifton spoke out against free trade, in the belief it would give the U.S. access to Canadian forests and lead to eventual annexation.[31]

MEANWHILE, AMERICAN explorers continued to dominate the race to the North Pole. With enthusiasm similar to an earlier generation's conquest of the Wild West, they viewed the Arctic as a new frontier, a place of high adventure, with the added incentive of obtaining honour and prestige for their country. References to Manifest Destiny were also evident in their rhetoric, emphasizing the expectation that eventually the U.S. would possess the whole of North America including the Arctic. Yet in terms of zeal, rhetoric and achievements, none compared to those of Robert E. Peary. A former officer with the U.S. Navy, Peary had taken an extended leave in 1886 to conduct his first Arctic exploration, which was followed by numerous others from 1893 to 1909. Although criticized for his aggressive self-promotion, he nevertheless was responsible for extensive mapping and collection of scientific data for northern Greenland and Ellesmere

Island. Peary claimed his quest was not driven by the desire for personal glory, but he believed reaching the Pole was a matter of national honour, "our manifest privilege and duty." The U.S. War Department agreed, as did President Roosevelt, who maintained ongoing correspondence providing encouragement and commendation. Canadian historian Clive Holland, however, suggests that one of Peary's letters to his mother revealed another side of the ambitious explorer, when he wrote, "I *must* have fame, and I cannot reconcile myself to years of commonplace drudgery." [32]

In the summer of 1908, Robert Peary sailed from Sydney, Nova Scotia, on ss *Roosevelt*, built to his specifications with American timber in an American shipyard. His sole destination was the North Pole, which he hoped to claim for the U.S. as its "natural northern boundary." His repeated emphasis on the importance of claiming American sovereignty over as much of the Arctic as possible suggested that Canadian concerns of possible encirclement were not entirely unwarranted. Finally on 6 April 1909, with great excitement, Peary wrote in his diary that he had finally reached the North Pole, where he unfurled the Stars and Stripes and claimed possession in the name of the United States of America. [33] Although Dr. Frederick Cook declared that he had reached the Pole first, Peary was initially accepted as the rightful holder of the honour, with President Taft quick to acknowledge that his success had "added to the distinction of our Navy, to which he belongs, and reflects credit to our country." [34] As uncertainty grew to whether either Cook or Peary had reached the Pole, Canadian officials were quite content to let the controversy rage without having to acknowledge the success of either party.

After 1909, Peary no longer actively participated in polar exploration but he was behind the scenes advising American explorers and pressing them to continue their search for uncharted islands. Dr. Donald MacMillan, a member of Peary's North Pole expedition, took up the challenge and led an expedition in search of "Crocker Land," a land mass that Peary claimed to have sighted north of Axel Heiberg. Pre-departure publicity emphasized that he hoped to find undiscovered lands to claim for the U.S. Allegedly with a presidential

Robert Peary at the North Pole. Although the original caption of this
photo taken on 1 April 1909 suggests that Peary was among those waving
their hands under the Stars and Stripes, text with a similar photograph
by the *National Geographic*, which co-sponsored the expedition,
describes the five figures as Peary's assistants and notes that the actual
location was approximately 30 kilometres from the North Pole.
S0014657, Royal Geographical Society, photographer unknown but likely Peary

endorsement, MacMillan set out for Ellesmere Island in 1913 on
an expedition lasting fifty-one months and covering 9,000 miles.
Although he failed to find any sizable uncharted islands, Canadian
sources believed that he might have discovered three small islands as
well as veins of coal on Ellesmere Island and Axel Heiberg.[35]

Meanwhile whaling activity had come to an abrupt halt in both
the eastern and western Arctic, replaced in some locations with trade
for furs and ivory. Yet because of Britain's vague description of the
lands transferred to Canada, the task still remained to protect British

claims to the Arctic Islands. Prime Minister Robert Borden and his Conservative government were not convinced that Laurier's concerns about Arctic sovereignty warranted the expenditure incurred by the Bernier expeditions. They were willing, however, to fund Vilhjalmur Stefansson's Canadian Arctic Expedition in 1913, on the proviso that he make a concerted effort to identify and claim previously undiscovered lands for Canada. Financial support was also rationalized as a means of eliminating foreign sponsors who had offered to fund his original proposed exploration, namely the American Geographical Society and the National Geographic Society.

Canadian officials appeared unfamiliar with the legal protocol attached to laying official claims of possession. Before Stefansson's departure, the Acting Under-Secretary of State for External Affairs read an article in the *Washington Post* that accused Britain of actively taking possession of new lands in the Arctic. Realizing that there was no record of correspondence granting authority for Stefansson to claim title for Canada, William J. Walker contacted officials in London for advice. On 10 May 1913, the British colonial secretary stated in a despatch to Canada's governor-general that under new interpretations of international law Canada could not claim possession of new lands without first obtaining written authority from Britain to do so, implying that Bernier's claims of possession might be invalid. The despatch went on to formally convey, "under advice of the Privy Council, such authority to the Governor General of Canada to take possession of and annex to his Majesty's dominions any lands lying north of Canadian territory." The colonial secretary also advised that "as it is not desirable that any stress should be laid on the fact that a portion of the territory may not already be British, I do not consider it advisable that this despatch should be published, but it should be permanently recorded as giving authority for annexation to the Governor General in Council." [36] Fortunately for historians, the correspondence was retained as evidence of the British approach in dealing with potential sovereignty problems—asserting publicly that the title was secure, while quietly taking action to correct any weaknesses—an approach later adopted by Canadian officials.

As it happened, Stefansson succeeded where MacMillan had failed, by discovering four previously unclaimed islands of reasonable size. Meighen Island was located northwest of Axel Heiberg, whereas Brock, Borden and Lougheed Islands were discovered west of Ellef Ringnes. With the exception of Brock Island, named after the head of the Geological Survey, the other islands were named after senior government leaders responsible for funding the expedition, a tradition dating back to the age of Martin Frobisher. The expedition might have been considered an unqualified success had it not been plagued by internal dissension and sinking of the expedition ship *Karluk*. Stefansson was a visionary and believed the Arctic would someday become the "Mediterranean of the North" because of commercial air routes between Europe and Asia. Although his tendency toward personal aggrandizement and continual pressure on the Canadian government to fund further explorations would make him unpopular in Ottawa, his lectures and books on the Arctic found a captive audience south of the border.[37]

Meanwhile, the demise of the whaling industry had left many Alaskan Eskimos without employment and access to goods such as flour, molasses, tobacco, guns and ammunition. As the demand for white fox increased, fur-trading posts soon replaced the whalers' supply of goods but often required the Eskimos to travel great distances to the nearest post. The loss of traditional hunting skills due to introduction of the rifle added to their increasing dependence on the white man for their very survival. Disease had already decimated their numbers and many camps were threatened with starvation because too many caribou had been killed to feed and clothe the whaling crews. In an attempt to increase their food supply, in 1890 the U.S. government initiated a reindeer herding project, with mixed results. The once vibrant, self-sufficient Eskimo communities were now often destitute, causing one Soviet scholar to blame "colonial exploitation promoted by American capitalism."[38] Consequences encountered in Hudson Bay and Cumberland Sound were similar, yet less devastating because of assistance provided by Catholic and Anglican missions.

Greenland Inuit, on the other hand, were even less affected as a result of welfare assistance and increased fish trade.

As the Hudson's Bay Company's trading posts in the eastern Arctic slowly expanded northward, they were joined by church missions to form the nucleus of tiny settlements, such as Lake Harbour (1911), Cape Dorset (1913) and Repulse Bay in Foxe Basin (1916). Private traders congregated in the Eclipse Sound area of northern Baffin Island, while the French-owned Reveillon Frères Company expanded its trade into northern Quebec and southern Hudson Bay. Aside from the sole police detachment that had moved from Fullerton Harbour to the site of a trading post at Chesterfield Inlet, the fur traders became the figures of authority to the Inuit; missionaries looked after their spiritual needs. The Canadian government was conspicuous by its absence north of Hudson Strait. New HBC posts also opened in the western Arctic from the Mackenzie Delta eastward to Coronation Gulf. Catholic and Anglican missions soon followed. In response to reports of Inuit violence, a police detachment was established at Tree River east of Bathurst Inlet.

In the High Arctic, the islands north of Lancaster Sound remained uninhabited except for occasional groups of Greenland Inughuit arriving at Ellesmere Island to hunt muskox or polar bears. Otherwise, there were no signs of "effective occupation" in the High Arctic by Canada or any other country. Even at more southerly settlements, the Canadian government made no effort to provide the Inuit with better accommodation, education or medical services as the Danes had done in Greenland. Instead, welfare assistance was left to the discretion of fur traders, health and education to the missionaries and housing to the Inuit.

Elsewhere in the circumpolar world, conflicts seemed easily resolved through bilateral or multilateral cooperation. A case in point was the 1911 Convention for the Preservation and Protection of Fur Seals, which had been prompted by concerns for the dwindling population of the sea mammal, coveted for its lush fur. Signed by Great Britain, Russia, the U.S. and Japan, the treaty prohibited pelagic sealing in the Bering, Kamchatka, Okhotsk and Japan Seas. In terms of establishing a precedent, the agreement specifically excluded aboriginal hunters from the ban. According to Donald Rothwell, a law professor at the University of Sydney, the treaty's success was attributable to the fact that it was "characterized by unique environmental factors, relatively simple government regulations, and an absence of new entrants."[39]

Specific disputes over sovereign rights in the Arctic were more difficult to resolve, particularly if valuable resources were involved as was the case with the remote Svalbard Islands. Because of the abundance of whales and walrus, sovereign authority over the islands and their surrounding waters had been contested at one time or another during the eighteenth and nineteenth centuries by Britain, Denmark, Norway and the Netherlands. When Russia protested Danish and Norwegian claims in 1871, there was a compromise agreement that the islands would be treated as *terra nullius*. At the end of the nineteenth century, discovery of coal threatened to reopen the dispute, particularly between Norway and Russia, which were actively mining in the vicinity of Longyearbyen and Barentsburg, respectively. The issue was finally settled by the Svalbard Treaty of 1920 concluded at the Versailles Peace Conference, in which Norway was recognized as "the territorial sovereign of the island" based on initial discovery by the Norse in the twelfth century. Signatories to the treaty, including Sweden, Denmark, Great Britain, the Netherlands and Russia/USSR, were allowed equal access to the territorial waters and ports, along with rights to mine or carry out other commercial and industrial operations. In return, participants in such a venture were expected to pay a royalty to Norway. To maintain its right to sovereign authority, Norway continually updated local regulations such as mining codes and provided infrastructure services.[40] The islands themselves are relatively barren, affording sparse food for only a few species of land-based mammals and no indigenous population. Although the islands are a popular site for scientific research, coal mining is still the only industrial activity, with mines still operated by Norway and Russia.

The integrity of the treaty will be tested if sizable amounts of more valuable minerals are discovered.

With the exception of the Stefansson and MacMillan expeditions, polar exploration had ceased during the Great War. Yet new technologies developed for military purposes provided even greater incentives to resume efforts at the war's end. Aviation advances, in particular, created visions of commercial polar air routes to Europe and Asia. Stefansson's stories of potential exploitation of resources added to the appeal. Although the honour of being first to reach the North Pole and traverse the Northwest Passage was now history, air travel offered easier access and a new form of adventure. Once again, the Arctic gained the attention of the American public. The U.S. government continued to reject the Sector Theory, declaring the High Arctic *terra nullius* open to exploration by all nations with the assumption that previously undiscovered lands could be claimed by the sponsoring nation.[41] Canada was at a clear disadvantage. With the exception of Captain Bernier, there was no avid interest or financial resources to support a private polar expedition. As before, it became the government's responsibility to ensure that there were no more uncharted islands in the Archipelago.

The same issue concerning *terra nullius* arose when Knud Rasmussen, a young Dane in charge of Greenland's most northerly trading post, declared that Ellesmere Island was a no man's land and that the only authority in the area was exercised through his station in northern Greenland. His written statement was made in response to a Canadian request for assistance from the Danish government to restrain Greenlanders from killing muskox on Ellesmere Island. The Danish note that accompanied Rasmussen's reply reiterating his position cautiously stated that the government thought "they could subscribe to what Mr. Rasmussen says therein."[42] In response, the Canadian government issued a formal protest on 13 July 1920 and referred the matter to the Advisory Technical Board (ATB), an ad hoc committee allegedly created to deal with "technical matters" related to northern affairs. The committee was composed of senior officials of agencies reporting to the Department of the Interior, some of whom had been involved in the Alaska boundary dispute.

While the issues were essentially the same as described in 1904 by King, the committee again reviewed the validity of British title to the Arctic Islands. As an additional reference, Under-Secretary of State for External Affairs Sir Joseph Pope provided the board with a copy of Oppenheim's *Treatise on International Law*. Although the treatise was published after King's report, the only difference appeared to be the finality of Oppenheim's assertion that if a period of time "lapses without any attempt by the discovering State to turn its inchoate title into a real title of occupation, such inchoate title perishes and any other State can now acquire the territory by means of an effective occupation." As before, the committee feared that British discovery claims were insufficient to maintain title to portions of the uninhabited Arctic Islands, particularly Ellesmere and islands to the west, where Norwegian Otto Sverdrup and American Donald MacMillan were reported to have made a number of recent discoveries.[43]

The situation acquired a sense of greater urgency that September, when Rasmussen announced plans for his Fifth Thule Expedition, which was to follow a route from Greenland across the Canadian Arctic to Alaska. Although the stated objective was to conduct scientific studies, Canadian officials feared there was a hidden agenda based on rumours that the Danish government was funding the project. After an initial report on Rasmussen's plans was presented to the ATB in September, Stefansson was asked to attend a meeting on 2 October 1920 to give his thoughts on the subject. His report was alarmist and exaggerated, describing Rasmussen's scientific study as a "commercial venture" designed to acquire the uninhabited Arctic Islands for Denmark. The self-serving aspect was clearly evident when he argued the need for further exploration, which he offered to undertake for the government. At the end of his presentation, members agreed that a special subcommittee should be set up to deal with the sovereignty question, chaired by Surveyor-General Dr. E. Deville and with J.B. Harkin of Dominion Parks as secretary. Other members included Dr. O. Klotz, J.J. McArthur and Noel Ogilvie, who had assisted in legal preparations for the Alaska Boundary Tribunal. Deville set out three points for the committee to study: the necessary steps required to secure Canadian title to the islands; a review of whether the lands were worth protecting; and the advisability of further explorations.[44]

Following the meeting, Stefansson was asked to meet with Prime Minister Meighen, his legal adviser Loring Christie and another cabinet member. In anticipation of the meeting, he submitted an outline of the steps that should be taken, which included further explorations, creation of a revenue cutter service, additional police posts on Baffin Island, further mapping and economic surveys and a policy to encourage further development involving private enterprise.[45] On 28 October 1920, Christie also wrote a lengthy report for the prime minister, outlining the legal arguments that supported Canadian claims. He noted that immediate attention should focus on Ellesmere Island as "action there seems urgent; action elsewhere seems necessary but not urgent." While he also argued that a further government expedition was required, he suggested that it be regarded as an extension of the Stefansson and Bernier expeditions "since they were designed and announced as an integral part of the policy making good Canadian claims to the northern islands," and that showing the "continuity of our policy [is] an important point."[46]

Sir Joseph Pope also reported to the prime minister after meeting with Stefansson, advising that he reject the explorer's suggestion that Canada lay claim to Wrangel Island north of eastern Siberia, but reiterating that the islands north of mainland Canada might be vulnerable unless claims were followed up by some form of effective occupation. He also supported the idea of setting up police posts on Ellesmere and reminded the prime minister that "in the past our territorial claims have suffered not a little by inaction and delay."[47] The latter comment likely referred to construction the previous summer of a police post at Port Burwell near the entrance of Hudson Strait, some fifteen years since first recommended.

A series of reports by the ATB's secretary further clarified the issues, defined the region's importance and proposed a number of actions to accomplish effective occupation. They recommended establishment of police posts in the High Arctic to enable regular land patrols and enforcement of game laws, with an annual government expedition to assist in setting up and supplying the new detachments. Other measures proposed included expansion of HBC posts throughout the Archipelago and possible transfer of Inuit families from overcrowded areas in the south to uninhabited islands in the High Arctic.[48]

Particularly disturbing that winter were newspaper reports that Donald MacMillan planned to search for uncharted lands west of Ellesmere with the object of claiming them for the U.S., or in another version that he intended to circle Baffin Island to map additional uncharted lands. It was also brought to the committee's attention that the latest *Century Atlas* had highlighted the U.S., Alaska and Ellesmere Island in the same colour. Parliament's initial response to news of the Fifth Thule Expedition reflected a sense of panic and lack of knowledge among some officials when they proposed that Canada should send an advance party to Ellesmere Island by hydroplane or dirigible from Britain, which was rejected outright by the Minister of the Interior.[49]

Conservative Prime Minister Arthur Meighen's preference had been for a more prestigious expedition by the famed British explorer Ernest Shackleton, but when Shackleton reported that he was unavailable, approval was finally granted to refit CGS *Arctic* for use as an annual patrol boat. After nine years as a lightship anchored in the St. Lawrence and largely dismantled, the ship was towed to a government dry dock for assessment. The refit proved to be a major challenge and costly. John Davidson Craig, a Dominion Lands surveyor and a member of the International Boundary Commission, was appointed to take charge of the overall preparations. His innocuous title of "advisory engineer" to the Department of the Interior reflected the secrecy attached to his position, as with the equally ambiguous name of the Advisory Technical Board. In the winter of 1920–21 the police, now renamed the Royal Canadian Mounted Police (RCMP), began making preparations for the construction and staffing of two

CGS *Arctic* in dry dock, C1921, was being refitted for an Arctic expedition
after having been stripped and anchored in the St. Lawrence River
as a lightship. Although compared to the HBC's supply ships the
government ship seemed outdated and minuscule, CGS *Arctic* made
four more trips to the High Arctic before being scrapped.

LAC, C-143189 from James Bernard Harkin Fonds, MG 30 E 168, vol. 1, file: May–December 1921 new police detachments, one on Ellesmere Island and the other on Baffin Island.[50]

Complicating the issues raised by the proposed Fifth Thule Expedition was a report that a white fur trader had been killed by Inuit in the vicinity of Admiralty Inlet on northern Baffin Island. The request from the trader's family in Newfoundland for a full investigation had been left unanswered, as the site of the incident was beyond the reach of the nearest police post at Chesterfield Inlet. To do nothing, however, would indicate to other countries that the police were incapable of enforcing law and order in the area. The proposed government expedition for the summer of 1921 provided a perfect solution and a contingent of RCMP officers were placed on standby for the journey north. One new detachment would be established on Eclipse Sound, a location that would allow for a proper police investigation.

Problems of enforcing Canadian laws among the Inuit had become a matter of increasing concern for the police amid reports of increasing violence. Apart from maintaining law and order to provide stability in the region, the ability to administer justice was considered critical to establish effective occupation throughout the Arctic. Episodes of Inuit violence within their own communities had been ignored in the past, but recently there had been a number of attacks on white men in the western and central Arctic. Sometimes the alleged murderers could not be found, but in the case of two Catholic priests killed in 1913, the police arrested two Inuit and brought them to trial. Originally they were given the death penalty, but this was commuted to life sentences of hard labour. In the end, the prisoners worked at a police detachment for only two years before being released back to their community, where they described how they had been provided with food, clothing, a warm place to live and material goods. Not surprisingly most Inuit perceived this form of punishment as tantamount to a reward. With Inuit violence again on the increase, the police believed that their prior leniency was responsible and hoped for a clear-cut case to prosecute as a deterrent against further violence.[51] The building of a police post in North Baffin provided just such an opportunity to bring the guilty parties to justice and at the same time show the world that Canada could assert its laws in more remote regions of the Arctic.

On 9 June 1921, the immediate crisis of the proposed Fifth Thule Expedition was unexpectedly resolved when a telegram arrived from the British Colonial Office to advise that the Danish government had provided written assurances that Rasmussen's expedition was strictly a scientific investigation and that "no acquisition of territory whatsoever was contemplated."[52] With an eye to costs, the Conservative government immediately halted preparations and deferred the expedition for at least a year. RCMP Commissioner Perry was momentarily at a loss about his pending police investigation until he learned that the HBC planned to open a trading post at Pond Inlet that summer. As a consequence, a lone police officer, Staff Sergeant A.H. Joy, was sent on the HBC supply ship to stay at the new Pond Inlet trading post for the sole purpose of investigating the death of the white fur trader. In the event Joy verified that a murder had taken place and that he could locate those responsible, he was ordered to take them prisoner and await further instructions.

Stefansson, meanwhile, had become disenchanted with the Canadian government, only partly for rejecting his offer to conduct further explorations. More irritating to him was the government's refusal to claim title to Wrangel Island, after the survivors of the wrecked *Karluk* had allegedly taken possession in 1914. Without the government's knowledge or approval, Stefansson created a private firm named the Arctic Exploration and Development Company and in 1921 sent a party of Inuit and a few white men to occupy the island. In spite of Stefansson's argument about the island's importance for future air routes, first to the Canadian government then to the U.S., neither country was prepared to claim the island. Finally on 19 August 1924, a Soviet warship, *Red October*, arrived at the island and raised the Soviet flag on a 36-foot pole, with "Proletarians of every country, unite!" inscribed at the base. A formal ceremony of possession took place the next day and a single American and twelve Inuit from Stefansson's private expedition were unceremoniously removed. Two years later, the Soviets sent a permanent party to occupy the island, consisting of sixty Chukchi with a former Red Army officer and his family, in the second known incident in Russian/Soviet history where Native people were used to protect claims to sovereign authority.[53] Having lost his credibility in Ottawa, Stefansson departed for New York City, where he continued his writing and public lectures until eventually he was hired by the U.S. government as an adviser on Arctic issues.

With the return of the Liberal government to power in September 1921, approvals were easier to obtain for the proposed Arctic expedition and construction of new police posts. Thus a year later than planned, CGS *Arctic* sailed from Quebec City in July 1922 with Captain Bernier again at the helm. This time, however, J.D. Craig was in overall command and accompanied by nine RCMP officers to build and staff the new detachments. On the first trip of what would be called the Eastern Arctic Patrol, the government party included Squadron Leader Robert A. Logan, sent by the Canadian Air Board to locate sites for future airfields, a surveying crew, a medical officer to report on the health of the Inuit and a cinema-photographer to record the activities of the expedition. There was no public send-off or press coverage and any radio communication was to be brief and in code. The government party, police and crew were under strict orders to maintain secrecy until the police stations had been built. For the same reason, all news releases were carefully censored by Ottawa officials.[54]

Rasmussen's claim that Ellesmere Island was a "no man's land" has often been cited as a wake-up call that forced the Canadian government to take responsibility for its Arctic islands. Partly true if applied to the Union and Conservative governments in power during the war and immediate postwar years, but in the mind of Liberal politicians, the new police posts and Eastern Arctic Patrol were merely a continuation of their policy set out in 1902.[55] The Liberal government under William Lyon Mackenzie King also enacted changes to management of the northern territories, largely a consequence of the discovery of oil in 1920 at Norman Wells on the Mackenzie River. Fearing a possible influx of prospectors as had occurred during the Klondike gold rush, Ottawa revamped the Northwest Territories Council and gave it increased powers to enact legislation. The Deputy Minister of the Interior was appointed commissioner of the NWT Council and the number of members was increased to include representatives of various departments involved in northern affairs. At the same time, the Northwest Territories and Yukon Branch was established within the Department of the Interior, under the direction of O.S. Finnie, a former Yukon gold commissioner. His mandate was to establish offices in the Mackenzie District and posts in the Arctic Islands, "where there was grave danger of our sovereign rights being questioned by foreign powers." Administrators, mining engineers, scientists and medical officers were assigned to staff offices throughout the Yukon and the Mackenzie District, whereas Finnie was located in Ottawa to better influence political decisions affecting northern Canada.[56]

In 1921 another outbreak of Inuit violence occurred in the western Arctic, not far from the site of previous murders but this time involving the deaths of four Inuit, an RCMP officer and an HBC trader. When added to Sergeant Joy's report that he was holding three prisoners for the alleged murder of a white fur trader near Pond Inlet, the news convinced the RCMP commissioner that previous leniency had resulted in complete disregard for Canadian authority. In consultation with the Department of Justice, two public trials were scheduled for the summer of 1923, one at Herschel Island in the western Arctic, the other at Pond Inlet in the eastern Arctic. The two Inuit on trial at Herschel were found guilty and later hanged. The trial at Pond Inlet, however, had greater significance for Arctic sovereignty because of its proximity to Greenland. Furthermore, a member of the Fifth Thule Expedition had reported to the RCMP detachment at Chesterfield Inlet that near Igloolik he had met one of the alleged murderers, who talked openly about killing the trader and seemed proud of his actions. Hence the trial at Pond Inlet would serve a dual purpose, namely to deter further violence by the Inuit and secondly to show Danish officials in Greenland that Canada was capable of enforcing laws and administering justice in the Arctic Islands.

With the court party wearing flowing black robes and accompanied by eight policemen in their scarlet dress uniforms, the spectacle

The first murder trial in the eastern Arctic was held in August 1923
at the Pond Inlet RCMP detachment on northern Baffin Island. During
a recess, members of the court party are seen here in in black gowns in
deep discussion with several police officers, the translator and officers
of the CGS *Arctic*.   LAC, PA-187325, Tredgold Collection

(*inset*) George Valiquette, seen here at Pangnirtung in September
1923, was the cinema-photographer hired by the Canadian government to
take movie films of the 1923 Eastern Arctic Patrol and the murder
trial for distribution in the United States and Greenland, as evidence
that Canada was "effectively occupying" the Arctic Islands.
    LAC, PA-207813, Louise Wood Collection

could not fail to impress those present, including Therkel Mathiassen of the Fifth Thule Expedition, who had arrived unexpectedly. Of
the three Inuit on trial, Nuqallaq, who had shot the fur trader on the
advice of others, was sentenced to ten years at Stony Mountain Penitentiary in Manitoba. Aatitaaq was acquitted for lack of evidence and
Ululijarnaat was sentenced to two years' hard labour at the Pond Inlet
detachment, again a punishment perceived by the Inuit more as a
reward. As further assurance that the world should know Canadian
justice was properly dispensed, a film of the trial was distributed by
Fox Films movie theatres in the U.S., with an additional showing of
the movie during the patrol's annual visit to Greenland the following
summer. In spite of good intentions, Nuqallaq was released from the
penitentiary in less than two years because he had contracted tuber-
culosis. In the expectation that the cold air would arrest the disease,
he was returned to Pond Inlet, where he died within a few months. As
one might have expected, an outbreak of the disease was reported the
following year. Yet the trial was considered a success since reported
incidents of Inuit violence throughout the eastern and central Arctic
had decreased dramatically since the event.[57]

Between 1922 and 1926, five new police detachments were built in
the eastern Arctic—at Craig Harbour on Ellesmere Island, Pond Inlet
on Eclipse Sound, Dundas Harbour on Devon Island, Pangnirtung on
Cumberland Sound and Lake Harbour on the southern coast of Baffin
Island. The number of HBC trading posts also increased, as did Anglican and Catholic missions. As a result, the region was slowly acquiring
permanent settlements, with sufficient patrols and administrative
actions performed by the police to ensure that Canadian sovereignty
was well protected by clear evidence of effective occupation.

The incentive to develop a more comprehensive plan would
require a more significant threat, as occurred in 1925 in the form of
a direct challenge from the U.S. Navy. Under the guidance of Dr. O.D.
Skelton as the newly appointed under-secretary of state for external
affairs, Canada's response adopted a more professional approach
based on a clearly defined strategy. Formerly the dean of arts at
Queen's University, Skelton had been recruited by Prime Minister

King, first as an adviser, then to replace Sir Joseph Pope as head of External Affairs. Skelton was a staunch nationalist and skilled negotiator. More importantly, he had the ear and respect of the prime minister to facilitate approval for immediate action. He also shared King's belief that Canada should become more directly involved in international affairs and less dependent on Great Britain.[58]

The foreign policies of Presidents Theodore Roosevelt, William H. Taft and Woodrow Wilson had all envisioned the U.S. Navy "as an active instrument of national policy which might be used for possible coercion of foreign powers."[59] Hence any direct involvement in Arctic exploration by the navy would be considered a serious threat to Canadian sovereignty. Wartime advances in aviation and short-wave radio communications had added to the potential threat, as the U.S. War Department was now convinced that air power would play a major role in defending the Arctic, perceived as necessary for the security of North America. Following the war, the navy retained responsibility for military aviation and, as a result, was under intense pressure to find uncharted lands near the North Pole as an advance defence post. Even though it had announced publicly that it was looking for islands "north of Alaska," its plans involved access through Ellesmere Island. Nancy Fogelson, a history professor at the University of Alaska, argues that the U.S. naval expeditions were publicized as a quest to seek new lands to gain public support, when in fact the Americans knew there was little hope of finding new territory.[60] If this were the case, then their objective must have been to acquire lands claimed by Canada in an area the U.S. classified as *terra nullius*.

In 1921 and again in 1923, veteran explorer Donald MacMillan resumed his explorations. One that attracted the attention of the U.S. Navy was his proposed expedition to Ellesmere Island, sponsored by the National Geographic Society and the Carnegie Institute. Secretary of the Navy Curtis Wilbur approached MacMillan to suggest that his plans might be coordinated with those of the navy to include aerial reconnaissance under the direction of Lieutenant Commander Richard E. Byrd Jr. MacMillan was commissioned and placed in charge of the expedition, with Byrd second in command and responsible for the

Prime Minister W.L. Mackenzie King on the porch steps of his home at
Kingsmere, Quebec, with his sister Jenna (Mrs. H.M. Lay) and Dr. O.D.
Skelton, 29 July 1923. King's close relationship with Skelton enabled the
latter to act quickly and decisively on Arctic sovereignty matters after
being appointed under-secretary of external affairs in 1925.

LAC, C-026031

navy's pilots, mechanics and aircraft—three Loening single-engine,
amphibian biplanes. The expedition included two ships: MacMillan's
schooner *Bowdoin,* and ss *Peary,* chartered by the navy to transport
the planes. Application of new technologies was also evident in use
of sophisticated shortwave radio communications and a k6 Fairchild
camera for aerial photography.

After first learning of the MacMillan-Byrd expedition from an
American newspaper, later confirmed from informal discussion
with Commander Byrd himself, Canadian officials feared that the
U.S. Navy might attempt to lay claim to Axel Heiberg and portions of
Ellesmere Island, where Canadian title was weakest. Certainly Donald
MacMillan anticipated such an event when he wrote to the Secretary
of the Navy to affirm that all lands discovered by U.S. planes "will be

claimed in spite of Canada's protest." [61] To deal with this and other Arctic sovereignty issues, the Canadian government created an inter-departmental committee, soon renamed the Northern Advisory Board by an order-in-council on 23 April 1925, essentially replacing the special subcommittee of the Advisory Technical Board. Meetings were chaired by either Deputy Minister of the Interior W.W. Cory or Under-Secretary of External Affairs O.D. Skelton, and attended by the deputy ministers of national defence, justice, customs and revenue, the RCMP commissioner and other high-ranking officials representing key interests in the north.

At the first meeting, the only item on the agenda was the proposed MacMillan expedition, with adviser James White warning that if Mac-Millan should succeed in finding new islands, "Canada would have trouble establishing title thereto." Under existing regulations, it was determined that MacMillan would require a permit from the Royal Canadian Air Force to land planes on Canadian territory, as well as permission from the Customs Department. It was also agreed that Cory, who happened to be in New York at the time, should try to meet with MacMillan and inform him of the permits required to land in Canadian territory. [62] In a separate memo to Cory, Skelton outlined the main questions raised at the meeting:

> First, the validity of Canada's claim to the Arctic Islands and of possible counter claims, and second, what steps could be taken to strengthen and assert Canadian sovereignty, whether by making the whole Archipelago a game sanctuary, or by amending the North West Territories Act to require a permit from all expeditions entering our territory, or further acts of administration by Interior, Customs, Royal Canadian Mounted Police and Indian Affairs officials. [63]

Unable to locate MacMillan, Cory instead had what appeared to be a very productive meeting with Commander Byrd, who assured him that "no expedition will go forward without the approval of the Canadian Government." On his return to Ottawa, however, Cory received a very polite but apologetic letter from Byrd, explaining that he had orders from Admiral J.P. Moffett that he was not to get involved with "that end of the Expedition." The Northern Advisory Board immediately set up a subcommittee to begin drafting a despatch to the British ambassador in Washington that included a request for further information about the purpose of the MacMillan/Byrd expedition. The inquiry included the assumption that "the United States recognizes Canada's claim to the territory indicated on our map of the North and that those in charge of the expedition will comply with Canadian Laws and Regulations."[64]

The subcommittee, meanwhile, had prepared a "Statement of Canada's Claims to the Arctic Islands" that set out the precise boundaries and a lengthy legal argument in their support. Included was a detailed description of police activities, other evidence of effective occupation and the permits required for visiting explorers. Significantly, the boundaries of Canada's northern hinterland were defined in accordance with the Sector Principle as "the area bounded on the east by a line passing midway between Greenland and Baffin, Devon and Ellesmere islands and thence northward to the Pole. On the west, Canada claims as the boundary the 141st meridian from the mainland of North America indefinitely northward without limitation."[65]

As required by protocol, the request for information required approval by the British ambassador in Washington before being forwarded to the U.S. State Department. A note to the ambassador suggested that, if deemed necessary, the "Statement of Canada's Claims" might accompany the request for information. Also included in the letter was an offer from the RCMP to provide assistance to the expedition while it was in Canadian territory. Skelton had taken a calculated risk in declaring boundaries that might be declared invalid if challenged in an international court of law. In a sense it was a bluff, as there was no evidence that the Canadian government had previously asserted any administrative acts in the northwestern portion of Ellesmere Island, nor that any Canadian had ever set foot on the Sverdrup Islands. The ball was now in the State Department's court. Would it protest Canada's claims? If so, on what grounds?

Forwarding correspondence from Canada's External Affairs to the U.S. State Department through the British ambassador was a tedious process that usually involved delays and requests for revisions. On 4 June, the letter along with the "Statement of Canada's Claims" was sent under the signature of Governor-General Lord Byng of Vimy to the British ambassador in Washington, Sir Esme Howard. To elicit immediate action, Skelton sent a coded telegram to the British chargé d'affaires in Washington on 12 June warning that Minister of the Interior Charles Stewart was preparing for a press interview in which he planned to outline Canada's Arctic boundaries and the legal basis for the claims.[66] The strategy worked. On 15 June, the British ambassador forwarded the despatch on to the State Department, along with the statement of claims.

Secretary of State Frank Kellogg replied a week later, confirming that the MacMillan/Byrd expedition would be flying over and establishing a base on Ellesmere, but he requested more information: "What was an R.C.M.P. post? Where are they established? How frequently are they visited? Are they permanently occupied and, if so, by whom?" On 27 June, the Canadian government replied with detailed information about the location of the police detachments and the extensive functions performed by the RCMP throughout the Arctic Islands. Kellogg formally acknowledged receipt of the note and the earlier one of 15 June, saying a reply would be forthcoming after various departments involved had had a chance to study the notes. This time, there was no further response.[67] Canada had followed the proper diplomatic procedures and clearly stated its case. The ultimate test would be whether Canada could enforce the new regulations should the U.S. State Department reject the claims as invalid.

When MacMillan received notice that he would be required to include the registration numbers of the planes and the names of the pilots when applying for a permit to fly over Ellesmere Island, he sought the advice of the Secretary of the Navy, who in turn advised the State Department. Canada's request complicated matters, as the U.S. government had always maintained it had not funded any of MacMillan's exploration activities. In this case, the registration numbers would prove the planes were navy property and the pilots actively employed in the service. Kellogg reportedly questioned the validity of the Canadian position and suggested that because of the nation's ties with Great Britain the Monroe Doctrine might be invoked "to curb Canadian expansion." After reconsideration, he admitted that application of the Monroe Doctrine would cause "strained relations for years to come." In the end, the State Department simply declined to respond.[68]

Meanwhile, Commander George Mackenzie of the Eastern Arctic Patrol was apprised of the American expedition and asked to look out for the two ships. With approval from the Danish government, ss *Peary* and *Bowdoin* had been anchored in Etah Harbour in northwest Greenland since the beginning of August. On the third, MacMillan received a radio message from the navy, warning that CGS *Arctic* was in the vicinity with an American reporter aboard and that under no circumstances should he be allowed to use the expedition's radio phone or interview either Byrd or MacMillan. The reporter, actually a Canadian on contract with Fox News, did not get an interview but he did manage to take some compelling photographs, as did others on board CGS *Arctic*. Further instructions arrived the next day, this time from the U.S. State Department, ordering MacMillan to obtain the necessary permits and avoid "an embarrassing situation by handling the matter informally and diplomatically as possible."[69] Either MacMillan did not receive the message or he ignored it. As a result, the matter was handled neither diplomatically nor informally.

By the time CGS *Arctic* arrived at Etah on 19 August, Byrd had already flown 6,000 miles on reconnaissance east across Greenland and west over Ellesmere as far as Axel Heiberg. He also landed supplies at Flagler and Sawyer Bays on Ellesmere's east coast. To his profound disappointment, bad weather forced cancellation of plans to set up further depots on the west coast of Ellesmere and the northern tip of Axel Heiberg. Commander Mackenzie sent his secretary to ss *Peary* with a message for Commander Byrd, tactfully offering to issue the necessary permits authorizing the expedition "to fly over Ellesmere Island and other Canadian territory and establish on

Amphibian plane piloted by Commander Richard Byrd, USN, approaching
the stern of the SS *Peary* chartered by the United States Navy. When CGS
Arctic met the MacMillan/Byrd Expedition in Etah Harbour, Greenland,
28 August 1925, Byrd had already flown reconnaissance flights over
Ellesmere Island and left a cache of supplies on the west coast.

LAC, PA-100618

such Canadian territory the necessary bases incidental to such flying
operations." Reportedly dressed in naval uniform, Commander Byrd
arrived on board CGS *Arctic* to report that he had been informed by
MacMillan that the expedition had already obtained permission
from the Canadian government "to carry on flying operations over
Ellesmere." Since Mackenzie was denied access to the navy's radio
to confirm this information and had no long-range radio of his own,
he was unable to verify whether permits had been issued after he
had left Quebec City. The Canadian officials departed unconvinced,
but unable to take further action. The patrol ship headed directly to
the site chosen for an RCMP depot at Kane Basin, where Mackenzie
reported that two of Byrd's planes had circled overhead as they were
unloading supplies.[70] A small shed was built for emergency supplies
until such time as a full detachment could be built and staffed.

As expected, Ottawa later confirmed that no such licence had been issued, whereupon a letter was sent to the State Department "calling attention to the incorrect statement made by Commander Byrd to the officer in charge of the CGS *Arctic*." The response was immediate but brief, simply that "the matter would be looked into." When questioned by the State Department, MacMillan claimed that Byrd "knew perfectly well" no permit had been issued and suggested that it was the National Geographic Society and naval authorities that had decided that they need not apply since the United States did not recognize that Canada had any claim to the lands.[71] As extraordinary as it appears, a naval officer had fabricated a story, whereas MacMillan, the senior officer, apparently ignored orders radioed to him by the State Department.

As expected, there was no further naval sponsorship of MacMillan's expeditions in search of unclaimed lands and no more suggestions by the State Department about invoking the Monroe Doctrine against Canada. Perhaps of greater significance, the navy also withdrew its financial support for Commander Byrd's plans to fly over the North Pole from Spitzbergen the next summer. Byrd did manage to get private funding and his mission was reportedly a success, but to MacMillan's disappointment he reported finding no significant land mass anywhere near the North Pole. Although the U.S. still refused to acknowledge Canadian title to northern Ellesmere and Axel Heiberg, it is significant that it made no attempt to challenge the claim in the international courts. In time, both Denmark's and Norway's recognition of Canadian sovereignty claims reinforced Canada's political right of authority.

Not waiting for another crisis, Skelton adopted a more proactive strategy to protect Canada's title. At the outset, an amendment to the Northwest Territories Act passed both Houses of Parliament in June 1925, requiring foreign scientists and explorers to apply for a permit to conduct research in northern Canada.[72] That winter, Inspector Joy conducted a major sled patrol from the police detachment at Craig Harbour, across Ellesmere Island to Axel Heiberg. Another protective measure was initiated in 1926, with creation of the Arctic

Islands Game Preserve, which covered the entire Archipelago and gave the police another vehicle with which to enforce Canadian laws. With reference to boundaries assigned by the Sector Principle, an External Affairs report explained that "the creation of this preserve and its appearance on our maps serves to notify the world that the area between the 60th and 141st meridians right up to the Pole is under Canadian sovereignty."[73] Essentially, Skelton had used legislation to "protect the Arctic environment" as a means to affirm Canada's authority over the area, a strategy that Prime Minister Trudeau employed forty-five years later when announcing the Arctic Waters Pollution Prevention Act.

In the summer of 1926, the Craig Harbour police detachment was closed and a new one built on the Bache Peninsula, almost directly under the flight path of Byrd's reconnaissance mission a year earlier. From here Inspector Joy and other officers accompanied by Inuit guides continued their extensive sled patrols, essentially covering the entire area explored earlier by Sverdrup and MacMillan. The new detachment not only provided physical evidence of a permanent settlement, but the police were also responsible for several administrative acts of government. By 1927, the Canadian government had a total of seven RCMP detachments on the eastern perimeter of the Archipelago, stretching from Port Burwell northward along the shores of Baffin, Devon and Ellesmere Islands. Slowly but surely, Canada was affirming its effective occupation over the Archipelago, something neither the U.S. nor Norway had attempted after their explorers had discovered uncharted lands. The police post at Bache Peninsula was closed in 1932 owing to supply problems because of ice conditions, at which time the Craig Harbour post was reopened. The Greenland Inughuit, meanwhile, continued to hunt on Ellesmere Island, a sovereignty issue that was finally resolved in 1949 by an exchange of notes between Canada and Denmark, allowing them to apply for a licence to hunt on the island.

Other measures that reflected Skelton's adept diplomacy included gaining Denmark's support of Canada's title to the Archipelago in return for Canada's and Britain's support of Danish claims to all of

Official photograph of the party who built the RCMP Bache Peninsula
detachment, August 1926. In attendance were police officers, members of
the government party on the Eastern Arctic Patrol and Inuit families from
Greenland hired to assist the police. Built to maintain Canadian Arctic
sovereignty, the remote detachment was closed after five years because of
difficulty supplying the post because of ice conditions. It was reopened and
relocated in Alexandria Fiord in 1953 and closed again nine years
later because of ice.   LAC, PA-111799, photographer D. L. Livingstone

Greenland. He was also indirectly responsible for negotiations that led to Norway in 1930 relinquishing claims to the Sverdrup Islands in return for Canada's purchase of the explorer's maps and journals for $67,000. With careful editing, a press release was drafted announcing the purchase in recognition of Sverdrup's scientific discoveries without admitting that Canada's sovereignty over the islands had ever been at risk. As it turned out, most of the maps and notes had already been used in the publication of Sverdrup's book *New Land* and were no longer available. As a result, Ottawa received only a few papers, photographs and thirteen notebooks. Decades later, however, Norway's recognition of Canadian sovereignty over the islands proved priceless on account of later oil and gas discoveries. Sadly, Sverdrup died only fifteen days after the agreement was announced. The compensation was passed on to his widow, who in turn donated a portion to the sponsors of his expedition.[74]

One measure that was discussed, but not acted upon, came from Major Robert Logan, formerly of the Canadian Air Board, who in 1922 had surveyed the airfields at Craig Harbour and Pond Inlet. Now retired and running Fairchild Aerial Surveys out of New York, Logan had heard stories at the Explorers Club in June 1925 about plans by the U.S. Navy to build air bases on Ellesmere and Axel Heiberg Islands. Concerned, he wrote to Prime Minister King, describing a plan to protect Canadian sovereignty by leasing lands to private companies for airports on the outer reaches of the Archipelago. He believed that issuing licences under international regulations would provide irrefutable proof that Canada was exercising its sovereign authority over the Arctic Islands with a view to commercial development. The concept was discussed by senior officials, but after consideration they informed Logan that while they appreciated his concern they already had a viable plan to deal with the American expedition that summer.[75] In retrospect, Logan's argument was similar to that used by the Canadian government in the 1980s to justify its sale of drilling permits to foreign companies for oil and gas exploration in the Arctic Islands.

Despite his many successful initiatives, Skelton was unable to gain Britain's support for Canadian recommendations on the definition of territorial waters for submission to the League of Nations Conference on Codification of International Law. The Canadian position that sought baselines and designation of internal waters for the Archipelago was at odds with that of Great Britain, which sought to protect its rights to unrestricted navigation elsewhere in the world. As expected, the British committee urged that all submissions be limited to clarifying existing laws of the sea. Otherwise, it was argued, if the interests of each nation were to be considered, it would result in a "deadlock, because those of weak naval powers would be diametrically opposed to those of strong powers"—a statement that foretold the reluctance of powerful nations to adjust the laws of the sea to a changing world.[76] The Canadian interdepartmental committee chaired by Skelton had included law professors and senior government officials. They had given it their best effort but were unable to influence Britain to make significant changes. Among attendees at the meetings was Lester B. Pearson from External Affairs, who became actively involved in a similar debate during his tenure as prime minister.

Skelton's fine hand was also seen in measures that increased Canada's authority to act as an independent nation. The first step in 1927 was to set up a Canadian legation in Washington with Vincent Massey as the first minister. Backed by Prime Minister King, Skelton's support of the 1926 Balfour Report led in 1931 to the Statute of Westminster, which established Canada as an equal nation within the British Commonwealth of Nations and with full responsibility for its foreign affairs. Historians have justly credited O.D. Skelton with raising the country's stature on the international stage, but few have considered that the protection of Canada's Arctic sovereignty may have served as a proving ground.[77] While Laurier and Sifton deserve recognition for the initial strategy aimed at protecting Arctic sovereignty, it was Skelton who was responsible for perfecting Canada's title.

IN MANY respects, the potential threats to Canadian Arctic sovereignty seem minor compared to Norway's direct challenge to Denmark's title to East Greenland. Norway's claim was historically based, dating back to the Norse settlement led by Eirik the Red and later to the Norwegian missionary Hans Egede, who was responsible for the 1721 recolonization of the island. Denmark based its claim on the Royal Navy's possession of Greenland in 1605, followed during the next century by the west coast settlements controlled by various Danish trading companies. The rift between the two countries widened in 1814, when Norway was transferred to Sweden because of Denmark's support for France during the Napoleonic Wars. At the time Norway had protested Denmark's continued authority over Greenland, but the argument was denied because of the Danes' long-standing administration of the colony. Anticipating a potential problem on the east coast frequented by Norwegian fishermen, in 1894 the Danish government established a settlement at Angmagssalik (now Tasiilaq) and extended the Royal Greenland Trading Company's monopoly to include the area. This failed, however, to halt the increasing activity of Norwegian hunters and trappers further to the north. For years their presence was seasonal but in 1908 they began wintering over.

On at least two occasions, the U.S. had approached Denmark about purchasing Greenland and the Danish West Indies. During the Great War, priorities shifted as President Woodrow Wilson sought a naval base in the Caribbean to protect the Panama Canal. Negotiations were reopened with Denmark, which agreed to the sale of the West Indies (now the Virgin Islands), but only if the U.S. agreed to support Danish plans to extend economic and political control over all of Greenland.[78] At the end of the war, Norwegian trappers resumed their activities but they now had competition from Danish trappers trading with the newly formed East Greenland Company. In an attempt to resolve the problem, an agreement was struck between Norway and Denmark with an exchange of notes in 1924, which allowed the Norwegians to continue hunting and trapping. Unfortunately, the substance of the exchanged notes differed. Denmark's version claimed sovereignty over all of northeast Greenland, whereas Norway's note declared the area *terra nullius*. By now Norwegian trappers were living year-round in crude huts stretched out along their traplines and spending the winter at a central station equipped with radio communications.[79]

Fearing Norway might attempt to lay claim to the area, in 1924–25 the Danish government transferred eighty-seven "volunteers" from Tasiilaq along with a few West Greenlanders and a Danish trader to create a new settlement on Scoresby Sound. As a further show of force, in 1929 Denmark sent a multi-year "scientific expedition" to East Greenland, composed of "three ships, twelve motor boats, two seaplanes and over a hundred staff." That same year, the Danish East Greenland Nanok Company began operations in the area, where it built a new central station and eventually added over fifty new huts. In retaliation, the next July Norway claimed occupation and sovereignty over a strip along the coast north of Scoresby Sound and in 1931 expanded its claim to include the coast of southeast Greenland between Cape Farewell and Tasiilaq. The dispute was finally settled in 1933 by the Permanent International Court of Justice in The Hague, with a decision that favoured Denmark and was justified because of the area being contiguous with long-established Danish settlements.

To confirm full authority over the island, in 1937 Denmark formally annexed North Greenland, which had been privately administered by Knud Rasmussen from his trading station at Thule. Historian Richard Vaughan reminds us that the "Polar Eskimos," as they were often called, were the last of their culture in the circumpolar north to be brought under the authority of a national state. He also maintains that the Norwegian and Danish trappers who lived in the otherwise uninhabited regions of northeast Greenland had done so simply because they "craved the adventure and solitude." In Vaughan's opinion, they were "real settlers," unlike traders arriving elsewhere in the Arctic from Great Britain, France and the United States, who he argues were only temporary residents.[80] While his is an intriguing observation, international law of the time only recognized nation-states as having rights to acquire sovereign title to lands.

By 1933, Denmark had secured sovereign title over Greenland, initially by court decision and acceptance by Canada, followed by its provision of administrative services for the entire island.

Other circumpolar countries, notably Russia/USSR, the U.S. and Canada, have avoided appeals to the International Court of Justice to settle Arctic sovereignty issues. Although the U.S. actively sought undiscovered islands in the Arctic, it did not unilaterally claim title to any portion of the region. Instead, the U.S. position maintained that the uninhabited Arctic Islands were *terra nullius*. Logically, if a country had no grounds to declare sovereign title to an uninhabited area, then it would be in its best interest to deny others authority. It is also logical that the two countries with the longest mainland coastlines bordering Arctic waters—Canada and Russia/USSR—would adopt the Sector Principle to claim sovereignty over the islands extending northward to the Pole. Since 1933, Canadian and Danish titles to their Arctic lands have remained secure. U.S. title to Alaska has never been challenged since its purchase.

Other aspects of the Soviet Union's sovereignty claims are comparable to the Canadian experience. Just as Canada's public declaration of its Arctic boundaries in 1925 was in response to a potential threat from the U.S., so too was the Soviet decree a year after Vilhjalmur Stefansson's aborted attempt to occupy Wrangel Island. The only difference was that there may have been more undiscovered islands within the sector claimed by the Soviets than in the area claimed by Canada.[81] Also similar to Canada's experience with the Northwest Passage was the Russian/Soviet claim that the Northern Sea Route and adjacent large bodies of waters were internal or territorial waters, a claim that remained unchallenged because of the ice-infested waters of the mid-section. Commercial shipping at the two ends of the northern route was common practice by the early twentieth century, but easily controlled at the entrances. Scientific expeditions during the Second International Polar Year (1932–33) were allowed to transit the Northern Sea Route with the government's consent if accompanied by Soviet icebreakers.[82] For both Canada and the Soviet Union, the only countries that appeared prepared to challenge the

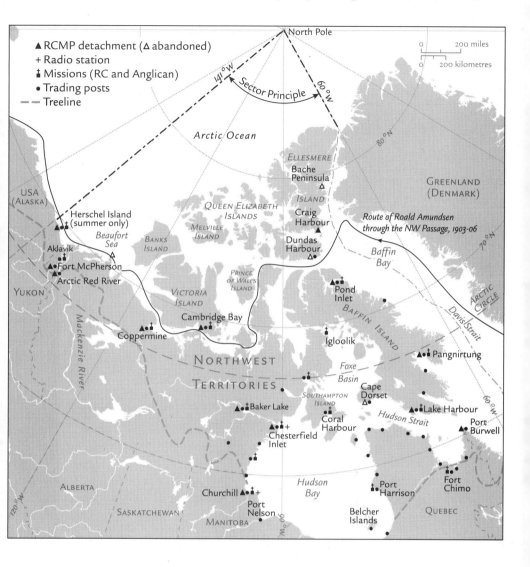

CANADIAN PRESENCE IN THE ARCTIC, C1933

Although Canada publicly claimed sovereignty over all the Arctic
Islands within the sector defined by extension of its mainland boundaries,
the relative absence of a Canadian presence in the High Arctic made
this region particularly vulnerable to a potential challenge to Canada's
sovereign rights. Budget restraints during the Depression also resulted in
the closure of a number of RCMP detachments and mainland trading posts.

status of their northern passages were their closest neighbours, the U.S. and Norway, respectively.

During the Depression years, the Conservative government was returned to power in Canada, with R.B. Bennett as prime minister. Subsequently a program of cutbacks and downsizing saw the Northwest Territories and Yukon Branch disappear and along with it the staff of dedicated northern specialists and plans to improve medical services and education for Native peoples. The Department of the Interior was diminished in size and later abolished. As a further cost-saving measure, the police post at Dundas Harbour on Devon Island was closed. To replace its sovereignty function, the Northwest Territories Council supported a colonization scheme that involved transporting twenty-two Inuit from Cape Dorset, another twelve from Pangnirtung and twelve more from Pond Inlet along with a clerk from the Hudson's Bay Company, to the site of the abandoned police post at Dundas Harbour. Finding trapping poor, the Inuit from Pangnirtung were returned home two years later and the rest went on to Arctic Bay. From there they moved to Fort Ross and eventually found a permanent home at Spence Bay.[83] Unlike the Russian and Danish governments in their relocations of indigenous peoples to establish sovereignty in uninhabited Arctic regions, the Canadian government did not provide housing, medical care or spiritual support. What might have seemed a good idea on paper failed because of flawed execution.

Cutbacks also occurred in Canada's Department of External Affairs, but Skelton was singularly successful in retaining the capable young recruits he had hired in the twenties. Individuals such as Hugh Keenleyside, Kenneth Kirkwood, Lester B. Pearson, Norman Robertson, John Read and Hume Wrong had all been involved in some aspect of defining policy on Arctic sovereignty. As a consequence, Canada was guaranteed another generation of similar commitment and foresight in the decades ahead. By 1931 Canada's title over the entire Arctic Archipelago appeared secure. The only outstanding issues were related to jurisdiction over the adjacent waters, air and ice, and the status of the Northwest Passage.

Although relatively passive in 1930s, the U.S. military never lost sight of the need for broader access to the Canadian Arctic and Greenland in order to adequately defend North America. Exploration and scientific studies continued throughout the interwar period. Of particular note were University of Michigan expeditions from 1927 to 1930 that included construction of a temporary airfield at Sondre Stromfjord in Greenland. German scientists were also active during the same period in both Greenland and Ellesmere Island. At the time, there were no suspicions that either the U.S. or Germany might use the knowledge obtained by their scientists for future military purposes.

The thirties also witnessed an apparent change in attitude among U.S. State Department officials toward Canadian sensitivities to sovereignty issues, whereas Canadian officials seemed more confident. At least publicly, diplomacy had acquired a relatively measured and more respectful approach compared to the bluster and aggressive posturing of earlier years. Canada's increasing independence from Great Britain might have partially responsible, but the change also may have been facilitated by the Office of Geographer, which was created to advise the State Department on boundary issues. Posthumously published studies by Samuel Wittemore Boggs, who held the office for thirty years, provide insight into American policy on polar regions throughout the world. Writing in 1933, Boggs acknowledged that "Canadian jurisdiction is rather effectively established throughout the known islands within the sector claimed by Canada." In reference to the Sector Principle, however, he recommended that the U.S. should challenge the concept if applied to yet undiscovered lands in order to "uphold the idea that sovereignty can be admitted only in relation to known territories." Boggs disregarded the importance of mineral resources in the Arctic, believing the potential for transpolar air routes was more important, but he was equally aware that sovereignty issues related to stationary ice and adjacent waters would require either bilateral or international negotiations to resolve disputes.[84] As evident in the role played by O.D. Skelton in defining

Canada's Arctic policy, Boggs's writings likewise suggested increased legal expertise within the U.S. State Department, a factor which may have moderated pressures on political decisions as a result of exaggerated or misinformed newspaper articles on both sides of the border. In the years ahead, Canada would also rely on the State Department to temper the more ambitious plans of the U.S. military.

ALTHOUGH NEITHER the U.S. nor Canada had approved an official Arctic policy, at least not publicly, both countries recognized the importance of abiding by international law in sovereignty disputes. With the contentious issues now the responsibility of legal advisers, there was a greater opportunity for peaceful negotiation to settle differences. Discussions on sovereignty were conducted most often behind closed doors, but there was no intended deception or intrigue. A degree of secrecy seemed necessary to avoid premature announcements appearing in the press.

For those who have criticized the efforts of officials and politicians in protecting Canada's Arctic sovereignty, the fact that the boundaries of the Arctic Archipelago are the same today as they were thought to be over a hundred years ago is evidence that Canada did not fail in its commitment to protect the legacy handed down by Great Britain. In some respects, the 1930s might be likened to the calm before a storm, as the next decade would bring unimaginable challenges to the circumpolar countries and the expectations implied in their sovereign authority.

(9)

WORLD WAR II,
1939—45

Aviation will have a greater influence on American
foreign interests and American foreign policy than any other
non-political consideration... We cannot remain unconcerned
as to the location of airports, present and post-war control of these,
and arrangements by which they are controlled and maintained.

ADOLPH A. BERLE, U.S. Assistant Secretary of State, September 1942[1]

. . . .

A S WAR clouds gathered over Europe in the late 1930s, neither
Canada nor Denmark gave much thought to how hostilities
might affect their respective Arctic regions. Even U.S. military
strategists were only somewhat more prescient when planning their
security strategy. As described by American military historians Stetson Conn and Byron Fairchild, the sole objective of the continental
defence policy established in 1939 was to prevent any hostile power
from establishing a base of operations in the western hemisphere,
including the land masses and islands of North and South America,
Greenland, Bermuda and the Falkland Islands. By their interpretation
"it was a natural outgrowth of American policy and practice under
the Monroe Doctrine."[2]

Greenland in particular posed a dilemma. Previously the idea
of purchasing the island from Denmark had been raised twice, first
by William Seward in 1869 and again during Theodore Roosevelt's
tenure in the White House. In 1916, however, the U.S. had agreed to an

official declaration recognizing Denmark's sovereignty over Greenland as part of its purchase agreement for the Danish West Indies. At the time, a Caribbean base to protect the Panama Canal was considered of far greater importance than the Arctic. Two decades later the situation had changed as a result of advances in aviation and submarine technologies. Hence in the summer of 1939, the U.S. Senate once again debated purchase of the world's largest island, but tentatively rejected the proposal after an aerial survey reported a lack of appropriate sites for military bases.[3] Of more immediate concern was Alaska because of the buildup of Japanese forces. At the time Arctic Canada was not considered a security risk.

The spread of war throughout Europe and subsequent German submarine activity in the North Atlantic soon changed the priorities of continental security. Once valued solely for its resource potential and national prestige, the North American Arctic suddenly acquired a new strategic significance. The fact that the U.S. had sovereignty rights to only a relatively small portion of the region necessitated negotiation of wartime agreements with its northern neighbours in order to execute a viable defence strategy. Plans were modified accordingly and again expanded after America's entry into the war with the bombing of Pearl Harbor. Within five years the Arctic and Subarctic regions of North America were dotted with new radar installations, weather stations, airfields and naval bases, most of them constructed, supplied, manned and operated by American forces. As U.S. military activities proliferated, Canadian officials became increasingly concerned about a *de facto* loss of sovereignty, particularly in the northwest where by 1943 there were an estimated 33,000 American soldiers and civilians, a number that exceeded the resident population of the Northwest Territories and Yukon combined.[4] Such concerns were not shared by the Free Danes, who actively sought and welcomed U.S. protection of Greenland and Iceland after the Nazi occupation of Denmark in April 1940.

Although U.S. military activities in the Canadian Arctic and Greenland were undertaken with official approval, the wartime agreements created a precedent in that they acknowledged the

Americans' right of access to foreign soil for the purpose of continental defence. Their increased military presence throughout the Arctic happened subtly, initially occurring under cover of wartime secrecy. Yet once the Soviet Union replaced Germany as a potential threat to U.S. security, the continued American presence in the Canadian Arctic and Greenland was inevitable. World War II simply accelerated the process.

While it may appear incongruous to devote a full chapter to a period of five years, compared to the decades and centuries covered in previous chapters, this anomaly is warranted because of the dramatic shift in national priorities that forever changed the strategic significance of the Arctic and its effect on sovereignty. At the same time, the U.S. discovered a "new frontier" upon which to test its many scientific and technological innovations. Unlike previous frontiers in American history, this was strictly a military frontier and located on foreign soil. Because of wartime secrecy, few details were generally known about the nature and extent of these activities, particularly in the High Arctic, yet they are critical to understanding the political tensions and future agreements negotiated with Canada and Denmark. This period in history was short, but the effects long-lasting.

THE NEUTRALITY Act passed by Congress in November 1939 was intended to protect the U.S. from becoming embroiled in yet another European war. At the time it was assumed that Greenland was secure because of Denmark's declaration of neutrality. Similarly, the inhospitable environment was thought to be a natural barrier against possible invasion, but advances in radio communications, radar, aviation and submarine technologies proved those assumptions were no longer valid. Immediately following the defeat of Denmark in 1940, Greenland's two resident governors rejected Germany's demand to capitulate and instead sought military protection from the Allies and assistance in obtaining food supplies. Britain and Canada were first to make plans to occupy Greenland in order to protect cryolite mine production, essential in the manufacture of their fighter planes. Assuming that British action might be considered a violation of the

USCGC *Comanche* anchored near the cryolite mine in Ivigtut Harbour,
Greenland, in September 1940, kept a close watch on ships loading the ore
bound for the U.S. During World War II, cryolite was a critical component
in manufacture of aluminum used in airplanes. Although
still neutral, the U.S. government authorized the Greenland Patrol to
protect the island from possible invasion by Germans after
the fall of Denmark in April 1940. LAC, C-139052

Monroe Doctrine, they assigned primary responsibility for occupation to Canada, whose chiefs of staff prepared a small expeditionary force known as Force X to defend the mine. Within weeks, however, the operation was cancelled after President Roosevelt directly appealed to the Canadian prime minister to desist, in the belief that intervention by either Canada or Britain might trigger a German attack on Greenland or elsewhere in North America.[5] Not willing to stand idly by, the Canadian government ordered a consulate set up at Godthab in hopes that food supplies might be traded for cryolite.

As it happened, on 3 June 1940 three ships converged near the mine on Ivigtut Fjord: the Hudson's Bay Company supply ship SS *Nascopie* from Canada, SS *Julius Thomsen* from England carrying Canada's newly appointed consul to Greenland and the U.S. Coast Guard cutter *Comanche*. The incident prompted an angry outburst from U.S.

Assistant Secretary of State Adolph Berle, who accused the Canadians and British of attempting to take control of the mine for their own use. A heated debate followed in the U.S. Senate as to whether the country should take over Greenland. Although the Monroe Doctrine might have been invoked to support the U.S. right to occupy Greenland, so far there had been no evidence of a German invasion of the island. In the end, maintaining neutrality took priority over security, but only as long as the U.S. could be guaranteed control of cryolite production.

As a result, its government agreed to set up regular coast guard patrols to supervise transport of the precious ore to American industries, thus avoiding direct military intervention that might threaten the neutral status of the U.S. and Greenland. With approval from the Free Danish Legation in Washington, the U.S. Coast Guard also loaned personnel and guns to guard the mine. To pay for the cryolite, the Americans agreed to supply food and other essentials to the Greenland communities and a U.S. consulate was opened at Godthab to facilitate the exchange. At the same time all available vessels were refitted and added to the Coast Guard patrol. This included the aged *Bear,* whose history included rescue of the Greely expedition in 1884 and patrol of the Alaskan coast as a U.S. revenue cutter at the turn of the century.

Meanwhile in June 1940, Canada had ordered the RCMP vessel *St. Roch* based in Vancouver to set out for the eastern Arctic by way of the Northwest Passage. The initial intent had been to provide support for Canadian occupation forces in Greenland, but the ship continued on its way after cancellation of Force X, ostensibly to provide support for the new consulate at Godthab and ensure safe passage for Canada's portion of cryolite bound for the aluminum industry in Arvida, Quebec. The ship took three years to reach its destination, at which time its services were no longer required. The return voyage in 1944 was completed in one season, making *St. Roch* the first Canadian ship to traverse the Northwest Passage in both directions. While the achievement added greatly to national pride, the episode also revealed Canada's lack of ice-reinforced ships to adequately protect its Arctic Islands.[6]

With the fall of Denmark and France threatening to bring the war to North America, agreement with Canada on defence cooperation was required to give substance to the informal statements made in the summer of 1938 by President Franklin Roosevelt and Prime Minister King. As a result, the Ogdensburg Agreement was signed by the two leaders on 17 August 1940, creating the Permanent Joint Board on Defence (PJBD) to deal with specific projects and approvals. Initially the board's composition appeared to ensure equality, with two chairmen and an equal number of senior military and state officials from each country. The PJBD was responsible for assessing military needs before making recommendations and requests for approval of various projects, which were then forwarded directly to the Cabinet War Committee in Ottawa or to the Office of the President of the United States.

The Ogdensburg Agreement heralded a new era in Canadian-American relations that required close cooperation undreamed of a decade earlier. Other than distancing Canada from Britain in discussions of defence strategy, the PJBD provided a forum that appeared to give Canada an equal voice in planning for North American defence in spite of being a lesser power. In practice, however, this was not the case, especially after the U.S.'s entry into the war. Most, if not all, projects originated with American military strategists, who then discussed them with their Canadian counterparts prior to forwarding a recommendation for government approval. With very few exceptions, wartime projects in the Arctic were planned by the American military and built with American money, manpower, equipment and technology.

When the United States was still neutral, accommodation and consensus came easily as both countries shared the same overriding objective of defeating the enemy. Later disagreement generally related to the degree of urgency, with the Canadians attempting to moderate or defer American plans for further consideration. Tensions inevitably happened, especially among U.S. military leaders, who were frustrated by decision delays, and members of the Canadian War Cabinet, who were overwhelmed by the size and cost of certain projects

RCMP *St. Roch* caught in the ice at Pasley Bay while traversing the
Northwest Passage, c1942. Compared to U.S. Coast Guard ships patrolling
the Greenland waters, the *St. Roch* appears small and antiquated. In spite of
its size Captain Henry Larsen placed the ship on record as being the first to
traverse the Northwest Passage from west to east and back again.

LAC, RCMP-e003894953

and equally frustrated to learn that some had proceeded without their
approval. With increasing difficulty, Canadian political leaders tried
to remain alert to any infringement that might have a lasting effect on
Canada's rights as an independent sovereign nation.

The U.S.'s indirect participation in the war effort grew rapidly as
panzer divisions rolled across Europe. As Axis victories mounted,
it was soon apparent that Britain would require assistance to defeat
the enemy. A month after the Ogdensburg Agreement was signed,
the "bases for destroyers" agreement was negotiated with Britain to
provide the U.S. with ninety-nine-year leases on air and sea bases
in Newfoundland, Bermuda and the Caribbean, in exchange for

fifty-one aged destroyers. Then in March 1941, the Lend-Lease Act was passed by Congress authorizing supply of aircraft and munitions to Britain. To facilitate air cargo transport and ferrying of large bombers across the North Atlantic, operation of Newfoundland's Gander and Stephenville airports was transferred to the United States Army Air Force (USAAF), which also assumed control over all American planes flying to Britain. The Hyde Park Declaration signed in April 1941 was essentially an economic corollary of the military pact between the U.S. and Canada, which agreed to share the resources of the two countries and coordinate production under the supervision of a joint economic committee. The agreement also offered an opportunity for Canada to overcome its shortage of funds required to purchase materials and parts for its war industry, which was also supplying munitions and equipment to Britain.[7]

Meanwhile the size and status of the Air Corps, now part of the USAAF, had grown steadily under the leadership of Commander General H.H. Arnold, until it was said to enjoy a "virtual autonomy in the War Department" by the time the U.S. officially declared war.[8] As might be expected, it was the veteran polar aviators, explorers and scientists who were most influential in the design of USAAF initiatives in the Arctic. The older generation, men like Vilhjalmur Stefansson, Professor William H. Hobbs and Sir G. Hubert Wilkins, were behind the scenes acting as consultants and lobbyists—Stefansson and Wilkins in particular with a view to creating postwar commercial benefits. Some taught at American universities, which led to a close relationship between military planners and academic institutions that facilitated applied research and the training of recruits. Others became more directly involved, such as Dr. Alexander Forbes (USN Reserve), Commander Donald B. MacMillan (USN ret.) and Dr. William S. Carlson, who conducted aerial surveys, charted access to safe harbours and designed military air routes respectively.[9]

Of particular note in terms of leadership and enthusiasm were Colonel Bernt Balchen, a Norwegian-born polar aviator who had accompanied the Byrd Antarctic expedition, and Lieutenant-Colonel Charles Hubbard, an engineer with extensive experience in northern

Labrador. Balchen joined the USAAF to take a lead role in Greenland defence and air search and rescue operations on the icecap, whereas Hubbard was commissioned to oversee establishment of Arctic weather stations and later appointed chief of the Arctic Section for the U.S. Weather Bureau. These men and others trained yet another generation of Arctic expertise, ensuring the U.S. military's ability to assume a permanent role in the region long after the war's end. Some projects verged on science fiction in terms of ingenuity and design. Some were unsuccessful, such as the attempt to burrow a tunnel from the Narsarssuaq air base in southern Greenland northward through the icecap in hopes of connecting with the airfield at Sondre Stromfjord.

Initially, American efforts were focussed on expanding the number of weather stations in the northeastern Arctic, a move warmly welcomed by Britain, whose air and naval defence depended on accurate meteorological forecasts. Most weather patterns in northern Europe originated in the North Atlantic, where the southward movement of Arctic air collides with the northward thrust of warm tropical air, making advance warning of disturbances critical for Allied commanders when planning air and naval attacks. Similarly, violent storms were often generated over the Greenland icecap, creating havoc for cargo ships and aircraft travelling across the North Atlantic. As a result, construction of Arctic weather and radio stations became a high priority to aid Allied forces in Europe and ensure safe delivery of munitions and planes to Britain. German military strategists were of the same mind and early on had secretly established weather stations on the northeastern shore of Greenland and later in Labrador.[10] The Soviet Union also expanded its Arctic weather stations and communication posts to support convoys of supply ships through the Northern Sea Route. Occasional disruptions by German U-boats and small cruisers took place, primarily in the Kara Sea, but without notable success.[11]

Discovery and capture of twenty Nazi troopers on Greenland's northeast coast in late August 1940 and the interception of another fifty Germans bound for the island fuelled concerns that they were

USCGC *Bear* setting out on Greenland patrol, c1941. "The *Bear*," as it was
affectionately known in U.S. Coast Guard history, was the oldest cutter to
see service in World War II. Originally built as a sealer in 1874, the steam-
assisted barquentine was purchased by the U.S. Navy to rescue the ill-fated
Greely expedition in 1884. In 1886, it was commissioned as a revenue
cutter and for thirty-eight years it patrolled the Alaskan waters during the
summer. In 1933, it was decommissioned and sold to Admiral Richard
Byrd for his expeditions to Antarctica. In 1941, *Bear* rejoined the U.S. Navy
with its masts cut and fully motorized, this time assigned to the Greenland
Patrol, and earned the distinction for the first U.S. capture of the war—
the German ship *Busko*, caught setting up a radio station on Greenland.
U.S. Coast Guard Military History, *Bear* 1885

intended to assist Hitler's anticipated amphibian invasion of England. That fall and winter, negotiations began in earnest to locate American bases on both Iceland and Greenland. War exempted diplomatic convention, with the result that an American survey party was already in Greenland when President Roosevelt announced in mid-April 1941 that an official agreement had been signed, placing the island under U.S. protection. Co-signatories on the agreement were Secretary of State Cordell Hull and Ambassador Henrik Kauffmann representing Free Denmark. Citing the Act of Havana, which authorized emergency unilateral measures for hemispheric defence, the U.S. claimed the right to deepen harbours, construct roads and fortifications and generally "to do any and all things necessary to insure the efficient operation, maintenance and protection" of all military facilities. Also included was a U.S. commitment to respect the laws and customs of Greenlanders and assist local authorities with regard to their welfare. The agreement was later approved by the two governors still presiding over Greenland.[12] Unlike the Ogdensburg Agreement signed with Canada, the 1941 bilateral agreement with the Free Danes granted blanket approval for all activities considered necessary to defend Greenland.

Meanwhile Iceland, once a colony of Denmark, was recognized under the Act of Union of 1918 as a fully sovereign state united to Denmark under a common king. At the outbreak of the war, the tiny state had also declared its neutrality. Barely a month after the German occupation of Denmark in April 1940, however, the island was occupied by British and soon Canadian forces because of its strategic location in the North Atlantic. Although Iceland was not geographically located in North America, representatives made an informal inquiry to the U.S. concerning possible protection, citing the Monroe Doctrine. Subsequently, an agreement was signed in July 1941 transferring responsibility for Iceland's defence to the U.S., but allowing for a joint command of British and American occupation forces. At the height of the war, foreign troops were estimated to be around 50,000, a number that equalled the male population of the island. Without any military forces of its own, on 17 July 1944 the

Icelandic government declared its status as an independent republic, but with provision for the U.S. to retain continued responsibility for the island's defence.

Meanwhile in the spring and summer of 1941, American survey expeditions were sent to Greenland to locate sites for air bases and weather stations to enable delivery of short-range fighters from Gander airport in Newfoundland to Reykjavik in Iceland and on to Prestwick, Scotland. The first choice, Narsarssuaq (Bluie West 1), lay at the southern tip of the island. Veteran polar explorer Commander Donald MacMillan USN came out of retirement to help chart the waters for supply ships. By mid-October 1941, a construction task force numbering over 650 men was hard at work on the airfield and construction of some eighty-five buildings, as well as numerous access roads and a temporary dock. In just over three months, an all-weather runway was ready for the arrival of its first plane. During this period, a naval base was also established near the mine at Ivigtut— at Grønnedal just west of Narsarssuaq.[13]

Even more ambitious plans were under way for the Canadian Arctic. With expectations of heavy traffic resulting from the Lend-Lease agreement, an alternative to the original air route utilizing Gander airport was believed essential, and possibly a third route. The immediate objective according to General Arnold was to connect the aircraft factories in the American west to Prestwick airport in Scotland by means of a "great circle route." Referred to as the Crimson Route, this airway would stretch from Great Falls, Montana, through the Canadian Arctic and on to Greenland, Iceland and Scotland. On 30 June 1941, an aerial survey party led by the president's son, Captain Elliott Roosevelt, was dispatched to Labrador and northern Quebec to locate sites for the new airfields, one in the general area of Lake Melville in southern Labrador and another in northern Labrador or Quebec. Further reconnaissance missions were later sent to Baffin Island and Greenland.

Much to Captain Roosevelt's surprise, a Canadian party from the Dominion Geodetic Survey was already hard at work at the western end of Lake Melville. Their selection of a site on Goose Bay near the

U.S. airfield at Narsarssuaq at the southern tip of Greenland, seen here
in July 1942, was built to provide a stopover and fuelling base for fighter
planes and escort bombers being ferried to the United Kingdom. Shortly
after U.S. entry into the war after the bombing of Pearl Harbor, planes
began to land routinely at the Greenland air bases on their way
to Prestwick, Scotland.   NA, DMG-XBB, Bernt Balchen Papers, file 7-D-2, #34

mouth of the Northwest River was admittedly the best location, but
Roosevelt was unconcerned as he believed that Canada had neither
the equipment nor the manpower to build an air base in time to meet
the demand. As it happened, RCAF engineers immediately set to work
on the runway and had it ready when the first plane landed at Goose
Bay in December 1941, two days after the attack on Pearl Harbor. In
addition to this site, Captain Roosevelt selected three other locations
for airfields: the first some five miles from the Fort Chimo fur-trading
post on the Koksoak River leading into Ungava Bay, the second near
the head of Frobisher Bay on Baffin Island and a third on Padloping
Island further north on Baffin's east coast. These weather stations and
adjacent airfields were called the Crystal stations, numerically designated I, II and III. A possible fourth site near the Torngat Mountains

in northern Labrador was rejected. Ironically, the latter was in roughly the same area where remnants of a German weather station were discovered forty years later.[14]

In mid-August 1941, President Roosevelt and Prime Minister Churchill met secretly on the British warship HMS *Prince of Wales*, anchored in Argentia Bay. Topics discussed included U.S. occupation of Iceland and General Arnold's alternative ferrying routes. Both apparently met with Churchill's approval. Within weeks, American troops arrived in Iceland to relieve the beleaguered British garrison and work began on expansion of Meeks Field near Reykjavik. At the end of September, five separate construction crews were dispatched in trawler convoys, three destined for the Canadian Arctic and two for Greenland. By November, three Crystal weather stations were completed using prefabricated units and the airstrip was cleared at Fort Chimo, ready for completion the following spring. The buildings erected in Frobisher Bay, however, were only temporary as supply ships had been unable to find the site selected by Captain Roosevelt. The Crystal III weather station was built on Padloping Island, but plans for an airstrip were cancelled because of unsuitable terrain.[15]

The other two convoys headed for Greenland, one arriving at Sondre Stromfjord (Bluie West 8), where construction began on a second major airfield as an alternative to the fog-prone Narsarssuaq base. The second convoy headed for Angmagssalik on the east coast of Greenland to build yet another landing strip for emergencies and as a base for rescue missions on the Greenland icecap. Eventually, there were thirteen U.S. weather and radio stations in Greenland, five on the east coast and eight on the west, all coded by number and designation Bluie East or West. In 1943, the USAAF built yet another weather station, this time at Thule in northwest Greenland (Bluie West 6), which was operated by the Free Danes. A USN loran radar station was also located at Frederiksdal.[16]

Following the bombing of Pearl Harbor on 7 December 1941, the U.S. moved quickly to mobilize for all-out war. Although not prompted by any crisis, plans to connect the central states with the Canadian Arctic moved ahead rapidly without consultation with

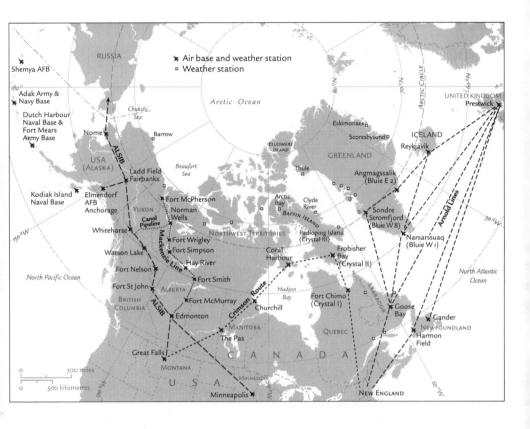

ARCTIC WEATHER STATIONS, FERRY

ROUTES AND AIRFIELDS IN WORLD WAR II

The eastern and western ferry routes carried Lend-Lease planes
to Britain and Russia, respectively. The ALSIB (short for Alaska-Siberia)
route is better known to Canadians as the Northwest Ferry Route, which
linked airfields along the Alaska Highway to Fairbanks. At Ladd Field,
Russian pilots took possession of the planes and flew them on to Siberia.
The Crimson and Mackenzie routes were never used for this purpose,
although the latter was used extensively to support construction of the
Canol pipeline and exploratory drilling for oil north of Norman Wells.

Canadian authorities. A number of polar experts, who had previously volunteered their time and advice, were now formally commissioned into the navy or air force. In February 1942, for example, Dr. William S. Carlson was commissioned as a lieutenant-colonel in the USAAF and asked to design an air route connecting the Crystal airfields to Great Falls, Montana, by way of Hudson Bay. Initially it was thought that the interior ferry route, referred to as the Crimson Route to differentiate it from the original North Atlantic or Arnold Lines, would provide more reliable flying weather and shorten the route from California by 600 miles. It was also argued that these bases might furnish the beginnings of a direct postwar air route to Russia.

Carlson chose sites at The Pas and Churchill in Manitoba, as well as Coral Harbour on Southampton Island in Hudson Bay. The airfields at Coral Harbour and Churchill were completed and runways paved in the summers of 1942 and 1943 but, like those at Frobisher and Chimo, they were never used for ferrying airplanes. An additional route was also recommended, extending from Detroit to Greenland and connected to Chimo by airfields at Kapuskasing and Moosonee. The PJBD's estimated cost for the additional routes and expansion of the Goose Bay facilities was roughly $200 million, a figure that stunned the Canadian War Cabinet. When verbal approval was tentatively granted, it contained the proviso that the U.S. would bear all costs of construction, maintenance, security and administration. By that time, the USAAF had withdrawn its plans for the Detroit route.[17]

The USAAF also utilized and re-equipped many existing Canadian and Danish facilities. The Free Danes in Greenland were reportedly eager to cooperate, but Canadians were reluctant to combine efforts, complaining that differences in British codes and procedures would make it difficult to communicate the collected data. American forces also preferred to work with their own men and equipment, resulting in a duplication of services as evident at Goose Bay, Labrador. Although the USAAF had warned that joint operation of the air base would be unworkable, the Canadian forces by December 1941 had completed a gravel runway, a weather station, hangars, warehouses

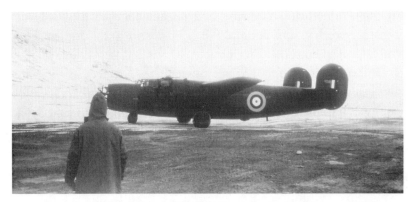

This B-24 Bomber (Liberator) was the first to land at Sondre Stromfjord
(Bluie w 8), destined for the RAF at Prestwick, Scotland, April 1942.
NA, DMG-XBB, Brent Balchen Papers, file 7-D-2, #34

and barracks. Two additional runways were added the next spring.
After the American airmen complained bitterly about "intolerable
conditions," they were eventually granted approval to construct separate facilities across from the RCAF base. In addition to a second set
of barracks, mess hall, officers' quarters, radio/weather huts, warehouses and hangars, the USAAF also expanded and resurfaced the
landing strips. In the end, there would be two air bases at Goose
Bay, under separate commands but sharing the same runways and
airspace.[18]

German U-boat activity in the North Atlantic made air transport
the preferred means to send planes to Britain. Long-range bombers
were able to make the flight from Newfoundland directly to Prestwick,
but fighter planes required at least one or two stops for refuelling.
Since the U.S. Eighth Air Command had arrived safely in Britain by
the summer of 1942 and was waiting for its planes, upgrades at Goose
Bay and completion of the airfields in Arctic Canada and Greenland
were now top priority. For a second summer in a row, a large convoy
of cargo ships and trawlers carrying men, equipment and supplies set
out, this time for Fort Chimo, Frobisher Bay and Coral Harbour. The
fleet was delayed, however, after a German U-boat sank one vessel
off Labrador and along with it some 6,000 tons of equipment and

supplies. Nonetheless, runways, hangars and ancillary facilities were constructed that summer and fall at Frobisher and Coral Harbour, with upgrades completed at Chimo.

The ships bound for Frobisher were further delayed as their first task was to transfer men and equipment from the temporary location on Crowell Island to a site further inland near the mouth of the Sylvia Grennell River. It was mid-August when the ships finally arrived at the new site, carrying 350 men, building materials and heavy construction equipment. By October a prefabricated village was in place, complete with barracks, officers' quarters, hospital, general store, mess hall, generator stations, assorted hangars and warehouse facilities, linked by a mass of power lines. As the ships departed that fall, the bulldozers were still hard at work clearing the runway.[19]

Greenland was considered secure by the fall of 1942, even though there were continual reports of German attempts to establish weather stations in the northeast. To assist in surveillance, Rear Admiral E.H. Smith, USCG, commander of the Greenland Patrol, had organized local trappers and Inuit to form a regular sled patrol along the east coast as far north as 77° N latitude. The first casualty from enemy contact on land occurred in March 1943, when a member of the sled patrol was killed by a party of Germans, who then attacked and destroyed the patrol's isolated station at Eskimonaes north of Scoresby Sound. In the process, Lieutenant Hermann Ritter, the commandant for German Greenland operations, was taken prisoner and turned over to U.S. authorities. Ritter, who had been a lieutenant in World War I, was a student of geology, teacher and author of books on the Arctic, which seemed to confirm Balchen's claim that during the interwar years "alleged German scientific expeditions had actually been studying the Arctic with an eye to future military use."[20]

Once it was verified that the enemy's base of operations was located on Sabine Island north of Eskimonaes, plans got under way to launch a bombing raid from USAAF headquarters in Iceland. Thus on 25 May 1943, a large German communications centre, weather station, storehouses and a supply ship anchored offshore in the ice were destroyed in an air attack led by Balchen in command of two large

B-24 Liberators and two smaller B-17 Fortress bombers. Bad weather and accidents delayed plans to deliver a follow-up landing party until mid-July, at which time two Coast Guard cutters carrying American ground troops were despatched from Iceland. Only one ship, USCGC *Northwind*, made it through the icepack to find that the Germans had been successfully evacuated and remaining buildings torched. They did, however, find a lone survivor who had been on a reconnaissance patrol during the evacuation—Dr. Sensse, a lieutenant in the German Medical Corps—who was immediately taken prisoner. The landing party also discovered two parachute kits that had been dropped and a newspaper dated 15 May 1943, suggesting the drop had occurred either just before the USAAF attack or as part of the subsequent evacuation of the base. Further exploration was cut short by the appearance of a German Junker aircraft which was successfully diverted by gunfire from the U.S. Coast Guard cutter.[21]

Upon his return to Iceland, Balchen learned more details about German activities on Greenland in an interview with Ritter, who had been commissioned in the German navy in early 1942 to set up a weather station in East Greenland to supply long-range forecasts to the Luftwaffe and U-boats in the North Atlantic. Similar information was provided to German merchant ships in the straits between Iceland and Greenland, which were carrying supplies from Norway to the South Pacific and Japan. Supported by the Danish ship *Hermann*, a German weather station on Sabine Island had operated from August 1942 until discovered by the Greenland sled patrol the next spring, relaying data from ground observations and *radiosonde* balloons to the German naval high command in Berlin. The twice-daily reports were sent in code by a radio, operated by diesel-powered generators and dynamos. The station was also responsible for relaying misinformation about the weather and location of emergency fields to American planes crossing over the Greenland icecap.[22]

Over a year later, yet another German weather station was discovered by the Greenland Patrol, this time on Shannon Island further north, where the men had dug themselves into caves and tunnels under a massive snowdrift. The Germans were again safely

German weather station hut discovered on Shannon Island in
East Greenland, 1944. The USAAF bombed the main buildings in 1943,
but missed the weather shack that broadcast weather information to the
homeland. The USCG discovered six tents pitched in the snow, sleeping
accommodations for seventeen men, large supplies of ammunition,
food and radio equipment that had been destroyed, suggesting that the
Germans had been picked up shortly before the Coast Guard arrived.

2009.01.08, C2-DA, USCG Collection, Arctic

Institute of North America (AINA) Photo Collection

evacuated, this time with no loss of men. In October 1944, however, another German base of operations was discovered further north by the U.S. icebreaker *Eastwind,* on an island near Danmarkshavn. This time all personnel were taken prisoner.[23] This constituted the sum of direct enemy combat on Greenland, seemingly trivial compared to the thousands of lives lost and hundreds of ships sunk by German U-boats in more southerly waters. Yet in terms of significance, the Greenland experience established the critical importance of an expanded network of Arctic weather stations and airfields for future continental defence.

While most four-engine cargo planes and bombers flew straight from Newfoundland to Scotland, a few flew in convoy with the smaller fighter planes, which required refuelling stops at bases in Greenland and Iceland. On the whole, the North Atlantic ferry route was an unqualified success in spite of initial problems. The first major test of Operation Bolero took place in June 1942, a delivery of planes for the U.S. Eighth Air Command at Prestwick. Of the eighteen bombers (B-17s or Flying Fortresses) that left Newfoundland on the first run, seven arrived at Narsarssuaq as planned; one landed at Sondre Strom-fjord; three came down along the coast of Greenland; seven returned to Goose Bay. The next month, six P-38 fighters (Lightnings) and two B-17 bombers came down on the Greenland icecap, but there was still no loss of life. By the end of 1942, the downed planes amounted to just over 4 percent. In 1943, the average had dropped to just over 1 percent of the more than 3,000 planes flying the North Atlantic route. The following year the number of flights almost doubled with even fewer crashes.[24]

The overall success rate of the rescue missions was remarkable. While sixteen planes were known to have crashed on the Greenland icecap from 1941 through 1945, only eight lives were lost. One search plane was wrecked and five men died attempting rescues. As described by Major Oliver La Farge, historian for the Air Transport Command, "Out of it all comes a picture of the risks men will run to save their fellows, and a story of sacrifice, suffering, endurance, and intense good-fellowship . . ."[25] The expertise of polar veterans stationed in Greenland proved invaluable and in turn they trained a new generation of Arctic enthusiasts, many eager to return to the Arctic after the war ended. A surprising number were caught up in the excitement of a frontier adventure, ready to face difficult challenges in the harsh environment, testing their endurance and mettle to the limit. In a sense, it was a quest like those in Roman and Greek mythology, but the distinguishing characteristics were stamped with the psychology of the American western frontier. These twentieth-century adventurers had discovered a new territory to challenge their pioneer instincts, not a settlement frontier but one of science and technology adapted for military purpose.

For the most part, the war in Greenland was waged against the environment and the heroes were the rescuers of pilots downed on the icecap or in icy coastal waters. Additional projects were undertaken in support of rescue operations and meteorological studies, including setting up a beachhead station on Comanche Bay on the northeast coast and two icecap stations in the interior to provide additional weather and radio communications. The latter were barely finished when a Flying Fortress crashed in the vicinity, setting off a bizarre rescue mission which ended with five dead, one disabled for life and the remaining men finally lifted off the glacier five months later. This and other stories were reminiscent of the heroic accounts of nineteenth-century polar expeditions. Yet they bore little relevance to the epic battles of World War II, where hundreds of lives were lost in a single day.

At remote weather stations, life was dreary, monotonous and lonely, spent in cold wooden buildings with a radio as one's only contact with the outside world. Elsewhere in Greenland, base personnel and pilots dealt with hurricane-force foehn winds (similar to chinooks), dust storms, unpredictable ice conditions and sea fog. But the frigid cold created the most serious challenge, mentally and physically. Critical to survival was morale, requiring a concerted effort to defeat the boredom and monotony of a polar winter. Balchen's men were encouraged to take part in all manner of sports: boxing, skiing, snowshoeing, hiking, hunting, fishing, dogsledding, football and even falconry. When winter darkness set in, there was a large library, movies, games, puzzles, pets of all sorts, Christmas celebrations and even a barbershop quartet. The mystique of the Arctic carried with it harsh realities and the Americans spent considerable time and effort and money to compensate. Not everyone enjoyed their experience. According to Lieutenant-Colonel Carlson, the response varied. "Some hated the place, others didn't mind it, a few really liked it. Some found it adventurous and exciting, others thought it dull, dreary, and unbearably monotonous. A few simply couldn't take it." [26] Those who thrived on the experience would return to the Arctic and assume key leadership roles during the Cold War. Canadian and Danish forces had no similar experience, which may account for their relative lack of enthusiasm for Arctic assignments in later years.

The wartime tales of Greenland were more about the American assault on the Arctic frontier where victory was survival. Yet for the first time in American history, the new frontier was on foreign soil—and would remain so—a fact that some U.S. military planners seemed to ignore when designing further plans for the Arctic before the war had officially ended. Others anticipated peacetime benefits from their experience, as described by Colonel Balchen in 1944:

But it was an important war, for the knowledge of the Arctic that we gained at the cost of these men who gave their lives on the Ice Cap, will insure the safety of tomorrow's aerial travel in the North. The bases and weather stations they fought to maintain, amid the darkness and silence and cold, will be future stops along the new air route to Europe. Some day our whole conception of geography will be changed; the earth itself will be rolled over on its side, and the spindle of the globe will run, not from Pole to Pole, but from one side of the Equator to the other. Then the Arctic will be the very center of our new world; and across Greenland and northern Canada and Alaska will run the commercial airways from New York to London, from San Francisco to Moscow to India. Today's highway of war will be tomorrow's avenue of peace. [27]

Similar thoughts were expressed by Assistant Secretary Adolph Berle, who wrote to the U.S. Secretary of State on 9 September 1942 claiming that "aviation will have a greater influence on American foreign interests and American foreign policy than any other non-political consideration." For this reason, he argued that close attention should be paid to "territorial relationships" and "diplomatic strategy" as "we cannot remain unconcerned as to the location of airports, present and post-war control of these, and arrangements by which they are controlled and maintained."[28] The objective of gaining commercial benefits may explain the haste and disregard for costs when building the northern airfields, particularly in Arctic Canada.

The phenomenal speed at which a project moved from concept to completion was facilitated in Greenland by the blanket approval granted under the Hull-Kauffmann agreement. For Canadian officials, however, expediency established a pattern that saw American planning and preparation taking place without consultation on the assumption that approvals would be granted at the final hour. Such was the case with the 1941 construction of the Crystal weather stations. Reportedly the Canadian War Cabinet was unaware that the weather stations even existed until May 1942, when approvals were requested to build adjacent airfields, possibly an afterthought as preliminary work on the airfield at Chimo had already begun.[29]

For Canada, O.D. Skelton's untimely death in January 1941 might have had even more dire consequences had it not been for men like Lester B. Pearson, Norman Robertson, Hugh Keenleyside, John Read, Hume Wrong and Escott Reid, who became what historian Jack Granatstein called "a meritocratic elite." Many had gained first-hand experience in protecting Canada's Arctic sovereignty in the 1920s and 1930s, prompting them to remain ever mindful of protecting those rights during the war years.[30]

After U.S. entry into the war in December 1941, PJBD requests for approval proliferated and were accompanied by a visible change in attitude. Canadian Under-Secretary of State Norman Robertson commented on the Americans' new sense of Manifest Destiny and a tendency to view "Canada as an internal domestic relationship."

Hume Wrong when posted in Washington complained of a loss of Canadian influence. Escott Reid later suggested that misunderstandings arose from Canada's failure to understand the degree of "independence of the Defense Department from the State Department." Unable to contribute proportionate funding or manpower for the projects, the Canadian War Cabinet felt pressured and reluctant to give immediate approval. Often recommendations from the PJBD would be referred back for revision. The American military, in turn, became increasingly impatient and frustrated, believing Canadian failure to grant immediate approvals was hindering the war effort.[31]

POLITICALLY AND militarily, a parallel situation occurred in the northwest, one that inevitably contributed to Alaska's growth and prosperity, but only secondarily to Canada's Yukon and Mackenzie Valley regions. Japan's military buildup in the North Pacific after 1936 had increased the vulnerability of Alaska's offshore islands, yet it was not until 1940 that Congress approved militarization of the territory, beginning with construction of naval and air bases—initially at Sitka and Kodiak Island, then Anchorage and Fairbanks—with the first troops of the Alaska Defense Command arriving in June 1940.

Initially, the War Department believed that Japan would not attack as long as Britain remained undefeated, but as Axis victories mounted in 1941 and the Japanese buildup increased, Alaskan forces were strengthened to defend the new naval bases. Modern aircraft, however, were diverted to Hawaii. That same year, the Alaska National Guard was activated, and with Canada's cooperation the airfields owned by the commercial Yukon Southern Airway were expanded to link Edmonton, Alberta, to Fairbanks, Alaska. This route was further upgraded the following year and became known as the Northwest Staging Route, for the most part built and financed by Canada. Initially intended to move troops and supplies to Alaska, it was later used to send Lend-Lease planes to Russia.[32]

Following the attack on Pearl Harbor in December 1941, tens of thousands of U.S. troops and civilians poured into Alaska to construct additional facilities. As a local initiative, Governor Ernest Gruening set up the Alaska Territorial Guard made up of Eskimos and Aleuts as unpaid volunteers to watch for enemy ships or aircraft along the coast. Canadian Ranger units were organized to serve a similar purpose in northern Canada. Then in March 1942, after a decade of failed negotiations, the Alaska Highway Act was signed by Canada and the U.S. with the latter accepting responsibility for the highway's construction and costs. Although the route of the pioneer road linked the airfields of the Northwest Staging Route, its value to the war effort was negligible. Publicized as a means to move troops and supplies to Alaskan military bases, the highway was never used for that purpose. One might conclude that the major benefit from the Alaska Highway Act was gaining Ottawa's consent to construction of a land bridge across Canada linking the U.S. with its northern territory. By terms of the agreement, however, maintenance and control of the portion built on Canadian soil would revert to Canada at the end of the war. This became a bone of contention for Ottawa when it was discovered in 1945 to be virtually impassable without major reconstruction.[33]

Then on 3 June 1942, Japanese planes bombed the U.S. naval base at Dutch Harbor in the Aleutians, and four days Japan later invaded and occupied the westerly islands of Attu and Kiska. The incident was allegedly kept quiet for reasons of public morale, as was the fact that the Japanese maintained occupation of the two islands for almost a year until they were finally evicted in the spring of 1943 by American forces assisted by the Royal Canadian Air Force (RCAF).[34] Even though the War Department believed the U.S. Navy was the primary target and had discounted the possibility of a direct Japanese attack on mainland Alaska, American military buildup in the northwest continued. In addition to improvements on the Northwest Staging Route, the PJBD submitted numerous other requests for highway construction and for weather and communication stations, all of which were beyond Canada's financial or manpower resources. Yet when presented with the possibility of a Japanese invasion, Ottawa had little choice but to allow the Americans to proceed at their own expense, with written guarantees that any facilities built on Canadian soil would revert to Canada at the end of the war.

Throughout 1942 and 1943, military activities continued at a feverish pace, including construction of ancillary airfields along the Mackenzie Valley, expanded oil drilling along the Mackenzie River, increased oil production and storage tanks at Norman Wells, more roads, telegraph lines, and weather and radar stations. By far the most ambitious and costly project was construction of an oil pipeline from Norman Wells on the east side of the Mackenzie River, across the steep mountain ranges in the Yukon, to a new refinery built at Whitehorse. A second pipeline connected the Whitehorse refinery to the port at Skagway on the Alaska Panhandle. Referred to as the Canol Project, it served no wartime advantage and was later suspected of being designed as an experiment to test the feasibility for future commercial use of carrying oil from the wells owned by the Imperial Oil Company on the Mackenzie River to be refined at Whitehorse, then loaded on ships at Skagway for transport to the southern U.S.[35]

New airfields along the lower Mackenzie Valley were originally built without Ottawa's approval but claimed to be critical to supply the Canol pipeline project. Additional requests called for a further expansion of these airfields to provide a secondary route to Alaska, based on the assumption that the Lend-Lease agreement with the Soviet Union might involve up to 60,000 flights. In the end, the yearly average was closer to 4,500, with the result that the Mackenzie route was only partially completed and never used for ferrying planes.[36] Only the Northwest Staging Route fulfilled its intended purpose of flying American troops, supplies and Lend-Lease planes to Alaska. Weather also had an adverse effect on activities in the Pacific northwest, with the result that accurate forecasting became almost an obsession. If American pilots distrusted British weather reports in the northeast, they were equally critical of Canadian meteorological stations in the northwest. In the end, the U.S. 16th Weather Squadron was established to cover Alaska and the Canadian west coast. As elsewhere in Canada, American-built facilities were described as "joint" military projects even though Canadian forces rarely participated. There was one covert operation, however, that had a decided wartime

A group of Curtiss P-40 Warhawks escorted a pair of Consolidated
B-24D Liberators over the Aleutian Islands in 1944. Advances in aviation
technology and operations on the Alaskan front would ensure
USAAF pre-eminence in postwar defence of the Arctic.
ID 73654850, photo by Dmitri Kessel, Time/Life Pictures/Getty Images

benefit: reopening of the Eldorado uranium mine on Great Bear Lake
to supply U.S. atomic research.

Other military activities in the northwest were more visible to the
local population and journalists. By the summer of 1943 the dominant presence of U.S. forces gave the impression of "an American
occupation" throughout the Yukon and Mackenzie Valley, an image
given full coverage in the Canadian media. Local accounts seemed
to welcome the arrival of the Americans, a view not shared by press
in the east. In response, the Canadian government launched a public
relations initiative to emphasize the "joint" nature of the military
activities and sponsored a National Film Board documentary film
about the Canol Project. The American media responded with their
filmed version of events, followed by an Associated Press release that
claimed the Canadian northwest was "now a military area under
control of the United States Army and will remain a restricted area
until the war is over." A subsequent article appeared in the *New York*

Times, with headlines claiming "U.S. Army Tapping Canada's Oil."[37] Meanwhile Canadian residents of the Yukon and Mackenzie Valley appeared to benefit from a period of economic prosperity, with the possible exception of some Native communities. Alaskans enjoyed a virtual boom time, the major exception being the Alaskan Japanese-Americans, who were transported to southern internment camps.

As a result of growing concern that Canadian authority was being ignored, in May 1943 a special commissioner reporting directly to the Canadian War Cabinet was appointed to oversee and act as a liaison for joint defence projects in the Yukon and Mackenzie Valley. Included in his mandate was the responsibility to report infringe-ments on Canadian authority and suggest appropriate policy and action to protect its sovereign rights. At the same time, reports that some facilities appeared extravagantly overbuilt for wartime use raised concerns in Ottawa that at least some projects had been built for future commercial use. While it is now broadly accepted that the Ogdensburg and Hyde Park Agreements inextricably bound Canada closer to the U.S. politically and economically, the Canadian govern-ment remained keenly alert to any diminution of its sovereignty.[38]

Yet the U.S. War Department continued to put forward new proj-ects, either ignorant of or simply ignoring Canadian sovereignty concerns. Military planners believed that the PJBD had provided the machinery to facilitate the necessary cooperation, described in the official history of the USAAF as "a practical arrangement" that "permitted decentralization to regional commanders to con-clude agreements required for the common defense."[39] Cognizant of growing tensions, the U.S. State Department commissioned a series of confidential studies in 1942 in an effort to gain a clearer under-standing of the Canadian people and the motivation behind their government's foreign policy. A preliminary report suggested that "Canada has always suffered from an inferiority complex about her southern neighbour" and was envious of the "wealth and vast scale of American enterprise and industry." A longer and more detailed study probed deeper into the influences affecting government poli-cies—none of them particularly flattering—but concluded that cooperation with Canada was attainable "as long as Americans are careful to remember the susceptibilities and sensitiveness of a small, but proud people."[40]

Finally in March 1943, after Ottawa's request for clarification concerning lack of approvals for certain projects, the American secretary to the PJBD informed the senior U.S. Army representative that the United States in fact did not "have blanket authority for construction of all war projects in Canada," and that "special permission of the Canadian government must be obtained for the construction of any proposed airfields." As a consequence, a number of earlier agreements were modified or confirmed by a series of letters between the two secretaries of the PJBD.[41] Even then, tensions continued during the remaining war years and into the postwar period, as American military commanders and their staff continued to dismiss the importance Ottawa accorded Canada's sovereignty.

A number of projects were abandoned because technology had made them redundant, as in the case of the Crimson Route, whose airfields were no longer required for refuelling after fighter planes were refitted with larger fuel tanks. Yet expansion of the Frobisher and Chimo bases continued throughout 1943, raising speculation in Ottawa that the Crystal airfields were built primarily for postwar commercial aviation. After an inspection tour in 1944, the British high commissioner, Malcolm MacDonald, prepared an official report on the Arctic airfields, describing the Frobisher base as maintained by a staff of eighty military and a few civilians, in accommodations built to house 800, and having two runways, one paved with asphalt, and a large hangar which doubled as a badminton court and gym. Basic facilities included officers' quarters, barracks, mess halls, kitchens and a twenty-five-bed hospital with a dental office, a modern operating room and an X-ray machine. There were also shops, a theatre and a coffee house, and for personal comforts, a barber shop, a laundry and a Turkish bath. A year later, a member of the U.S. Coast Guard saw a more humorous side of the story when he reported even fewer Americans at the site, who local Inuit believed were hiding in the Arctic and leaving their women and children at home to fight the war.[42]

The weather station at Chimo had also expanded into a full-sized air base, with two asphalt runways, hangars, warehouses, housing facilities to accommodate 700 and a hotel for visitors. Like Frobisher, the airfield at Chimo was rarely used, with the result that by the summer of 1944 there were fewer than 160 American military and civilians on site. A Canadian scientist arriving in 1946 was overwhelmed by the size and extravagance, describing the base as stretching two and a half miles along the shore and a mile deep, with wide roads, full airfield facilities, numerous cars and trucks, telephone and electricity, rows of huts and barracks and a block of administration buildings. The large leather chairs in the hotel reminded him of what one might expect in a senior common room at Oxford. Facilities built at Coral Harbour and The Pas were smaller, with accommodation for fewer than 500 men. At Churchill, there was only one runway but it was longer, wider and made of concrete, whereas base facilities were larger with accommodations for over 1,500.[43]

When considered in total, there seemed no end of excessive expenditures without any discernible wartime benefit. Aside from the Canol pipeline, which was likely the most extravagant project if measured against its fifteen months of dubious operation, another at Narsarssuaq in Greenland was equally bizarre: miners were brought from Michigan to drive a large tunnel into a mountain for storage of dynamite and bombs, but it was never used because of heavy moisture buildup. Unsubstantiated reports have suggested that the original intent was to connect the base with either the cryolite mine at Ivigtut or the airfield at Sondre Stromfjord.

To support the expansion of Arctic weather stations, there was a major increase in university training programs for meteorologists and radio operators. In 1940, for example, the Massachusetts Institute of Technology (MIT) had graduated roughly 400 qualified officers and enlisted men as meteorologists, but at the end of the war the number had increased to over 6,000. A similar situation occurred in connection with radar technology. Initially, the Air Corps claimed its systems were inferior to the British and that its trained technicians were in short supply. Once again, MIT was called upon to conduct

Aerial view of Crystal II Air Base at Frobisher Bay, 1946. Although not as lavish as described in the British high commissioner's report, this was a sizable airfield that was never used to ferry planes to England. According to the agreement signed in 1944, the base was to be turned over to the RCAF after the war. This did not happen and instead a reduced USAAF staff remained and began to upgrade the buildings. Abandoned trucks and other debris can be seen on the lower left of the photograph. Wartime agreements did not require the U.S. to remove waste or debris from a military site. LAC, PA-164470, photographer J. Whitley

an extensive research and training program for the USAAF. Other university studies were sponsored by the National Defense Research Committee and later by the Office of Scientific Research and Development.[44] These projects not only created opportunities for ongoing funding of graduate research, but also encouraged continued links between the universities and the military. No one, it appears, questioned the emphasis on Arctic-related projects and training, even though the U.S. had relatively little Arctic of its own.

The American military was also directly involved in Arctic research, particularly with regard to survival techniques and specially adapted materials. New clothing and equipment required testing, as did methods of servicing new equipment and vehicles. In response, the USAAF set up various research and training facilities, including an experimental station at Fairbanks, Alaska, and a cold-weather training centre at Buckley Field in Colorado. Recognizing the need for ongoing research and data collection, polar scientists promoted the idea of an Arctic information and research centre. The concept was approved and subsequently expanded to cover other areas of extreme climate, with the result that on 20 September 1942, the War Department formally established the Arctic, Desert, and Tropic Information Center (ADTIC), reporting to the Air Force Proving Ground Command. The addition of desert regions and the tropics was never clearly explained, although likely related to the location of other American air bases on foreign soil. In addition to collecting information and conducting studies on operational techniques, the centre produced maps and survival manuals. The ADTIC was deactivated in 1945, then resurrected in 1947 to accommodate the U.S. Air Force's research needs for its postwar continental defence program.[45]

If 1943 marked a turning point in the fortunes of war, it was also a year of political reassessment, when leaders in both Canada and the U.S. began to think in terms of the postwar implications of military activities in northern Canada. In September 1943, a special committee of the U.S. Senate chaired by Senator Harry S. Truman was set up to investigate the escalating costs of the National Defense Program. When it was rumoured that the Truman Committee would recommend that the U.S. seek postwar benefits from wartime oil and airfield investments on foreign soil, Ottawa took swift action to protect Canada's economic independence and obtained cabinet approval to reimburse the United States for costs of the Mackenzie Valley airfields. The goal was to "re-Canadianize" American operations throughout northern Canada. In a separate report released the following January, the Truman Committee confirmed the rumours by recommending a revision of contracts to ensure that the U.S. would obtain postwar benefits from its wartime investments in Canadian airfields and oil production.[46]

With the two opposing objectives now openly declared, negotiations between the two countries began in earnest. At the outset, it was apparent that Prime Minister King and External Affairs officials were determined to remove the dominant American presence from northern Canada. In addition to the weather stations and airfields, the government announced that it was also prepared to reimburse the U.S. for the cost of the Canol pipeline and ancillary facilities. As King wrote in his diary, he "held strongly with one or two others to the view that we ought to get the Americans out of further developments there, and keep complete control in our own hands," otherwise "with the United States so powerful and her investments becoming greater in Canada we will have great difficulty to hold our own against pressure from the United States."[47]

Ethically, the U.S. was bound by the terms of the wartime agreements to return the permanent installations facilities to Canadian control at the end of the war. From Ottawa's perspective, reimbursement was considered a just and honourable means to repay the U.S. taxpayer for construction costs on Canadian soil. Similarly, Canadian officials argued that the Canol Project was approved as a wartime measure and not intended for peacetime commercial benefit. The terms of the latter agreement included the early withdrawal of U.S. military and civilians, with Canada having the first right of refusal in the event of sale. As a conciliatory measure, a strategic oil reserve was created if required for the future defence of North America. The disposition of Canol was concluded by an "exchange of notes" on 7 June 1944. Further negotiations led to an agreement on 27 June 1944 for reimbursement of costs for airfields and weather stations elsewhere in northern Canada, including those located in the Arctic. A supplementary agreement in March 1946 added weather stations along the Alaska Highway and a few miscellaneous items. The cost to Canada, including assumption of almost $30 million in debt for work done on behalf of the U.S., was over $123.5 million for twenty-eight airfields and fifty-six weather stations. For the eastern Arctic bases alone, the cost amounted to just over $71 million.[48]

Not included in the agreement was the Canadian portion of the Alaska Highway, which was to revert to Canada at the end of the war. In September 1944, when Washington suggested that Canada should take over its final construction, Ottawa had refused because the original agreement had stipulated that the U.S. would complete the road to approved standards. Six months after the end of the war, Canada finally took control of the highway but for years it remained a military road under control of the Canadian Army, until such time as the Royal Canadian Engineers were able to rebuild it to meet acceptable standards for public use.[49]

To implement the "Canadianization" strategy, Ottawa had planned to have the Department of Transport and the RCAF take control of the Arctic weather stations and airfields, but this would require a prolonged period of time due to a lack of adequately trained personnel. Other attempts to prevent foreign control of commercial air routes across Canada included creation of the government-owned Trans-Canada Airlines and support for the creation of an international civil aviation authority.[50] The Canol Project was more easily resolved. The pipeline from Norman Wells to Whitehorse closed in the spring of 1945 after a short, lacklustre performance complicated by breakdowns, leaks and spring floods. Described by one cynic as "a monumental junkyard to military stupidity," the assets were sold piecemeal for a mere fraction of the estimated $134-million cost.[51]

To some Americans, plans to "re-Canadianize" wartime airfields meant the end of a dream that had envisioned "great circle routes" over the North Pole, connecting major U.S. cities with those of northern Europe and Asia, as they did not believe Canada had the manpower, finances, technology or initiative to develop such routes. The American business magazine *Fortune* took a more pragmatic view. Noting that the agreements to build Arctic airfields might have been considered "a diplomatic coup" at the time, the author suggested that because of the recent Canadian purchase, "the United States may have to bow out of the North Atlantic" unless a plane could be designed to fly direct from New York to Britain, which of course is exactly what happened.[52] With the war nearing an end, the public's attention was understandably on peacetime opportunities. Even concerns arising from Stalin's stance at the Yalta Conference did not alter the fact that the USSR was considered an ally. Weary of war, most North Americans looked to the United Nations to halt further aggression.

The wartime agreements had created a precedent by allowing the U.S. easy access to Greenland and Arctic Canada for purposes of continental defence, but the precedent also had a flip side in that further rights of access and cooperation could be achieved only through bilateral negotiations that provided assurance that both Denmark's and Canada's sovereign rights were protected. Neither shared the view that militarization of the Arctic would be required in peacetime. Even the atomic bombs dropped on Hiroshima and Nagasaki raised no immediate concerns that other powers might develop similar technology to trigger a nuclear arms race. Just as Canada and Denmark each believed their Arctic sovereignty was secure in the 1930s, they also believed their wartime agreements had ensured that it would remain so in peacetime.

IN MANY respects, World War II represented a pioneer phase in military development of the Arctic. In the words of U.S. General Curtis LeMay, when summing up the objectives of the USAAF, "Our frontier now lies across the Arctic wastes of the polar regions."[53] This same theme was reiterated directly and indirectly by so many that the message became commonplace in American rhetoric. Yet few Danes or Canadians recognized or understood the American fascination with the Arctic and the commitment of U.S. military scientists to expand upon their wartime research. The Arctic frontier had not yet been "conquered" in the traditional sense of development. Instead, technological changes continually presented new challenges that demanded new forms of assault. Just as aviation advances made the Crimson Route obsolete before it was operational, the years ahead would witness longer-range bombers, nuclear-powered submarines and guided missiles armed with atomic warheads, all requiring even more

U.S. military truck graveyard near Ross River, Yukon. Although the U.S.
was permitted to remove any or all equipment after the Canol pipeline
was shut down, most remained on site. When I drove along the westward
leg of the Canol Road in 1980, rows of rusty trucks were gathered on the
roadside—a reminder that the U.S. was not responsible for removing
leftover equipment or disposing of waste material from military sites on
foreign soil. Eventually the Yukon government cleared away the discarded
equipment and covered the dumps. The toxic wastes left behind at
DEW Line sites were more problematic and more difficult to clean up.
Photographer Shelagh Grant, 1980

innovative means of advance detection and interception. Time and
again, military planners would return to drafting tables to redesign
new Arctic defence strategies to meet changing technologies, only to
discover that plans still on the drawing board were already redundant.

Without prior consultation or approval of the U.S. State Department, Congress, Canada or Denmark, American military planners
had allocated a key role for the Arctic in their postwar security strategy. Hence no one, other than the strategists themselves, anticipated
that there would be a continued presence of American forces in
Arctic Canada and Greenland after the war had ended.

(10)

POSTWAR AND
COLD WAR, 1946—91

The development of long-range aircraft has completely
changed our world. Places that are the farthest apart by ordinary
geography are much closer by air over the Pole... The Arctic
is no longer a cold spot but the "hot spot" on this planet.

COLONEL BERNT BALCHEN, USAF, 1954[1]

. . . .

CONSIDERED IN retrospect, defence activities in the Arctic during
World War II were only a harbinger of what was to come. Just
when American militarization of the region appeared in decline
at the end of the war, the trend reversed in the next decade and resulted
in an even greater U.S. presence. Although the Soviet threat of attack
during the Cold War was the major cause for the increase, there were
secondary factors involved, such as strategists' long-term plans for the
Arctic region, the Pentagon's influence on the U.S. government and
the rapidity of technological advances. The Soviet Union also factored
the Arctic into its postwar defence strategy, including increased aerial
surveillance with both offensive and defensive capabilities. Eventually nuclear-powered submarines were added, capable of launching
nuclear missiles at the United States from undetected locations. As
might be expected, both the Soviet Union and the U.S. cited the other's
military buildup to justify preparations for retaliatory action. Unfortunately, Canada and Greenland lay between the two superpowers and
in the path of the most direct routes of attack.

With advances in aviation and the dominant role played by airpower in World War II, increased American military presence in the Arctic was virtually inevitable. As five-star General H.H. Arnold of the USAAF warned in 1946, should a third world war occur "its strategic center will be the North Pole."[2] From a broader perspective, Colonel Bernt Balchen, a former commander of the U.S. forces in Greenland and later founder of SAS Airlines, claimed that "the Arctic is to us what the Mediterranean was to the Greeks and Romans—the center of the world."[3] As new technologies and world politics dramatically increased the Arctic's strategic importance, both Denmark and Canada with their limited military and financial resources would be challenged to preserve their sovereign authority.

Although the primary objective of any American defence strategy was to protect the United States, it required the cooperation of Canada and Denmark to establish U.S. military bases in the Arctic. As reflected in newspaper articles, Canadians were critical of letting the American military back into their country after paying for their anticipated departure. For this reason, once postwar agreements were negotiated and approved by the Canadian government, there were also carefully crafted press releases that downplayed the military aspect and emphasized the "joint" and civilian nature of new projects. Free Danes and Greenlanders, on the other hand, considered American forces their protectors during the war and a valued source of supplies. Although the wartime agreement with the U.S. was expected to terminate at the end of hostilities, the Danish government was equally cautious about announcing revisions to the original terms. As a result, even today the general public in both Denmark and Canada is unaware of the full extent of American activities in the Arctic during the Cold War, and possibly less informed about the precise nature of the agreements that established the Americans' right to remain there. In peacetime, as in war, the interests of national security justified the right of governments to maintain secrecy.

Although the North American Arctic was still sparsely populated in the early 1950s, there were pronounced economic and demographic differences between northern Canada, Alaska and Greenland.

Alaska with an area of almost 1.5 million square kilometres was the largest and least populated territory in the U.S. Yet compared to Greenland's land mass of 2.2 million square kilometres and Canada's Northwest Territories and Yukon in excess of 3.9 million square kilometres, Alaska was by far the smallest in terms of size but with more than double the population, estimated in 1950 to be roughly 138,000 including civilian and military. All three were dwarfed in size and population by the Soviet north, which had the longest Arctic coastline of all circumpolar countries. According to a 1964 USSR statistical handbook on the far north, the area amounts to approximately 10.9 million square kilometres with a population estimated in 1959 at over 2 million, most residing in urban areas associated with resource development. Yet like Alaska and Canada's northern territories, the vast majority of the Soviet north lay within the Subarctic region, whereas Greenland's population of just over 20,000 in 1950 was located entirely in a treeless Arctic environment.[4]

As might be expected, wartime activities had a far greater impact on the economic growth of Alaska compared to northern Canada and Greenland, largely because of the massive influx of military personnel during the war years and approximately $3 billion of expenditures on airfields, naval bases, roads, weather stations and communications networks. According to the 1939 census, Alaska's civilian population had been roughly 72,500, a number which more than doubled at the height of the war. Yet even with the postwar decline in military activities, the 1950 census recorded 112,000 civilians and another 26,000 military personnel.[5] Additional federal spending on infrastructure after the war and the infusion of new capital for Cold War projects created what Alaska historian Stephen Haycox describes as "a free world military bastion."[6]

During the postwar period, Alaska clearly placed economic development as a priority over environmental and Native concerns. In one instance, Indians' rights to their lands were disregarded when contracts were issued to lumbering companies for huge areas of forested lands to feed new pulp mills. Similarly, Aleuts, who had been forced to evacuate the Aleutian Islands after the bombing of Dutch Harbor, waited almost forty years before receiving reparation for destruction of their homes and property. Yet Eskimos, as they are still called in the U.S., benefited considerably from the war, in terms of both respect and regular wage employment, as members of the armed forces or labourers at construction sites. In 1945, an anti-discrimination bill passed by the territorial legislature paved the way for the election three years later of two Eskimos to the Alaska House of Representatives—a far cry from the experience in Arctic Canada, where Inuit were not granted a federal or territorial franchise until 1953 and in the eastern Arctic had no opportunity to exercise their vote for another six years.[7]

Civilian pressure for statehood mounted steadily after the war. In spite of resistance from the U.S. Defense Department, Congress eventually passed the Alaska Statehood Act in December 1958, with the result that on 1 January 1959, Alaska officially became America's forty-ninth state. With statehood came an unexpected challenge. The act had allotted 103 million acres to the new state. At the time of signing, however, Alaskan officials were unaware that Section IV denied the state rights to lands that might be subject to Native title, a provision included in all statehood acts since the Civil War. Native Alaskans began to file land claims, causing a temporary halt to development, including along the oil-rich North Slope of Prudhoe Bay. How the conflict was resolved and the implications for Arctic sovereignty are detailed in the next chapter.

Compared to the Alaskan experience, wartime activities in Canada's Northwest Territories and Yukon had a lesser long-term effect on local economies, with the possible exception of communities along the Alaska Highway. Arguably, there was a lasting impact on St. John's, Newfoundland, around Gander airport in Labrador and on Churchill, Manitoba. With the exception of Frobisher Bay, however, U.S. activities had relatively little effect on communities near Arctic weather stations and airfields, largely because the Canadian government discouraged, and in some cases prohibited, Inuit employment. By comparison, most Greenlanders prospered during the war, not because of military activities, but because of the trade agreement with the U.S. After the fall of Denmark in 1941, Governor Eske Brun had taken over administration of Greenland with the support of the two provincial councils. Through his careful application of American credits for fish and cryolite against purchases of supplies and material goods, island residents escaped the economic hardships suffered by other countries. Similarly, continued prosperity during the Cold War was initially related more to Denmark's support of the economy than to U.S. military activities.

In 1946, with an eye to Iceland's declared independence, the Greenland governors and councils presented the Danish Parliamentary Committee on Greenland with a number of demands, including an infusion of capital and greater independence. Denmark complied through a series of legislative acts culminating in two amendments to the Danish constitution in 1953, which officially made Greenland a province of Denmark with equal privileges for Danes and Greenlanders. The island was now divided into three districts. The heavily populated West Greenland was granted an elected council and the right to send two elected members to the Danish Parliament. With additional funding for the fishing industry, manufacturing facilities, new homes, schools and medical services, Greenlanders in all districts continued to prosper with additional benefit in later years from American purchases of local goods and services.[8]

Although not usually considered part of the western hemisphere, Iceland also played a key role in the defence of North America during the war and postwar years. Although its northern coast borders on the Arctic Circle, the island has a much warmer climate than Greenland or Arctic Canada due to the Gulf Stream surrounding it on the east and west. Iceland was a semi-autonomous colony of Denmark before the latter was occupied by German forces. Iceland was initially defended by British and Canadian forces, but in July 1941 the U.S. officially took over responsibility for its defence while sharing command with Great Britain. At the height of the war, it was estimated that British and American troops exceeded the male population of the island. Then in June 1944 Iceland declared its full independence. Two years later its government terminated the wartime defence agreement with the U.S., with the exception of certain rights to the Keflavik air base at Reykjavik. Although having no military forces of its own, Iceland became a charter member of the North Atlantic Treaty Organization (NATO) in recognition that its location at the juncture of the Atlantic and Arctic Oceans provided a natural base for the organization's naval operations. Following the outbreak of the Korean War, however, and at NATO's request, Iceland signed a new agreement in May 1951 that again placed the defence of the island in U.S. hands.

The United States faced two entirely different situations when negotiating postwar military agreements with its immediate neighbours to the north. In 1945, Denmark ratified the 1941 agreement with the U.S. with only minor changes. Although efforts were made to restore the Danish navy to its prewar status, the war had left the country without airplanes or trained pilots. In the spring of 1946, a Greenland Naval Command was stationed at Godthab and the following year Denmark requested renegotiation of the 1941 agreement. On learning more about the Soviet threat, Danish authorities realized that they lacked the financial resources, manpower, ships and planes to protect the island in the event of an attack. Pending further review, American forces were allowed continued control over weather stations and certain military bases.[9] Like Canada, Denmark also sought other means of protection and in April 1949 became a founding member of NATO. The Soviet detonation of an atomic test bomb that August created a new urgency on the part of both countries to revise the 1941 agreement.

Negotiations began immediately, resulting in a new agreement in 1951 that granted the U.S. the right to operate existing defence facilities in Greenland and to establish additional bases as needed under the provisions of the NATO Treaty.[10] In recognition of Danish sovereignty, the flags of both countries were to fly at all military bases, the division of responsibility at each site to be determined by separate agreements. In the event operation of a base became a U.S. responsibility, Danish military personnel were assigned to the American commanding officer for purposes of consultation. Otherwise, without compensation or "prejudice to the sovereignty" of Denmark, the U.S. was entitled to build and operate facilities at selected sites, improve harbours, entrances and anchorages, and control traffic of all aircraft, ships and submarines. Where Denmark retained responsibility for other defence facilities, the U.S. was allowed to attach American military personnel to the Danish command and if deemed necessary construct additional facilities and carry out activities as long as these did not interfere with Danish activities. There was no specific reference to a proposed air base at Thule, as it was covered by the terms of the general agreement, which did specify the turnover of the U.S. naval base at Grønnedal to Denmark, with provision for free access of American ships and aircraft as required.[11]

Subject to parliamentary approval in Denmark, the agreement was signed on 27 April 1951 in Copenhagen. Although specific terms might be modified by mutual consent of both countries, the agreement itself was to remain in force for the duration of the North Atlantic Treaty. A number of provisions might be interpreted as representing a certain *de facto* loss of sovereignty for Denmark. U.S. military and civilian personnel or corporations were to be exempt from Danish taxation or other levies imposed on Greenland residents. Similarly, all imported materials, equipment and other supplies for military bases were exempt from customs duties or taxes, as were goods purchased in Greenland. The U.S. government also retained legal jurisdiction over American bases with the exception of cases where Danish nationals were found guilty of committing an offence. As required, American forces, ships and aircraft were granted free movement by land, air and sea. Although Denmark agreed to provide all available topographical maps, geodetic surveys and aerial photographs, U.S. forces were granted the right to conduct additional surveys and take photographs if needed. Of particular note were the provisions of Article 6, which stated that "every effort will be made to avoid any contact between United States personnel and the local population which the Danish authorities do not consider desirable for the conduct of operation under this Agreement"—a provision that gave legal authority in 1953 for relocation of Inuit families residing near the new Thule Air Base to Qaanaaq, over 100 kilometres to the north.[12]

Perhaps to avoid a scenario similar to Canada's repayment for American facilities built on Canadian soil during World War II, the 1951 agreement between the U.S. and Denmark clearly defined the terms of ownership in the event of termination. Specifically, all facilities and equipment at military bases provided by the U.S. "shall remain the property of the Government of the United States of America." All removable property and facilities erected by the U.S. "may be removed from Greenland free of any restriction or disposed of in Greenland" in consultation with Danish authorities. Of particular significance to current problems of contaminated military waste sites in the Arctic, the agreement also stated that "any areas under this agreement need not be left in the condition in which they were at the time they were thus made available."[13] Signing of the agreement allowed for immediate construction of a large air base at Thule in a sparsely populated area of northwest Greenland, as well as reactivation of the U.S. air bases at Sondre Stromfjord and Narsarssuaq.

The year 1951 also marked the formation of the Royal Danish Air Force after it acquired surplus Spitfires and a Catalina from NATO countries. The Catalina was used primarily for surveillance along the Greenland coast, with new planes added over the course of the next twenty years. The Royal Danish Navy also employed frigates and other inspection vessels to protect the Greenland fisheries. Volunteer sled patrols, which played such a key role during the war in locating German weather stations in East Greenland, were reorganized in 1950 to become SIRUS, the official military sled patrol responsible for surveillance of the uninhabited east coast northward from Scoresby Sound. When added to the joint participation at many weather stations and quasi-observer status at U.S. bases, the Danish contribution to Greenland's defence was not inconsequential.[14]

By comparison, negotiating postwar agreements with Canada proved more difficult because of public sensitivity toward any potential threat to its Arctic sovereignty, a view shared by bureaucrats and politicians. With the repayment in 1944 for wartime facilities built in northern Canada, the government gave official notice that it intended to remove all vestiges of the American wartime presence. The U.S.

War Department, however, was equally unwilling to accept an end to its active role in the Canadian Arctic. Even prior to the end of the war, the U.S. chiefs of staff were pressing for a peacetime security plan to replace the wartime ABC-22 agreement on joint defence, a position strongly supported by senior Canadian military officers but not by Canada's political leaders.[15] The Permanent Joint Board of Defence (PJBD) continued to act as the conduit for all American proposals. The direct link between the board and the Cabinet War Committee (renamed the Cabinet Defence Committee after the war) also meant that Canadian politicians were privy to knowledge of military plans well in advance of their U.S. counterparts and in some cases, the State Department. Yet because of the secrecy attached to national security, the cabinet committee's discussions on American plans and their implications for Arctic sovereignty were not necessarily shared with the full cabinet or members of Parliament.

In February 1945, the Canadian Working Committee on Post War Hostilities presented a position paper to the PJBD on possible future defence relationships with the U.S. The Canadian War Cabinet approved the concept of continued joint cooperation in principle, but only with the proviso that all military facilities in Canada and New-foundland remain effectively under Canadian control. By the end of the year, however, the situation had deteriorated. Not only had Stalin acquired firm control of portions of eastern Europe formerly occu-pied by Germany, but Soviet defector Igor Gouzenko had revealed a major spy network throughout North America and plans by Stalin to develop a nuclear bomb. Initial hopes that the UN could stem further aggression now seemed remote with the USSR holding a veto on the Security Council. Resigned to the inevitable, in December the Cana-dian government agreed to further discussions on a mutual defence arrangement.

Central to the U.S. military's postwar security strategy was devel-opment of a network of weather stations and airfields across the Arctic from Alaska to Greenland. The plans originated in a wartime study conducted by MIT and sponsored by the Research Board for National Security. The Arctops Project, short for "Arctic topography," envisioned a network of Arctic weather stations and airfields as the key component of a major scientific research program designed to collect information on the region and its potential resources through mapping and aerial photography, experimentation with communications and radar technology, as well as inventories of wildlife and minerals. These permanent stations would also form the basis of future "great circle transpolar flyways." The potential of commercial benefits was likely desirable to sell the idea to the U.S. Congress, but the rationale if made public would have raised red flags for both Danish and Canadian governments. Almost as an afterthought, the report suggested that approvals from Canada and Denmark would be "essential since these latter governments control the majority of the land mass under consideration." [16] To emphasize the urgency, an attached circumpolar map showed the large number of weather stations in the European and Soviet Arctic compared to the few in North America.

Perhaps in hopes of allaying Canadian concerns of an increasing American military presence, the weather station proposal took on a civilian character in early January 1946 when Lieutenant-Colonel Charles Hubbard left the USAAF to join the U.S. Weather Bureau in Washington. As a result of his intense lobbying, a bill authorizing construction of a joint weather station network finally passed Congress on 12 February that same year. Within two months, Hubbard had finalized specifications for the buildings and transport requirements, operational timetables and even lists of personnel. Unlike the civilian proposal presented to Congress, however, his working plans depended on USAF planes and personnel along with assistance from the U.S. Navy and Coast Guard, with the military having the final decision on priorities and alternate arrangements. As explained by Hubbard, "It seems probable that the considerations of national security which lie behind the authorization for an Arctic weather network are of more immediate concern than the procurement of meteorological data for civilian purposes." [17] Assuming that Canadian approval would be forthcoming, Hubbard began purchasing necessary supplies and loading the navy supply ships anchored in Boston Harbor.

Hubbard assumed that the joint weather station network would be an all-American project, paid with U.S. funds, utilizing U.S. equipment, transportation, manpower and surplus supplies left over from the war. He mistakenly believed that any participatory interest Ottawa might have was a matter of "national prestige," hence the inclusion of "joint" in the name. He had also assumed that future plans were such that it was doubtful if the Canadian government could afford joint participation over the longer term.[18] Hubbard's arguments sounded logical from an American viewpoint, but he greatly misunderstood Canadian desire for involvement. It was far more than a matter of "national prestige."

In the spring of 1946, the postwar Cabinet Defence Committee (CDC) was already debating the political and sovereignty implications of the proposed Basic Security Plan prepared by the Canada-United States Military Cooperation Committee. A "general appreciation" of continued mutual defence cooperation had been submitted to the CDC as the thirty-fifth recommendation of the PJBD, along with a detailed planning document. The latter spelled out the details of a security scheme that included an extensive radar system across northern Canada, an expanded network of airfields, interceptor aircraft and other anti-aircraft defences. Phase II of the plan proposed setting up a "Combined Air Defence Headquarters with operational control of all continental air defence forces," essentially the basis of the North American Air Defence Command (NORAD) agreement signed twelve years later.[19] The Basic Security Plan was far more ambitious than the wartime agreement and ultimately involved far greater costs and manpower. Moreover, it was designed to be permanent.

Because of its alleged civilian purpose, the U.S. Weather Bureau's proposal had been submitted separately to the Canadian government, but the CDC immediately recognized the part it played in the overall plan and refused to consider it in isolation. As a consequence, a decision on the joint weather station network proposal was deferred for a year to allow further consideration and revisions to the overall security plan. Postponement of the weather station on Melville Island was met with enthusiasm in the Canadian press, as evidenced by an article in the *Financial Post* on 29 July 1946, under the headline "Ottawa Scotches U.S. Plan to Man Weather Bases in the Canadian Arctic." The news was fed to the press, perhaps to quell criticism in an earlier article condemning the security proposals, titled "Canada Another Belgium in U.S. Air Bases Proposal." Other papers and speeches picked up the theme and criticism mounted with repeated references to the "Maginot Line."[20]

Reports that the United States Air Coordinating Committee planned to probe unexplored regions of the Archipelago in hopes of finding and claiming undiscovered islands only heightened fears of Canada's senior politicians, particularly the suggestion that the committee should consult the State Department as to whether the U.S. government would support such a claim if occupied by an American weather station. In response, the legal division of External Affairs warned against any public assertion of the Sector Principle lest it imply doubts as to the validity of Canada's sovereignty. A report from the Department of National Defence added to the caution, stating that because Canada had not attempted to effectively occupy lands in the High Arctic, claims here were "at the best tenuous and weak." Moreover, Canada could "no longer reasonably expect to maintain her Arctic territories in state of vacuum, and hope at the same time to preserve her sovereignty over them in absentia . . . [She] must now either herself provide essential facilities and services in her Arctic territories or provide them cooperatively, or abandon almost all substantial basis to her claims upon them."[21] The report went on to recommend that for any new facility built in the region, "full title and control should be retained by Canada, and this fact should be well publicized," and that "a majority of the personnel employed should be Canadian." Concerns were also raised that refusal to cooperate might encourage the U.S. to claim some uninhabited islands "as their own territory by right of occupation."[22]

While the "general appreciation" of continued mutual defence cooperation was approved in principle, the detailed security plan was rejected. Senior officials in Ottawa were faced with a dilemma. According to James Eayrs, "The Soviet Union was the enemy, war a possibility, bombers were a threat, the polar corridor the route."[23] What had once been a simple question of protecting Arctic sovereignty was now perceived as a threat to Canada's independence as a nation. In retrospect, former diplomat John W. Holmes saw the Arctic frontier as having created a double-edged sword for Canadian security policy, in which the objective was not only to protect the country against a potential aggressor, but also to defend itself "on another plane against their defenders," in this case the U.S.[24] Holmes had also reminded Canadians earlier that "history did not make the United States and Canada friends; it made them natural antagonists from the eighteenth to the nineteenth century. It took the Germans and then the Russians to make them allies."[25] To find consensus between the two countries required discussion between the president and the prime minister, followed by negotiations between members of the U.S. State Department and Canada's External Affairs.

Meanwhile numerous other projects had been forwarded to the CDC for approval, including continued U.S. operation and expansion of existing Arctic airfields, remobilization of the Goose Bay base, revitalization of existing weather stations, more aerial reconnaissance flights, naval operations and a new chain of loran radar stations.[26] Hubbard's frustration mounted over Canada's failure to approve the weather station on Melville Island, as equipment and supplies had already been loaded on USN ships. All other necessary clearances had been approved, including USAF flights between Alaska and Iceland (Operation Polaris), expansion of the loran program, continued operation of existing Arctic weather stations and USAF control of the airfields at Mingan, Chimo and Frobisher. Also approved were the USN reconnaissance and scientific explorations utilizing the marine landing parties and aircraft of Task Force 68, sometimes referred to as Operation Nanook.

Since plans for the summer of 1946 included setting up a fuel cache and airfield near the Danish weather station at Thule (Bluie West 6) in Greenland, Hubbard decided to offload supplies and personnel for the proposed Melville Island station at Thule. The USN Task Force 68 was composed of two cargo ships, an aircraft tender, three long-range flying boats, an icebreaker and an ice-strengthened survey ship, all of which arrived on 22 July 1946 at Thule on North Star Bay. Nearby were a small Danish weather station and a trading post once managed by Knud Rasmussen. The ubiquitous Charles Hubbard was on location to direct operations. Navy personnel and construction crews worked together to erect Quonset huts and prefabricated buildings, while army engineers prepared an emergency landing field. The eleven members of the U.S. Weather Bureau assigned to the new station were joined by eleven technicians from the Danish station, who provided general supplies but no equipment. The official placed in charge of the Thule station was an American. The USN task force then escorted Hubbard on an extensive sea and air reconnaissance of northern Greenland and the outer islands of the Archipelago. The entire mission was accomplished in less than six weeks.[27]

Hubbard's otherwise detailed report did not mention whether the U.S. had permission from Denmark to build the new airfield or whether it was assumed under the old 1941 agreement. Nonetheless no one thought to notify the Danish weather station of their pending arrival; staff thought they were being invaded when the flotilla of supply ships arrived in North Star Bay.[28] The fact that the following year Denmark suddenly requested that American bases be returned to Danish control suggests the likelihood that official permission had not been granted.

Not to be upstaged by American activities planned for the summer of 1946, the Canadian Army was also active in the Arctic that year. Beginning in February, the army carried out an overland expedition, code-named Operation Musk-Ox, to test cold-weather clothing and equipment. The long trek originated at Churchill, circled northwest to Victoria Island, then south to Great Bear Lake, and ended at Port Nelson in May. The entire operation was said to have involved about 400 men and estimated to have cost millions. Actual participants on the trek, however, numbered fewer than fifty and involved only ten vehicles especially adapted to polar conditions, including DC-6 tractors, American Studebaker M-29 Weasels and Canadian armoured snowmobiles. The RCAF also carried out an aerial reconnaissance

USN Task Force 68 unloading supplies and equipment to build a new
airfield and weather station at Thule in northern Greenland, summer 1946.
Danish staff manning the existing weather station were not informed
of the U.S. plans and initially thought they were being invaded.

National Archives, Washington, DC (NA), Donated Material Group (DMG)

Charles Hubbard Collection, XCJH, 17/7/1

that summer, photographing an area covering over 400 square miles
of the Canadian Arctic, reportedly "to establish a wide ranging Canadian presence."[29] There were no reports of previously undiscovered
islands from either Canadian or American sources.

The question of Canada's commitment to a joint defence agreement remained unresolved that fall. With Canada's large size, small
population and limited financial resources, the risks attached to military dependence upon a powerful neighbour at times seemed greater
than the possibility of an enemy attack from the north. U.S. military
strategists were of a different mind. Having little sympathy for Canadian sensitivities about sovereignty, they believed that if Canada was
unable to adequately defend its Arctic, then surely its government

would be grateful for U.S. protection. They claimed to have no particular wish to own the land, they just wanted use of it, exclusively if
possible. If they were refused permission, then perhaps there were
unclaimed islands which could be occupied for the purpose.[30]

The USAF Intelligence Service was called upon to report on the
"Canadian problem," with specific reference to the legality of Canada's
sovereign claims to St. Patrick Island, Melville Island and Grant Land,
the latter known to Canadians as northern Ellesmere Island. The
report warned that based on precedence Canadian jurisdiction over
the entire Archipelago would likely be sustained in an international
court, but suggested that "the United States could present a fairly
well documented legal defense in support of any action its Government wished to take" with regard to the uninhabited islands. While
acknowledging grave political implications of such action that might
be interpreted "as a usurpation of Canadian territorial rights," the
report suggested that the U.S. would not "be compelled to remain idle
if it seemed probable that penetration of this area was threatened by
a potential enemy." It concluded, however, that the immediate objective would be to gain Canada's full cooperation by "assurance that
the United States has no intention, now or in the future, of claiming
sovereignty over any section of the Canadian Arctic." For U.S. military planners, the prospect of leaving the Arctic unprotected until
hostilities appeared inevitable was unthinkable, particularly in light
of the events leading to World War II still fresh in memory. Much of
the Archipelago was unknown territory, requiring research, mapping and surveys. Arctic equipment must be developed and tested,
and men trained in the techniques of polar warfare. Thus the report
concluded that an all-out effort must be made to gain Canada's cooperation, even if it meant delaying plans for a joint air command and
an offensive air base in Arctic Canada as set out in the Air Annex that
had accompanied the Basic Security Plan.[31]

The U.S. State Department, however, was not prepared to discuss
sovereignty issues in formal negotiations, lest it lead to an attempt to
obtain American acceptance of the Sector Principle.[32] As noted earlier, legal experts in Canada's External Affairs Department were of the

same mind, albeit for different reasons, and recommended that officials avoid disputes over validity of Canada's sector claims until the Archipelago was fully occupied. Reflecting the urgency of the matter, the U.S. State Department arranged for a meeting at the White House between Prime Minister King and President Truman to discuss the future defence of North America. Each was provided in advance with the agenda items and his government's positions.

At the outset, Truman stressed the importance of an adequate continental defence system and how it might be explained "without mention of boundaries." He offered assurances that the United States would assume "an equitable portion of the cost," that Canada's relationship in the Commonwealth would be recognized and that any arrangement would be in accord with the principles of the UN. King was unusually candid about concerns of sovereignty and the negative attitude of the Canadian public toward militarization of the Arctic. Truman responded with the suggestion that the civilian aspect of the weather stations might be emphasized and that the additional air bases in Canada "could be established under the cloak of civil aviation, but in such a manner that they could rapidly be taken over for military purposes." In the end, the two heads of government agreed to proceed with final negotiations, to be held on a diplomatic rather than military level.[33] Had King wished to pay the full cost of defence facilities built on Canadian soil, the timing could not have been worse. Because of rising imports from the U.S. and falling exports to the U.S. and Europe, there was only one way to fund social welfare measures such as baby bonuses and unemployment insurance promised in the 1945 election and that was through drastic cuts in military spending.[34] More than likely the American president was fully aware of the situation.

Political negotiations followed, with agreement on the terms finalized on 17 December 1946 and formally announced on 12 February 1947. To avoid possible conflict with the UN Charter and adverse reaction from the Soviets, it was agreed that the public announcement would be discreet and general, referring only to an agreement in principle. It was also agreed that initial phases of defence preparation would be carried out, where possible, "under civilian cover," including the weather stations, loran radar installations and various research projects. Accordingly, the Prime Minister's announcement to Parliament emphasized that there was no formal treaty or pact, nor would there be "Maginot lines of large scale defence projects." Instead, he defined the northern program as "primarily a civilian one to which contributions are made by the armed forces." [35] For Pentagon strategists, it was the first hurdle of many in the years to come, but it was also the most important as both countries knew that it would be virtually impossible to reverse the agreement. As noted by Canadian political scientist Andrew Richter, the Declaration of Principles on Defence Cooperation as agreed upon in 1946 would "guide the framework of North American defence" until 1958 and establishment of the North American Air Defence Command (NORAD). [36]

On 28 January 1947, the Cabinet Defence Committee approved the Joint Arctic Weather Station program (JAWS), which would take place over the next three years and include nine stations in all. The station on Banks Island was removed from the priority list, as were plans to enlarge facilities along the Mackenzie airway. Instead, the U.S. Weather Bureau now planned to use Goose Bay and Thule as supply bases. Canada agreed to pay the costs of permanent facilities and supply half the staff. There was no formal exchange of notes. Instead arrangements were to be agreed upon at the beginning of each year. Officially, the "officer in charge" was a Canadian; in practice there was also an American "executive officer" unofficially in charge. Charles Hubbard continued to organize and supervise the construction, maintenance and supply of these weather stations, in cooperation with the USN and the USAF. [37]

The JAWS agreement was not announced in Parliament until March 1947, with C.D. Howe as minister of reconstruction and supply providing a rather misleading version of the situation: "The United States has therefore undertaken to assist Canada in the establishment and operation of these northern stations which will, of course, be under the control of the Canadian government which will supply the officers in charge." [38] To its credit, Canada gradually increased its participation in the program, but not until 1972 did the RCAF and the Department of Transport assume full responsibility for resupply of the weather stations.

Once Canadian approval had been granted, plans went into effect immediately. On 7 April, the stores and equipment cached at Thule were airlifted to the west coast of Ellesmere Island, where the Eureka weather station became the first in the new JAWS network. By 7 PM that night, a Jamesway hut had been erected and a rough airfield cleared, with radio and meteorological equipment fully operational. As per the agreement, four Canadians and four Americans were assigned to the station.[39]

That summer, Hubbard joined USN Task Force 69, which included USS *Wyandot* and *Whitewood*, along with the icebreaker *Edisto*. The first task was to resupply Thule and Eureka, then build a new station and airstrip on Melville Island, before setting up an automatic weather station near Dundas Harbour. When heavy ice conditions prevented the task force from reaching Melville Island, Hubbard reluctantly selected an alternative site at Resolute Bay on Cornwallis Island. Within two weeks of the first delivery to Resolute, almost 300 tons of supplies and heavy machinery had been unloaded and construction was well under way on the buildings, airfield and a two-mile graded road connecting the landing strip to the base site. For the first time, three Canadian observers joined over a hundred American officers, enlisted men and construction crews. Another first was use of three Canadian prefabricated wooden buildings to house regular staff and equipment. The Americans supplied five Quonset huts, two Jamesways, construction vehicles, equipment and all technical apparatus and supplies for weather and radio communications. Although Resolute was a second choice, it proved to be an excellent site. Along with Thule, it became a major centre of supply operations for the satellite stations.[40]

The successful construction of Eureka by airlift prompted similar plans in the spring of 1948, for Mould Bay on Prince Patrick Island and for Isachsen Island just west of Ellef Ringnes. Additional sites were explored, then rejected for reasons of cost, inaccessibility and doubts about available Canadian personnel. Air reconnaissance began early that spring, followed by the arrival of men and equipment, with the two new stations completed before summer. The USN task force that year, assisted by two icebreakers, *Edisto* and *Eastwind,* each with two helicopters, had hoped to supply all four stations and select two more sites, until ice damage to *Edisto* forced a change of plans. By air, however, a promising location was identified at the northernmost tip of Ellesmere Island, where construction supplies were cached before the ships dropped off supplies for Eureka and Resolute.[41]

Meanwhile, there was growing concern in Ottawa about the increasing numbers of American personnel stationed in the Canadian Arctic. Asked if the wartime weather stations were still under U.S. military control rather than civilian as requested, the USAF admitted that American control continued at Clyde River, Arctic Bay and Frobisher Bay on Baffin Island, and at Chimo, Mingan, Indian House and Mecatina in northern Quebec. When notified that Canada planned to take over these stations, U.S. Major-General Guy Henry expressed surprise, as he doubted that Canada could provide adequately trained meteorologists. The situation differed at Goose Bay, where the RCAF officially operated the air base, even though there were upward of 500 USAF officers and men remaining by permission of the Newfoundland government.[42]

To coordinate Canadian military and civilian activities in northern Canada and monitor sovereignty issues, in January 1949 yet another senior-level committee was established, vaguely similar in structure and purpose to the 1920s Northern Advisory Board, but with major military representation reflecting the changing character of the Canadian Arctic. The Advisory Committee on Northern Development (ACND) consisted of the deputy ministers of transport and of mines and resources, the under-secretary of state for external affairs, the secretary to the cabinet, the Canadian chairman of the PJBD and the chiefs of general staff and air staff. Their mandate was to "advise the government on questions of policy relating to civilian and military undertakings in northern Canada and to provide for effective coordination of all government activities in the area."[43]

As outlined in the opening remarks at the first ACND meeting, coordination was considered key to maximizing Canadian control of defence activities. Also implied was responsibility for monitoring the progress of "re-Canadianizing" American defence facilities. After five sessions, at times marked by divisive debate, the committee ceased to meet when it was discovered that for security reasons the answers to questions concerning the number of American troops stationed in the Arctic would not be made available to members of civilian departments.[44] Yet Ottawa was determined to increase Canadian participation, despite a seemingly continual stream of new projects being forwarded for approval.

In addition to the joint weather station program in 1947, the Canadian government also approved three new loran stations, again with the understanding that American control would be transferred when trained Canadian personnel became available. This time, Canada was responsible for the buildings and their construction, with the U.S. supplying construction equipment, vehicles, technical equipment and advice, as well as commanding the airlift. Loran technology was a wartime invention, an electronic navigational aid for pilots in unfamiliar territory. Operation Beetle was the code name for the airlift supplying the new station located at Cambridge Bay on Victoria Island. Churchill was designated its supply base. That summer, two RCAF North Stars and fourteen USAF C-54s transported over 400 tons of equipment and supplies.[45]

Other loran stations were built at Kittigazuit on the eastern shore of the Mackenzie Delta, and at Sawmill Bay on Great Bear Lake. Two additional stations were located in Alaska. The equipment for the experimental system was inordinately costly. Together, the three new stations were reported to have cost well over $50 million, with the U.S. paying the major portion. Not surprisingly, the project was cancelled in 1950. Officially it was stated that benefits did not justify costs. Unofficially the new version that had been developed to overcome magnetic interference proved inadequate and inaccurate.[46] That same year approval was granted for the first of three new radar lines, the Pinetree Line, which initially included sites in British Columbia, southern Ontario and Quebec, and the Atlantic provinces, irregularly north of the 50th parallel, then north along the Labrador coast to Frobisher Bay. Construction began in 1951 and was completed by 1954, with the U.S. agreeing to supply two-thirds of the manpower and costs, estimated at $450 million.[47]

In the postwar period, independent polar research had been relatively minimal compared to wartime government and military studies and was conducted primarily under the auspices of the newly formed Arctic Institute of North America (AINA). Based in Montreal, the AINA also sponsored studies by Canadian government agencies, under contract through various departments or the Defence Research Board. The American military, on the other hand, provided its scientists with unprecedented financial support and equipment for a variety of research and exploration. In 1947, the Arctic, Desert, and Tropic Information Center was reactivated to provide a research program for the USAF. Understandably, its primary focus would be on the Arctic for the next ten, perhaps twenty, years. The earliest projects, notably Mint Julep and Ice Cube, studied glacier and sea ice for use as temporary landing fields. Other experiments were carried out by the army and navy. The highly secret Devon Ice Cap Project in 1948, for instance, involved dynamiting the glacier and touched off urgent inquiries as to its purpose, including from Inuit hunters who thought they were being bombed. Subsequently, a memo from the Canadian Embassy in Washington suggested that the U.S. Army might defer renewal of the project.[48]

A number of permanent research and training stations were established in the Arctic regions, three of note in 1947: the Joint Canadian-United States Experimental Station at Fort Churchill; the USN Arctic Research Laboratory at Point Barrow, Alaska; and the USAF Arctic Polar Survival and Indoctrination School at Nome, Alaska.[49] At the end of the war, the American air base at Fort Churchill had been turned over to the Canadian Army and the RCAF, with the understanding that it would be a joint research and training centre for Arctic warfare techniques. In the summer of 1946, American authorities asked that Canada expand and upgrade facilities to include housing for an additional 500 American personnel, as well as married quarters, schools, a new water system and better sanitation. Aware of Canada's budget limitations, the U.S. War Department agreed to provide financial assistance to meet costs, and the U.S. Army Corps of Engineers furnished the construction crew. By 1950, further expansion resulted in accommodation for 1,299 men and 200 married couples. The Churchill location was preferred over the training centre at Fairbanks because of the rail link, the more severe Arctic climate, the shorter distance from the central and eastern U.S. and longer daylight hours.[50] The base also included small rocket-launching sites, under control of the Canadian Army until 1959, at which time the range was turned over to the U.S. Army. In 1966, the facilities at Churchill were transferred again, this time to the National Research Council of Canada.[51]

There were numerous other U.S. military studies and expeditions in the Arctic during this period, many identified by intriguing code names such as Operation Frostbite, Operation Nanook, Task Force Frigid, Task Force Williwaw, Exercise Firestep, Project Ski Jump, Project Icicle and Project Snowman. Some were conducted annually, such as the USN task force expeditions that supplied weather stations and air bases under the code name Operation Nanook, and the USAF weather reconnaissance, or Ptarmigan flights.[52] At that time, the Canadian Army Signal Corps operated only one radio station in the High Arctic, at Cambridge Bay on the southern shore of Victoria Island. Canadian Army exercises also took place during those years, such as Operation Musk-Ox in 1946, referred to earlier, as well as Exercise Moccasin in 1947–48, and Exercise Igloo, Exercise Sun Dog 1 and Operation Ennadai in 1948–49, but they focussed on equipment-testing and survival techniques and did not involve great numbers of men, ships or planes.[53] By comparison, American military exercises seemed massive, like the USN Operation Microwex off the Alaskan coast in February 1949, involving 18,000 officers and men, 30 ships, 2 aircraft carriers, 59 airplanes and 2 helicopters. Others involved lesser but still sizable manpower, such as the U.S. Army's Task Force Frigid near Fairbanks, Alaska, in 1947 with 1,500 officers and men, and Exercise Firestep in April 1951 with 1,000 men from the U.S. Army 82nd Airborne Division alone, assisted by USAF and U.S. Army ground forces.[54]

If American military exercises were held on or over Canadian territory, Ottawa asked that observers be invited. Press releases to the Canadian media always noted the presence of observers, sometimes described as "with Canadian participation." Not until February 1950 and Exercise Sweetbriar along the Alaska-Yukon border did Canadians participate in equitable numbers. In this instance, over 5,000 men were involved, almost half Canadian, utilizing 978 motor vehicles and 100 planes. According to Dr. O.M. Solandt of Canada's Defence Research Board, Sweetbriar not only allowed for testing of the latest equipment and technologies, "it also provided a most important opportunity for gaining experience in joint and combined planning for a truly integrated Canada-United States Army-Air Force Command."[55] American pressure for a unified U.S.-Canadian command continued, with full support from the RCAF, but was strongly resisted by the Canadian government.

Meanwhile, another experiment was under way. In 1948, Colonel Bernt Balchen had been recalled to active service and was stationed at Elmendorf Air Base near Anchorage, Alaska, to train the 10th Air Squadron in search and rescue techniques on the frozen icepack. As part of the 1950 exercise, a crew landed on an ice floe north of Barter Island in the Beaufort Sea and erected a radio station and research lab.[56] This was not a first in terms of originality as Ivan Papanin had undertaken a similar experiment for the Soviet Union before the war. From a polar station set up on a small island north of Franz Josef Land, Papanin had flown to the North Pole and landed on a large ice floe on 21 May 1937, where he set up a research station with electrical power provided by a windmill. After drifting southward toward the eastern Greenland coast, he was evacuated nine months later. In 1950, the Soviets resumed erection of research stations on the drift ice, usually beginning north and east of Wrangel Island and numbered North Pole 2, 3 and so forth. A few drifted past the North Pole and ended up off the shores of northeastern Greenland.[57]

USAF Ice Island Research Station Charlie in 1959. Recognizing
that the Russians had been establishing research stations on
large ice floes since 1950, the USAF followed suit. After success with
Fletcher's Ice Island, another was set up in 1959, named Charlie.
This time, the project ended in near disaster when the large floe suddenly
began to break up, necessitating an emergency evacuation.
NA-DMG, William S. Carlson Collection, XWSC-TK 675

In an attempt to keep pace with Soviet research, the U.S. Navy set
up oceanography stations on the sea ice, first Project Ski Jump I in 1951,
followed the next year by Ski Jump II. Also in 1952, the USAF established a more permanent scientific station on a large ice island that had
broken off from the coast of Ellesmere Island, five miles by nine miles
and floating some 100 miles south of the North Pole. Known as T-3
or Fletcher's Island, this particular site was occupied on and off over
the next seven years. In 1959, a similar station was erected on Charlie, which ended in near disaster when the ice floe suddenly began to
break up, necessitating an emergency evacuation. The success of these
ventures and similar Soviet ice stations that had floated into Canadian
waters raised new concerns in Ottawa for its sovereignty over territorial waters and specifically—who owns the sea ice?[58]

In 1949 there had been a temporary halt on expansion of the weather station program, partly due to bad weather but also because of a shortage of manpower, supplies and aircraft and the loss of the icebreaker *Eastwind,* which was disabled in a fire. That same year, heavy ice conditions prevented the naval task force from reaching Eureka, Mould Bay and Isachsen, necessitating resupply by air. But the lull in activity was only temporary. After this success in airlifting supplies to remote locations, plans for 1950 included yet another first—the most northerly permanent weather station in the world—at Alert on the northern tip of Ellesmere Island. A new pattern of supply was also established. The USN task force ships would only be required to stop at Resolute and Thule to unload cargo, which would then be airlifted to remote weather stations: from Resolute to resupply Mould Bay and Isachsen, and from Thule for Alert and Eureka. Now larger than the eighty-bed Thule Air Base, Resolute could accommodate over 100 military personnel and transients. With the RCAF announcing it would assist in the airlift for the first time, there were a total of 136 flights carrying over 700 tons of cargo and involving thirty-three officers and eighty-eight enlisted men.[59]

An aura of excitement surrounded the establishment of Alert, noticeable even in the reports by veteran Weather Bureau chief Charles Hubbard. Along with three other American officers and one Canadian, Hubbard was with the initial party that landed on the ice near Alert on Easter Sunday, 9 April 1950. All supplies left by the reconnaissance party two years earlier, including a tractor, were found to be in excellent condition, so work began immediately to prepare a temporary shelter and landing site for the large cargo planes. By mid-April planes began arriving with workers and supplies, nonstop around the clock. Within weeks all building and housekeeping supplies, 450 drums of diesel and motor gasoline, another D-2 Caterpillar tractor, radio and scientific equipment and two years' supply of food had been unloaded and stored. The temporary airstrip on the ice proved too dangerous by late May, requiring remaining supplies to be dropped by parachute. By late August, a gravel runway had been completed and all major buildings erected, with technical services in place and functioning. The outermost limits of Arctic Canada were now circled by weather stations and, more importantly, by permanent radio communications. For all intents and purposes, the exercise appeared to be an unqualified success, an extraordinary achievement for science and man in his assault on the formidable High Arctic.[60]

But the mission's success was never celebrated, for on 31 July 1950 an RCAF Lancaster crashed during a parachute drop at Alert, bringing instant death to its occupants. Aboard were eight Canadians and one American—Colonel Charles J. Hubbard. Attempts to remove the bodies failed when a Canso sent to bring them back also crashed. Thus Hubbard, who had spent the last decade of his life designing and supervising construction of the Arctic weather stations, would be buried at the site of his last achievement, the most northerly permanent post in the world.[61] Alert remains today a tribute to his tireless devotion to Arctic meteorology. Perhaps equally significant, this was the last official joint Canadian-American weather station built. In time, Alert was turned over to the RCAF, but even today the station is supplied through the USAF base at Thule, Greenland.

Meanwhile, there were far more ambitious plans afoot. Colonel Bernt Balchen, when stationed in Alaska, was convinced that the U.S. would require a large air base in the High Arctic from which to deploy interceptor aircraft as well as search and rescue squadrons. From his previous experience in Greenland, he believed that the Thule weather station offered the best site and could be used in future commercial routes. To test his theory, he suggested a reconnaissance flight over the Pole to Thule and on to Norway. With approval from General Hoyt S. Vandenberg, Air Force Chief of Staff, on 23 May 1949 Balchen and his crew left Ladd airfield in Alaska aboard a Douglas C-54 and headed for Norway. Upon nearing the North Pole, Balchen took over the controls and circled twice before heading to Thule, the site he had recommended to General Arnold in 1942 as a prime location for a large runway. On return from Oslo, he flew non-stop to New York City to prove theoretically that both New York and Washington, DC, were vulnerable to a Soviet attack if the USSR established a base in Norway. In a press conference, he also argued that civil aircraft

The original weather station at Alert, c1959. The site chosen for
the last in a series of Joint Arctic Weather Stations (JAWS) was in Dumbell
Bay on the northern coast of Ellesmere Island. Initially operated jointly
by the Canadian Department of Transport and the U.S. Weather Bureau,
the adjacent wireless station was taken over by the Royal Canadian Corps
of Signals in 1958, and in 1972, responsibility for the entire operation
was turned over to Canada. The military component increased during the
Cold War, with population peaking at over 200 in the 1980s. Nine
crosses marking gravesites on a hill alongside the runway are a stark
reminder of the crash of an RCAF Lancaster in the summer of 1950,
which took the lives of eight Canadians and one American—
Charles J. Hubbard, chief of the U.S. Weather Bureau.

Courtesy troywoodintarsia.com, photo by the late George Dingwall, WO2

(*inset*) The nine crosses.

Courtesy David R. Gray, photographer

could make the trip but would require search and rescue facilities and an emergency landing base in the High Arctic. That December, he presented his proposals to U.S. Secretary of the Air Force Stuart Symington and argued the urgent need for a joint USAF-RCAF command to execute search and rescue operations. By now, the Soviets had successfully detonated their first atomic test bomb.[62]

With the Korean War occupying the U.S. chiefs of staff, it was not until January 1951 that Symington's successor, Thomas K. Finletter, ordered Balchen to report to the Pentagon as a special adviser to study the "feasibility and desirability of construction, operating, and protecting bomber staging bases" in the Arctic. As it happened, Balchen had already written a detailed report on the merits of the Thule site for the Glover Committee, a group of strategic planners meeting in December 1950 to determine locations of future Arctic air bases. As a result, Balchen's report had already been approved when he arrived in Washington.

With Finletter's full support, Balchen was named Air Force project officer for Operation Blue Jay, the name given the top-secret project. As the U.S. Army Corps of Engineers began preparing for the massive undertaking, diplomatic negotiations were initiated with Denmark for permission. By the time a new defence agreement for Greenland was signed by the two governments in April 1951, Balchen, accompanied by 400 army engineers and contractors, had been at Thule for almost two months to survey what would become the largest air base in the entire Arctic. Under terms of the agreement, Denmark had set aside 339,000 acres or 287 square miles for the U.S. air base.[63]

The advance party was followed in July by 120 ships carrying 300,000 tons of cargo and 12,000 men, while airlines contracted by the USAF carried an additional 19,000 passengers and cargo. Working around the clock, in sixty-two days the men had built row upon row of barracks, fuel storage tanks, warehouses, office buildings, heated hangars and a 200-by-10,000-foot runway, which had its first test landing in mid-September. A year later, four F-9 interceptor fighters arrived and the air base was declared fully operational. Buildings were constructed with preformed Clements panels, used

COLONEL BERNT BALCHEN, USAAF (1899–1973). The Norwegian-born polar aviator came to the U.S. in 1931. Joining the USAAF in 1941 as commander of Task Force 8, Balchen supervised construction of the Sondre Stromfjord airfield in Greenland and directed a number of dramatic rescues of planes downed on the icecap. Later he went overseas to provide assistance to the Norwegian underground. From 1948 to 1951 he commanded the 10th Air Rescue Squadron headquartered in Alaska, until he was transferred to Washington where he planned and directed construction of Thule AB in 1952. Allegedly he was denied promotion because he dared to suggest in his autobiography that Admiral Richard Byrd did not actually fly over the North Pole. Upon retirement in 1956, he continued to serve the USAF on special assignments. Awarded high honours in many countries, Balchen is one of the few Norwegian-born to be buried in Arlington National Cemetery—in a plot next to Admiral Richard Byrd.

Image 50531295: Hank Walker/Time Life Pictures/Getty Images

commercially for large walk-in refrigerators. A 1,000-foot pier was constructed from eight barges towed from the Gulf of Mexico, placed on caissons and stabilized alongside a rock-filled causeway. Construction firsts also included erection of the buildings on stilts to protect against permafrost damage, the world's largest saltwater distillery and the second-tallest radio tower. So began the most bizarre and costly American undertaking in the Arctic to date, which had been described in a prior press release simply as "some rehabilitation and construction work." After stories leaked to the press from workers returning home, Balchen escorted thirty-six journalists in October 1952 to examine the completed base. Subsequent articles appearing in *Life* and *Reader's Digest* emphasized the base's strategic and commercial importance.[64]

By 1953, the main base covered 2,600 acres, with 82 miles of roads and fuel tanks with a capacity of roughly 100 million gallons to support interceptor bombers and allow for mid-air fuelling. Initially, the base was defended by a ring of anti-aircraft guns, manned around the clock and alerted to possible attack by radar atop a nearby mountain. Originally placed under the North Eastern Air Command in 1952, the Thule air base was transferred to the Strategic Air Command five years later. That same year, 1957, the anti-aircraft guns were replaced by four Nike missile-launching systems, two each on North and South Mountains, with forty-eight nuclear warheads stored at the base. The Nike launch sites were shut down three years later, after the airbase was considered adequately protected by interceptor aircraft. Also in 1960, the Thule base was designated an air defence base now that longer-range aircraft had eliminated the need to use the facility as a forward support base. That year, the replacement value of the buildings was estimated at over $2 billion.[65]

During the first decade of operation, the base expanded to include gas stations and modern bus service, housing for upward of 12,000 and a well-appointed hotel. There was also a fifty-bed hospital, a laundry and dry cleaning plant; mess halls and officers' clubs; libraries, a bowling alley, chapel, gymnasium and movie house; a post office,

Unloading trucks and equipment at Thule for Operation Blue Jay.
The ships, equipment and manpower used in construction of
the USAF air base were likely unprecedented in peacetime.
EI 92302856; photo by U.S. Army Corps/Time & Life Pictures/Getty Images

numerous bars, a hobby shop and bank; grocery, drug and clothing
stores; even a watch repair shop and an American Express office. To
relieve the boredom, there was a radio and television station, and a
newspaper, the *Thule Times*. Heat, water and sewage travelled along
utilidors to and from buildings. Street signs, traffic lights and police
maintained a semblance of civil order. At one side of town, large
paved runways led to several oversized hangars; on the other lay
ocean piers and submarine berths. On the hill behind stood a long
row of gasoline storage tanks. Two primary power plants were aided
by four auxiliary heating plants. At the height of operations in the
early 1960s, the base and its outlying camps housed around 10,000
personnel. Thanks to infinite financial resources, scientific expertise,

Helicopter view of barracks, hangars and fuel storage tanks
at U.S. Thule Air Base, 1 October 1953. Within a year,
a gigantic air base had been carved out of a polar desert.
EI 50672446, photographer George Silk/Time & Life Pictures/Getty Images

trained technicians and the Danish government's cooperation, the ultimate dream of U.S. postwar planners had become a reality.[66]

Regrettably, the messianic drive of the USAF ignored the fact that the Arctic wilderness the military had acquired might be the homeland of the Inughuit, as northern Greenlanders were called. The consequences became evident in 1953, when the U.S. government annexed land adjacent to the Thule Air Base and 116 resident Inughuit were evacuated to Qaanaaq 120 kilometres north. Since the relocation was in accordance with the 1951 defence agreement and had Danish approval, responsibility for the move was attributed to Denmark.[67] It did not appear out of character at the time since protection of the Greenlanders from disease and potential abuse by foreigners had been central to Denmark's policy for centuries. The need for protection, however, did not apply to Danish nationals, many of whom had been hired by the USAF and other agencies as housekeepers, cooks, dishwashers and drivers and to do a variety of menial jobs.[68]

In the interim, debate continued in Canada and the U.S. about adequate radar protection. As noted above, in 1951 the two countries had approved construction of the Pinetree radar system, with the provision that all stations on Canadian soil would be built under Canadian supervision, with rights to the sites vested in the Crown and allowing Canada's eventual takeover of their operation. Two-thirds of the costs were to be borne by the U.S., with many stations initially manned by American personnel. At Ottawa's request, the terms of the agreement were kept secret for a number of years to avoid public criticism.[69]

Yet no sooner had construction on the Pinetree Line begun than military planners raised concerns about its capability and location. In 1951, Professor G.A. Woonton at McGill University in Montreal demonstrated a superior technology that allowed a continuous line of protection, initially referred to as the McGill Fence. Then in the summer of 1952, the USAF-sponsored Lincoln Summer Study Group at MIT introduced the idea of two new radar lines located further north to provide backup for the Pinetree Line. Concerned that enemy bombers might steal across the polar skies undetected, the group argued the need for a more sophisticated radar system designed to give advance warning of an aerial attack from remote areas of the Arctic. President Truman, in the last days of his presidency, gave approval in principle and directed the Defense Department to begin work on designing an early warning system.[70]

Much to the consternation of U.S. officials, Canada continued to resist approval of new projects. In November 1952 an internal memo, classified as secret, was prepared by the State Department for an upcoming visit to Ottawa to discuss the proposed radar project. Referring to Canada's continual delays in granting approvals, the memo suggested that part of the problem was that the Canadian government did not have "the sense of urgency of the U.S. and appear not as seriously concerned by the Russian threat." The memo concluded with a note of obvious frustration: "I believe the Canadians should appreciate the fact that the U.S. does not wish to station U.S. troops in Canada merely because we like to spend millions of dollars, nor because we wish to infringe on Canadian sovereignty. The two countries have agreed that we constitute a single unit for defense purposes. It is because of geographic and strategic necessities that so many installations have to be located in Canada." [71]

Meanwhile, the Canadian government was wrestling with other priorities. Apart from the question of Arctic sovereignty, a major portion of military expenses and manpower was allocated to support Canada's commitment to NATO and the Korean War. Yet another legal assessment, this time by Dean Vincent C. MacDonald of Dalhousie University Law School, was received in February 1950 and immediately classified as top secret with limited distribution. While its conclusion essentially repeated earlier reports that Canadian policy must rely on "effective occupation alone" to protect its title to the Arctic Islands, the MacDonald report provided more explicit details as to what actions were required to achieve that goal, with direct reference to providing inhabitants with "the normal benefits of Canadian citizenship and numerous provisions for their special needs." [72]

The idea of employing Inuit at remote Arctic weather stations and airfields had been discussed by various government agencies since 1948, including the ACND and NWT Council. When the Eskimo Affairs Committee was created in 1952 to deal with welfare-related problems, the debate became even more divisive, with one side arguing the benefits of maintaining a vibrant fur-trading economy and the other in support of introducing more wage employment. On several occasions, it was suggested that Inuit families might be moved from areas of poor fur resources to the High Arctic under RCMP supervision. Inevitably the debate became part of the larger discussion on how best to protect sovereignty in new defence project areas. By 1952, sovereignty concerns were again a priority as a result of the proposed new early warning system, which threatened to bring even more Americans to the Canadian Arctic and create a *de facto* loss of sovereignty similar to what had occurred during World War II.[73] As explained to Lester B. Pearson, by then secretary of state for external affairs, the probable consequence of the proposed new radar stations was "that the number of U.S. citizens in the District of Franklin will probably be substantially greater than the number of white Canadians." A later projection estimated that there might be 1,200 U.S. military and civilian personnel compared to 140 Canadian.[74]

In February 1953, the Advisory Committee on Northern Development was reactivated, with the secretariat given specific instructions "to examine all defence projects and, wherever Canadian participation is considered insufficient, to so advise the Deputy Minister" with the option to employ Inuit where possible.[75] As a result, plans were made to send five Inuit families to the Resolute air base from Fort Chimo, where they had previously been employed at the wartime airfield. Seven other families from Port Harrison, Quebec, were to be resettled on Ellesmere Island near a proposed radar site on Coburg Island, along with three families from Pond Inlet to help them adapt to a completely new environment. Plans were abruptly changed after the RCAF at Resolute sent notice that the Inuit would require separate quarters such as they were accustomed to at Chimo and that neither the RCAF, the USAF nor the Canadian Weather Bureau was prepared to foot the bill. Instead the seven Inuit families assigned from Port Harrison and three from Pond Inlet were divided between camps set up near the Resolute air base and at Grise Fiord near the Craig Harbour police detachment. To ensure that they did not become dependent on assistance while they adapted to the new environment, their camps were located several miles from the police posts.

Although other families were allowed to join the original relocated families in following years, the hardships endured and the government's refusal to allow them to return home led to a Royal Commission of inquiry in the 1990s and eventually an award of compensation. Unlike the Russian government, which resettled indigenous peoples on Arctic islands to assert sovereignty claims in the late nineteenth and early twentieth centuries, the Canadian government made no attempt to provide housing or basic services at the time of transfer. Coincidentally, the Canadian relocation took place within weeks of the evacuation of Greenland Inughuit families from their homes near the Thule Air Base, a resettlement which was also later protested and for which reparations were made.

In August 1953, reports that the Soviets had successfully tested a thermonuclear bomb suddenly raised the issue of national security to one of urgency, in the knowledge that the effects of a hydrogen bomb could devastate an area up to ten times larger than the target zone of a conventional atomic bomb. Negotiations on new bilateral defence agreements resumed in earnest. That December, Prime Minister Louis St. Laurent announced the reorganization of his government to give the new Department of Northern Affairs and Natural Resources prominence in recognition of Canada's increased interest in northern regions. To his cabinet, however, he explained that it was now "important for Canada to take measures that will make clear and effectively maintain Canadian sovereignty throughout the area."[76] Still mindful of the public's negative attitude toward any increase in militarization in the far north, his government formally requested through the PJBD that restrictions be placed on publicity about American activities in the Canadian Arctic.[77]

Although the former American policy of retaliation was now replaced by one of deterrence, installation of more sophisticated radar protection could no longer be deferred, with the result that two new lines were now proposed. In hopes of minimizing overall expense, Ottawa agreed to take responsibility for the costs and construction of a southern line. Utilizing the technology developed at McGill University, the Mid-Canada Line generally followed along the 55th parallel and was manned by Canadians. Ninety unmanned stations and eight large control stations were built between 1954 and 1957 and became fully functional by January 1958. In the mid-1960s the line proved too expensive to operate and the stations were closed. In the interim, a second phase of the Pinetree Line was built between 1957 and 1964 to fill in the gaps of the existing line in the Canadian prairies and northern Ontario. For the most part, these were also paid for by Canada and manned by the RCAF.[78]

After President Eisenhower had given his approval in February 1954, negotiations with Canada resumed over shared responsibility for a more northerly radar system. Finally on 5 May 1955 an agreement was reached on "Establishment of a Distant Early Warning System in Canadian Territory" and effected by an exchange of notes. The proposed DEW Line was to extend from the northwest coast of Alaska, then roughly follow the 69th parallel from the Yukon coast to Cape Dyer on the east coast of Baffin Island. Although these stations were paid for, planned, built and initially manned by the U.S., Canada would be consulted as to their location and Canadian laws were to be respected, including customs and immigration regulations. Title to the stations was retained by the Crown, with provision for Canadian takeover if so desired. Other terms covered protection of the Inuit, telecommunications policy and hunting regulations. The agreement also allowed for a small airfield at each site for purposes of supply and maintenance. The cost to the American taxpayer was reported to have been over a billion dollars. In this instance, Colonel Balchen failed to convince his superiors that it would be far less costly and more effective if the line were built along the outer rim of the Archipelago. A separate agreement with Denmark provided for sites on Greenland, extending from Sondre Stromfjord to Angmagssalik, with two located on the icecap.[79]

Particularly significant in the original DEW Line agreement with Canada were provisions under paragraph 13 in the attached annex requesting that American forces avoid contact with local Inuit unless they were employed with prior approval by Canada's Department of Northern Affairs and Natural Resources. The rationale, that the Inuit were susceptible to disease and other negative effects from close contact with the white man, was similar to Denmark's explanation for keeping American military activities at arm's length from Greenlanders. This clause was eventually relaxed and many Canadian Inuit eventually gained employment at DEW Line stations. Although there were a few reported abuses, some historians have suggested that Canadian protectionist policies likely benefited the Hudson's Bay Company more than the Inuit.

Distant early warning radar station Dye 2 on Greenland icecap, seen here in
1970. Built ten years earlier, the structure was six stories high and hung 30
feet above the snow on eight support columns. Dye 2 was disbanded in 1990.

NA-DMG, William S. Carlson Collection, XWSC-T3-B-7

For the multiple-layered radar system to be effective, it required
a team of interceptor aircraft in readiness to respond to warning
of an attack. These were composed of both USAF and RCAF planes,
stationed at strategic locations in Alaska and Canada, and coordinated under a single command. Although the Canadian government
had rejected the concept of a unified command when it was first
proposed in the draft Basic Security Plan in 1945, the situation had
changed. Active negotiations began in 1954 for a North American air
command, with the Canadian government insisting on direct consultation and shared command. Again, the U.S. military officials were
far less conciliatory toward Canadian views than their State Department, as evidenced by one officer's complaint that since "the U.S. has
95 percent of the sites to be protected and 95 percent of the equipment, why should we consider a joint commander with Canada. All
we need is permission to station forces in Canada." [80]

Although a tentative agreement had been approved pending further discussions, the overwhelming defeat of the Liberal minority

government in 1957 ended the stalemate when Conservative Prime Minister Diefenbaker, reportedly without consultation with External Affairs officials, approved a unified air command. Once the government was committed, there was no option but to defend the concept. An exchange of notes establishing the North American Air Defence Command (NORAD) took place on 19 May 1958; the agreement was debated in Parliament in June and officially took effect that July. The USAF would command the new entity, with an RCAF representative acting as deputy commander. While the bilateral agreement was harshly criticized by the Liberal opposition and the media as a major loss to the nation's independence, most experts agree that it was inevitable once Canada had committed to a defence program involving radar and interceptor aircraft. Although the terms suggested that Canada would be consulted prior to an offensive action, it was proven during the Cuban Missile Crisis that "consultation" might mean notification after the fact and not participation in decision-making.[81]

Joseph T. Jockel, a respected authority on Canadian-U.S. defence relations, viewed the years of negotiations leading up to the NORAD agreement as a learning experience during which "Canadians and Americans, in coping with a new and unparalleled threat, also coped with each other." He also reminded his readers that under the NORAD agreement, "it was the first time since Canada left its colonial status behind that control over Canadian forces located in Canada would no longer be in Canadian hands alone."[82] Yet in the end, both countries achieved their primary objective of preventing a Soviet nuclear attack. While NORAD may have contributed to a *de facto* loss of Canada's sovereign authority over its airspace, the fact remains that Canada could not have defended its territory on its own. Since its inception, the agreement has been amended on numerous occasions in accordance with changing circumstances. In 1981, the name was changed to North American Aerospace Defense Command in recognition of the Americans' increasing reliance on outer space technology for warning systems and surveillance. The last revision took place in 2006 with provision for changes as necessary.

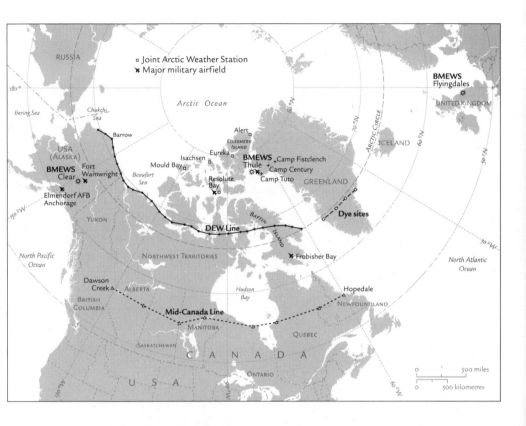

DEFENCE ACTIVITIES IN THE ARCTIC DURING THE COLD WAR

With costs only partially shared with Canada and Denmark, the
United States invested large sums of money, manpower, equipment
and technology in the Arctic to defend the continent against possible
invasion by the Soviet Union. The exception was the Mid-Canada
Line, which was built, paid for and manned by Canadians, then
disbanded in the mid-1960s. Costs were shared for the Pinetree
Line (not shown on the map), which roughly followed the 50th
parallel, with some stations initially manned by American personnel.

Two men sitting in an ice tunnel at Camp Tuto, near Thule AB, Greenland,
c1956. The tunnel was built as part of preliminary research for Project
Iceworm, a concept designed to construct a series of tunnels under the
icecap to create a network of mobile nuclear missile launch sites. The
movement of glacier ice proved too powerful and the project was cancelled.

EI 50679357, photographer Carl Mydans, Time & Life Pictures/Getty Images

While Canada was immersed in political debates over the DEW Line and NORAD, massive undertakings were under way near the Thule Air Base. While the base was still under construction, advance parties were sent out in search of easy access onto the icecap. One such site was located some 14 miles west of Thule, where Camp Tuto, short for "Thule Take Off," was established by the U.S. Army Polar Development and Research Center as the primary staging ground for all icecap operations. Completed in 1954, the camp consisted of more than fifty prefabricated buildings, which included a library, mess hall, chapel, theatre, bar, store and post office, and was serviced by an airstrip. From Tuto, a three-mile gravel road allowed heavy land vehicles to mount the incline to the edge of the icecap. At the camp, the U.S. Army Corps of Engineers excavated two large tunnels, one directly into the ice extending several hundred yards into the glacier and the other into the permafrost. The primary purpose was for research, such as testing equipment, survival techniques and glacial studies, with the objective of building a much larger structure under the inland ice. The tunnels were also used for storage of food, equipment and "ammunition." Additional radar stations were built at Site I north of Thule and at Site II some 200 miles west on the inland ice, although the latter was abandoned within a few short years after being crushed by the wind and shifting ice.[83]

In 1953, the first overland expedition by motorized vehicles was completed to Greenland's east coast, the round trip taking a full forty-eight days. The first outpost camp built on the icecap was called Fistclench and was roughly 220 miles east of Thule, with accommodation for over 100 men. It was built in 1955 primarily for summer research projects. The engineers stationed at Fistclench took the Tuto experiments a step further and dug five shallow tunnels into the ice, which were roofed with arches and covered with corrugated sheeting and finally snow. Like Tuto, albeit more primitive, Fistclench camp also had dining facilities and a post office, store, theatre and bar.

According to historian Richard Vaughan, the concept of motoring over and tunnelling into the icecap was a product of "Bernt Balchen's vision of Greenland as a gigantic aircraft carrier" lying in the path of a potential Soviet attack.[84] The creativity and scientific applications inspired by his dream were never more evident than in the construction of Camp Century, over 150 miles from the Thule Air Base. Originally conceived to lie 100 miles west of Tuto, hence its name, Camp Century was relocated because of ice conditions to a site 138 miles from the base of operations, some three to four days' travel by land vehicles. Built in 1958, the camp was situated in tunnels under the ice to house military personnel, ample food and equipment, even a plane and weapons, and powered by an atomic generator with enough fuel to provide heat and light for two years. The unique experiment was described as "a refuge from nuclear bombs" by former USAAF Colonel William Carlson in 1959, suggesting it might serve as a bomb shelter if Thule were attacked:

> Camp Century was dug with coal-mining machinery and has sixteen streets, railways, hot and cold running water, flush toilets, dormitories, cafeteria, gymnasium, workshops, a post exchange, a chapel, a hospital and one hundred human inhabitants. Camp Century is free of dust, traffic noises, and changing weather. Building temperatures are set at 60° [F], and the temperature in the streets is kept at 20°. The power source is a portable nuclear reactor, capable of producing 1,500 kilowatts and built at a cost of $6,300,000.[85]

Three years later, more details and photographs appeared in two books and a film produced by the U.S. Army, which claimed the primary purpose was for research. Often referred to as the "city under the ice," the camp was not technically under the ice, but built in twenty-one deep, wide trenches covered as at Fistclench and topped with three feet of snow. Only ventilators and escape hatches were visible from above.

The largest tunnel, known as Main Street, was 1,100 feet long, 26 feet wide and 28 feet high. Thirty prefabricated wooden buildings with accommodation for 200 were set within the tunnels, three feet above the ice and four feet from the walls to prevent melting. They

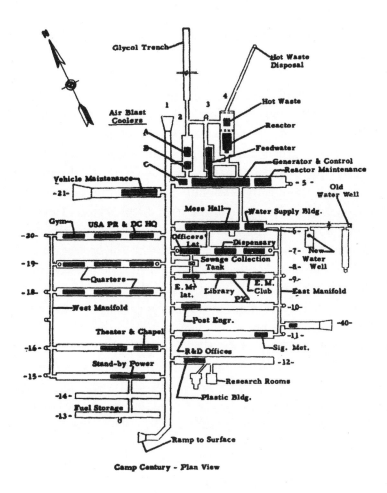

Camp Century - Plan View

Layout of Camp Century, 1960. Although written descriptions gave
an impression of comfort and luxury, interior photographs seemed
claustrophobic, with rectangle-shaped wooden buildings built end to
end in long narrow, windowless, snow-lined tunnels. The unique feature
was the portable nuclear generator used to provide heat and light.
The camp was abandoned in 1963 after the tunnels began to
collapse from the force of the ever-moving glacier ice.

U.S. Army Material Command, CREEL, Technical Report 174

also housed research labs and repair shops, dormitories, mess halls, food storage, a post office and store, a pharmacy, barbershop, laundry and library, as well as a theatre and club for relaxation. Roughly 10,000 gallons of fresh water was obtained daily from a deep pit dug in the ice into which steam was injected. One research team successfully drilled down to the floor of the Greenland ice sheet and extracted valuable cores of ice with dust particles and air pockets that represented more then 120,000 years of climatic history.

Recent studies suggest that the primary purpose of Camp Century was to determine the feasibility of constructing a giant nuclear missile system under cover of the inland ice—Project Iceworm—involving upward of 4,000 kilometres of tunnels and deployment of 600 nuclear missiles on mobile launchers. The project never proceeded beyond the planning stage, at which time it was cancelled due to unstable ice conditions.[86] Completed in 1960, filmed in 1961, Camp Century was evacuated in 1965, the nuclear generator removed and the facility closed because of structural weaknesses caused by unexpected movement of the glacial ice. In spite of the extraordinary achievements by its engineers and scientists, the U.S. Army met defeat in its attempt to conquer the Greenland icecap. Camp Century might best be described as a truly ingenious but exorbitant failure.

Before the DEW Line was declared fully operational in 1957, the potential of nuclear-armed, intercontinental ballistic missiles once again spawned a new invention. The first fully automated Ballistic Missile Early Warning System (BMEWS) installation was built near Thule. The other two sites, one in Alaska and the other on England's Yorkshire moors, allowed the U.S. to avoid Canadian insistence on active participation and shared control.[87] Since the project was built by RCA Services for NORAD, Canada also signed a BMEWS agreement regarding the use of Canadian airspace, modelled on the DEW Line agreement. While neither agreement explicitly recognized Canadian claims to the Arctic, sovereignty expert Gordon W. Smith claimed that they represented "as least *de facto* recognition," which could be reasonably interpreted as complete and permanent.[88]

In Greenland, BMEWS facilities were built on a high ridge, approximately 12 miles from the Thule Air Base. Completed in 1961, the dominant features were the four gigantic scanners, each longer than a football field and fifteen stories high. Scanners were connected to the transmitter and administration buildings, nine in total, by a labyrinth of tunnels housing personnel and equipment. Described as the "most massive technological undertaking in history," its cost in 1960 dollars was reportedly $5 billion. The BMEWS was designed to give adequate warning of an impending attack as part of U.S. deterrence policy—sometimes referred to as "mutually assured destruction" or MAD—so its existence and capabilities were purposefully not kept secret.[89] As testimony to the success of U.S. policy, almost fifty years has passed without a nuclear attack. Space surveillance capability was added in 1961 with a satellite tracking system known as Det 3, one of nine worldwide stations. While able to track intercontinental ballistic missiles (ICBMs) and submarine-launched ballistic missiles (SLBMs), neither the BMEWS nor satellite surveillance could locate and track Soviet nuclear submarines travelling under the sea ice.

The potential threat of Soviet nuclear submarines prompted the Americans to develop similar capabilities. Two models were designed by the U.S. Navy during the 1950s: a "fast attack" vehicle approximately 360 feet long and a larger "boomer" capable of launching a long-range ballistic missile on Moscow. Soviet nuclear submarines posed a similar threat to American cities. In 1958, USS *Nautilus* was the first submarine to travel from the Pacific Ocean under the North Pole and on to England, for the most part submerged under the Arctic Ocean. Celebrating yet another American achievement, the crew were honoured with a tickertape parade in New York, public relations suggesting the voyage had fulfilled Jules Verne's fantasy vision as told in *Twenty Thousand Leagues under the Sea.*[90] That same year, USS *Skate* began surfacing exercises in the Arctic icepack, and in 1959 it successfully pushed its way through the ice at the North Pole. This feat was followed in 1960 by USS *Seadragon*'s submerged transit through the full length of the Northwest Passage. There were now suggestions of using submarines for cargo carriers as an alternative to the Panama Canal. While U.S. submarines contributed another viable means of retaliation in the event of a nuclear attack, they also added to the deterrence factor in Cold War defence strategy. When submerged under the ice, British, American and Soviet nuclear submarines likely posed a threat to Danish and Canadian sovereignty, but it was theoretical rather than visible. Unless they came up for air, no one above knew they were there.

Without nuclear submarines of their own or effective means of detecting a foreign presence, Canada and Denmark knew that their territorial waters were easily violated. In 1987, Canada's Conservative government's white paper on defence, *Challenge and Commitment,* signalled the intent to acquire three or more nuclear submarines capable of travelling under the ice-covered waters. When the proposal was withdrawn two years later, the U.S. Navy was reportedly relieved. As J.T. Jockel explained, "Quite simply, the U.S. Navy does not welcome the prospect of partners in Arctic antisubmarine warfare and is more than willing to be relied upon alone in Canadian Arctic waters." [91] Still determined to protect its sovereignty, Canada instead explored satellite and underwater detection technologies to enable identification of foreign submarines.

Station Nord on the northern coast of Greenland had been built for the U.S. Air Force during the Cold War as a weather station and emergency airfield. It was closed in 1972, then reopened in 1975 under control of the Danish Defence Command and staffed year-round by at least four officers. The rationale for Denmark's decision to reopen the facility was explained in terms of sovereignty: Station Nord represented the only Danish-owned and -operated gateway to northeastern Greenland for scientific research. [92] While only a minor event, nevertheless the resumption of Danish authority over Station Nord illustrates how the Danes were gradually reasserting their sovereign authority over all of Greenland by assuming control of other air and naval bases, DEW Line sites and weather stations.

By 1965, a general downsizing had also taken place at the Thule Air Base after several fighter squadrons had been deactivated. As a

Nuclear submarines HMS *Tireless* (in the foreground) and USS *Pargo*
surfaced at the North Pole in early summer 1991. American and British
subs, the latter as a part of a NATO commitment, routinely patrol under the
ice of Canadian waters in search of Russian submarines. In this instance,
crews of both submarines met on the ice and played a friendly game of
cricket, the pitch just visible to the right of the *Tireless* conning tower. Crew
members also built a diagonal boundary line between the two subs, which
they jokingly referred to as the "international boundary line." Under-ice
submarine patrols are not without peril. In 2007, HMS *Tireless* suffered
an explosion and the loss of two men while submerged in Canadian
Arctic waters.   Courtesy Michael Pitt, Plymouth, England, photographer unknown

result the resident population was reduced to 3,370 in 1968, including
those employed at the BMEWS and satellite tracking stations. In 1982,
Thule was redesignated as an Air Force Space Command base, in recognition of its changing character. When I visited Thule Air Base in
1984 with the Canadian Institute of International Affairs, it was obvious that the base itself was still active, but with noticeable changes.
Coach buses were fewer in number now that the resident population
had dwindled to a little over 1,300, yet other services appeared the

same and large bombers continued to roar down the runway. BMEWS installations still stood proudly on a hill, accompanied by an Air Force Satellite Control facility, reflecting the ever-changing state of technology. The majority of the original barracks, however, lay abandoned in various stages of disrepair. In 1984, there were a little over 200 USAF officers and men still living on the base with their wives and children. Danish construction and maintenance workers now constituted a majority of residents, hired through a Greenland contracting company partially owned by the Home Rule Government. As of 2008, the 821st Air Squadron was still in charge of the air base, largely as caretakers for the "sleeping giant," but also to provide support for resupply missions to Canadian weather stations at Eureka and Alert and the Danish research station at Station Nord.[93]

At the same time, Canada was gradually assuming full control of the American-built facilities in the Arctic Islands and on the mainland. Yet even with the numerous safeguards written into the DEW Line agreement, the dominant presence of U.S. personnel and reports of failure to display the Canadian flag gave rise to periodic media criticism that Canada again had lost *de facto* control of its Arctic. Nonetheless, the Canadian government took incremental measures to reduce the impact of the American presence, initially in 1959 by sending a detachment of RCMP officers to supervise the DEW Line and in 1961 by taking over operation of the remaining Pinetree stations.

In 1971, the Trudeau government placed a major emphasis on sovereignty protection in its white paper on defence, resulting in the Canadian Air Force nominally assuming peacetime responsibility for air defence in the east and for interceptor aircraft flying over the western provinces. Eventually, the air defence plan was reconfigured to allow Canadian commanders control of all Canadian airspace during peacetime. Under the Mulroney government, the U.S. presence in the Arctic continued to decline after the DEW Line was replaced by the North Warning System, comprising fifteen long-range radar installations, of which eleven are in Canada, in addition to thirty-four unattended, short-range radar units. The new system was designed to be operated on Canadian soil by Canadians as part of the 1985 North American Air Defense Modernization Agreement.[94] With the collapse of the Warsaw Pact in 1991 and disintegration of the Soviet Union, the Cold War was considered over. Nonetheless, the warning systems are still on twenty-four-hour alert.

Denmark's approval of the North Warning System occurred much later, largely because of political dissension over a nuclear accident off Greenland's coast which had occurred without anyone immediately notifying the Danish government. The incident took place in 1968, when a B-52 bomber armed with four hydrogen bombs caught fire and crashed on the ice roughly seven miles from the Thule Air Base. According to a BBC report, the incident took place at 16:45 local time on 21 January with only one reported fatality. The intense fire, it was claimed, had ruptured one or more of the bombs it was carrying and spread radiation over a wide area. The fire also melted the ice and caused the plane to sink to the bottom, carrying with it any bombs that had not exploded. Straightaway, forty-seven men in protective clothing were dispatched by dog team to locate the site, search for survivors, remove traces of military technology and account for all the bombs. In the end, it took 700 men over nine months and a mini-submarine to locate and remove the contaminated material from the crash site, including over 500 million gallons of snow and ice. U.S. officials claimed all the bombs were accounted for, but later admitted that one pound of plutonium had been released into the environment. Shortly after the crash, Secretary of Defense Robert McNamara ordered the removal of nuclear warheads from all continuous alert flights, which were later curtailed and ultimately suspended. Recent investigations have suggested that one bomb was not accounted for and may still rest somewhere on the ocean bottom.[95] The U.S. continues to refute this allegation.

Perhaps naively, the Danish people believed that interceptor bombers flying over Thule would not be armed with thermonuclear warheads because of their government's non-nuclear policy. In spite of subsequent angry protests in Copenhagen, the initial explanation that the plane was on a routine flight over the Canadian Arctic and had attempted an emergency landing at Thule appeared to satisfy Danish officials and no further action was taken. Later, the nuclear arms question resurfaced when the U.S. requested approval to modernize the radar systems at Thule. In 1993, an internal investigation revealed that at the time of the crash, bombers with nuclear warheads had routinely circled the Thule Air Base as part of the airborne alert program called Chrome Dome. When the U.S. government finally admitted that nuclear weapons also had been deployed at the Nike missile sites near Thule, the Danish government decided to break the news to the public to avoid further scandal over what now is now referred to as the "Thulegate" affair. A further investigation was commissioned, this time conducted by the Danish Institute of International Affairs, which concluded that the Danish government had exercised two versions of its nuclear policy with regard to Greenland: a public policy that banned nuclear weapons and a secret policy that accepted them. Beset by complaints of cancer and other illnesses from Danes and Greenlanders who had worked at the site after the crash, the Danish government finally authorized payment of $15.5 million to settle workers' claims. Even then, debate over the new radar plans for Thule continued, now with Greenland's Home Rule Government actively involved.[96]

Eventually the ability to apply use of the Thule Air Base to reduce Denmark's contribution to NATO won over the pragmatists. After a further round of negotiations, a supplement to the 1951 defence agreement was signed with the U.S. on 10 August 2004 at Igaliku, a small village in southern Greenland. Signatories included U.S. Secretary of State Colin Powell, Danish Foreign Minister Per Stig Møller and Premier Josef Motzfeldt for the Home Rule Government. Inclusion of the latter marked a new chapter in Greenlanders' demands for greater say in foreign policy. The document was described as "a modernization of the 1951 agreement," with U.S. military activities in Greenland now confined to the Thule Air Base. Another significant change was the stationing of a representative of the Home Rule Government at the base to consult with the base commander on local matters.[97] For the Americans the agreement was critical to allow upgrade of the BMEWS installation and other radar systems as part of the North Warning System. Significantly, there was no specific reference in the agreement to deployment of nuclear weapons on Greenland soil. With the exception of a similar debate in Canada, which ended when Prime Minister Pearson gave his approval, Ottawa tended to avoid public criticism of joint defence agreements by restricting most discussions to the Cabinet Defence Committee.

Meanwhile, in Alaska there was no perceptual downsizing of the military presence during the Cold War as had occurred in Canada and Greenland. During the peak years, there were 200 fighter interceptors based in the state, along with 16,000 air, army, navy and coast guard personnel reporting to the Alaska Command (ALCOM). In recognition of the importance of air power, the commander-in-chief was a member of the USAF. ALCOM was deactivated after the Vietnam War and was replaced by a new Alaska Command formed in 1989 as a sub-unit of the Pacific Command and headquartered at the Elmendorf Air Base. At present the combined forces total upward of 46,000, with the commander also in charge of the Alaskan NORAD region.[98]

The reduction of American forces in Canada and Greenland after 1965 could be attributed partly to the failure of Camp Century but more directly to deployment of combat units to Vietnam that year. Another factor involved was escalating competition in space exploration between the two Cold War antagonists, beginning in October 1957 with the Soviets' successful launch of *Sputnik 1*. This event led to creation of the National Aeronautics and Space Administration (NASA) with virtually unimaginable financial support to overcome the initial Soviet advantage. Within two decades, the "space race" became an integral part of the cultural, technological and ideological rivalry between the two countries, with military applications also changing the nature of defence activities in the Arctic. Money that might have been allocated to polar science and technology programs in the United States and Soviet Union was now diverted to their respective space programs. The competition continued until 1975, when the U.S. *Apollo* and Soviet *Soyuz 19* met and docked in outer space to carry out combined experiments. For Americans and Russians alike, the space frontier captured the public's imagination in much the same way as British Admiralty polar explorations had inspired Britain and the Western world over a century earlier. This time, however, the heroes were astronauts, not military figures.

For Canada and Denmark, the pause in American activity provided ample opportunities to take over operation of the Arctic weather and radar stations, yet the end of the Cold War provided a disincentive to spending more than absolutely necessary on military initiatives. With the exception of the "Thulegate" affair, tensions between Denmark and the U.S. seemed more muted, possibly because of geography and world politics. Greenland may be situated in North America, but Denmark is first and foremost a European nation which has relied on NATO and the Scandinavian countries to support its interests on both economic and military fronts. While Canada had hoped membership in NATO would reduce American influence in defence matters, it never quite succeeded because of NATO's willingness to delegate the primary responsibilty for North American defence to the U.S.

Arctic sovereignty issues between Canada and the United States have deep historical roots. Although memories dim, Americans still tend to view Canada as a relatively minor economic power in control of a large piece of undeveloped northern real estate. Canadians, on the other hand, are still sensitive to perceived intrusions on their sovereign rights. In this regard, the Cold War provided an exceptional opportunity for the two nations to settle their differences peacefully through bilateral negotiations and to allow unresolved issues—such as rights of transit through the Northwest Passage—to remain so without acrimony.

(11)

ARCTIC OIL AND ABORIGINAL
RIGHTS, 1960—2004

It is for the Great Powers to decide, by their policies and their
plans, whether... development can be conducted in an atmosphere
of friendly cooperation between all the Arctic nations, and with
a resultant benefit to all, or whether the Northern Hemisphere is
to become an area of national rivalries, fears and ambitions.

LESTER B. PEARSON, December 1945[1]

. . . .

MILITARY ACTIVITIES during the Cold War may have brought
changes in Arctic transportation, communications and land
use, but in the last half of the twentieth century it was discovery
of new resource wealth that played the key role in economic, political
and social development of the North American Arctic. Since the age
of Martin Frobisher, the search for gold or other valuable resources
had attracted countless adventurers to the Arctic Islands. This time,
however, it was not gold but oil and gas that inspired a new generation of fortune hunters to lay claim to vast tracts of land and offshore
waters. A major oil discovery on Alaska's North Slope in the winter of
1968–69 unleashed a combination of forces that forever changed the
course of Arctic history. Comparable to a bursting dam, the discovery
released a reservoir of competing interests: the oil and gas industry,
various environmental groups, commercial shipping and government vessels, as well as aboriginal land claims and demands for the
right to self-government. Before major development could take place,

the United States and Canada would be forced to resolve the question of aboriginal title to traditional lands and at the same time deal with their conflicting positions on the marine boundary in the Beaufort Sea and use of the Northwest Passage.

After preliminary assessment of Greenland's hydrocarbon resources proved disappointing, the oil and gas companies focussed their attention first on Alaska, then elsewhere in the Arctic. Fearing irreparable harm to their environment, the Inuit across North America responded with a call for a unified voice to counter adverse political decisions of their southern-based nation-states. To some, it appeared that history was slowly coming full circle as the Inuit joined together to renounce the vestiges of colonialism and regain control over their ancestral lands and waters. While progress was slow, their incremental success in the 1970s and 1980s laid the foundation for major changes in governance in Alaska, and especially in the Canadian Arctic and Greenland, that were thought impossible only decades earlier.

Although American corporations dominated exploration activities in Alaska, Canadian companies played a major role in the Arctic Islands with the full support of their government and general public during a period of heightened nationalism. By now most Canadians had accepted the notion that their country's "northernness" gave them an identity distinct from that of the U.S. Taking the so-called "myth of the north" a step further, John Diefenbaker as leader of the Conservative Party promised new oil and mineral discoveries in his 1958 "Roads to Resources" campaign. Not surprisingly, the idea that their country's future prosperity might lie in development of its northern hinterland caught the imagination of many Canadians and in turn increased public sensitivity to any incursion on their country's sovereign authority.[2] In response to intense media coverage about potential threats, Ottawa would again be required to adopt defensive measures to safeguard the nation's Arctic sovereignty. The same period marked the rise of environmental activism, which manifested itself in campaigns to protect remaining wilderness areas of northern Canada and Alaska. Generally these efforts coincided with increasing pressure from northern indigenous peoples for recognition of their rights of ownership to traditional lands and need for improved living conditions. Yet in spite of the domestic issues that threatened to slow Arctic oil and gas development, it was the sovereignty question that firmly tied economic growth to foreign policy and ultimately forced circumpolar countries to seek international support through the UN Law of the Sea Conferences.[3]

AT THE outset of the Cold War, Canadian sovereignty over the Arctic Islands and mainland was considered relatively secure. The status of adjacent waters and polar ice was tenuous, however, as evidenced by the growing number of American and Russian research stations on ice floes drifting into Canadian waters, or the passage of USS *Nautilus* under the polar icecap in 1958 and two years later USS *Seadragon* through the Northwest Passage. After the failure to codify international maritime law in 1930, a number of states relied on unilateral declarations to define the territorial waters within their jurisdiction. In 1937, for example, Ottawa claimed exclusive authority over Hudson Bay and Hudson Strait as historic Canadian waters. Although the U.S. never officially recognized these claims, neither did it officially challenge them, implying tacit recognition of Canada's authority. Then unexpectedly in September 1945 President Truman issued two unilateral declarations in the form of official proclamations. The first claimed exclusive jurisdiction over the continental shelf lying within 200 nautical miles of the U.S. coast, whereas the second declared the right to establish protected fisheries zones in its adjacent waters. Inadvertently, the two proclamations undermined subsequent American protests against unilateral declarations by other countries and encouraged more states to declare exclusive rights of authority and increased limits of their territorial seas.[4]

Previously, disputes over maritime jurisdiction and violation of rights were brought by consenting countries before the International Court of Justice at The Hague, where decisions were based on conventions and customs, general principles of law, previous decisions and the teachings of learned publicists. In practice, however, the major portion of international law developed through state action, which was then absorbed into the body of customary law. As a result, the status of Arctic waters as defined by past decisions was open to several interpretations and ambiguous conclusions. The first successful attempt in fifty years to codify international maritime law took place at the UN Conference on the Law of the Sea held in 1958 at Geneva (UNCLOS I) and at a second conference held in 1960 (UNCLOS II). Four conventions drafted at the first meetings defined the limits of territorial seas, contiguous zones, the continental shelf and the high seas. Upon approval of participating countries, these four came into force independently between 1962 and 1966.[5]

As agreed upon at UNCLOS I, there were five main categories of offshore waters: internal waters, territorial seas, contiguous zones, the continental shelf and the high seas. "Internal waters" were defined as gulfs or bays surrounded by a single state and delineated by a baseline not to exceed six miles drawn between the headlands. No rights of innocent passage were accorded in these waters. "Territorial seas" were described as the waters adjacent to a coastal state over which it had complete sovereignty. Here ships may be accorded innocent passage during peacetime, unless they endanger "peace, good order and security." While it was agreed at UNCLOS II that the outer limit should not exceed 12 miles, this was not included in the written convention. A "contiguous zone" could be declared beyond the limits of a territorial sea for purposes of exercising control over customs, fiscal, pollution control, immigration or sanitary regulations, but otherwise freedom of innocent passage was not restricted. An exclusive economic zone to incorporate fishing rights would be defined at later meetings.

The "continental shelf" was described as the extension of coastal land forms lying beneath adjacent waters. The 1958 convention confirmed the American claim to jurisdiction and control of its natural resources up to a depth of 200 metres and 200 nautical miles beyond the coast, with limits extended in a later revision. "High seas" or international waters were defined as those beyond the territorial seas, which included contiguous zones and above the continental shelf. Here full rights of passage applied, as governed by *res communis*, except for specific regulations pertaining to contiguous zones and continental shelves.[6]

Some questions remained unresolved or ambiguous, such as the outer limits of continental shelves or interstate boundaries of territorial seas and contiguous zones. Limits were generally measured from the low-water mark, except in the case of adjacent islands or an archipelago. Although not specifically defined by convention, drawing baselines along a median equidistant between headlands was acceptable but with a caveat that allowed for special considerations. Significantly, there were no changes to existing laws regarding international straits or answers to the question whether landfast ice was an extension of an island's land mass. Nonetheless the four conventions were a beginning, with the expectation that multilateral negotiations would continue to clarify further questions. The most contentious issue for Canada and the U.S., then and now, was the status of the Northwest Passage. Washington claimed it was an international strait, defined as a passage of water used for commercial navigation between two areas of high seas and where innocent passage could not be suspended under existing maritime laws. Ottawa argued that the passage had never been employed as a commercial route and fell under the status of internal waters, where rights of innocent passage were restricted.

Following return of the Liberal government to power in 1963, Prime Minister Lester Pearson suggested enclosing the Archipelago with straight baselines, citing the 1951 *Anglo-Norwegian Fisheries* case as a precedent. The U.S. rejected the proposal and the Canadian request was traded off for concessions in fishery policies on the east and west coasts.[7] For the U.S. Navy, in particular, it was important that all waters beyond the three-mile territorial seas and particularly the Northwest Passage be designated as international waters to provide full freedom of navigation. At the time, the only ships sailing Arctic waters were naval and coast guard vessels, local supply ships and CGS *C.D. Howe* on the Eastern Arctic Patrol, which may explain why Pearson apparently gave little thought to the possibility that the passage might ever be used to transport oil and gas.

Although oil seepages had been reported in the Alaska Territory long before its purchase by the U.S. in 1867, the first wells drilled thirty years later proved commercially unviable. By 1911, however, several wells in the Katalla district were found to contain sufficient oil to be refined and shipped to Cordova by tanker. This short-lived venture revealed the high cost of extracting Alaskan oil and transporting it south. Although most production had halted by 1920, Congress created a large oil reserve on the Arctic coast, generally referred to as the Naval Petroleum Reserve No. 4. Oil discoveries along Canada's Mackenzie River in 1920 had posed the same problem of transporting the product to southern markets. The Canol Project during World War II, considered an experiment to test the feasibility of a pipeline connecting the interior to the coast, fell just short of being a complete failure.[8] Yet the concept still offered a better option than tanker transport, which was significantly more hazardous and only seasonal.

The U.S. Navy assisted by the U.S. Geological Survey continued a postwar drilling program that led to discovery of a large field on the Kenai Peninsula. In the late 1950s, a number of large oil companies appeared on the scene, notably the Richfield Oil Company of California, as well as Phillips, Marathon, Unocal, Shell, Mobil, Chevron and Texaco. Oil production and further drilling activity in Cook Inlet brought rapid economic growth to the region, fuelled by the arrival of thousands of transient workers. When production eventually declined, the consequences of the boom and bust cycle were felt more keenly by Native communities, a problem that had plagued Alaska since the gold rush.[9]

After Alaska attained statehood in January 1960, pressure mounted for the state to sell drilling permits on the 103 million acres assigned under the Statehood Act. That same year, before selection of state lands took place, the Secretary of the Interior designated another 8.9 million acres of coastal plains and mountains in northeast Alaska as the Arctic National Wildlife Range to protect its "unique wildlife, wilderness and recreation values." As expected, Alaska's selection of state lands initially began on the North Slope between the naval petroleum reserve and the wildlife refuge. The selection process, however, came to an abrupt halt in 1965 when the Secretary of the Interior froze further acquisitions after learning that an obscure section in the Alaska Statehood Act denied the right to claim any lands that might be subject to Native title. That same year, indigenous groups banded together to form the Alaska Federation of Natives (AFN) to facilitate settlement of their land claims. The AFN, which included those of Indian, Aleutian, Yup'ik and Inupiat descent, put forward a proposal that included title to lands traditionally used for hunting and fishing and $500 million in compensation. Unexpectedly, they also proposed that the money be invested in local corporations of which Native Alaskans would become shareholders and receive annual dividends. At the time, it was expected that the process of settling the land claims would take years, if not decades.[10]

Meanwhile the Geological Survey of Canada had also identified sites with hydrocarbon potential in the Arctic Islands. By June 1960, Ottawa had issued exploration permits for 40 million acres throughout the islands and adjacent mainland, mostly to small Canadian companies but also to a few American firms such as California Standard, Texaco and Union Pacific. The first exploratory well was drilled at Winter Harbour on Melville Island in the summer of 1961, along with two more in 1963 at Resolute Bay and Bathurst Island. Although these efforts proved that drilling was feasible in a polar environment, the disappointing results suspended further testing. As a result, the larger U.S. companies concentrated their efforts on developing plans in Alaska and the North Sea, which promised faster returns on their investments.

Then in 1967, a relatively unknown Canadian company, Global Marine, filed for drilling rights in 2 million acres of offshore waters, which sparked another rush for permits, this time in the waters of the Archipelago.[11] To offset growing American investment in offshore leases, Ottawa had provided financial assistance to the newly formed Panarctic Oil Company, consisting of a number of small Canadian companies committed to exploratory drilling in the High Arctic. Unhampered by the secrecy that had shielded U.S. military activities in the Arctic from public scrutiny, the Canadian media gave full coverage to potential problems should U.S. companies be allowed to dominate exploitation of Canada's Arctic oil and gas resources, stoking nationalist sentiments to a fevered pitch. Not surprisingly, in the wake of public optimism rose the old shibboleth of Arctic sovereignty.

The focus of attention was back on Alaska in early 1968, after the Atlantic Richfield Company (ARCO) announced that it had discovered a major oilfield at Prudhoe Bay on Alaska's Arctic coast. After additional exploratory wells yielded similar results, it was estimated that the North Slope had the potential of becoming the largest oil-producing field in North America. Within months, ARCO was joined by Standard Oil of Ohio (SOHIO) and Humble Oil (now part of Exxon-Mobil) to lobby for a speedy resolution of Native land claims to allow for construction of an oil pipeline stretching 800 miles from the Arctic coast to the deep-sea port at Valdez on Prince William Sound. Drilling continued at a feverish pace on lands held under existing permits, with the results further increasing estimates of proven resources. For residents of Alaska, the oil discovery promised yet another bonanza, although this one would be managed with more economic sophistication to accrue longer-term benefits to the State of Alaska. Even today, Alaskans pay no state sales taxes and relatively low property taxes.

The announcement of the Prudhoe Bay discovery was initially greeted with enthusiasm by Canadian oil interests and the government, in expectation of similar finds in the Beaufort Sea and Mackenzie Delta. By the end of 1968 the entire offshore waters of Canada's Arctic mainland and the Archipelago had been leased for exploration, for the most part to Canadian companies. Of greater significance for future energy policy was the change in Liberal leadership in April 1968, when Pierre Elliott Trudeau replaced Lester Pearson as prime minister, a change that marked an end to the internationalist approach to foreign relations, which had been based on compromise, cooperation and mediation. Other changes had also taken place. For the most part, the Ottawa mandarins of the war years had retired and been replaced by those with lesser experience in management of Canadian-American relations and Arctic sovereignty.

Yet because Congress increasingly perceived issues between Canada and the U.S. as "quasi-domestic in character, to be resolved at the professional level" rather than the political level, this diverted public attention from more contentious issues and gave an outward appearance of improved Canadian-American relations.[12]

The prospects of major oil development in the Canadian Arctic inspired visions of imminent prosperity. Still buoyant from the nation's centennial celebrations, most Canadians were unprepared for obstacles that would test the expectations set by a newly defined nationalism. To most Canadians in 1968, Trudeau was a breath of fresh air, an intellectual and an idealist whose outlook was not moulded by the Depression and war years. One of his first undertakings as prime minister was to order an extensive review of the government's foreign policy, followed by a major reorganization of the Department of External Affairs. A new foreign policy was declared as an extension of national policy, a shift in emphasis to self-interest that coincided with a similar change in Washington. Inevitably this led to a period of unsettled Canadian-American relations as the interests of each country rarely complemented the other's. The first confrontation arose over sovereign jurisdiction in Arctic waters. Any action that hindered U.S. naval and shipping mobility in the Arctic or elsewhere in the world was considered a serious threat to American military and economic power. For Canadians, the issue was one of sovereignty. Americans perceived it a matter of national security and a threat to American capitalism and free enterprise.

Since existing government institutions were considered inadequate to deal with the multifaceted issues affecting the Canadian North, the Task Force on Northern Oil Development was created in 1968, with a mandate to gather all information available on northern oil potential and alternative means of transporting the product south.[13] In the belief that a pipeline would be of greater benefit to the Canadian oil industry than tanker transport, the task force spent considerable time studying a proposed oil and gas corridor along the Mackenzie Valley or, as an alternative, across Alaska to meet the Alaska Highway, then following it through the Yukon and B.C. to connect with existing pipeline grids in Alberta. Either route involved a pipeline on Canadian soil, which, it was thought, might provide leverage in influencing American policy and at the same time protect their oil exports to the U.S. The issue became more complicated when the U.S. assumed that Canada's offer of cooperation was a preliminary step toward a continental energy policy.[14]

Without advance warning, the Trudeau government was presented with a direct challenge to Canada's Arctic sovereignty in October 1968 when Humble Oil announced in the press that its oil tanker ss *Manhattan* would be refitted and upgraded to a Class 7 icebreaker in preparation for a trial run east to west through the Northwest Passage. According to the company, the objective was to prove that a supertanker with icebreaking capabilities could carry oil from Alaska to east coast ports. Suspicious that the U.S. Navy might be funding the project and aware of Washington's refusal to acknowledge Canadian jurisdiction over the passage, the Canadian media had the makings of a sensational story.

The authors of *Arctic Front*, however, claim that the sovereignty threat posed by the ss *Manhattan* was not quite as serious as it appeared. There had been a history of U.S. Coast Guard ships transiting the Northwest Passage since 1957, when three vessels, USCGC *Spar, Storis* and *Bramble*, sailed east from Alaska and were welcomed by HMCS *Labrador* in Bellot Strait.[15] In anticipation, the *Labrador* had made the transit from east to west a year earlier. Reportedly, relations between the two countries' coast guards have always been courteous if not amicable. The difference in 1969 was that ss *Manhattan* was a commercial vessel.

Yet according to Captain T.C. Pullen, who served as Canada's official representative on the *Manhattan* voyage, not only had the company and the U.S. Coast Guard consulted with Canadian officials, but they also had requested that a Canadian Coast Guard vessel accompany them and the ship's master had agreed to fly the Canadian flag when appropriate. Thus it was no surprise when Prime Minister Trudeau announced in the House of Commons, 15 May 1969, that the voyage posed no threat to Canada's legal status in the Archipelago's waters.

The hook that allowed the media to capitalize on a potential threat to Canadian sovereignty was the refusal of the U.S. government to request official permission to enter the passage. To do so would have acknowledged U.S. acceptance of the fact that the waters were Canadian, a position it had always rejected for reasons of continental defence.[16] Canadian foreign affairs officials were fully cognizant of the U.S. position and up until then had not considered it serious.

Although Ottawa initially attempted to downplay the incident, the story took on a life of its own. By February 1969 numerous articles about the *Manhattan's* proposed voyage had appeared in the Canadian press, with pointed questions about sovereign jurisdiction and government inaction. Media coverage continued at a feverish pitch of indignation not witnessed since the Alaskan dispute at the turn of the twentieth century. The issue also was raised repeatedly in the House of Commons, with the opposition leader claiming that U.S. maps now indicated American ownership of potentially oil-rich islands in the Archipelago.[17]

Word spread rapidly around the world, and the Soviet Union's *Pravda* reported that "the U.S. military has been rapidly encroaching on the sovereignty of that state [Canada]."[18] Canada's initial response seemed almost comical. In the old tradition of "showing the flag," in late April the Governor-General was sent on an Arctic tour. This was followed by Trudeau's first official statement on Arctic sovereignty, which affirmed Canadian authority over the islands and territorial waters, along with the right to explore and exploit the continental shelf. In response to criticism that more assertive action was required, an official note was sent to the American Embassy in May, further defining the Canadian position. The reply was explicit: the U.S. did not recognize Canadian sovereignty beyond the three-mile limit of territorial waters and claimed the right to innocent passage and freedom of the high seas in the remainder, including the Northwest Passage. Intense discussion and debate continued in Ottawa, with a spokesman for the Standing Committee on Indian Affairs and Northern Development suggesting the Archipelago be enclosed within baselines to ensure all adjacent waters were internal to Canada. While the primary concern was sovereignty, he argued that such an action could also be justified as a means of preventing marine pollution that would require sovereign authority to enforce necessary regulations.[19]

A few parliamentarians took matters into their own hands. Chartering a plane, they flew over SS *Manhattan* as it entered Lancaster Sound in early September and radioed a message in French and English to the captain, welcoming the ship to Canadian waters. Others embarked on the HMCS *Labrador,* the Royal Canadian Navy icebreaker, and met *Manhattan* near Resolute Bay, where they were allowed to tour the ship. At one point, CCGS *John A. Macdonald* was called in for assistance after the U.S. Coast Guard icebreaker *Northwind* developed engine problems and was rerouted to a coastal channel. On the return voyage, another U.S. icebreaker, *Staten Island,* joined the two vessels, but when the convoy experienced further problems with heavy slush in Viscount Melville Sound, the Canadian CCGS *Louis St. Laurent* came to the aid of all three. The Northwest Passage inflicted one final insult on *Manhattan* when it collided with an iceberg in Lancaster Sound, putting a hole in its plating with subsequent loss of ballast.[20] The American media proclaimed the voyage a historic success, whereas Canadian officials were haunted by visions that someday the passage might be choked with oil tankers.

What seemed surprising in this case was the failure of Prime Minister Trudeau to back down as other Canadian leaders had done in the past. Perhaps he saw an opportunity to test the American position in hopes the U.S. might relent, or simply to test the degree of international support for Canada's position. Whatever his thoughts, Trudeau kept them to himself.

While government officials explored the options available to assert sovereign jurisdiction, the Department of External Affairs notified Canadian embassies around the world of the government's official position: that the *Manhattan* experiment was welcomed by Canada and the status of the Arctic waters was not at issue. The message included explicit instructions that references to differences of opinion with the U.S. were to be minimized. The department also

Supertanker SS *Manhattan* owned by Humble Oil (today part of
ExxonMobil) on its traverse through the Northwest Passage in 1969.
S000091, Royal Geographical Society Photo Collection, London

issued a general warning against making any assertion that would
encourage open confrontation with the U.S.

Meanwhile, Prime Minister Trudeau assembled a team of legal
advisers that included Ivan Head, J. Alan Beesley and Allan Gotlieb
to evaluate the various recommendations and suggest appropriate
action. Suggestions ranged from drawing baselines around the Archipelago, expanding the icebreaker fleet or taking full control of the
DEW Line, to generally increasing government activity in the Arctic.
In the end, the Prime Minister's Office, on the advice of the legal
team, overrode the advice of External Affairs officials and opted for
a functional approach by declaring the right to enforce pollution
control in offshore Arctic waters, based on the rationale that it was
Canada's responsibility to protect the fragile environment and indigenous people against potential degradation caused by tanker traffic.
In the throne speech on 23 October 1969, the Governor-General reiterated the government's serious concern about the Arctic ecology
and announced pending "legislation setting out measures necessary to prevent pollution in the Arctic Seas" and "other methods of

protecting Canada's ocean coasts."[21] In November, news that Pan-arctic Oil had discovered a major gas field at Drake Point on Melville Island simply added to concerns about future tanker traffic and its effect on the marine environment.

In essence, Trudeau's action of making a unilateral declaration, then seeking international acceptance, was a strategy first employed by O.D. Skelton in 1925 when he publicly declared Canada's jurisdiction over the Arctic Islands, then waited five years before Denmark officially recognized the claim. In 1969 Trudeau was more cautious and sought support internally and externally in advance of submitting the necessary legislation to Parliament. Initially internal division threatened to stalemate the proposed action, when foreign affairs and military officials argued against open confrontation with the U.S. Others supported the initiative, swayed largely by strong nationalist and environmental arguments.

Recognizing that support from the international community would be critical to counter U.S. opposition, Canadian politicians lobbied other countries on the need for special regulations to protect the fragile Arctic environment. By now, the argument had shifted from sovereign rights to concerns for the Arctic ecology and indigenous population. Responding to Canada's invitation to the international community to support a special Arctic pollution prevention regime, the U.S requested bilateral discussions, initially on the environment then broadened to include Arctic resources and related transportation issues. Trudeau, however, had already met with U Thant, the UN secretary-general, to discuss Canada's proposed actions, at the same time as his minister of transport was explaining the situation at the International Maritime Consultative Organization in Brussels. In Ottawa, Mitchell Sharp as secretary of state for external affairs had met with Soviet Foreign Minister Gromyko to discuss the possibility of Canadian-Soviet cooperation in the Arctic. Canada's argument for anti-pollution measures rested on the moral obligation of a country with potentially vast oil and gas reserves to protect the vulnerable Arctic environment on behalf of the world community. Arctic sovereignty was minimized during these discussions and only obliquely referenced when the Department of National Defence announced plans for a mobile Arctic strike force, new military detachments in the northwest, six new airports along the Arctic Circle and plans for military exercises in the Arctic Islands.[22]

Three events occurred early in 1970 that forced the Canadian government to immediate action: first, the discovery of oil on the Tuktoyaktuk Peninsula in the Northwest Territories, followed by the breakup of the Liberian tanker *Arrow* off the Nova Scotia coast, causing a major oil spill, and finally, the announcement by Humble Oil of *Manhattan*'s second voyage. Aware of the inordinate influence the U.S. Navy had on American policy and Canada's inability to detect, let alone regulate, the travel of submerged nuclear submarines, the Canadians agreed that proposed regulations would exempt military vessels in hopes of moderating Washington's criticism. Hence the proposed bill would define a maritime zone of water and ice extending from Canada's Arctic coastline, over which strict anti-pollution regulations would be enforced on all ships except naval or government vessels.

In prior discussions, the U.S. State Department stood firm in its rejection of the proposed legislation, which only strengthened Prime Minister Trudeau's resolve to defend his country's rights as an independent nation. When he phoned the White House to alert the President to introduction of the bill the following day, Secretary of State William Rogers returned his call and warned that the U.S. would defy any such regulations, "with a submarine if necessary." Enraged at the threat, Trudeau reportedly replied that pollution concerns were related to oil tankers, not submarines, and "if you send up a tin can with a paper-thin hull filled with oil, we will not only stop you, we'll board you and turn you around. And if we do so, Mr. Rogers, we'll have the world on our side."[23] While the remainder of the conversation returned to a more conventional tone of diplomatic respect, the incident suggests that there are occasions when strong language may be more effective in countering the threats of a superpower than the gentle art of diplomacy. Media may alarm; the public may express outrage; but the success of any government response will depend on extensive preparation and above all a leader's resolve to stay the course. More often than not, it is the human dimension in an Arctic sovereignty conflict that ultimately directs the outcome.

The following day, 8 April 1970, two bills were introduced in the Canadian House of Commons. The first, Bill C-202, the Arctic Waters Pollution Prevention Act (AWPPA), created a 100-nautical-mile offshore zone over which Canada had the authority to enforce anti-pollution regulations. As a measure to buy time needed to obtain international support, the AWPPA was accompanied by a reservation that excluded any related dispute from arbitration by the International Court of Justice. The second, Bill C-203, amended the Territorial Seas and Fisheries Act to extend the limits of territorial waters from three miles to twelve, a measure which seemed reasonable since only twenty-five nations still held to a three-mile limit, whereas sixty-six had extended the limit to twelve miles.[24]

President Nixon's immediate response was to announce import quota cuts of Canadian oil and threaten further retaliation should the legislation pass. Subsequent high-level negotiations between Ottawa and Washington failed to find common ground. Although the Humble Oil Company had agreed to a list of stipulations for *Manhattan*'s second voyage, including prior inspection of the ship, the U.S. government firmly refused to accept Canadian authority over the Northwest Passage. In defiance, Congress announced authorization for the "most powerful ice-breaker fleet in the world" to eliminate the need for foreign-flagged ships. The House of Commons responded by passing the bill unanimously and the Senate by granting approval within eight days of its introduction. The only criticism within government was that the measures might be inadequate.[25] Opinions by Canadian legal experts were equally positive, with one suggesting that the AWPPA was "the most significant unilateral action on the international marine environment ever taken."[26] With a few exceptions, American opinion was negative.

By now, Humble Oil's *Manhattan* had already departed on its second voyage and completed the traverse without incident. This time, however, the ship had a Canadian observer on board and was accompanied by CCGS *John A. Macdonald*, whose captain had the responsibility to end the voyage if the situation warranted.[27] This acquiescence to Canadian requests suggested that if U.S. commercial ships were willing to comply with necessary regulations, other foreign vessels might be equally cooperative. Canada may have won a significant battle but the full brunt of the diplomatic wars lay ahead, as the issue was now politicized.

Before legislation passed the Canadian Senate, the U.S. unexpectedly proposed to convene a multilateral conference that June, with the object of establishing an international regime for Arctic waters that met American priorities. Canada was invited to attend, but would have no part in preparing the invitation list or the agenda. Through active lobbying, Ottawa garnered sufficient support to block the conference, with a curious division of support. Of the fourteen countries the U.S. had invited, only the Netherlands seemed in favour. Among circumpolar countries, the Soviet Union, Iceland, Norway and Sweden opposed the conference, whereas Denmark, along with Belgium, Britain and Japan, requested clarification of the terms of reference. Also opposed were Italy, Latin American coastal states and two "flag of convenience" shipping states, Panama and Liberia.[28] As a result, the U.S. switched strategies and called for another Law of the Sea Conference to deal with jurisdiction over the seabed, the limits of territorial seas, international straits and marine pollution. The UN complied and announced plans for UNCLOS III to begin in 1973, with an agenda that eventually included pollution control in ice-infested waters.

The Arctic Waters Pollution Prevention Act may best be described as a functional exercise of special rights to achieve recognition of sovereign authority. Considered in conjunction with concurrent changes in the Canada Water Act, the Inland Water Act and the new land-use regulations of the Territorial Lands Act, the AWPPA was, as Trudeau had promised, a foreign policy extending from national policy.[29] When combined with Bill C-203 to extend territorial seas, the overlapping jurisdiction essentially gave Canada authority to enforce extensive anti-pollution controls on all ships entering Arctic waters.

At the same time, expansion of the territorial seas to 12 nautical miles effectively created two gates in the narrows of the Northwest

Passage, at Barrow Strait and Prince of Wales Strait, where the distance between the islands was less than 24 miles, indirectly supporting the claim that the Northwest Passage was not an international strait, thus subject to Canadian regulations. Even then the status was not permanently resolved, as classification of an international strait was partly determined by the number of foreign ships traversing the channel, and that number was increasing yearly. The hotly contested reservation, meanwhile, was rationalized on the grounds that marine and environmental laws had failed to reflect the technological changes of the previous decade. In other words, the AWPPA was not in violation of international law, but in advance of it. From the perspective of political scientist Peter Dobell, "The measure of the government's success was that it achieved the rhetoric of confrontation without having to face an actual confrontation." [30]

Although the AWPPA was passed in 1970, it was not proclaimed for another two years, during which time detailed regulations were drafted to carry out the intent of the legislation. Ships entering the contiguous zone were required to conform to Canadian standards of construction and navigational procedures. Regulations regarding icebreaking capabilities differed according to the season and ice conditions in the sixteen designated Shipping Safety Control Zones. Pollution prevention officers were given the authority to halt vessels failing to meet the required standards and, if appropriate, to seize their cargo. Regulations also included a ban on dumping waste into the water and the requirement that foreign owners provide proof of financial responsibility and civil liability. To manage the traffic regulations in both the eastern and western Arctic, a voluntary reporting system called NORDREG was set up in 1977 and applied to all vessels over 300 tons. A clearance request was to be submitted twenty-four hours in advance, to include route and destination, followed by daily reports to the Canadian Coast Guard Traffic Centre at Frobisher Bay (now Iqaluit). The centre, in turn, was responsible for exercising control over a ship's navigation as well as providing pertinent information and services. [31] Even though it was voluntary, the Canadian government claims NORDREG has rarely been violated.

Meanwhile, Denmark and Canada took a critical first step in resolving potential conflicts over marine boundaries when they negotiated an agreement in 1973 that officially defined the boundary line between Greenland and the Arctic Islands. Effectively dividing jurisdiction over the continental shelf, the line was set equidistant from each coast, using baselines across large inlets or straits with adjustments made for the location of offshore islands. The new boundary line was approximately 1,500 nautical miles in length but extended only as far as 83° 13´ N latitude—in other words, up to but not including the Lincoln Sea. Nor did the agreement apply to the waters around Hans Island, which was jointly claimed by Canada and Denmark. Recognizing that there might be problems determining the precise location of the line, Article 3 of the Canada-Denmark Agreement prevents either party from issuing exploratory permits adjacent to the boundary. The agreement also had the distinction of being the first bilateral agreement to define Arctic maritime boundaries.[32]

In the interim, oil drillers had accelerated their activity in the Arctic Islands following Panarctic's discovery of gas at Drake Point. Additional gas fields were identified at nearby Hecla and on King Christian, Ellef Ringnes and Thor Islands. So far, there had been no major oil discoveries other than a small field on Cameron Island. Eventually, Panarctic came under the wing of Petro-Canada with the federal government acquiring a 45 percent equity stake. Other companies also increased exploratory drilling, including Elf, British Petroleum, Texaco, Gulf, Imperial Oil, Dome and Atlantic Richfield, but with only modest results. By 1971, offshore permit holders began combining their drilling programs under the management of Suncor. Further consolidation followed in the late seventies, when the Arctic Islands Exploration Group was formed from Esso, Gulf, Panarctic and Petro-Canada, which committed to spend a further $80 million on exploration and research. With only the gas fields indicating commercially profitable reserves, attention now turned to finding how best to bring the product to southern markets.[33]

American companies involved in the Prudhoe Bay oil discoveries had already experienced objections to their pipeline proposal to transport oil from the Arctic coast to a deep-sea port on the Gulf of Alaska. With problems encountered during the *Manhattan* voyages and the regulations implicit in passage of the Arctic Waters Pollution Prevention Act, the pipeline option was considered the only alternative. By now ARCO had joined with British Petroleum and Humble Oil to create the Alyeska Pipeline Company to design, build and operate the Trans-Alaska Pipeline System (TAPS). Applying pressure on both federal and state governments to speed up Native land claims negotiations, the oil companies succeeded where the Alaska Federation of Natives had failed. Following intense negotiations, a modified version of the AFN's proposal was accepted. On 17 December 1971 President Nixon signed the Alaska Native Claims Settlement Act (ANCSA), to the delight of the state, the oil companies and most, but not all, aboriginal communities.

Under ANCSA's terms, the U.S. government agreed to pay $462.5 million over eleven years, and the state agreed to pay a further $500 million from its royalty revenues, the latter measure designed to ensure continued support for oil production from the Native population. In return for extinguishing all aboriginal title to their lands, Alaskan Eskimos, Indians and Aleuts received roughly 44 million acres of land divided among 220 villages and 12 regional corporations. While the communities held only surface rights to their lands, the Native-run corporations would hold full title and subsurface rights and be responsible for their administration and for cash payments received from the federal and state governments. Natives were expected to become shareholders in the corporations and receive annual dividends from profits. A "Native," according to the act, was defined as a U.S. citizen who had at least a quarter Indian, Aleutian or Eskimo ancestry.[34]

The Alaskan settlement was considered historic, not only for the speed at which it was negotiated, but for provision for subsurface rights to a portion of the land award, a first in North America. More importantly, it inspired other indigenous groups in northern Canada, including Inuit, to demand settlement of their land claims ahead of any oil and gas or other major development taking place on their traditional lands. As a European nation, Denmark had no historical precedent acknowledging aboriginal rights, in either northern Europe or Asia. Greenlanders' primary objective was to attain Home Rule Government, similar in structure and powers to a territorial government in Canada, but in line with the devolution of power that eventually resulted in Iceland's full independence as a separate nation-state.

Increased compensation in the final Native Alaskan settlement is generally credited to the efforts of an Inupiat named Charles Edwardsen Jr., commonly known as Etok, who was born and raised in a North Slope community and educated in government residential schools. At the root of Etok's determination was his belief that the U.S. purchase of Alaska had been illegal because it failed to gain prior approval of the Native population and was not followed by a treaty agreement similar to those that regularized colonization of the other forty-eight states. Possessing unusual charisma and aggressiveness at the age of twenty-two, Etok organized the Arctic Slope Native Association (ASNA) in 1961 to advance Inupiat interests, then hired a lawyer to present the group's claims to both state and federal authorities. Two years later, he threatened to pull ASNA out of the AFN unless the leaders agreed to negotiate a larger parcel of land. Even then, when the AFN ratified the agreement, the Arctic Slope Native Association voted against it, protesting that the North Slope Inupiat would receive only 10 percent of their traditional lands.[35]

Displeased by the Inupiat lack of influence on oil development, Etok took a first step toward local self-government when he acquired approval in a local referendum to convert six towns on the Arctic coast into a borough with its own elected council. Former Alaska state senator Eben Hopson became the borough's first mayor. When the courts finally ruled in 1976 that the 7,200-square-mile borough with its 6,000 residents was legal, the decision marked the first instance of Inuit local self-government in Alaska. Immediately the borough levied a tax on every barrel of oil leaving the North Slope, money that would be used to improve Inuit living conditions and help fund the first meeting of the Inuit Circumpolar Conference, held in 1977 at the North Slope community of Barrow, Alaska.[36]

Native land claims settlement was only one of several hurdles delaying construction of the Trans-Alaska Pipeline System (TAPS). Increasing pressure from environmental groups had resulted in passage of the National Environmental Policy Act (NEPA) in 1969, requiring an Environmental Impact Statement (EIS) in advance of all major federal projects that impacted on human life. As part of the TAPS review, evaluation of an alternative route through Canada was also required. The following year, several environmental groups and five Native villages launched separate lawsuits citing inadequate protection of the land and wildlife, prompting a federal judge to issue an injunction against construction until the lawsuits were settled. When the U.S. Secretary of the Interior released a draft EIS on the proposed pipeline two years later, it raised another storm of protest from environmental groups which subsequently banded together to form the Alaska Coalition. While the statement recognized the need for a gas pipeline connecting to the southern states by way of Canada's Mackenzie Valley, it argued that the oil pipeline should be on Alaskan soil and under American control to improve the import/export balance, provide a benefit for American shipping and create jobs and income for Alaskans.

Believing the state contained America's last major wilderness area and must be preserved, environmentalists argued that the project had contravened NEPA and demanded a thorough study of the pipeline's potential impact on the environment and further evaluation of alternative routes through Canada to avoid destruction in Alaska's wilderness and pollution of America's west coast waters. The review was expected to delay construction for years.[37] Unexpectedly, the Department of the Interior released a final EIS in March 1972, rejecting an alternative Canadian route as taking up to six years longer to complete than the Alaskan route. The six-volume report also stressed the urgent need to expand domestic production to reduce dependence on foreign oil. As a result the federal injunction was lifted, only to be overturned by an appeals court that ruled that the right-of-way corridor was too narrow.

Debate and indecision ended abruptly on 17 October 1973 when the Organization of the Petroleum Exporting Countries (OPEC) announced an embargo on oil exports to the U.S. in retaliation for American support for Israel in the Yom Kippur War. A month later, President Nixon signed the Trans-Alaska Pipeline Authorization Act. Federal authorization for the pipeline right-of-way followed in January. Construction began in April with the haul road (now Alaska State Route 11) completed by September. The rapid pace was costly but effective. In June 1977, oil began flowing along the 800-mile-long pipeline to Valdez on Prince William Sound.

Alaskans celebrated the event as an outstanding achievement, despite the fact that it was grossly over budget—approximately $8 billion for a total workforce of 70,000 paid high wages to meet the completion date, state-of-the-art technology to meet environmental demands, massive infrastructure that required a large fleet of heavy construction vehicles and specialized equipment required for early completion. When reaching peak production ten years later, the pipeline met its promise of supplying well over 20 percent of domestic needs. For Americans, the project had achieved its purpose; for Canadian environmentalists, there was a sense of relief that all-too-frequent oil spills would not occur on their soil.[38] The overall lesson learned was that pipeline construction was costly but once approvals were granted it was virtually impossible to halt if there was a continued demand for oil. Although the seventies offered an optimum environment for energy megaprojects, these developments also aroused fear and mistrust in indigenous communities that lay in their path.

Successful settlement of Alaskan Native land claims in 1971 encouraged northern indigenous groups throughout Canada to demand a halt to major projects until their land claims were settled. The first case of note was in northern Quebec, where Cree Indians and Inuit joined environmentalists to protest the Quebec government's decision to proceed with the James Bay hydroelectric project. The megaproject involved damming several major rivers draining into James Bay, which would cause massive flooding of traditional hunting and trapping lands. A well-publicized court case in 1972–73 was followed by an injunction halting further construction until land claims were settled. Although the ruling was overturned within weeks by a higher court, the publicity garnered wide public support for Inuit and northern Cree as Canadians became more knowledgeable about northern aboriginal peoples, the history of treatymaking in North America and its origins in the 1763 Royal Proclamation.

After several years of intense negotiations, on 11 November 1975 the Quebec Cree and Inuit signed the James Bay and Northern Quebec Agreement, which gave them ownership to 5,400 square kilometres of land or 1.3 percent of the total under negotiation, as well as specified hunting, fishing and trapping rights on adjacent lands. They also acquired a measure of control over health, education, policing and justice. In return for $225 million to be paid over a period of years, the Cree and Inuit agreed to extinguishment of all aboriginal rights to remaining lands. Some Native groups reacted negatively to the agreement, believing that it had placed a higher priority on a cash settlement compared to land rights, economic support and a voice in future development. Amending agreements later addressed some deficiencies and problems in implementation.[39]

Even then, the Inuit of northern Quebec were not satisfied with the status quo and held on to the dream of someday creating a self-governing territory within the province. The Inuit-owned Makivik Corporation, which had been established as an elected body to implement the terms of their agreement, was particularly successful in administering the Kativik School Board and other agencies set up to manage various responsibilities granted to the Inuit under the James Bay Agreement. One agency, the Kativik Environmental Quality Commission, played the lead role in blocking the proposed Great Whale project. Gradually, but with tenacity and continued negotiations, Quebec Inuit gained increasing control over local services as they moved toward their objective of self-government. With the inherent difficulties in dealing with the split jurisdiction of provincial and federal governments, progress was slow. As a result, the

Offshore oil rigs built on a man-made island in the Beaufort
Sea are connected to land by a bridge, allowing for oil to be
carried along the Trans-Alaska Pipeline year-round, a costly process.
Companies now hope to transport oil by tanker during the summer
when the ice melt is sufficient to guarantee safe passage.

EI #78623844, *National Geographic* photographer James Blair/Getty Images

ultimate goal of establishing Nunavik as a self-governing region
within Quebec would be delayed until the next century.[40]

The aboriginal rights movement in Canada began with the
southern-based Indian Eskimo Association established in 1955, a
predominantly non-Native organization led by an educated elite dedicated to improving the lives of the nation's indigenous peoples. By
1973, it had metamorphosed into a more appropriately named Canadian Association in Support of Native Peoples, but not before it had
encouraged the formation of numerous Native organizations, including the Council of Yukon Indians, the Dene Association, the Inuit
Tapirisat of Canada (ITC) and the Committee for Original People's
Entitlement (COPE) representing the Inuvialuit of Canada's western

Arctic. At the outset, it was apparent that the Inuit preferred to proceed on their own without the support or collaboration of Métis or
Indian organizations. Although initial focus was on the settlement
of land claims, the longer-term goal was self-government. Further
organizations were set up to provide the infrastructure required to
negotiate agreements on Nunavut and more recently for Nunatsiavut (Labrador). Settlement of these claims took longer to negotiate
as there were no urgent development projects to pressure the government, as occurred in Alaska or Quebec. Although the Supreme
Court ruling on the *Calder* case in 1973 gave legitimacy to the concept
of aboriginal rights to traditional lands, the major breakthrough did
not occur until 1982, when section 35 of the Constitution Act, 1982
confirmed official recognition of aboriginal rights, thus enabling the
Inuit to negotiate their concerns rather than having to rely on the
courts.[41] As a result, subsequent land claims settlements were not
only expedited, but also included measures that allowed Inuit a voice
in future socio-economic development and protection of the wildlife
upon which their lives depended.

As part of a general movement that originated in the U.S., environmental protest groups were also on the increase in Canada. As with
American concerns over disappearing wilderness in Alaska, Canadian
organizations focussed on the far north and in particular on energy-
related developments. In response, in 1972 the Department of Indian
Affairs and Northern Development (DIAND) announced a new federal policy for northern Canada entitled "Northern Canada in the 70s"
that included as one objective the "maintaining and enhancing of the
northern environment with due consideration to economic and social
development."[42] That same year, the Mackenzie Valley Pipeline Inquiry
was set up to evaluate the impact of a proposed gas pipeline extending
from the Beaufort Sea to connect with the Alberta system. Commissioned by Justice Thomas R. Berger of the British Columbia Supreme
Court, the inquiry took three years to complete its investigation before
issuing a report entitled *Northern Frontier, Northern Homeland*.

In the interim, the commissioner travelled from village to village
along the route, interviewing Natives about their use of the land and

the effect a pipeline might have on their lives. With the Canadian Broadcasting Corporation (CBC) providing full coverage of events, it was likely the most publicized event of the decade. Berger asserted that the inquiry was "not simply a debate about a gas pipeline and energy corridor," but a debate on "the future of the North and its peoples." He warned that "the choice we make will decide whether the North is to be primarily a frontier for industry or a homeland for its people." The report released in May 1977 described the pipeline's potential destruction of the environment and adverse effects on aboriginal communities. Among the many recommendations, the most important was the call for a moratorium on the project for at least ten years to allow for a fair and just mediation of aboriginal land claims.[43] Ottawa heeded Berger's warning. In spite of several attempts to revive the project, as of 2009 the Mackenzie Valley Pipeline remains where it was left in 1977—awaiting environmental approval.

Seeking another option, the Canadian government established another pipeline inquiry in April 1977, this time to look into the Alcan project, a proposed gas pipeline running south from the North Slope to connect with the Alaska Highway and across the southern Yukon and northern B.C. Chaired by Kenneth M. Lysyk, the Alaska Highway Pipeline Inquiry was "directed to prepare a preliminary report that identified the principal social and economic implications of the proposal and the attitudes of the Yukon people." An Environmental Assessment Review was established at the same time to prepare a statement on the environmental impact of the Alcan project. Both reports were to be delivered before 1 September. Even with limited time constraints, Lysyk interviewed over 500 witnesses at community hearings and reviewed numerous briefs and exhibits. Presentations by the Council of Yukon Indians, in particular, expressed grave concern about the pipeline and requested that the project be denied approval until land claims had been settled. The commissioners agreed.[44] As expected, given the forceful arguments in the Berger report, neither was this proposal approved. Nor was it discarded. In 2007, the Trans Canada Pipeline Company resurrected the proposed route in its application to the State of Alaska to build a gas pipeline from the Beaufort Sea south and along the Alaska Highway.

Amid the confusion of cross-purposes between oil development activities and Native demands for settlement of land claims, the third session of the UN Conference on the Law of the Sea (UNCLOS III) had convened in 1973, with the first meeting held at Caracas, Venezuela. For Canada, three main issues demanded resolution: the status of the Arctic Ocean, the legal definition of the Northwest Passage and the special rights of Arctic coastal states to control pollution of their adjacent waters.[45] Once it was apparent that there would be no prior agreement with the U.S. on these issues, Ottawa had turned to the UN Conference on the Human Environment held in 1971 at Stockholm to seek international support. With Canada playing an active role in the preparatory sessions, the Stockholm Conference unanimously accepted the twenty-three principles and the Statement of Objectives on the Marine Environment proposed by Canada, including recognition of the special interests of coastal states in preventing pollution of the marine environment. Issues not endorsed, but referred to the Law of the Sea Conference, were the concept of coastal pollution control zones, the rights of coastal states to refuse passage of ships not complying to international standards and delegation of international authority to coastal states to exercise control over pollution. So far Canada's success was only partial. The major battles lay ahead at UNCLOS III.[46]

The energy crisis of 1973, caused by the sudden rise of OPEC prices, the Arab oil embargo and the possibility of energy shortages, raised concerns that Canada's Arctic pollution prevention measures might be a luxury the world could not afford. After peaking in 1973, drilling activity in the Arctic Islands had dropped off dramatically due to disappointing results and anticipated transportation problems. Tensions between Canada and the U.S. over the status of the Northwest Passage diminished somewhat as other issues such as fisheries and seabed mining gained in importance.[47] Of greater importance at that moment was the growing unrest in Quebec that had created a more immediate sovereignty crisis.

Seven years of negotiations at the UNCLOS III meetings saw many compromises and trade-offs. Although the Revised Composite Negotiating Text (RCNT) of 1980 awaited approval by the American government, progress toward establishing a consensus on environmental law had been substantial. With Canada's priority the prevention of Arctic pollution, its legal team adopted a functional approach to coordinate climate and geopolitical concerns with those of seabed mining, fisheries, shipping, environmental concerns, potential exports and defence. Although each point was defended in isolation, the Canadian team was forced to acquiesce on broader issues related to freedom of the seas because of demands by countries with major shipping interests.[48]

Canada succeeded, however, in having an Arctic clause, Article 234, incorporated into the negotiating text, acknowledging that Arctic waters deserved special consideration and that affected coastal states were authorized "to establish and enforce non-discriminatory laws and regulations" to prevent and control pollution in their adjacent waters. The RCNT also proposed a 200-nautical-mile exclusive economic zone, which legitimized Canada's 1977 unilateral claim to a 200-mile Arctic fisheries zone, and port-state enforcement, which would allow Canada to prosecute ships violating international standards. Unfortunately, boundary disputes related to the continental shelf were left in limbo because of the ambiguous wording of Article 83, which stated that agreement between two affected states should be based on "equitable principles, employing the median or equidistance line where appropriate."[49]

To obtain consensus on the Arctic clause, negotiators were forced to make compromises that weakened Canada's jurisdictional claims. To meet the demands of Soviet Russia and the U.S., for instance, Article 236 granted government and military vessels exemption from environmental regulations, including the ban on dumping waste. Agreement to accept an International Seabed Authority over the polar basin appeared to be a pragmatic concession to prevent American encroachment, but in the end the proposed authority and related issues required further negotiations and amendments before U.S.

acceptance. The most serious compromise was Canada's agreement that the "right of innocent passage" through international straits would be replaced by the right of "transit passage" or sea lanes passage, which gave foreign vessels virtually the same freedom in an international strait as on the high seas. Should commercial traffic through the Northwest Passage increase considerably, Canada could only exercise control under Article 234 and only over non-government ships that violated international anti-pollution standards.[50] So far, Trudeau's strategy of making a unilateral declaration and waiting for international support had only partially succeeded. Even then, there were no guarantees that the UN could prevent a superpower from defying international law if it was in its best interests.

EVEN WITHOUT precise information on the ecological damage that might result from an oil spill, the Inuit across North America were already fearful of the effects that supertankers or pipelines might have on the marine environment. By far the most influential organization to pressure governments of Arctic countries was the Inuit Circumpolar Conference, later renamed Inuit Circumpolar Council (ICC), composed of representatives from Alaska, Arctic Canada and Greenland, with a small delegation of Inuit from Chukotka province in eastern Siberia attending in later years. Not surprisingly, the driving force behind creation of the ICC came from the Inupiat of Alaska living on the North Slope.

The idea of establishing a permanent inter-Arctic organization was first discussed in 1973 at the Arctic Peoples' Conference in Copenhagen, convened to discuss how to provide a unified voice against policies dictated by southern nations. Carl Olsen of Greenland and Etok from Alaska convinced Charlie Watt, a Canadian delegate at the time preoccupied with implementation of the James Bay treaty, to join them in establishing an all-Inuit organization. Also in full support of the idea was former Alaska state senator Eben Hopson, the grandson of a British whaler who had settled at Barrow in 1886. Hopson was responsible for planning the first meeting to be held in his hometown and for finding funds to cover delegates' costs of transportation and accommodation. In the end, a good portion of the expenses were provided by the North Slope and Arctic Slope Corporations. As the lead lobbyist against the International Whaling Commission's attempts to ban subsistence hunting of the bowhead whale, Hopson perhaps had a more personal motivation than other delegates, but he found strong support among all Inuit delegates when concerns for the environment were joined with aboriginal rights to self-government and ownership of traditional lands. As mayor of the new North Slope Borough, Hopson also understood the importance of an elected local self-government in having the authority to voice community concerns to senior levels of government.[51]

Although delegates came from a variety of communities with diverse living conditions and history, the common denominator at the meeting was cultural. They all shared common ancestors, language and such traditions as food preferences, hunting and fishing practices, clothing, dogsleds and kayaks, drum dancing, storytelling and so on. According to Danish reporter Philip Lauritzen, who accompanied the Greenland delegation, the site chosen for the first meeting was equally significant. The tiny village of Barrow had begun to take form in the 1880s with the arrival of three whalers from Liverpool by the names of Brower, Hopson and Gordon, all of whom married Inupiat wives, learned their language and became part of the Native community. Although Gordon later moved on and settled in northern Quebec, descendants of all three families played key roles in the formative years of the ICC. Equally significant was the age of the delegates. With the notable exception of Hopson, who was in his fifties, many were in their twenties, educated at government or church boarding schools and determined to right past wrongs. In essence, time and circumstance had conspired to bring together a common threat, a group of educated young Inuit and the experienced leadership of a few to ensure success of the venture.

The first meeting of the Inuit Circumpolar Conference opened on 12 June 1977, with Eben Hopson presiding. Attending were eighteen official delegates from Greenland, twenty from Alaska, eighteen from Canada, along with a host of observers and the entire population of

On the right, the former state senator and executive director of the Alaska
Federation of Natives, Eben Hopson, is speaking to Joseph Upicksoun,
president of the Arctic Slope Native Association, at a North Borough
executive meeting, 1970. Hopson actively promoted the Eskimo right to
hunt whales and in 1977 was a major force behind creation of the Inuit
Circumpolar Conference (now Council). He died just before the ICC
charter was officially signed at the 1980 meeting in Nuuk, Greenland.
ASL-NL-4, Alaska State Library Photograph Collection

the town. Hopson's opening remarks were in English and to the point,
that creation of an Inuit circumpolar organization was "the only
means whereby we can secure an efficient and successful protection
of our common Arctic environment." He explained that the underlying purpose of the new organization was to encourage all Inuit to
seek forms of self-government that would give them a voice in the
development and management of all Arctic resources on land or sea,
as opposed to relying on courts to communicate their concerns.[52]
The ideals espoused in the keynote address were lofty and raised high
expectations among delegates, most of whom were young, enthusiastic and determined to preserve their culture from assimilation into

a white man's society. Little did they realize that they were on the threshold of a whole new concept of Arctic sovereignty.

Discussions followed in small groups and plenary sessions until the first and most important resolution was presented on the third day. With a preamble that affirmed the need for Inuit to express their concerns and their right to self-government, a resolution was passed that officially established the ICC. An interim planning committee made up of four delegates from each country was to draft a charter, reviewing its substance with Inuit communities and establishing a ratification procedure to take place at a second meeting to be held in three years' time. The resolution also detailed the items of concern to be included in the charter: protection of the environment, preservation of language and culture, improved transportation and communications connecting all Inuit, consultation on government policies and proposals affecting their lives, wildlife management, improvement of living conditions, development of a comprehensive Arctic policy and establishment of sufficient sources of funding to ensure the operation and future existence of the organization.[53]

Further discussions the following day resulted in seventeen more resolutions. Dissent arose on only one issue: inclusion of a resolution that the Arctic be used for peaceful purposes and that military operations, testing of weapons and on-site disposal of wastes, whether chemical, biological or nuclear, be banned. A few Alaskan delegates objected, with Hopson arguing that denying the importance of military defence was illogical. "Our governments are responsible for defending our country, the whole country and therefore also our country . . . The environment must be defended as far as possible, but without a defense system we cannot even be sure of possession of any environment."[54] Nonetheless, the resolution carried with only a third of the Alaskan delegation voting against the motion. Hopson, however, had raised a key point. Only a mature nation had the military capability to protect Inuit lands against a potential enemy invasion.

A number of resolutions dealt with the environment, one specifically demanding that Inuit be allowed to review and approve the technology involved in any new resource development. A final resolution requested that the ICC encourage attendance of Siberian Inuit and that their government should be approached to obtain their approval. A proposed budget of $1.5 million was to cover expenses for the coming year, including preparation and approval of the charter and creation of national offices in Alaska, Canada and Greenland. Funding was sought from selected oil and gas companies, foundations, government agencies, mainline Arctic churches and environmental groups. Although the Danish, Canadian and American governments gave nominal support to the new organization, few senior politicians took their resolutions and determination seriously, perhaps a miscalculation considering the major influence the ICC would have on future Arctic affairs. A committee was set up to prepare a draft charter and gain approval from the Inuit communities throughout the Arctic. According to sources at the Eben Hopson Museum, Canadian Mary Simon, vice-president of Makivik, was largely responsible for writing the draft charter.

Eben Hopson and the Inupiat of Alaska's North Slope may have been the first to call for Inuit self-government to save their environment, but Greenlanders were first to achieve a major breakthrough with creation in 1979 of the Home Rule Government. Greenlanders use the term "home rule government" in reference to self-government with powers similar to those of the Canadian territories. In Canada, devolution of power is based on a set of criteria that includes population, economic stability and non-reliance on federal subsidies before a territory is elevated to provincial status that includes full control over and revenue from the area's natural resources. In Greenland, the 2009 Self-Rule Government is similar to provincial status in Canada except that revenue from resources is shared. Denmark retains full control of foreign policy, currency and security. By virtue of U.S. government structures and policies, the Alaskan Eskimos appear to be limited to the local municipal or borough form of self-government.

Greenland's Home Rule Government came about as a result of angry protests by bright young Inuit who had been sent to Copenhagen for their secondary education. The major source of discontent

The 1980 Executive Committee of the Inuit Circumpolar Conference
photographed at Nuuk, Greenland. L-R: Oscar Kawagley (Alaska), Jimmy
Stotts (Alaska), Lars Chemnitz (Greenland), President Hans-Pavia Rosing
(Greenland), Mary Simon (Canada), John Amagoalik (Canada),
Aqqaluk Lynge (Greenland). It is a reflection of the commitment of
these educated young Inuit that four would serve as presidents of the
International ICC (Stotts, Rosing, Simon and Aqqaluk), whereas John
Amagoalik is generally considered the founding father of Nunavut.

Courtesy Inuit Circumpolar Council, Greenland

was rooted in Danish policies of the 1960s that were intended to
make Greenlanders more self-sufficient by making the fishing industry the mainstay of the island's economy. Modernization of the
industry required centralizing in a few larger centres with new warehouses, processing plants and port facilities for the expanded fishing
fleet. Expected to become part of the labour force, hunters and their
families were encouraged to move from their tiny coastal communities to large, cost-efficient apartment complexes built in the fishing
ports, where schools and health services could be provided at a reasonable cost. Promising students would be sent to Copenhagen for
secondary education, requiring hundreds of new teachers to teach
the children Danish at the primary level of education. Then in 1964,
to entice the thousands of Danes needed to build the infrastructure
for the new economy and teach the children, the Danish Parliament

passed legislation guaranteeing considerably higher wages than those paid to Greenlanders for the same work. As might be expected, the newcomers treated the Inuit as second-class citizens, which in turn gave rise to increased violence, alcohol abuse and suicide.

Inevitably a new generation of young people educated abroad became active politically, demanding an end to discriminatory wages, protection of Greenlandic culture and more say in governing their affairs. Initially taken aback by the demands, the Danish Parliament realized something had gone wrong in spite of its good intentions. In 1975, a commission was appointed with equal representation by Danes and Greenlanders to review the situation and present proposals for home rule. The commission's work was completed within three years. Following a referendum that saw 10,000 Danes and 30,000 Greenlanders fully endorse the proposal, the new Home Rule Government was officially established in January 1979, with the first elections held that April.[55]

At the time, Greenland's Home Rule Government was considered the most progressive and far-reaching form of government to be granted to a predominantly indigenous population. While the Danish government retained full responsibility for defence, foreign policy, the judiciary, currency and initially the police, Greenlanders gradually acquired control over a wide variety of social affairs, such as culture, the media, educational policy and schools, labour legislation, municipal affairs, housing and the right to levy taxes and customs duties. The most unique characteristic of the Home Rule Act was the provision that all areas of government, excluding the responsibilities specifically assigned to Denmark, could be taken over by the Greenland government when it so wished, with funds made available for their administration. In following years, the Home Rule Government also shared or took over responsibility for the Royal Greenland Trading Company (KGH), its fish-processing plants and large trawlers, health services and the state-run construction and civil engineering organization. A pro-active "Greenlandization" policy also saw the disappearance of Danish names from signs and maps, reintroduction

High-rise apartments surround old town in Nuuk, capital of Greenland.
Built to accommodate Greenlanders moving from outlying camps, they
now dwarf the small houses in the old town. A statue of Hans Egede, the
Norwegian missionary responsible for the first Danish settlement
on the island, stands on a high hill overlooking the harbour.

CE 2677; photographer Carsten Egevang, ARC-PIC Greenland

of the Inuit language into schools, the offering of higher education
courses in Greenland and even withdrawal from the European Economic Community. By 1983, the number of Greenlanders had risen to
40,000, with the Danish population remaining stable at 10,000.

Thus it was with great pride that the second meeting of the Inuit
Circumpolar Conference was held in 1980 at Nuuk, now the seat of
the new Home Rule Government. Here the official charter was formally adopted and a thirty-two-year-old Greenlander, Hans-Pavia
Rosing, was elected its first president, a position he held for six years.
Working committees were also set up to deal with specific issues
such as the environment, education, language and culture, science
and traditional knowledge and whaling. Of particular concern were
proposals to bring gas finds in the High Arctic into production, creating major tanker traffic through Lancaster Sound and Davis Strait.

Concerned about the detrimental effect the ships would have on the whale population, President Rosing led a delegation to Ottawa to protest the proposed Arctic Pilot Project.

By 1980, it was estimated that over $800 million had been spent on oil and gas exploration in the Arctic Islands without a cent of return. Although oil reserves were less promising, the larger gas fields with roughly 9 trillion cubic feet of provable and probable reserves were considered commercially viable. Even then, the problem of transporting the gas in either condensed (CNG) or liquefied form (LNG) posed serious environmental concerns. With the Mackenzie Valley Pipeline now on hold because of the ten-year moratorium on development, attention turned to Petro-Canada's Arctic Pilot Project (APP), which involved a pipeline through Melville Island, then transport to eastern seaports by tanker through Lancaster Sound and Davis Strait. As part of environmental review procedures, Canada's National Energy Board began public hearings into the potential impact of the project on the fragile Arctic environment. In 1982, the ICC delegation presented their case against the proposal, citing a probable adverse effect on the whale population. Whether influenced by the presentation or by high interest rates, this project also died on the drawing board. Several attempts have been made to revive it, but with no success.[56]

IN 1980, Donat Pharand, a leading authority on Arctic sovereignty, maintained that the only assured method of guaranteeing exclusive sovereignty over all waters of the Archipelago would be to enclose the islands by drawing baselines around the perimeter. After the U.S. icebreaker *Polar Sea* traversed the Northwest Passage in 1985 allegedly without prior notice or permission, Canada finally drew the baselines and officially declared all waters lying within as internal waters.

As was the case in the SS *Manhattan* incident, the information fed to Canadians about the USCGC *Polar Sea* voyage was equally misleading. Plans for the transit had been discussed in advance by the U.S. officials and the Canadian Coast Guard. Based in Seattle, the *Polar Sea*

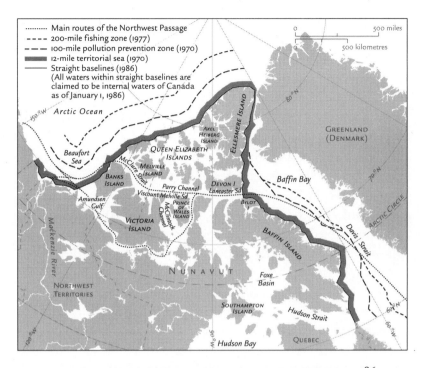

LIMITS OF JURISDICTION IN CANADIAN ARCTIC WATERS, C1986
In addition to the boundaries of jurisdiction set out by the
Arctic Waters Pollution Prevention Act and the Law of the Sea
Treaty, in 1986 Canada officially drew a line around the Archipelago
and declared all waters within to be internal waters.

had been assigned to replace the damaged USCGC *Northwind* for the
1985 resupply of the Thule Air Base. Instead of making its way south
through the Panama Canal, the U.S. Coast Guard suggested that the
ship might go north through the Northwest Passage to ensure it
reached the eastern Arctic in time for the supply mission. As argued
by the authors of *Arctic Front,* there was no intent to challenge Canadian authority. It was simply a pragmatic solution to an unexpected
problem and Canadian officials were pleased to cooperate. As agreed
in advance, three Canadian observers would be on board the U.S.
vessel as observers, pollution controls were in place and the ship

would be accompanied by CCGS *John A. Macdonald* in areas of heavy ice. In the end, the U.S. icebreaker set out from Seattle for Greenland by way of the Panama Canal, and returned westward through the Northwest Passage.[57]

Once again, however, news of the intended voyage caught the attention of the Canadian media, which joined federal opposition parties in mounting an angry protest against the U.S. government for directly challenging Canada's sovereign authority over its Arctic waters. Academics, Inuit leaders and national interest groups joined in to criticize the Canadian government for allowing it to happen. Once again, an exercise of cooperation between the two coast guards was transformed into an Arctic sovereignty crisis. To appease irate Canadians, Prime Minister Mulroney announced government plans to build a Class 8 icebreaker that would be four times more powerful than CCGS *Louis St. Laurent*. Promising the armed forces would do their part, Minister of National Defence Perrin Beatty announced plans to acquire up to a dozen submarines and lay a fixed sonar detection system to monitor foreign submarine activity—promises, like so many others in the past, which would never be fulfilled. The opposition parties, which initially had criticized the Conservative government for inaction, turned the tables and complained that the measures were too costly and would drain money needed for social services from the Treasury.

Whether the baseline strategy will be effective over the long term is debatable, but it did prompt immediate negotiations with the U.S. and resulted in the bilateral Arctic Cooperation Agreement in 1988, which pledged that all navigation by U.S. icebreakers in waters claimed by Canada to be internal would be "undertaken with the consent of the Canadian government." While the agreement did not advance Canada's position on the Northwest Passage, it prevented any damage future American actions might have.[58]

The UN Convention on the Law of the Sea, sometimes referred to as the Law of the Sea Treaty, was officially signed in December 1982, but did not come into force until ratified by the governments of sixty countries, as occurred twelve years later. At the outset, President

The U.S. Coast Guard icebreaker *Polar Sea*. When the ship traversed the
Northwest Passage in 1985, protests in the Canadian media and Parliament
prompted the Conservative government to draw baselines around the
entire Arctic Archipelago and declare the passage an internal waterway.
The U.S. rejects this position, claiming the right to freedom of passage
through the strait. USCG Historic Photo Gallery, Icebreaker Fleet, Polar Sea I

Reagan refused to sign the treaty because it was inconsistent with the basic free-market principles of private property, free enterprise and competition. Of particular concern to Republicans were the powers invested in the International Seabed Authority and the proposed sharing of profits from deep-sea mining beyond the 200-mile continental shelf limit. The U.S. Navy, on the other hand, generally supported the treaty as it guaranteed peacetime navigational rights for military vessels. As work began on a revision to address its objections, the U.S. was granted provisional participation. Yet in spite of the changes, in 1986 the revised treaty was again defeated in the Senate.[59] Canada, meanwhile, was comfortable with the growing number of ratifications and in 1985 withdrew the reservation against submission of the AWPPA to an international court. By the end of 2008, the treaty had been ratified by over 150 states, including Russia in 1997 and Canada in 2003, with the U.S. now the only Arctic country refusing to ratify the convention.

As it happened, the special Arctic clause of the Law of the Sea Treaty initially proved ineffective in preventing oil pollution in the Arctic, partly because international law was ahead of the necessary research and technology required to develop adequate preventive and cleanup measures. When the AWPPA was introduced in 1970, there had been little research into the consequences of oil pollution in the Arctic. This was partially remedied over the next decade as a result of environmental impact studies by government agencies and the private sector in Canada and the U.S. By 1980, over $100 million had been invested in Arctic environment research, including the $7-million Arctic Marine Oilspill Project.[60] Yet in light of overall costs of development, the investment in environmental research and pollution control was minuscule compared to the billions invested in oil and gas exploration, production and transport.

The ineffectiveness of Canadian regulations in preventing oil pollution was all too apparent. After the AWPPA came into force, two major blowouts of Arctic gas wells occurred, one at Drake Point on Somerset Island and another on King Christian Island. The Drake blowout took a year to bring under control, allowing inestimable amounts of hydrocarbon waste to seep into the land and adjacent waters. Similarly in 1977, leakage from an offshore well in the Beaufort Sea was reported to have been in excess of 2,000 trillion cubic feet of gas each day. In another instance, the failure of Canadian regulatory bodies to act effectively delayed cleanup for nine months after *Edgar Jourdain* ran aground off Hall Beach, spilling roughly 90 tons of oil into Foxe Basin. While seemingly minor compared to the 42 million litres of crude oil spilled when *Exxon Valdez* hit a shoal in Prince William Sound, the incidents served as a reminder that ultimate responsibility for cleanup of an oil spill rests with the country claiming sovereign authority over the region, a reality that politicians too often ignore when contemplating potential revenues to be earned from leases and drilling permits. Also too often forgotten are the obligations of Arctic sovereignty that require protection for inhabitants of the region and the marine life upon which many still depend for subsistence.[61]

AT THE third ICC General Assembly held in 1983 at Iqaluit on Baffin Island, work began on preparing an official Arctic policy. That same year, two important events took place. The ICC was granted status as a non-governmental organization (NGO) by the United Nations Economic and Social Council and, at the request of Alaska's North Borough, the ICC agreed to co-sponsor a review of the Alaska Native Claims Settlement. Former justice Thomas Berger was appointed to head the commission, with a broad mandate to examine and report on the socio-economic status of the Alaskan Natives, the history and intent of the ANCSA, historic U.S. policies and practices in the settlement of land claims, the functions of Native corporations and the significance of the act with regard to indigenous people throughout the world. The commission travelled to their communities throughout Alaska and in 1985 published its findings in *Village Journey,* a book that attracted worldwide attention. Harsh criticism was directed at the structure of the Native corporations that failed to protect their lands from potential takeover by outsiders and denied children born

An undated photograph released in 2004 by the U.S. Coast Guard shows
the freighter *Selendang Ayu*, broken in two parts off the coast of Alaska.
Heavy waves and harsh weather threatened the salvage effort of the broken
vessel that leaked thousands of gallons of oil, a subtle reminder that there
have been disasters occurring in Arctic waters other than the ss *Valdez*.
EI-51855123, U.S. Coast Guard, Getty Images

after 1971 the right to become shareholders. Berger also called for a
more community-based form of self-government and improved
social conditions.[62]

Publication of *Village Journey* prompted the U.S. Department of
the Interior in 1985 to initiate its own status report on the ANCSA,
prepared primarily from information supplied by contractors. In
1989, Congress passed several amendments to the act that addressed
some concerns about the structure of the corporations and ownership of the lands, but the Department of the Interior firmly denied
that the agreement had stipulated any social obligations. In its view,
the ANCSA was an outstanding success. If measured solely in monetary terms, perhaps it was. In 2004, it was reported that the Alaskan
Native corporations collectively employed over 12,000 people,

claimed assets totalling $2.9 billion and had distributed over $45 million in dividends.

Compared to those in Alaska and Greenland, Inuit negotiations for land claims and increased self-government were negotiated piecemeal across the Northwest Territories, Quebec and Labrador. As government officials gradually became more attuned to the idea, Inuit were taking a more proactive role in government. In 1977, for instance, Willie Adams became the first Inuk appointed to the Senate, a position he held for more than thirty years. Two years later, Peter Ittinuar would be the first Inuk elected to Parliament.

Although funding had been provided to Canadian Inuit groups to prepare their land claims, it was not until 1982, when section 34 of the repatriated Constitution Act of Canada affirmed the legitimacy of aboriginal rights under the Charter of Rights and Freedoms, that negotiations began in earnest. That same year, a territory-wide plebiscite confirmed that Northwest Territories residents agreed to a division to create a separate Nunavut territory. As a result, the Tunngavik Federation of Nunavut was created to pursue negotiations for the new territory, while the Inuit Tapirisat of Canada continued work on land claims. The only stipulation made by the Inuit of the central and eastern Arctic was that the two agreements be signed simultaneously.

For Canadian Inuit, the first comprehensive land claims settlement north of the 60th parallel was the Inuvialuit Final Agreement (IFA) in 1984, in which the Inuit of the western Arctic agreed to give up exclusive use of their ancestral lands in return for title to 35,000 square miles of land including 5,000 with subsurface rights, financial support, participation in environmental impact studies and co-management of fish and other wildlife resources. The Inuvialuit Regional Corporation (IRC) and various subsidiaries were created to administer the rights and benefits of the agreement. In 2007, the IRC reported a net income of $35.2 million, of which over $3.8 million would be distributed to beneficiaries over the age of eighteen.

An agreement in principle on creation of Nunavut was signed in 1990 and finalized two years later after a referendum had approved the boundary separating the new territory from the remaining

Northwest Territories. On 25 May 1993, the final land claims agreement was signed, followed in June by passage in Parliament of the Nunavut Land Claims Agreement Act and the Nunavut Act calling for the creation of the new territory by 1 April 1999. In the interim, the Nunavut Implementation Commission worked on the structure and responsibilities of the new government. The land claims settlement was by far the largest in Canada in terms of both land and financial compensation. The Inuit gained title to 1.9 million square kilometres of land and water, with subsurface rights to over 35,000, plus a sum of $1.9 billion to be paid over fifteen years. The Nunavut Trust was established to manage money transfers and to oversee investment and distribution of the money to the various communities, whereas the elected Nunavut Tunngavik Incorporated was responsible for ensuring that provisions of the land claims agreement were fully implemented.

Initially, the Nunavut government was made up of nineteen elected representatives, who in turn elected a member to become premier. The first was Paul Okalik, a young lawyer, and the second and most recent, Eva Aariak, a newcomer to the legislature who had extensive experience in government administration, most recently as language commissioner. By design, there are no political parties and for the most part decisions are reached by consensus. Initially, elected members were responsible for ten departments and eleven boards, commissions or agencies, with a staff commensurate to the workload. To outsiders, the government might appear top-heavy for a population of around 25,000, but it is deemed necessary because of the many diverse interests and size of the region.

Nunavut is the only territory or province in Canada that has no roads connecting its twenty-six communities, most of which are located in the Arctic Islands. In 1998, Inuit constituted more than 80 percent of the population. Iqaluit, the capital, had the largest population, with Bathurst Inlet the smallest, having only eighteen permanent residents. Although travel by boat or snowmobile is feasible between a few communities, airplanes are the primary form of transport, carrying passengers and supplies, including perishable foods. Once a year, large freighters, referred to as the Sealift, bring in heavier goods. Although tourism, mining and small businesses provide some jobs, government is by far the largest employer. Many Inuit still depend on hunting and fishing. Although presently the responsibilities are consistent with a territorial government, the determination to move toward provincial status was evident in the 2008 signing of a protocol to establish the framework for negotiating devolution of power by means of a federal transfer of province-like responsibilities for lands and resource management.[63]

Two other major agreements in principle were signed by Canadian Inuit around the turn of the century. The Labrador Inuit Association had been negotiating a land claims settlement with the governments of Canada and Newfoundland since 1977, but made little progress until 2001 when an amendment to the Canadian Constitution changed the name of the province to Newfoundland and Labrador to recognize the distinctiveness of the two regions. That same year, an agreement in principle was signed that recognized Labrador Inuit traditional land use in northern Labrador and northeastern Quebec. With ratification of the final agreement completed in May 2004, the following December the Labrador Inuit Land Claims Agreement Act was passed, and it came into force in 2008.

The act established the Labrador Inuit Settlement Area, totalling 28,000 square miles of land and 18,000 square miles of adjacent coastal waters. With the exception of clear title to 6,100 square miles within the settlement area, the Inuit will not own the remaining lands and seas but will have special co-management rights on their use and a percentage of provincial revenue earned from mining activities. Another 3,700 square miles at the tip of the Ungava Peninsula will be set aside for the Torngat Mountains National Park Reserve. In return for extinguishing their aboriginal title, the Inuit received $140 million to be paid over fifteen years and another $156 million to implement the deal. The Labrador Inuit Constitution provides for two levels of government: the Nunatsiavut government and five community governments. The legislature building will be located at Hopedale and the administration centre at Nain. All 5,300 members of the Labrador Inuit Association will share benefits, including the Kablunângajuit or mixed-bloods and those not living in the settlement area.[64]

After an earlier false start, the Inuit of Northern Quebec resumed negotiations in 1997 toward their second comprehensive land claim agreement, which would include a Nunavik regional government. Signing of a political accord led to the appointment of a commission to make recommendations on the design of Nunavik as a self-governing region within Quebec. Following the commission's report Makivik, representing over 10,000 Inuit, worked with the Canadian and Quebec governments to create a framework agreement in 2003 that set out the negotiation process and principles of the new government. A land claims agreement signed on 1 December 2006 created a Nunavik Inuit Settlement Area, which included 80 percent ownership of the islands and intervening waters offshore from Quebec, along with annual royalties on resource development to be paid by the federal government.

On 5 December 2007, an agreement in principle was signed as the next step toward formation of a Nunavik government. With the implementation committee now at work, this elected, non-ethnic regional government took shape, under the jurisdiction of the province of Quebec. The seat of government will be at Kuujjuak, with an assembly made up of twenty-one members, including the mayors from each of the fourteen Inuit communities, the chief of the Naskapi First Nations, plus five regionally elected members who will form an executive council with a government leader. The latter five will be responsible for implementing assembly decisions and for the four departments which will oversee local and regional affairs, administration and finance, health and social services, and education, all of which will replace existing agencies established under the James Bay and Northern Quebec Agreement. The final agreement will include a capital transfer of $40.1 million over ten years, plus an additional $38.7 million to cover implementation costs.[65]

With Inuit land claims agreements now including shared control over land use and resource management, it became readily apparent that the Inuit interpretation of aboriginal rights included a sovereign right attached to their historic occupation and use of Arctic lands and waters, bringing a whole new dimension to the term "Arctic sovereignty." Noting that Ottawa also had promoted the idea of Nunavut as a measure to protect Canada's Arctic sovereignty suggests that both the government and the Inuit believed they were reinforcing their sovereign authority over the Arctic, although those beliefs were arguably based on somewhat different interpretations.

The ICC continued to broaden the scope of its activities in the latter half of the twentieth century, yet without losing its key focus on Arctic environmental issues and aboriginal rights to self-government. In 1985, for instance, the ICC became an active participant in the UN Working Group on Indigenous Peoples and played a key role in drafting the Universal Declaration on the Rights of Indigenous Populations.[66] After twenty-two years, the declaration was finally adopted in September 2007 by the UN General Assembly. The organization was also gaining international recognition, as in 1988 when it received the UN Global 500 Award for its framework document on an Inuit conservation strategy and sustainable development. That same year, the executive council travelled to Chukotka in Russian Siberia to request approval from Soviet authorities for their Inuit to participate in the ICC. A year later, the Chukchi Inuit attended the meeting as observers, and in 1992 they were full participants in the General Assembly held in Inuvik in Canada's western Arctic.

In June 1991, the ICC hosted the first Arctic Leaders Summit in Denmark, and it was an active participant in an environmental conference referred to as the "Finnish Initiative" held that same year at Rovaniemi, Finland. The latter conference brought together eight Arctic countries—Denmark, Canada, Norway, Sweden, Finland, Iceland, Russia and the U.S.—to discuss environmental concerns. A signed declaration at the conclusion of the meetings outlined an official Arctic Environmental Protection Strategy (AEPS) designed to reduce contamination and pollution of Arctic lands and waters. Of particular importance to their underlying goal of self-government was ICC's participation in the UN Conference on Self Government in

September 1991, which resulted in a document, *The Nuuk Conclusions*, that outlined twenty-six internationally accepted principles for self-government. Of significance in advancing both aboriginal rights and environmental policies was ICC's success in lobbying for the right of indigenous peoples to participate in the 1992 UN Conference on the Environment and Development held in Rio de Janeiro, Brazil.

Throughout the years, the ICC's activities remained consistent with its original objectives: of advancing the Inuit right to self-government as a means of protecting their environment. From an Inuit perspective that aboriginal right was a sovereign right retained through historical occupancy of Arctic lands and waters, hence in their view an adjunct of Arctic sovereignty. In his history of the ICC written in 1993, Aqqaluk Lynge, a long-time member of its Executive Council and of Greenland's Home Rule Government, attempted to remove any implied threat in the term "right to self-government" when he argued that the objective was not future separation but "participation, rather than exclusion from the system." He also argued that Inuit rights to their lands and their distinct culture should not deny them "the same standards of living as those enjoyed by others within the federal states." Aqqaluk believed that self-reliance had been the "major driving force" behind their physical and cultural survival throughout the centuries and that is why today "Inuit throughout the Arctic, have a common interest in gaining control over the political and economic development in Inuit territories." For political and legal purposes, the ICC identified Inuit traditional lands based on historic land use and occupancy. In Aqqaluk's opinion, the dispute in Greenland over Inuit rights to their traditional lands and its resources had been settled with a compromise, with the terms of the Home Rule Act acknowledging that Greenlanders had "fundamental rights" to their lands. Management of mineral resources, however, would be a shared responsibility of the Danish and Home Rule governments through a joint committee administered by the Danish Ministry of Energy, with each party having a veto.[67] While the arrangement appeared acceptable to all parties at the time of writing, within a little more than a decade the Greenlanders were considering full independence from Denmark, a situation described in the next chapter.

As expected, the ICC's objectives of increased self-government did not find favour among world superpowers such as Russia or the U.S. The Canadian government, on the other hand, perceived these demands within its political traditions as a first step in the normal devolution of government. Denmark also saw these changes in government from a European perspective as a natural transition from colonial rule. For the Inuit Circumpolar Council, creating policies by consensus agreement was made more difficult by the fact that the Inuit resided in three distinctly different nation-states (four if counting Russia), each with its own peculiar history and attitudes toward its indigenous peoples. As a consequence, over a decade passed before the ICC's long-awaited *Comprehensive Arctic Policy* was officially introduced in 1992. Perceived as a critical first step to Inuit self-determination, the general policy and its many subsets were a means of setting out Inuit values and concerns as a basis for a prescribed course of action. For this reason, they are considered a living document that will be applicable amid changing circumstances and priorities in the years ahead.[68]

The policies described in the document were expansive and broad-reaching, ranging from security and disarmament issues, to subsistence rights and sustainable economic development, to self-determination and to social and cultural issues affecting health, education and language. By far the largest section of the document was devoted to environmental issues, the key concern that had prompted the creation of the ICC. Thus it is not surprising that environmental protection would appear as the first principle in the document, which states "a fundamental objective of the Arctic policy is to protect the delicate environment, including the marine and other resources on which Inuit depend."[69] Nor was it surprising that environmental issues would still be uppermost in the minds of Alaskan Inupiat of the North Slope Borough where the idea of a circumpolar Inuit organization originated.

The Arctic National Wildlife Range east of the North Slope Borough had been signed into law in 1973 by President Nixon and remained a controversial issue for the state of Alaska. In 1980, the Alaska National Interest Lands Conservation Act (ANILCA) renamed the reserve the Arctic National Wildlife Refuge and more than doubled its size, but added a provision that would allow the northern coastal portion to be opened for oil production with congressional approval. The first attempt to gain approval for drilling in the range occurred in 1983, after OPEC announced an embargo on exports to the U.S. Pressure increased again in 1986, as Prudhoe Bay production declined and oil prices crashed, causing Alaska's economy to suffer a major downturn. With widespread unemployment, reduced income, lower property values and failures of small companies and banks, the Alaskan government was under siege to take measures to restore the state to prosperity. The rift between southern-based environmentalists and Alaskan residents played out in increased political tensions between the federal and state governments. With one-third of Alaska's economy dependent on oil development, state officials believed that the only hope for future prosperity depended on tapping the oil fields of the wildlife refuge.[70]

As economic conditions deteriorated, Native corporations, oil interests and state officials found common ground, whereas the Inupiat conviction that increased self-government would protect the environment now appears less certain. Moving forward to the present, the message by Mayor Itta of the North Slope Borough in 2009 suggests an intent to accommodate conflicting interests when he describes working "closely with the oil industry, state, and federal agencies to make sure that everyone can benefit from the resource wealth of this region without sacrificing the natural gifts that have sustained Inupiat culture for thousands of years."[71] The aims of the ICC seemed to offer an end to what Oran Young described as "internal colonialism and economic dependence."[72] However, the Alaskan Inupiat may be caught in the boom and bust conundrum of a nonrenewable resource economy driven by forces beyond their control.

While the ICC was gathering momentum and influence on the world scene, there were signs that other northern interest groups were also seeking support to combat the dominant influence of larger nations. Multilateralism along an east-west axis was adopted by circumpolar countries, as evident in establishment of the Nordic Council (1972), the Council of the Baltic Sea States (1992), the Barents Euro-Arctic Council (1993), the Northern Forum and the Council of Arctic Parliamentarians. Paralleling this movement was proliferation of structured, non-governmental organizations (NGOs)—partially as a result of environmental concerns, but also as a means of advancing social, health and educational concerns—associations such as the Association of Circumpolar Universities, the International Arctic Science Committee, the International Congress of Arctic Social Sciences and the International Union for Circumpolar Health, to name only a few.[73]

Although many organizations were created to investigate economic or educational opportunities, the focus shifted dramatically over the past two decades to an emphasis on environmental concerns that, in turn, led to the establishment in 1991 of the Arctic Monitoring and Assessment Programme (AMAP).[74] Environmental questions were also the driving force behind creation of the Arctic Council in 1996, to include Russia, Canada, Finland, Norway, Sweden, Iceland, Denmark (representing Greenland) and the U.S. (representing Alaska). Canada chaired the council for the first two years under the direction of the Canadian Ambassador for the Arctic and Circumpolar Affairs, Mary Simon. In the planning stages, there had been great expectations that this body might be a unified voice for the circumpolar nations. Then the U.S., as a precondition of its reluctant participation, insisted that the council exclude discussion related to defence or military issues, regardless of whether they were relevant to environmental questions.

Participation in the Arctic Council also led to closer bilateral ties. As a case in point, Iceland opened an official embassy in Ottawa in May 2001, followed six months later by Canada establishing an embassy in Reykjavik. After Canada chaired the first two years of the council, the U.S. followed, then Finland and Iceland. Initially, the Scandinavian countries and Canada were recognized as the major advocates and financial supporters of this new organization. Ironically, it was an

Icelandic Canadian, the Arctic explorer Vilhjalmur Stefansson, who once predicted that the Arctic Ocean would become the "Mediterranean of the North." Perhaps not in the way he had envisioned, but in terms of political alliances, that day may be fast approaching.

In the last two decades, the dialogue on Arctic pollution has been unprecedented among non-government and government agencies, and particularly evident in working groups of the Arctic Council. Research initiatives have been widespread and findings conclusive. Yet in spite of the number of international agreements aimed at reducing pollutants entering the Arctic, implementation of remediation policies has been slow. Although the Arctic Council has taken a strong stand on the need for both environmental protection and sustainable development, these two policies sometimes prove incompatible. As well, other political ties may limit the degree to which member nations are able to support the policy directives of the Arctic Council, such as membership in the European Union, or as signatories to the North American Free Trade Agreement.[75]

Of increasing concern was the reluctance of some countries to accept the seriousness of global warming and its consequences. This was particularly evident in heavily industrialized or developing countries, where economic considerations took priority over the environment. Inuit leaders, on the other hand, were fully cognizant of the potentially disastrous effect on their lives and were at the forefront in demanding recognition and new policy directives. One of the most vocal was Sheila Watt-Cloutier, chair of the International Inuit Circumpolar Council. Speaking in Milan, Italy, in 2003 to a UN conference on climate change, Watt-Cloutier described the recent impact on the Canadian Arctic and argued that "human-induced climate change is undermining the ecosystem upon which Inuit depend for survival." Referring to the Arctic as "the barometer of the globe's environmental health," she warned that what was happening to Inuit today "will happen soon to you in the South."[76]

The most conclusive study on global warming was the Arctic Climate Impact Assessment (ACIA), an international project of the Arctic Council and the International Arctic Science Committee

Sheila (Siila) Watt-Cloutier, former president and international chair
of the Inuit Circumpolar Council and nominee for the 2007 Nobel Peace
Prize, has worked tirelessly to show the world the connections between
human choices, enormous environmental changes and impacts on
communities and cultures. Most recently, she has focussed on climate
change and has brought a petition to the Inter-American Commision
on Human Rights proving the links between dramatic Arctic
warming and violations of human environmental and cultural rights.
Courtesy Sheila Watt-Cloutier; photographer Stephen Lowe

(IASC), a non-governmental organization that facilitates cooperation
on Arctic research. Funding for the ACIA secretariat was provided
by the U.S. National Science Foundation and the National Oceanic
and Atmospheric Administration. Initially, American delegates had
agreed to accept the study's findings. In February 2004, however,
the U.S. government reversed its earlier position and announced
it would not support the Arctic Council's policy recommendations
based on the ACIA report. Watt-Cloutier refused to take no for an
answer. In written testimony to the U.S. Senate Committee on Commerce, Science and Transportation, which met to hear a briefing on
the upcoming ACIA report, she reiterated her argument, claiming
that because of changes caused by global warming, "Inuit are facing

the beginning of a possible end of a way of life that has allowed us to thrive for millennia." Repeating the ACIA's view that "what happens in the Arctic will occur elsewhere in the world a decade or two later," Watt-Cloutier again warned that "without immediate action, not only are Inuit in peril, but the entire planet is at risk."[77] Unlike other countries of the G7, both the Canadian and American governments were influenced by the arguments of their respective oil and gas industries and refused to commit to a major reduction of greenhouse gases as set out in the Kyoto Protocol.

While there has been some success in combating pollution in Arctic regions, such initiatives are exceptionally vulnerable in times of a global economic or military crisis. In the end, how Canada, Denmark, the U.S. and other circumpolar nations deal with Arctic pollution and global warming, whether by capitulation or resistance to economic arguments, will depend largely on how the rest of the world views the Arctic and its importance. Will they be perceived as "homelands" or simply economic or military "frontiers"? Will the impact of climate change on the Arctic and its peoples be ignored or traded off for perceived advantages of global warming in other regions and by other countries?

THE NEW east-west relationships among circumpolar countries were driven in part by the need to seek solutions to common concerns, but also to provide a counterbalance to the dominant influence of southern interests, sometimes within their own nation-states. Successes in achieving cooperation and support for shared objectives were facilitated by a prolonged period of economic stability and peaceful coexistence of the world superpowers. Should this balance be disrupted, newly shared policy initiatives may not translate into meaningful actions. By the turn of the twenty-first century, the strength of the new east-west dynamic against inherent south-north influences had yet to be tested during a time of global crisis, a circumstance that soon changed.

Oil and gas discoveries and the creation of the Inuit Circumpolar Council marked the beginning of a significant new era in the history of the North American Arctic. No longer would proposed extraction of the region's resources go uncontested. More importantly, by virtue of its mandate and membership, the ICC essentially removed Greenland from its primarily European status and firmly established the island as an integral part of the North American community.

PART IV

THE TWENTY-FIRST CENTURY

AT THIS point, a reader might ask why the history of Arctic sovereignty is relevant to current issues faced by circumpolar countries. Granted, the map of the Arctic has remained relatively unchanged over the past century, yet going back further in time, changes did take place. While none involved outright war, there were a number of influences that triggered challenges to the status quo and in a few cases resulted in major shifts. In virtually every instance, the operative word was "change." Whether they were changes in climate, technologies, economic conditions, balance of world power or demand for Arctic resources, when two or more converged, their effect multiplied. Most changes had consequences, suggesting general patterns of cause and effect that bear consideration going forward.

From a historical perspective, major climate change frequently acted as a catalyst for shifts in authority or possession. Not only did a warming trend initiate arrival of the first inhabitants in the Arctic and a cooling period lead to their demise, but changes in temperature continued to influence commercial interest in the region's resources. With few exceptions, warming spells prompted stiffer competition, cooling periods a decline. The latest warming trend is again inciting increased competition because of easier access to the resources and lower shipping costs through the northern sea routes, rather than by way of the Panama or Suez Canal. As a result, there is growing support from European and Asian countries to have the Northwest Passage and Northern Sea Route declared international straits, as opposed to internal waters claimed by Canada and Russia.

As Sheila Watt-Cloutier convincingly argued in the keynote address at the 2030 North Conference held in Ottawa in June 2009, "Arctic sovereignty and climate change are two sides of the same coin." To Canadians, the statement implies that the warming trend has made their sovereign rights in the Arctic more vulnerable to challenge. For non-Arctic countries, climate change has opened opportunities to gain sovereign rights previously denied.

Historical relevance also relates to the different character of the Arctic countries, each moulded by cultural traditions, ambitions, experiences and long-standing rivalries. Taking the United States as an example, American history professor Thomas R. Hietala, writing about the concept of Manifest Destiny, argues that "however striking the changes in American life since the Jacksonian era, the persistence of certain principles and biases—the consistency of much of American political and diplomatic 'culture' over several generations—ties the present to the past, and links both to the future."[1] The same holds true for Canada and Greenland/Denmark. The key to understanding the rationale behind government actions lies in the social and political history of each country.

As a case in point, American assertiveness, individualism and libertarianism characterized most government actions in the nineteenth century, motivated in part by their belief that someday the entire continent would be unified under one flag. Peaceful annexation of British North America failed to materialize, yet during World War II and the Cold War, the United States slowly but surely expanded its hegemony across the Arctic regions, by assuming the major responsibility for continental defence.

The North American Arctic is once again threatened, this time by potential pollution from increased commercial shipping. Should Canada fail to provide the means to enforce necessary regulations to protect the environment, will the U.S. again step in and assume responsibility? And if so, what are the implications for Canada's Arctic sovereignty?

There have also been ongoing changes in the interpretation of what North Americans now broadly define as Arctic sovereignty. Beginning with the simplistic concept of "homeland" held by the Palaeo-Eskimos and the Inuit, to one of absolute power of authority in the Middle Ages, we have since added layers of subcategories, such as *de jure* and *de facto* sovereignty. At the same time, the term has been expanded to include authority over adjacent waters and ice cover, the air above and the seabed below. More recently, recognition of the Inuit's rights to their lands and self-government has been added to the discourse. Arctic sovereignty is no longer simply a legal right to land ownership, but has developed into a broader concept characterized by many shades of grey.

Of particular significance was the interpretation of international law early in the twentieth century, which stipulated that discovery claims must be followed by certain government actions to meet the criteria of "effective occupation." By including administrative acts, this interpretation implied responsibility for a region's indigenous peoples and their environment. In other words, Arctic sovereignty was no longer simply a right, but a responsibility.

In this context, Canada is faced with the question of whether the interests of the country as a whole should take precedence over its parts or whether such a concept is simply a remnant from the days when colonialism was an acceptable adjunct of imperial ambitions. The United States, by granting Alaska full statehood, and Denmark, by establishing the new Self-Rule Government in Greenland, effectively ended the former colonial dependency of their Arctic hinterlands. So far, Canada has expressed no urgency to take similar action.

There are other factors that have influenced changes in Arctic sovereignty. New technologies—whether improved seagoing vessels to navigate ice-strewn waters or advanced equipment to detect and extract the area's resources—added further incentive to explore and exploit. While current interest in seabed mining creates added value for the region, it also multiplies the number of non-Arctic countries seeking to share in the economic benefits, either directly from minerals that might be extracted from unclaimed seabed of the Arctic Ocean or indirectly through shipping, supply of equipment and technological services. Understandably, some multinational corporations will benefit from the melting sea ice and may consider any delay in mitigation of man-made causes an advantage.

Paralleling the increasing value of Arctic resources were changes in the demography of developed countries. Fuelled by industrial growth, urban areas expanded along with demands for new building materials, energy sources and technologies. In Canada and the United States, immigration added a multicultural character to many larger cities. This may translate into a change in public attitudes toward the once romanticized Arctic of the twentieth century.

Should the Arctic lose its allure as a unique, sparsely populated wilderness, will the broader international community consider the region little more than an underutilized wasteland, rich in resources, hence a potential source for global prosperity? To counter such ideas before they take root, the media may be the most valuable tool available to engage widespread support for protection of the fragile Arctic environment—this said with a word of caution, as the press can also be a conduit for misinformation provided by lobbyists and interest groups.

One final factor that has influenced public perception of the Arctic is "the human dimension." Although often used in reference to the indigenous peoples, whose traditional use of Arctic lands and waters provides added support to their respective countries' claims to sovereignty, the phrase may also be considered in the abstract to refer to the visionaries who were responsible for changing the map of the Arctic. A few names come to mind: Eirik the Red, Martin Frobisher, Hans Egede, Sir John Barrow, William Seward, Robert Peary, Roald Amundsen, Bernt Balchen; or in Russia, Vitus Bering and Ivan Papanin. Veneration of these men led to the belief that the Arctic was an integral part of their respective countries' national identity. For the Inuit, there is Eben Hopson, recognized as the founding father of the Inuit Circumpolar Council.

Significant by their absence, no Canadians are among them. Yet it became a point of national honour that Canada's sovereign rights in the Arctic be protected, but without any real understanding of the costs. At present there appears to be a general absence of vision and commitment—except among Inuit leaders, which may well be a harbinger of the future.

THE HISTORY lessons end where the present begins—a threshold we must cross over to reach the future. The following chapters examine the current situation and recent policy statements, with thoughts on how decisions and actions might change the map of the North American Arctic.

(**12**)

BEGINNING OF A NEW ERA

The Circumpolar North has begun to acquire an identity of its
own in the minds of policymakers and scholars alike. Yet this region
cannot be understood properly as a cockpit or as an arena or global
commons. Instead it belongs to the class of shared resource
regions, a category of areas that is acquiring more prominence
as the attention of policymakers shifts increasingly to issues
involving human/environment relations.

ORAN R. YOUNG, 1992[1]

. . . .

THE FIRST decade of the twenty-first century witnessed a much different world than anticipated only a few years earlier. The end of
the Cold War raised hopes for world peace, economic growth and
prosperity. In North America, this was also a time of increased immigration, scientific breakthroughs and new technologies, medical
advances and broader educational opportunities, new industries and
global trade. Expanding urban centres created a construction boom
of high-rise office buildings, apartment complexes and condomini-
ums, along with more arts and entertainment facilities to serve the
ever-increasing population. The industrial sector, in particular, created a voracious demand for materials and energy. New companies
proliferated. Others grew into international conglomerates. Global-
ization became the new byword for national prosperity.

Heightened concerns about pollution gave way to new fears—of
terrorist attacks, violent weather patterns, massive flooding, drought
and forest fires. Elsewhere, we witnessed continued unrest, bloody

violence and eventually full-blown wars in Afghanistan and Iraq. While there were ample warnings of adverse consequences of a potentially irreversible warming trend, few predicted the sudden economic downturn that led to a major global recession. By occurring together, climate change and recession placed additional pressure on circumpolar countries to choose between protection of the Arctic environment and the temptation to accelerate oil and gas development as an economic stimulus. The first decade of the twenty-first century marked the beginning of a new era, one that will require wisdom and foresight to bring political and economic stability to a rapidly changing world.

AMID THE economic prosperity of the 1990s came the realization that the world might be encountering a sustained warming trend that could prove irreversible unless there was coordinated global action to mitigate unnatural causes. Initially the trend was considered part of a normal cycle, but at the turn of the century, meteorologists and scientists began to warn of unusual acceleration of Arctic temperatures, in part caused by release of increasing amounts of carbon dioxide and other greenhouse gases into the atmosphere. Exactly what percentage of the causes was man-made is still under debate, but it was enough to create a "tipping point" in the Arctic, which resulted in a chain reaction that has accelerated the rate of ice melt and warming of the air. Most scientists concur that the rate might be slowed by new technologies and alternative energy sources but likely is not reversible in our lifetime, if ever. To do nothing will simply make the situation worse. Some alarmists warn of possible worldwide instability, local unrest, insurrections and perhaps even global war. Others claim that such concerns are exaggerated and there is no impending crisis.[2] Exaggeration and misinformation from both sides have confused the debate as has the diversity of personal experience.

Effects of climate change have been experienced in varying degrees throughout the world but nowhere so dramatically as in the Arctic. Here, the permanently frozen ice cover is rapidly shrinking, pack ice is fast disappearing, large blocks of the ice shelf are breaking off and huge glaciers are melting faster than scientists had predicted only a few years ago. Of increasing concern is the amount of methane, twenty-five times more potent than carbon dioxide, which is being released into the atmosphere as a result of melting permafrost. Scientific studies are under way to determine how much of the accelerated ice melt is attributable to methane and what measures might be taken to prevent its release into the atmosphere. Other factors are also contributing to the warming Arctic air currents and waters, such as the unusually high winds associated with climate change driving the broken icepack into the Atlantic and Pacific Oceans and reducing the ice cover's normal cooling effect on the Arctic waters. As well, the thinning ozone layer around the North Pole has increased the intensity of the sun and in turn the rate of evaporation. As a result of the disappearing snow and ice cover, less of the sun's energy is reflected back into space, creating a spiral domino effect with no sign of reversal. Scientific studies now confirm that the surface air temperature over lands just north of the Arctic Circle trended upward for the last two decades, with the year 2007 marking a high at 2°C or 3.6°F above the average temperature at the turn of the twentieth century. This is occurring in spite of the fact that the present tilt of the earth's axis should have created a general cooling period.[3]

Complicating the picture is the fact that the warming of the Arctic surface air is variable, as are the depth and area of sea ice. In 2008, the NASA Earth Laboratory discovered a slight moderation in the Arctic warming trend, with the recorded surface air temperature increasing from the mean by only 1.5°C compared to the previous year's 2.0°C. When the Earth Laboratory report was considered alongside 2008 reports from the NASA Goddard Institute for Space Studies that the United States had experienced on average one of the coldest years in the past decade, skeptics suggested the trend might be reversing. Unfortunately not all findings were positive. NASA satellite observations in 2009 showed further decrease in the permanent sea ice—ice two years or older—with first-year ice amounting to 70 percent of the total compared to 40 to 50 percent in the 1980s and 1990s. The new ice which forms each year is much thinner and more vulnerable

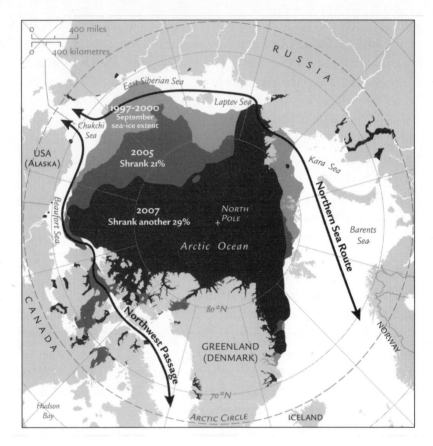

SHRINKING ARCTIC SEA ICE AND POTENTIAL NEW SHIPPING ROUTES

Maps can be informative but they must be interpreted accurately to have any meaning. This map is derived from observations by special imagers and microwave scanners on NASA's Aqua satellite that have been compared with the archived maps and statistics at the National Snow and Ice Data Center. The minimum extent of sea ice shown on this map represents only September averages and is not a solid, but a combination of large sheets, icebergs and smaller bergy bits and growlers. As climate conditions vary each year, the minimal extent may occur any time between August and October.

A change in wind direction also causes ice to push together or drift apart, creating continual variability in sea ice area and regional differences. For more information see websites for the NASA Earth Observatory and the National Snow and Ice Data Center.

to summer melt, which partly explains an apparent increase in floating ice that posed difficulties for shipping in the summers of 2008 and 2009.[4]

Former ICC president Sheila Watt-Cloutier has repeatedly warned that the warming trend experienced in the Arctic is akin to "a canary in a mine shaft," a harbinger of more dire consequences elsewhere in the world. The rationale for this statement rests in scientific evidence that the melting sea ice and especially the glacier ice on Greenland will ultimately affect more southerly regions. How much and when is speculative. Some scientists predict that the melting of Greenland's icecap will eventually raise sea levels throughout the world; others are more cautious in their predictions. Although to date climate change has not had nearly the same negative effects on temperate regions, scientific climate modelling suggests that global warming will increase incrementally over the next century, possibly with devastating consequences for the poorer developing countries. The debate still rages as to how high the temperature will rise globally and how soon.[5]

The Yup'ik Eskimos on Alaska's west coast were among the first to report a major upheaval in their lives attributed directly to warmer temperatures which had melted the coastal ice and frozen soil that once acted as natural barriers to ocean storm surges. As a result of severe erosion caused by flooding, the village of Newtok was abandoned and its 340 residents relocated to higher ground nine miles away. The U.S. Army Corps of Engineers estimated the cost of relocating the village at $130 million and warned that twenty-six other Alaskan villages were in immediate danger, with possibly sixty more facing a threat over the next decade. Problems with the runway and access roads as a result of melting permafrost were also reported at Salluit in northern Quebec, which may eventually require relocation of the town.[6]

There were other unexpected consequences. The ecological balance of the Arctic is under threat, the most publicized concern being the polar bears' ability to adapt. A more imminent worry is the arrival of southern predators, such as killer whales now sighted in Foxe Basin, which pose a threat to existing marine life. Humpback whales have been observed far north of their normal habitat, in one instance in an area destined for future offshore oil rigs. Even Russian scientists felt the effects in the summer of 2008 when they were forced to request emergency evacuation from their research station on a drifting ice floe. Although they had used similar floes annually for over fifty years, this time their ice island had melted to a small fraction of its original size a full six weeks before their planned departure.[7]

Alaska did not stand idly by. In 2006, state lawmakers formed the Alaska Climate Impact Assessment Commission to examine existing and likely effects and make recommendations on how to address the negative consequences. Unfortunately, the commission decided to focus on means of adaptation rather than mitigation. The causes of global warming were also not included in their investigations, since the oil industry, which is a major emitter of carbon dioxide, is the primary driver of the state economy. Warning that "climate change presents unavoidable challenges to the citizens of Alaska," the commission's final report stated that "the convergence of immediate threats, substantial human need, and prohibitive costs presents decision-makers at all levels of government with daunting challenges." A sub-cabinet group was formed to study the report released in March 2008. At the time of writing, there was still no official response.[8]

Greenlanders, on the other hand, experienced an unexpected advantage from the warming trend; they are now growing fresh vegetables to replace imported varieties and their sheep are producing fatter lambs. Although they too have suffered damage to their villages and roads, they appear much more resilient and are actively seeking new opportunities in mining and oil and gas development made possible by the shrinking ice cover. With the U.S. Geological Survey estimating the island's oil and gas reserves to be the nineteenth-largest in the world, Greenlanders hope to share in the wealth and gain financial independence from Denmark. The disappearance of the ice cover from most of southern Greenland has made the goal more realistic. Other opportunities range from tourism to freshwater exports and hydroelectric development.

Inuit elsewhere are demanding a greater say in resource development as part of their rights to self-government. The rationale for their position is set out in the ICC's Declaration on Arctic Sovereignty in April 2009, which declared that "industrial development of the natural resource development of the Arctic can proceed only insofar as it enhances the economic and social well-being of Inuit and safeguards our environmental security."[9]

Meanwhile, those living in more temperate regions of the United States witnessed little more than increasingly violent weather systems marked by unusually heavy precipitation, high winds, hurricanes and tornadoes that left floods and destruction in their wake. Given their experiences, it is difficult for them to relate their problems to those in more arid regions, where lowered water tables were causing drought, and in California and British Columbia, where major forest fires burned out of control fuelled by high winds. It was equally hard to convince Canadian residents in northeastern Ontario that global warming was upon us when heavy snow fell in early November 2008 and again the following April. Even though scientists have explained time and again that this is all part of global warming, there are still naysayers who claim lack of evidence. Some have suggested that Canada and temperate zones of the U.S. will benefit from growth of the boreal forest. Others strongly disagree. A few believe "geo-engineering" may be a solution, with the Arctic to be used as a testing ground for possible adverse effects. Meanwhile global carbon emissions have increased 3.5 percent annually since 2000, a huge increase from the average 0.9 percent yearly increase in the 1990s.[10]

The dispute over the cause of global warming should have ended with the 2007 report by the UN-sponsored Intergovernmental Panel on Climate Change (IPCC). Signed by over 100 senior international scientists, the report confirmed that the warming trend was "irrevocable" and more than likely caused by greenhouse gas emissions. Even with successful mitigation, the report predicted, the warming trend would continue to increase over the next few decades, and it warned of dire consequences unless there was immediate action to reduce emissions. It also highlighted the need for more research and education on means of adaptation.[11] Yet President George W. Bush with the full support of the Republican Party still refused to ratify the Kyoto Protocol signed by Democratic President Bill Clinton or to legislate sufficient measures to slow the increase of harmful emissions. Instead, the primary responsibility for reducing greenhouse gas emissions was delegated to individual states.

The Kyoto Protocol, which had been negotiated in 1997 and came into force in 2005, was designed to coordinate the efforts of industrialized nations to reduce greenhouse gas emissions and thereby slow the rate of global warming. Depending on their degree of industrialization, thirty-six nations were given individual reduction targets for 2012 based on their 1990 levels of emissions. Seven of the eight Arctic countries ratified the Kyoto Protocol. Only the U.S. refused. Highly industrialized western European countries with their dense populations took on the challenge, initially with remarkable success. By 2004, Denmark's reductions were reportedly ahead of plans to reach its Kyoto target, whereas the U.S. had increased its level of emissions by more than 20 percent.[12]

Canada's record was abysmal. A Liberal government had ratified the protocol in 2002 but managed only minimal reductions in emissions while in office. By the time the Conservative Party came into power in 2006, the level was still 29 percent above Canada's Kyoto target. Using figures from 1990 to 2006, Environment Canada estimated that 80 percent of national greenhouse gas emissions were derived from production or consumption of fossil fuels, of which only 27 percent came from commercial transport and personal vehicles.[13] With Canada's economy largely dependent upon the oil and gas industry, these figures should come as no surprise. Having openly campaigned against the Kyoto Protocol, the newly elected Conservative government slashed the environmental budget in 2006 and declared that its policy would focus on clean air and water in the residential and commercial sector.

When threatened with a ruling of non-compliance by the Kyoto enforcement agency, in early 2007, the Canadian government finally submitted its first report, which claimed progress but lacked statistical information. Only after a meeting with a team of UN experts to review the submission did Canada agree to create a national inventory of emissions and submit an annual report.[14] As expected, a recent update by Environment Canada reported that by the end of 2007 emissions had risen to 33.8 percent above the 1990 level, with most of the increase coming from the energy industries and transportation sectors, particularly oil sands production.[15] Yet the Canadian government continued to argue that its target was set unfairly high, that the country's contribution to overall greenhouse gas emissions was only about 2 percent of the world total and that China, the U.S., the European Union, Russia, Japan and India were the major emitters.[16] Ottawa neglected to acknowledge that Canada was one of the highest emitters on a per capita basis.

The outlook for the Arctic environment might have been bleak had it not been for the 2008 election of Barack Obama as president of the United States. His commitment to cut greenhouse gas emissions in the United States by 14 percent by 2020 was supported by the Democrats' American Clean Energy and Security Act, introduced in the House on 30 March 2009.[17] The overall goal, according to the Chair of the Energy and Commerce Committee of the House, was "to strengthen our economy by making America the world leader in clean-energy and energy-efficient technologies." Given the difficulty in getting health care reform passed in the Senate, the clean energy bill inevitably will face similar resistance. Protests against the bill mounted in 2009, led by several U.S. organizations including the Committee for a Constructive Tomorrow, funded by ExxonMobil and wealthy Republicans, and a group called Energy Citizens backed by the American Petroleum Institute.[18] Should this bill or a similar one pass with a cap-and-trade mechanism, Canada as America's major trading partner may have little choice but to adopt a similar plan. Even then, such measures will have no immediate effect on the ice melt in the Arctic.

The full extent of the anti-green campaign was revealed in a recent book by the president of a highly respected public relations firm with the assistance of an investigative journalist. *Climate Cover-up* exposes the orchestrated scheme to discredit the scientific reports on global warming and confuse the public debate. The primary industries involved were the oil and coal companies in the United States and the tar sands operations in Canada. Using leaked memos and investigative techniques, the authors show that the campaign's so-called scientific experts were actually paid lobbyists. For months, the media recounted the misinformation, creating a phony climate change debate and mass confusion. By mid-November, the Associated Press appeared to be the first newswire to check the facts with its own statistical study which confirmed the clever use of language and selective evidence used to debunk the UN reports.[19] The latter item appeared in a small column in the inner pages of the *Globe and Mail* in mid-October—a stark contrast to the front-page headlines some American newspapers had granted the anti-green movement.

In an attempt to bring consensus among the world's major political leaders, UN Secretary-General Ban Ki-moon invited twenty-five to meet on 22 September 2009 to discuss climate change. President Hu Jintao of China was among the attendees and for the first time described how his country intended to reduce emissions through increased use of solar power and applying new techniques to trap and bury carbon dioxide emissions. The key question facing world leaders is how to pay for cutting greenhouse gases in both developed and developing countries. A study funded by the Toronto-Dominion Bank in late October compared the effect on the Canadian GDP over the next decade of the Conservative government's current plan to reduce greenhouse gas emissions with a more drastic reduction considered necessary by environmental groups. Both plans would reduce the estimated growth of Alberta and Saskatchewan, which would still be growing at a rate more than double that of any other province.[20]

By the end of October 2009, the general consensus of the media and political pundits was that there would be no definitive agreement on a plan to replace the Kyoto Protocol at the Copenhagen Conference on Climate Change in early December 2009. Two countries listed as having problems in coming to an immediate agreement were Canada and the United States, the latter because the Senate had still not approved the U.S. clean energy bill. Signing such an agreement is even more problematic for Canadian Prime Minister Harper as the power base of his party is in the west, which is dependent upon continued oil sands production to fuel the growth of the regional economy.

One area in which Canada has made headway is with the Arctic and Marine Oilspill Program (AMOP), which was initiated by Environment Canada and partners from other circumpolar countries. Research over a period of thirty years has focussed on detecting oil spills in a polar environment, understanding their effects and improving preventive and cleanup measures. An annual conference brings together researchers from around the world to share their findings on these three critical aspects of oil spills.[21] The rapid ice melt in the Arctic may provide easier access to carry out cleanup measures, but will have no immediate effect on making the polar ecology more resistant to degradation. Furthermore Canada has neither the equipment nor the manpower to deal with a major oil spill.

The current trend in climate change has raised Arctic sovereignty issues which previously were not considered urgent by Canada or Russia because the ice had severely restricted commercial shipping. Now both countries are faced with the prospect of increased use of Arctic sea routes and global pressure to designate the Northwest Passage and the Northern Sea Route as international straits. To control traffic and enforce its regulations, Russia has announced an increase in military presence to support its large fleet of icebreakers. Canada is caught unprepared because it repeatedly deferred building its enforcement capabilities owing to costs. Now, because of the economic recession, Ottawa has even less capital to expend and will be vulnerable to a *de facto* loss of sovereignty if unable to enforce Canadian marine regulations in the Arctic. Denmark, on the other hand, has already increased its fleet of ice-strengthened vessels used to patrol Greenland waters.

ANOTHER CHANGE not fully understood by southerners is the degree to which the Inuit and Eskimos have taken back control over their lives through new forms of self-government. Given that they always considered themselves inseparable from the environment, it was natural that more control over resource use would be central to negotiations of land claims agreements. The Inuit represent a large majority of the population in the resource-rich lands in the North American Arctic, roughly 80 percent, yet few southerners recognize the implications of their increasing influence on decisions for future development.

The degree of control has been somewhat mixed across North America. In Alaska, the Inupiat have used their elected boroughs to pressure state and federal officials into accommodating their demands for subsistence hunting rights and protection of bowhead whales, the latter still central to their culture and identity. At the same time, however, they receive a portion of the royalties earned by the state government from oil production, which inevitably creates a potential conflict of interest with ecological concerns. Pressure for full recognition of aboriginal rights of Alaskan Indians and Eskimos resulted in the 1999 State Administrative Order No. 186 that recognized the right to a tribal government in what was loosely described as "Indian territory." As a result, their land claims settlement, which originally had been an attempt to assimilate Alaskan Natives, became a "permanent institution of Native empowerment." [22]

The Inuvialuit in Canada's western Arctic negotiated a final land claims agreement in 1984 that included co-management of "resource-use conflicts," essentially gaining an equal voice in the environmental review process for resource development. With whale hunting also central to their culture, it was understandable that they would be cautious about offshore drilling. Thus, after they approved winter drilling programs on the landfast ice off Tuktoyaktuk Peninsula, it came as a surprise in 1990 when the Inuvialuit halted a Gulf Oil offshore drilling program in the Beaufort Sea. To ensure their own interests took priority, they established the Inuvialuit Petroleum Corporation, which in turn created the Inuvik Gas Project to build a

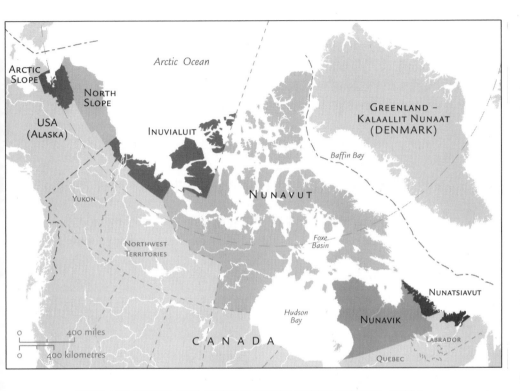

INUIT AND ESKIMO SELF-GOVERNMENT IN NORTH AMERICA, C2009
Eskimos in Alaska and Inuit in the Canadian Arctic and Greenland have
achieved various forms of self-government over the last decade. Alaska's
North Slope and Arctic Slope have borough governments
with a legislative assembly and planning commissions, similar to a county
within American states. In Canada, the Inuvialuit and the people of
Nunavik and Nunatsiavut all have regional self-governments within their
respective territories or provinces. Nunavut, which is over 80 percent
Inuit, is a democratic self-governing territory, whereas Greenland's
new Self-Rule Government with its large Inuit majority has powers
similar to if not greater than provincial powers in Canada.

pipeline from a nearby gas field to Inuvik. This resulted in major savings and cleaner energy for their town. In the interim, the Inuvialuit Regional Corporation wisely invested its land claims money and proceeds from its business ventures, enabling a distribution in 2007 of roughly $1,000 to each beneficiary enrolled in the program. This amounted to about 15 percent of the net profit, allowing the remainder to be reinvested to guarantee protection of the capital for future generations. With an agreement in principle already in place, the Inuvialuit negotiated a Process and Schedule Agreement in 2007 for a full regional self-government.[23]

Similar negotiations took place between the federal and provincial governments and the Inuit of northern Quebec and Labrador. Both groups received approvals for regional self-government within their respective provinces and as of 2009 were in the process of implementation. The new entities will be called Nunavik and Nunatsiavut respectively and both include shared responsibilities for fishing and mining. The most celebrated achievement was creation of the Nunavut Territory in 1999, which coincided with the ratification of the Nunavut Land Claims Agreement. The territory's area is vast, covering one-fifth of Canada. As pointed out by Thomas Berger, "If Nunavut were an independent country it would be the twelfth largest in the world." Like Greenland, Nunavut has a democratic public government with voting privileges extended to all residents, of whom over 80 percent are Inuit.

All appeared to run smoothly until negotiations broke down for funding the second phase of the implementation contract. At the request of the Premier of Nunavut, the President of Nunavut Tunngavik Inc. (NTI) and the Minister of Northern Development, Thomas Berger was appointed as conciliator to review territorial needs and means of facilitating the implementation process. In his final report, Berger dealt with the need to increase Inuit participation in government, which led to the broader issue of providing adequate education to prepare Inuit for employment in government administration and other sectors. Recognizing the urgency of the problem in the face of climate change and the prospect of accelerated resource

Council chamber of the Nunavut Territorial Government reflects the great pride the Nunavummiut have in their new government. Note the translation machines on the desks, which allow for simultaneous translation in both Inuktitut and English. Courtesy Nunavut Government, Office of the Premier

development, he recommended greater federal support for a major overhaul of the educational system at a cost of $20 million a year to guarantee that children were instructed in Inuktitut and had equal capabilities in English as their second language. The need to recognize Inuktitut as Nunavut's official language was compared to recognition of French in Quebec to allow its people to feel "at home" in their own country. Berger emphasized the need for "a unified Arctic strategy for sovereignty and industrial development . . . founded on the long-term interests of the Inuit," and wrote that "no affirmation of Canada's Arctic sovereignty will be complete unless the people of the Arctic—the Inuit—are partners in the task." [24]

Apparently there was no official announcement by Ottawa that it was willing to support the recommendations. Although substantial transfer payments for education and health have since resumed, this did not halt a billion-dollar lawsuit brought by NTI against the federal government for breach of contract in implementing the land

claims agreement. At issue is the deficit in funding for Inuit education and training to enable Inuit to fully participate in activities of the
Nunavut government. In the summer of 2009, the lawsuit was still
outstanding. On a more optimistic note, the Nunavut government
was officially granted the right to establish Inuktitut as the official
language within the territory of Nunavut after the Canadian Senate
passed the Nunavut Official Languages Act on 11 June 2009.

Greenland's Home Rule Government, established in 1979, has
long been considered a model of orderly devolution of Inuit rights
to self-government. Its advanced program of education also allowed
Greenlanders greater employment opportunities. Recently, a new
and much enlarged university was built at Nuuk to encourage Greenlanders to seek a post-secondary education in their own country,
rather than in Copenhagen. In part, it was tied to the Home Rule Government's determination to diminish Danish influence on the lives of
young people.

Greenlanders seemed content with the political relationship with
Denmark until the mid-1990s, when a Danish researcher reported
nuclear contamination in the waters offshore from Thule Air Base,
apparently as a result of the 1968 crash of a U.S. B-52 bomber carrying four hydrogen bombs. The Danish government eventually
compensated surviving workers—Danes and a few Greenlanders—
in amounts of less than $3,000 U.S. each. Yet anger continued toward
the American and Danish governments for keeping the incident
secret and resulted in the Home Rule Government delaying approval
to upgrade Thule Air Base. Finally an amendment to the original
postwar agreement was signed in 2004 by representatives of the
United States, Denmark and Greenland, but resentment lingered.

In the interim, the Inughuit families who had been forcibly
removed and relocated at Qaanaaq to allow expansion of Thule Air
Base attempted to regain their lands from the American military.
Calling themselves the Hingitaq 53 (meaning "deported in 1953"),
they argued that there was insufficient wildlife to sustain them at
Qaanaaq and took their case to the Danish courts. After a series of
appeals and support from Greenlanders and the Inuit Circumpolar

The new university built at Nuuk was designed to encourage young
Greenlanders to obtain a post-secondary degree at home rather
than abroad. CE-6504, photographer Carsten Egevang, ARC-PIC, Greenland

Council, the Danish Supreme Court upheld an appeals court verdict
in November 2003 and the relocated Inughuit were offered compensation of 17,000 kroner each (approximately $3,000 U.S.). Still
displaced, they took their case to the European Court of Human
Rights in Strasbourg, just days after Denmark and the U.S. signed
the agreement to modernize the air base. Although they returned a
portion of the land adjacent to the base, the U.S. Air Force and politicians distanced themselves from the legal proceedings, saying it was
a matter between Greenlanders and the Danish government, claiming the latter was responsible for their removal.[25] The Inughuit appeal
to the Court of Human Rights was later rejected.

To reduce apprehension over new plans for Thule Air Base, USAF
Group Commander Colonel Lee-Volker Cox toured twelve Greenland communities in eighteen days to explain how activities at the
base benefited the island and the Arctic in general. On the list were
lucrative contracts with Greenland companies, financial benefits
from taxes, training programs and employment opportunities for

Greenlanders, logistical support for postal services, as well as pro-vision of a departure base for scientific expeditions and medical emergency services. The public relations initiative appeared success-ful, but resentment toward the Danish government persisted, with Inuit claiming that they had been kept in a state of colonial depen-dency because of the trade monopoly, allegedly enforced for their protection from foreign abuse. Greenlanders also demanded an apol-ogy from Denmark for an experiment conducted in the 1950s, which saw specially selected children sent to Copenhagen for schooling and indoctrination of Danish values. Most ended up in orphanages and put out for adoption. Many developed social problems, some died young. As reported by *Sermitsiaq Newsletter*, the Danish prime minis-ter refused to apologize, arguing that the days of colonialism are past, "today is different." Yet as Malcolm Gladwell argues in *The Tipping Point*, sometimes it's the little things that trigger a change in society.[26]

To Denmark's dismay but likely no surprise, the referendum on 25 November 2008 saw over 75 percent of Greenland's electorate vote in favour of independence. While non-binding on the Danish and Home Rule governments, the vote provided the basis of negotiations for a new "Self-Rule Government" which came into force on 21 June 2009. The preamble of the Danish Parliament's Law of Self-Rule for Greenland states that "the inhabitants of Greenland are recognized as a people according to international law, with a right to indepen-dence if they so wish after referendum and further negotiations with Denmark." All internal matters are now the responsibility of the Greenland government, including the environment and resource development. Exceptions are foreign affairs, security, the Supreme Court and the coast guard. The Greenlandic language—Kalaallisut—is now recognized as the island's official language. Of particular significance was the agreement that income from future resource development would be shared with Denmark, until such time as the Greenland government could repay the amount of the annual grants provided by Denmark, estimated in 2009 to be around $650 million U.S. annually. Increased responsibility, however, has come with increased costs to establish a local judiciary, law enforcement and correctional system, in addition to the debt incurred by government-owned industries during the recession.[27] Another drain on the treasury will be the accumulated debt, which the Self-Rule Government announced was far greater than anticipated.

Most observers saw the referendum vote as part of a nation-building process and an expression of self-confidence by the 57,000 residents, over 85 percent Inuit. Many in the Home Rule Government, however, believed the results were a major step toward full independence, which Premier Hans Enoksen hoped would take place in 2021 to mark the end of 300 years of Danish rule. But as Mark Nuttall explains in an article in *Indigenous Affairs,* it was Greenland's rapidly melting ice cover that made such a dream seem possible.[28] With improved access, new economic opportunities emerged, ranging from offshore exploitation of oil and gas in Davis Strait to the opening of more mines to extract valuable mineral resources such as gold, rubies and diamonds. Increased mineral production in Greenland also has implications for Canada's claims to the Northwest Passage. As described in *Sermitsiaq Newsletter,* 20 July 2009, the London Mining Company expects that in three to four years it will be producing iron ore from a mine 140 kilometres northeast of Nuuk and employing 300 local workers. The company plans to sell the ore to China at a reduced cost from savings made by shipping through the Northwest Passage.

Not all Greenlanders were enthusiastic about the new resource developments and prospect of independence. Aqqaluk Lynge, international vice-president of the ICC, in an interview for the *Guardian* suggested that independence was still a long way off and that Greenlanders should not rush things. "We need to avoid conflict and assess exactly what the resources and options are before we make decisions."[29] To some, like Josef Motzfeldt, then a member of the Home Rule Government and former minister of foreign affairs, it will be a matter of choice. "We have to choose on the one hand between unrestricted exploitation of our resources in order to gain independence, and on the other hand the protection of our nature, which is so dear to us in order to maintain our cultural heritage."[30] Others were more dismissive, such as a member of the Danish Parliament who was quoted in the *Economist* as saying the "Greenlanders have been brainwashed by unprecedented propaganda." [31]

The election on 2 June 2009 resulted in a resounding defeat for the Siumut party, which had controlled the government since the inception of home rule. As reported in *Sermitsiaq Newsletter* on 7 and 29 June 2009, the Siumut loss was attributed to abuses of power and unwarranted expense accounts, rather than its aggressive economic policies. When the coalition government led by the Inuit Ataqatigiit party officially took over on 21 June 2009, the new premier, Kuupik Kleist, cautioned that full independence was a long way off and that the immediate objective was to carry out the new mandate of Self-Rule Government in cooperation with the Danish government. He also took personal responsibility for the environment portfolio after Denmark rejected Greenland's request for special opt-out clauses from new carbon emission targets. Within six months, the situation changed. Following the Copenhagen Conference on Climate Change in December 2009, *Sermitsiaq News* reported that Kleist had been successful in getting approval for only a 5 percent cut in carbon emissions by 2020, and that mining and other industrial developments would be exempted. Denmark's acceptance of Greenland's right to establish an independent climate policy represents yet another step toward full independence.

Prior to the referendum, agents of foreign companies had descended on the island, opening a virtual treasure chest of resources. In the summer of 2006, prospectors discovered 236 diamonds in West Greenland, the largest of which was said to weigh 2.4 carats. An Australian company offered to develop a uranium mine in southern Greenland, with an expected life of forty years and production capacity to take advantage of greater export opportunities to China. A Canadian company hoped to open a molybdenum mine in eastern Greenland and the U.S. Geological Survey estimated that the Rift Basin in East Greenland holds over 31 billion barrels of oil and gas, and the waters off the west coast possibly up to 110 billion more. In 2008 the American ExxonMobil and Chevron, Canada's Husky

Oil and Encana, Britain's Cairn Energy and Denmark's Dong Energy either purchased or were bidding for drilling rights. From a historical perspective, Greenland's once closed economy was now declared "open for business" for foreign companies in search of new investment opportunities.

More disconcerting were Alcoa's plans to build an aluminum smelter on Greenland's west coast that would require construction of two hydro power plants and flooding of caribou calving grounds and historical sites. The company estimated construction could begin in 2012 and would require between 2,000 and 5,500 foreign workers to build the infrastructure over a period of four years—with only 600 jobs available for local residents over the longer term. As Nuttall observed, "Greenland is on the verge of capitalist penetration by multinational corporations and the beginning of new forms of dependency relations." [32]

Others also spoke out critically. Greenland-born Professor Minik Rosing of the University of Copenhagen questioned the wisdom of buying independence with resource development. "With such a small population we could be overwhelmed by people coming to work here. We should be cautious of suddenly finding ourselves in the minority." He was not alone. Aqqaluk Lynge reiterated similar views, suggesting that Greenlanders should not buy their independence at the expense of their environment. While stating that it was up to the people to decide on independence, he warned that "the demographic influence of the large industrial projects" raised the question whether by 2012 the Greenlanders would still be "a majority in their own country." [33] Added to immigration problems is the issue of carbon dioxide emissions; the proposed Alcoa smelter alone was estimated to produce 450,000 tons annually. As of 2009, the Alcoa project was still under an extended review process with various communities. In the end, it will be up to the new Self-Rule Government to decide whether to approve or reject the proposal. At last report, the proposed uranium mine was rejected—but only tentatively. [34]

While there has been a groundswell of support for halting further Arctic oil and gas development, there are now marked differences of opinion between young and old. In April 2009, delegates to the United Nations Indigenous Peoples' Global Summit on Climate Change agreed that emissions must be drastically reduced by 2050 but were split on how the target should be achieved. Youth delegates, in particular, called for a moratorium on new oil and gas drilling and a phasing out of all fossil fuels, whereas others wished to retain the right to develop their own resources. Their report was to be submitted to the Copenhagen conference in December 2009.

A key issue was clarified a week after the summit when the Inuit Circumpolar Council issued its Declaration on Arctic Sovereignty on 28 April 2009 in Tromso, Norway, to coincide with Arctic Council meetings. Calling for closer cooperation and partnerships between the Arctic countries and the Inuit in developing their resources, the declaration stated that "issues of sovereignty and sovereign rights in the Arctic have become inextricably linked to issues of self-determination" and that "Inuit and Arctic States must, therefore, work together closely and constructively to chart the future of the Arctic." Aqqaluk Lynge, as president of Greenland's ICC branch, stated that this was "not an Inuit Nunaat declaration of independence, but rather a statement of who we are, what we stand for, and on what terms we are prepared to work together with others."[35] In essence, the Inuit are asking to be full partners in all discussions on Arctic affairs.

In Canada, the Nunavut government has also requested further devolution of powers to include more benefits from the territory's natural resources, but with no suggestion of wanting full independence. Nor has the government signalled an interest in offshore oil and gas development. Instead, a recent study recommended large-scale mining projects and expansion of the fishing industry. There are already a number of new mines in various stages of development, offering employment opportunities and a degree of environmental protection. These include a diamond mine on the Nunavut mainland, a gold mine near Baker Lake and one near Hope Bay, as well as a large iron ore mine proposed in the vicinity of Mary River in northern Baffin Island. Diamonds were also discovered 60 kilometres northeast of Iqaluit. At present, it appears that the only mine project to offer direct benefits to the Inuit in the form of royalties is the proposed uranium mine inland from Whale Cove on Hudson Bay. Nunavut previously voted to ban all uranium mining, but the restriction was lifted in 2008 following NTI's partnership with Kivalliq Energy Corporation.[36]

With Greenland now sharing resource revenues with Denmark, there is a reasonable assumption that Nunavut Territory and the new regional self-governments will pressure Ottawa for similar agreements. Thomas Courchene writing in the *Globe and Mail* challenges the federal government's argument that revenue from the territorial resources is needed to cover transfer payments. Using 2004 data for the Northwest Territories as an example, Courchene argues that Ottawa's revenue from mining activity in the territory was actually larger than the transfer payments that year. He also shows how additional revenue is lost through use of temporary workers who pay income tax to their home province and not to the territorial governments. If these revenues were shared, as in the case of Greenland, or accrued directly to the territorial governments, as in Alaska, he suggests that the three territories would be freed of much of their dependence on federal funding.[37]

Now that Inuit have a much greater voice in development of their resources, mining and energy companies may be faced with higher costs for environmental assessments and anti-pollution measures. How this will affect future development of Arctic resources is speculative, but bears close watching. Moving forward in the twenty-first century, Arctic sovereignty, resource development, environmental protection and Inuit rights to self-government will be inextricably tied to economic prosperity at both national and local levels.

CHANGES IN media coverage of Arctic issues also reflect the beginning of a new era. A century ago, American and Canadian dailies were successful in arousing public anger over the Alaska Boundary Dispute. Arctic sovereignty became a hot topic and ensured the sale of newspapers. Alarmist headlines still appear today, but the major difference is the global nature of coverage, which not only includes

Aerial view of the Mary River Project owned and operated by Baffinland
Iron Mines Corporation, 27 February 2008. Based on excellent assay
results, the project feasibility study is completed and has moved into the
environmental impact assessment phase. Pending regulatory approvals,
construction was to begin in mid-2010. Proven resources suggest the
mine will have a life of twenty-one years with potential for expansion and
will provide jobs for approximately 450 at the mine and port facilities at
Steensby Inlet. Lump ore will be mined, which does not require processing,
thus creating a significantly lower carbon footprint as well as no tailings
or waste, other than what is generated by the employees.

Courtesy Baffinland Iron Mines Corporation

the circumpolar countries, but also extends to Europe, Japan and even China. Most newspaper articles now tend to be more factual, based on scientific reports and studies rather than political opinion. So broad and extensive is the coverage that the authors of *Arctic Front* were able to write about events and issues of the last couple of years referencing only newspaper and magazine articles.[38] The Canadian media has also changed its focus. Arctic sovereignty is no longer confined to discussion of conflicts between Canada and the United States. Instead most articles centre on climate change as the key driver in a frantic race to claim ownership of the Arctic's mineral-rich seabed and freedom of passage through northern sea routes, with passing reference to related sovereignty issues.

In Canada, particularly, a major difference from the past is the part played by the academic community. Instead of writing papers and articles to present to themselves at conferences and in academic journals, political scientists and historians have begun to reach out to the general public in op-ed articles, with sophisticated and sometimes divergent arguments on how Canada should protect its Arctic sovereignty. Even former politicians such as Lloyd Axworthy and Senator William Rompkey have joined the growing list of contributors. Academics are also frequently interviewed on televised news broadcasts. The obvious question is how effective they are in influencing public opinion, especially in times of recession when the majority of Canadians have more immediate financial worries. If their influence on public perception is limited, academic experts will have little effect on political decisions, especially those of a minority government which is always more sensitive to views of the electorate.

In one case, however, expert opinion did seem to make a difference. In April 2008, Hans Corell, former United Nations undersecretary-general for legal affairs, wrote an op-ed article for the *Globe and Mail* and appeared on Canadian and American television. He was responding to recent articles that had emphasized the competition for Arctic resources and the possibility that Russia's military expansion in the far north might lead to renewal of the Cold War. Corell rejected the premise, claiming there were clear rules governing the Arctic and that if they "were respected by all states, in particular by the United States, there should be no risk of the Arctic descending into armed conflict." He also dismissed the incident of planting the Russian flag at the North Pole as "irrelevant," suggesting that stability in the Arctic might be better served by U.S. ratification of the Convention on the Law of the Sea.[39] The American press, in particular, took note and the idea of renewed conflict with Russia was largely put to rest, indicating that intervention by senior statesmen can provide a moderating influence on journalism and subsequently public opinion.

Another notable difference, especially in the Canadian media, is the increasing criticism of political statements and government actions on Arctic issues. The Access to Information Act and the ease with which reporters can travel to the Arctic have made it far easier to identify political rhetoric that does not match realities. One case in point was Prime Minister Harper's tour of the Arctic in August 2009, which was accompanied by a number of reporters and photographers to ensure full coverage of how the government's newly released Northern Strategy was being implemented. Virtually all reporters on the tour responded with negative reports. Paul Wells of *Maclean's* magazine was perhaps the most critical. Titled "The Cold Truth: Why Harper's Tough Talk on Arctic Sovereignty Is Empty," his article describes how the much-touted joint military exercises near Iqaluit instead proved that the armed forces were unable to carry out manoeuvres as planned, because the single-hulled HMCS *Toronto* could not handle the floating ice, bergy bits and growlers, in Davis Strait. Photographs of soldiers crawling along the snow with machine guns made the whole exercise appear farcical. Unknown to Wells, the Greenland Command, with its new ice-reinforced patrol ships *White Bear* and *Ejnar Mikkelsen,* had at that same time successfully reached 80° N latitude near Hans Island before being stopped by ice—proof that his criticism was justified.[40]

Media opportunities to influence public opinion are no longer confined to newspapers. Recent television documentaries about the Arctic serve a similar purpose, as do articles in magazines such as the

Economist, Newsweek, Time, Maclean's and the *Walrus.* Once the Arctic was a land of mystery isolated from southern eyes; now spell-binding images of polar landscapes appear in the living rooms of southern audiences around the world in magnificently illustrated coffee-table books or television specials. Artistic photographs and expert opinions may have an impact on public opinion, but in Canada they seem to have inspired more political rhetoric, more promises of future plans and little concrete government action.

Also marking a significant departure from the past is the major leadership role played by Canadian Inuit women in advancing interest in the Arctic and its people. In addition to the outstanding contributions made by Sheila Watt-Cloutier and Mary Simon, as discussed earlier, in 2008 Eva Aariak became the first woman to be elected premier of Nunavut by fellow members of the legislature. In her first year, she surprised southern skeptics by her ability to control the legislature with a velvet glove, while navigating through a muddle of conflicting issues to set a clear-cut, no-nonsense course of government action. There are other young Inuit women throughout Arctic Canada who are showing similar leadership qualities. Yet it was the young Inuit men in the 1970s who, with uncanny determination, set the stage for negotiations that ultimately led to the creation of Nunavut and the various regional self-governments. They also caused a cadre of academics to take greater interest in this seeming "mission impossible," and they in turn inspired interest by others in a variety of disciplines. Aided by authors, poets and artists, it appeared the Arctic would become embedded in the Canadian psyche as an integral part of the nation's identity.

A succession of government leaders joined the bandwagon with promises of major investments to support the Inuit and strengthen Canada's Arctic sovereignty. There were some achievements, but not many. Although Nunavut was not officially established until 1999 under the Liberal government, the Nunavut Land Claims Agreement had been negotiated by the Conservative government, signed by Prime Minister Mulroney in May 1993 and promoted in the media as a key measure to support Arctic sovereignty. Academics seemed more mindful of the fact that without the land claims agreement, the federal government was unable to issue licences for mining or oil and gas developments. Understandably, this is not something politicians wish to acknowledge.

The late 1980s through the 1990s saw the emergence of a cooperative spirit among the circumpolar countries that led to the creation of many government and non-government agencies dedicated to sharing information and technology on the Arctic. Shared projects multiplied. Cooperation was also evident with the signing under the Mulroney Conservative government of the Canada-U.S. Arctic Cooperation Agreement in 1988 and the Canada-Russia Arctic Cooperation Agreement in 1992. The latter unfortunately lapsed in 1999 and apparently was not renewed by the Liberal government. The Arctic Council was an initiative that began with discussions between Soviet President Mikhail Gorbachev and Canadian Prime Minister Brian Mulroney. Its creation in 1996 was considered a major step in establishing a united voice for the circumpolar countries. The media in all the Arctic countries, less so in the U.S., gave the new council their full support. For the most part, news of the Arctic during this period was "good news." To revive this former spirit of cooperation, support of all the circumpolar political leaders will be essential.

In Canada, the Liberal government which came into office in October 1993 appeared supportive of Arctic policies initiated by the previous Conservative government. Mary Simon, an experienced and respected Inuit leader, was appointed the country's first circumpolar ambassador in 1994 and played a key role in advancing Canadian concerns at the Arctic Council, which came into being two years later. In 2000, the Liberal government introduced the first official strategy for the Arctic, which was included in *The Northern Dimension of Canada's Foreign Policy*. The policy emphasized the importance of leadership, partnership and dialogue with northerners. Environmental and social concerns were to take priority over military activities. By now there were severe pollution problems in the Arctic to deal with and cleanup of toxic wastes at abandoned military sites proved costly. Then concerns about global warming entered the scene, raising potential implications for Canadian oil and gas industries. Old commitments were generally honoured if already in the budget, but new expenditures in the Arctic went on hold or were stretched out over a longer period of time.

For Canada, dreams of "what might have been" began to crumble earlier, when major investments in infrastructure to protect Arctic sovereignty became victims of partisan politics and/or budget cuts. Plans for a nuclear-powered icebreaker were dropped; plans for a fleet of nuclear submarines were shelved; orders for search and rescue helicopters were cancelled. Cheaper alternatives were sought and in most cases without success. Whether Conservative or Liberal, a newly elected party in power tended to wash the slate clean of its opponents' plans and promised a new set of its own. Traditionally "peace-minded," most Canadians welcomed any reduction in military spending. The media reported and military experts complained. After election of a Conservative minority government in 2006 and again in 2008, Prime Minister Harper made strong political statements about protecting Arctic sovereignty with lists of future plans to achieve that goal. Some of the items were left over from previous budgets; some were merely promises; some involved feasibility or scientific studies; many related to the Subarctic and had little to do with strengthening Arctic sovereignty. As a result, little "new money" was actually spent on or in the Arctic.

Contrary to popular opinion in Canada and the United States, the most serious threat to Arctic sovereignty is not external, but the "enemy within"—the lobbyists who have so confused the climate change debate and in so doing its relationship to protecting sovereign rights in the Arctic waters. The direct effects of climate change in the Arctic are very real, not imagined. Consequences elsewhere are more diverse and not easily gathered under a single heading. As noted before, reducing the man-made causes of the warming trend will not likely halt the process within our generation, but it will prevent possible disaster for many smaller, developing countries which do not have the financial ability to adapt to the changes.

CLIMATE CHANGE and Arctic sovereignty issues are still newsworthy throughout the world. For the circumpolar countries especially, the importance of responsible journalism on Arctic issues is paramount as it is the only means to reach a broad audience and, if appropriate, expose irresponsible government actions. In the face of the personal adversity suffered by many during the current economic depression, it is critical that the public be fully informed of the issues and the consequences of failing to invest in clean energy and other means to reduce greenhouse gases, as well as in the infrastructure required to protect their country's Arctic sovereignty. The two issues are inextricably tied together, as noted earlier—"two sides of the same coin." Success or failure in bringing about world cooperation to resolve an impending crisis will depend on the wisdom and foresight of the major political leaders in the global community to place the future of the planet ahead of national interests.

(13)

CONFLICTS AND CHALLENGES

Many predictions have been made about the opening of the Northwest
Passage to make the area navigable for normal cargo shipping. Some believe
it will happen in just five years, others say 2030, while there are those who believe
that it won't happen until even further down the line. But in reality, it is only
necessary to look at what the industry and markets are doing. If it pays to
do so, then industries will declare that new shipping routes are open.

ADMIRAL NILS C. WANG, RDN, September 2009[1]

. . . .

THE CURRENT warming trend created a new urgency among
circumpolar countries to settle their ongoing disputes over sovereign rights and jurisdiction. As long as the ice cover had restricted
commercial shipping, a number of conflicts were put on the back
burner, the nations involved simply "agreeing to disagree." Rapid
ice melt changed all that. Other countries now want free access to
the northern sea routes and any unclaimed seabed—and the pressure is growing. A number of new policy directives have been issued
to clarify positions and objectives, which in turn have brought new
pressure on Arctic countries to defend their rights. A few have opted
to reinforce their military capability to protect their interests. How
this will play out over the next decade is uncertain, but it will require
dedicated leadership on the part of all circumpolar countries to settle
their own disputes and at the same time ensure that their rights are
fully protected from southern competition.

In the winter of 2008–9, there were four announcements of
new or revised Arctic policies, three of them presented as official

documents. Canada's initial announcement of its northern policy in February was followed by an official document in July. The European Union was first to present its new policy, justified by the fact that five of the eight Arctic countries were directly or indirectly associated with the EU. Just prior to leaving office, President George W. Bush signed a new U.S. Arctic policy directive, and the Russian Federation followed with its own Arctic policy, published without international fanfare on the web. Canada likely had no other choice but to come forward with a policy of its own. All the above pledged to uphold their respective sovereignty claims in the Arctic and all referred to the importance of new resource development in the region. With the exception of the American assertion that the Northwest Passage and Russia's Northern Sea Route should be designated international straits, most sovereign rights were only generally defined.

The European Union

On 20 November 2008, the Commission of the European Communities issued a communiqué on its policy for the Arctic, prepared at the request of the European Parliament and released a fortnight after Greenland's referendum on independence. With the stated objective of obtaining observer status on the Arctic Council, the European Parliament claimed to be in support of the council's work in protecting the Arctic environment, but was "open to the development of [the Arctic's] potential as a future supplier of sustainable energy resources." The European Commission justified its right to intervene in Arctic affairs by the fact that three member states are Arctic countries: Denmark, Finland and Sweden, with Iceland and Norway participants in the European Economic Area. The communiqué also noted that Canada, Russia and the United States are strategic partners of the European Union and that other member countries have vested interests in the high seas of the Arctic Ocean, which lie beyond their national jurisdiction and whose seabed was managed by the International Seabed Authority.[2] As additional justification for intervening, the commission pointed to recent climate change as a "threats multiplier" that alters the "geo-strategic dynamics of the Arctic with potential consequences for international stability." As a consequence, it believes that "Arctic challenges and opportunities will have significant repercussions on the life of European citizens for generations to come," thus it is "imperative for the European Union to address them in a coordinated and systemic manner, in cooperation with Arctic states, territories and other stakeholders." [3]

The commission set out its policy under three major headings: protection and preservation of the environment; promotion of sustainable use of resources; and enhancement of multilateral governance. Each was discussed in detail under "policy objectives" and "proposals for action." Environmental measures were straightforward, with emphasis placed on the need for impact assessment, adequate monitoring and cooperative management of "disaster response." There was no mention of how these measures would be enforced. Indigenous peoples' traditional dependence on wildlife for subsistence was to be "protected" and provision made for their "free, informed consent." There was no mention of aboriginal rights to self-government and equal participation in decisions on future developments.

In terms of resource development, the commission called for guiding principles to ensure "a level playing field and reciprocal market access" for European countries. Not surprisingly, since the EU has one of the world's largest merchant fleets, a good portion of this section was devoted to transport and the work of the International Marine Organization. With the objective of reducing shipping distances between Europe and Pacific countries, the commission defended "the principle of freedom of navigation and the right of innocent passage in the newly opened routes and areas" across the Arctic. The global dimension of Europe's shipping industry is not generally known to North Americans, so the implications were unclear. Most Finns and Norwegians, however, are likely cognizant that their once thriving shipyards and technical services are now operated by STX, a private enterprise owned by a South Korean conglomerate.

The European Parliament had recommended a "standalone policy" on Arctic governance and urged the commission "to take a proactive role in the Arctic." Thus the final section on "Enhanced Arctic

Multilateral Governance" was designed to ensure that the EU is involved in all organizations responsible for supervising and managing Arctic affairs. Declaring at the outset that there was "no specific treaty regime for the Arctic" and that "no country or group of countries have sovereignty over the North Pole or the Arctic Ocean around it," the EU policy set out its critique on the current state of affairs. In its opinion, "the main problems relating to Arctic governance include the fragmentation of the legal framework, the lack of effective instruments, the absence of an overall policy-setting process and gaps in participation, implementation and geographic scope."[4] To rectify the problems, the commission proposed a new Arctic governance system to ensure security and stability, strict management of the environment, respect for the precautionary principle and sustainable use of Arctic resources with open and equitable access for all. Application for permanent observer status on the Arctic Council was considered an important first step. The eight Arctic countries disagreed and rejected the EU's request in May 2009.

In conclusion, the European Commission maintained that its policy would provide a structured and coordinated approach to circumpolar affairs and enhanced multilateral governance of the Arctic, open avenues of new cooperation with non-Arctic states and "establish the right balance between the priority of preserving the Arctic environment and the need for sustainable use of resources." This last statement suggests the EU might be offering a sustained or reliable market for Arctic resources. While concern for the environment was frequently referenced in the policy, so was the importance of developing the Arctic's resources to meet the needs of the European countries. The question of Greenland's future status was stated in two short paragraphs. The first attested to the fact that Greenland is "part of Denmark," hence one of the Overseas Countries and Territories associated with the EU and a candidate for financial assistance through the Annual Action Programmes. The "proposed action" was directed toward enhancing cooperation "to make the EU an even more important partner for Greenland in managing its fragile environment and the challenges confronting its population."[5] From the commission's perspective, it appears that Greenland is a European country and its resources should be shared with other European countries—a warning, perhaps, against any imperial notions the U.S. might entertain.

United States Policy

The United States responded more quickly than anticipated. On 9 January 2009, just days before leaving office, President George W. Bush signed a new Arctic policy, the first revision in fifteen years. The revised policy was justified by the recent requirements of homeland security and defence, the effects of climate change, increasing activity in the region, the work of the Arctic Council and "growing awareness that the Arctic region is both fragile and rich in resources." Admirable among the policy objectives were those ensuring that "economic development in the region [be] environmentally sustainable," that institutions promoting cooperation among the eight Arctic countries be strengthened and that the indigenous peoples of the Arctic be involved in decisions affecting them.[6]

As expected, the primary focus was on national security, with the warning that the U.S. "is prepared to operate either independently or in conjunction with other states to safeguard [its] interests." Listed among the items of particular interest were missile defence, early warning systems, strategic deterrence, maritime security operations and freedom of navigation and overflight. Because of increasing activity in the region, the U.S. was prepared to establish a more active presence in the Arctic and "project sea power throughout the region." Its position on the status of the northern sea routes was unequivocal. "Freedom of the seas is a top national priority. The Northwest Passage is a strait used for international navigation, and the Northern Sea Route includes straits used for international navigation; the regime of transit passage applies to passage through those straits. Preserving the rights and duties relating to navigation and overflight in the Arctic region supports our ability to exercise these rights throughout the world, including through strategic straits."[7]

The policy directive was to be implemented by projecting "a *sovereign* maritime presence in the Arctic in support of essential United

States interests" (emphasis added) throughout the entire Arctic region. Together, these statements constitute a direct challenge to sovereign authority claimed by Canada, Denmark and the Russian Federation. The U.S. also reiterated its position on the unresolved maritime boundary in the Beaufort Sea, based on a line at right angles from a baseline equidistant from projecting headlands, rather than accepting the Canadian assertion that it should follow the median line of the boundary between the Yukon and Alaska. A maritime boundary dispute with Russia was noted, with the reminder that once the Russian Federation ratified the 1990 bilateral agreement the treaty would enter into force.

The United States also responded directly to the EU proposal for enhanced multilateral governance by declaring that "an 'Arctic Treaty'—along the lines of the Antarctic Treaty—is not appropriate or necessary." The policy also asserted that the Arctic Council "should remain a high-level forum devoted to issues within its current mandate and not be transformed into a formal international organization, particularly one with assessed contributions." Otherwise the 2009 directive claimed to promote cooperation in scientific research, to provide effective infrastructure to protect the environment from adverse effects of increased commercial shipping, and to take appropriate measures to ensure energy resources were developed in a responsible manner to avoid destruction of the environment. On the last issue, the U.S. policy affirmed the importance of cooperation in recognition "that most known Arctic oil and gas resources are located outside of United States jurisdiction." Although the directive stressed the importance of protecting the fragile Arctic environment, proposed measures referred to adoption of new technologies and stricter surveillance rather than restriction of shipping activities. Otherwise the accelerated warming trend was seen as an opportunity to advance U.S. interests, with no suggestion of reducing greenhouse gas emissions or slowing the pace of further Arctic oil and gas development.

Another item of note was the recommendation that the Senate should approve the 1982 UN Convention on the Law of the Sea to give the U.S. "a seat at the table" in discussions that might affect the protection or advancement of its interests in the Arctic. In this context, special mention was made of national security issues, maritime mobility of armed forces, U.S. rights over valuable seabed resources and health of the oceans. The directive also endorsed all necessary actions to establish the outer limits of the American continental shelf as permitted under international law. In essence, the new policy supported U.S. interests in the Arctic, with a commitment to cooperate with existing organizations and abide by established international law. By U.S. interpretation, existing laws would support designation of the Northwest Passage and the Northern Sea Route as international straits. Although President Bush promised financial support to implement the policy, he left it to executive departments and agencies to establish budget priorities. Since he was a lame duck president on his way out of office, the question may arise whether he overreached his authority in signing the document. As it stands, however, the new directive is officially in force until replaced.

Canadian Policy

Canada's Arctic policy, as announced by the Minister of Foreign Affairs in February 2009, followed principles similar to those set out in *The Northern Dimension of Canada's Foreign Policy* in 2000 by the former Liberal government, with the Arctic still sufficiently blended with the Subarctic to create only generalized guidelines. Shortly after, the Canadian government launched a public relations initiative that sponsored events and exhibitions in Europe to promote Inuit art and culture as a means of publicizing the human presence in the Canadian Arctic—a central argument used in support of its sovereign claims. This new public relations policy was a deliberate move to send the world a message that Canada was a responsible steward of its Arctic regions in addressing ecological and aboriginal issues. In the words of Canada's foreign minister, Lawrence Cannon, "Canada is an Arctic nation and an Arctic power," and his message to all foreign countries was an affirmation of the country's "leadership, stewardship and ownership in the region."[8]

In response to mounting criticism for the lack of an official document, on 26 July 2009 three cabinet ministers held a press conference
at the Canadian Museum of Civilization to announce the publication of *Canada's Northern Strategy: Our North, Our Heritage, Our Future.*
The most striking difference from previous announcements was a
departure from the confrontational approach, with Foreign Minister
Cannon declaring that "we're going down a road toward co-opera-
tion and collaboration." Cannon was joined by Indian and Northern
Affairs Minister Chuck Strahl and Minister of State for Science Gary
Goodyear, and the thrust of their message was the oft-repeated assertion that the Harper government has made the Arctic "an absolute
priority." Attached to the policy was a list of "Recent Northern Strategy Commitments" in support of that statement. There was little
new on the list. Most items referred to completed projects, ongoing
projects already funded or ones still in the planning stage. After CBC
News broke the story, it was followed two nights later by interviews
with Arctic sovereignty experts. Michael Byers soundly criticized the
document, pointing out that there was little in the way of new initiatives and no mention of programs that had been cancelled, such as
the Northern Watch pilot project designed to test new surveillance
technologies in the High Arctic. In his opinion, it was a repackaging
of old projects and future promises. Rob Huebert generally agreed
but suggested the list was important as a means of holding the government accountable.[9]

The strategy document describes four priorities—"exercising our
Arctic sovereignty; promoting social and economic development;
protecting the North's environmental heritage; and improving and
devolving northern governance." At first glance, the strategy appears
impressive, comprehensive and aggressive, one that would assure
Canadians that the government had left no stone unturned. The local
and national press disagreed. Why the criticism? While *Northern
Strategy* offered a comprehensive blueprint that married needs with
initiatives, newspaper op-eds and articles characterized it as a compi-
lation of previous commitments, most of which had seen little or no
action. As a point of comparison, the *Globe and Mail* carried an article

the same day that described Denmark's plans to expand its military capabilities in the Arctic.[10] Overall, the lofty statements and political rhetoric in the strategy document were ignored; it was the list of "recent commitments" that inspired the criticism. It appears that the media expected new actions and new funding.

Instead, ongoing projects were funded by "old money" with the exception of an additional $17 million from the Department of Transport's 2008 stimulus package for a two-stage project to build docks for fishing boats at Pangnirtung, a project decades overdue. Evidently stage two will take place sometime in the future. Some initiatives were still in the planning stage. Others were revised to meet budgetary restraints, such as a Canadian Forces Training Centre at Resolute Bay, which will now be located in old government buildings. The new deep-sea port once intended for Iqaluit will become a refuelling centre utilizing the abandoned wharves at the former Nanisivik mine. The only "new news" was that the northern economic development agency, CanNor, would be based in Iqaluit, with branch offices in Whitehorse and Yellowknife. When the CanNor money is divided between the three territories, the funding available to Nunavut will be minimal compared to its needs. Jeffrey Simpson, writing in the *Globe and Mail*, suggests the strategy was worth building on, but skeptically notes a number of broken promises, such as the 2006 election promise of three new, heavy-duty icebreakers, now downgraded to a less expensive medium-range vessel.[11] At the time of writing, no tenders had been issued for the icebreaker.

Inherent in the list of initiatives are the realities of budget constraints. The deepwater harbour promised to Iqaluit has been cancelled. The eight ice-hardened patrol boats had already been reduced to six, and a week after release of the *Northern Strategy* document, the whole project was deferred because of costs. The Defence Minister also announced new Arctic surveillance aircraft, but it appears that the aircraft is a single Bombardier Dash-7 such as those used by the Department of Transport on the east and west coasts. Since then, the government has announced the approval of six new coast guard patrol ships, but only for use in southern waters. A writer for the

CCGS *Martha L. Black* and HMCS *Fredericton* anchored in Frobisher
Bay in readiness for Canadian joint military exercises in summer of 2008.
So far, the exercises can be undertaken only in relatively ice-free
water because Canadian naval vessels lack ice-strengthened hulls.
Courtesy photographer Chris Windeyer, Iqaluit

Economist saw the situation as inevitable and pointed to the problems
of a minority government during a recession, when "the overwhelming majority of voters live in the south," concluding that "Mr. Harper
will surely continue to try to make a little money go a long way in the
north."[12] Meanwhile Canadian military exercises in the Arctic will
likely continue each summer, attempting to keep pace with those carried out by the Danes, Russians and Norwegians.

Russian Arctic Policy

Although Russia is not a North American country, the Russian Federation's Arctic policy is included here as it was issued in response to
the EU and U.S. policies. On 27 March 2009, Russia's *Fundamentals of
State Policy on the Arctic Up to 2020* was posted on its Security Council's
official website. The document had been prepared earlier, debated
in the Security Council and signed by President Dmitry Medvedev

on 18 September 2008. With the stated intention of working with the other circumpolar countries to "preserve the Arctic as a zone of peace and cooperation," the plan was surprisingly transparent and forthright. The primary focus was on the need for expanded military surveillance within Russia's own maritime boundaries, considered necessary because of an anticipated increase in shipping and competition for offshore resources as a result of the rapid ice melt. Noting that the Northern Sea Route is now the shortest and safest link between western Europe and East Asia, Russian authorities believed that added protection was imperative for their northern ports, and tighter military and border control necessary to prevent smuggling, poaching, terrorist activities, even potential invasion. Their proposed action plan entailed increasing their military presence, border guards and coast guard throughout the region.[13]

To allay fears of renewed militarization of the Arctic, retired Admiral Vyatcheslav Popov, head of the Commission on Maritime Policy in the Russian Parliament, explained that the purpose was not to create a new strike force but to optimize the existing military to accomplish new tasks. He also stated that the plans included expansion of forward-based airfields in the region and that the proposal to strengthen security measures would be discussed at a ministerial meeting of the Arctic Council. Popov also stressed the importance of seabed mining on the continental shelf for Russia's future prosperity, adding that "about 20 percent of Russia's GDP and 22 percent of Russian exports are produced" in the far north.[14]

Nonetheless, the Canadian, American and even British press initially interpreted the policy as an aggressive act by the former Cold War enemy. Complaints were also levelled at pending Russian legislation that would provide for strict regulations on traffic in the Northern Sea Route, including the right to restrict foreign military vessels, expulsion of ships in violation of environmental regulations and levying of fees for use of Russian icebreakers to ensure safe transit through the passage. The Canadian press brought the Minister of Foreign Affairs into the fray, with Lawrence Cannon declaring that his own country's ambitions were not to militarize the Arctic but

The Russian nuclear icebreaker *Yamal*, with shark's teeth painted on the bow, is followed by the much smaller CCGS *Louis St. Laurent* and USCGC *Polar Star* as they head toward the North Pole. Russia's large icebreaker fleet is indicative of the importance the Russian Federation and the Russian people attach to the Arctic and particularly the Northern Sea Route. Costs of maintenance have been partially offset by offering cruises to the North Pole for tourists.   United States Coast Guard; photographer Steve Wheeler

simply to protect Canadian sovereignty. He went on to assert that "Canada will not be bullied" by the Russians, a statement that made headlines across the country. That night, the Russian ambassador to Canada appeared on CBC Television, protesting that "we don't want to bully anybody," that his country was not aiming for an "outlandish power grab" and that the two countries had more in common than other Arctic states. Reaction by readers varied, with one commentator suggesting that Canadian bickering with the Russians was non-productive, whereas the combined efforts of the two countries in any multilateral negotiations would be "unbeatable."[15] Ottawa must have agreed since its official policy document released that July committed the Canadian government to seek cooperation with all the circumpolar countries.

Comparison of the Arctic policy statements of the U.S., Canada and the European Union, in conjunction with the official policy of the Russian Federation, leads to a number of key observations. Common to all is omission of any reference to the Inuit Circumpolar Council's own Arctic policy. The lengthy document presented and approved in 1992 is likely the most comprehensive and far-reaching policy to date, covering an array of issues ranging from the environment, sustainable development, social welfare, culture, security and aboriginal rights to self-government and cooperation among the circumpolar countries. Prepared by and for the Inuit who inhabit the North American Arctic, it required a decade of research and discussion to achieve consensus. Their concerns go far beyond simply protecting their wildlife resources for traditional subsistence livelihood.[16] Yet neither Canada, the U.S. nor Denmark through the EU referred to the document, nor did they consult directly with the ICC before releasing their own Arctic policies. With the Inuit/Eskimos making up roughly 80 percent of the population in the North American Arctic, it seems inconceivable that any official Arctic policy was prepared without the direct participation of Inuit political leaders.

Canada's Arctic policy also has a problem of focus. By purposefully defining a "northern strategy," the government includes many activities in the Yukon and Northwest Territories, which obscure how little direct economic benefit from current initiatives will accrue to the residents of the Arctic. While the government claims that one of the priorities is to advance social and economic development for northerners, most of the budgeted Arctic-specific initiatives, such as support for scientific research of the International Polar Year, construction of an icebreaker, satellite surveillance technologies and feasibility studies, actually provide jobs and income to southerners or southern-based industries. In this context, one might consider whether the costs of protecting Arctic sovereignty are compatible with Ottawa's vision of the "North as a healthy, prosperous region." Vision and actions appear disconnected. With so much planned for the future, claims of protecting Arctic sovereignty seem little more than "paper sovereignty," which could be cancelled by a new party taking power. Should this scenario continue, Canadians may wake up someday to discover that some other country is in *de facto* control of their Arctic waters.

The latest American policy is focussed entirely on Arctic issues, but says little about Alaska. Instead, the bulk of the document relates to enabling effective security throughout the North American Arctic. As a consequence, it seems somewhat disingenuous for the American media to criticize the Russian policy of defending its own Arctic waters when the U.S. has assumed the right to defend Canadian and Greenland air and waters where its authority is derived though bilateral agreements. Public perception aside, the U.S. Arctic policy declares the country's interest in the Arctic is derived from its responsibilities for defence and the environment, as opposed to the Canadian and Russian policies that saw exploitation of their resources as being essential to their countries' future prosperity. Even the EU's policy stressed the importance of the Arctic to the economic security of its member countries. Seemingly forgotten is the fact that an economy based on non-renewable resources is not sustainable over the longer term and could subject the small Arctic communities to a boom and bust cycle.

A factor common to all recent policies is the commitment to cooperation: through UNCLOS as a means of settling disputes and the Arctic Council as a watchdog on the environment. Yet in the Russian and American policies, the goal of cooperation often appears secondary to the emphasis on military requirements, whereas the EU and Russian directives also stress the importance of resource development and shipping interests. The very few references to indigenous peoples in these policies, especially the EU's statements that they are to be "consulted" and their traditional cultures "protected" in future resource development, suggest there is little commitment to advance their economic prosperity. The Russian, U.S. and EU policies, in particular, appear to represent the interests of their southern-based governments at the expense of their Arctic hinterlands. *Canada's Northern Strategy*, on the other hand, fully incorporates social and economic well-being of Canada's northern people into its objectives, with promises to "work closely with the indigenous people." Commitments and vision are commendable in creating a road map for the future, but the financial means to implement them may not be available anytime soon. Unfortunately, Canadian politicians have a history of making promises—followed by little or no action. In the interim, circumpolar countries would do well to translate their commitment to cooperation and preservation of the environment into action and allow Inuit and other indigenous people direct participation in the policy-making process.

Ongoing and Potential Conflicts

In spite of the 1982 UN Convention on the Law of the Sea, there are still a number of outstanding jurisdictional disputes in the North American Arctic, all but one related to adjacent waters. As of 2009, ongoing areas of conflict include the status of the Northwest Passage; ownership of Hans Island, lying in Kennedy Channel midway between Ellesmere Island and Greenland; the marine boundaries between Canada and the U.S. in the Beaufort Sea; and the boundaries between Russia and the U.S. in the Bering Sea. Although not related to North America, the status of Russia's Northern Sea Route is discussed here as a point of comparison. In recent years, a great deal has been written on the subject by experts in international law and Arctic sovereignty.[17] The intent here is to summarize the ongoing disputes and potential conflicts.

The Northwest Passage

The longest-standing dispute in the North American Arctic is the status of the Northwest Passage. While there are a number of routes through the Arctic Islands which might be traversed under certain conditions, only two are considered navigable (see map p. 377). Canada maintains that the Northwest Passage is an internal waterway based on historic title. This claim was reinforced in 1986 when Minister of External Affairs Joe Clark announced the drawing of baselines around the Archipelago and declared that all waters within those lines were "internal waters." Sovereign jurisdiction also applied to the airspace above.

The U.S. took an opposing position, claiming that the passage is a commercial waterway between two high seas and that transit of all foreign vessels cannot be restricted by Canada. Initially, the U.S. position was based on the decision of the International Court of Justice in the 1949 *Corfu Channel* case, which defined an international strait as any waterway connecting two high seas and used for international shipping. The 1958 Territorial Seas Convention confirmed that innocent passage of foreign ships cannot be suspended in straits used for international navigation. Then in 1982, Article 37 of UNCLOS III created a transit passage regime which allows commercial vessels to pass through international straits with minimal interference, providing they do not adversely impact on the sovereign rights and interests of coastal states. Neither the Territorial Seas Convention nor UNCLOS Article 37 clarifies the amount of traffic required to meet the functional criteria of being "used for international navigation." [18]

By geographical definition, the two major routes of the Northwest Passage do, in fact, connect the Atlantic and Pacific Oceans by way of Davis Strait in the east and Bering Strait in the west. Yet for years Canada argued that because of its minimal use by commercial vessels the passage did not meet the functional criteria for international shipping. As long as either route was largely unnavigable because of ice, there was no pressure from the international community to clarify its status. As a result, Canada and the U.S. appeared willing to "agree to disagree" and had reached a compromise to allow unfettered transit of American government and military vessels under the 1988 Arctic Cooperation Agreement. The situation has changed. Commercial traffic, whether cruise ships, cargo ships or local supply vessels, has multiplied dramatically in the past ten years. With the ice rapidly melting in the passage and offering a shorter and safer route to Asia, many western European countries and China now support the American position.

Many experts believe traffic will increase steadily and easily meet the established criteria for an international strait. In this event, foreign ships would have transit rights and could pass freely as long as they do not stop ashore and do comply with international maritime regulations, some of which are more rigid than those legislated by the Arctic Waters Pollution Prevention Act. As of 2009, it was still unclear whether additional amendments to UNCLOS will be required to ensure Canada can enforce its anti-pollution measures in the Northwest Passage should it be recognized as an international strait. Of more serious concern is whether Canada can enforce those regulations and whether it would have the full cooperation and support of the U.S. to do so. In Bush's policy directive in January 2009, the U.S. stated its intention to provide effective infrastructure to protect the environment from the adverse effects of increased commercial shipping. Whether this will include an offer to step in and protect the Canadian Arctic is unclear. Should that happen, there would likely be concessions that would lead to further *de facto* loss of Canada's sovereign authority. Meanwhile, commercial shipping through the passage is increasing. The advantage of a shorter and safer alternative to the Panama Canal was self-evident when a Russian icebreaker and tug towing a dry dock were observed en route from Vladivostok to Bermuda.

The Arctic Waters Pollution Prevention regulations of 1977 and 1985 were generally accepted by other countries and were upgraded in 2009 to meet standards set by the International Maritime Organization and the International Association of Classification Societies. With the Canadian rights of control over the Northwest Passage now questioned under existing laws of the sea, some advisers are recommending that Canada establish a more effective monitoring system for enforcement of marine regulations and shipping standards. Even then, scientists argue that new regulations must be updated regularly to incorporate new technologies and address shortfalls.[19]

Donat Pharand, a recognized expert on Arctic sovereignty, believes that there is still insufficient use of the Northwest Passage to classify it as an international strait, but admits that should such a degree of use develop, Canada should take immediate steps to ensure it has the ability to protect the environment and general security of the area. In addition to safeguards already recommended by the Canadian government, he suggests that negotiations should begin immediately between Canada and the U.S. for a transit agreement for American merchant ships to protect against international terrorism. Otherwise, he fears "unrestricted freedom of navigation in an international strait" could have dire consequences for both countries. Most Canadian experts on the subject agree, with varying emphasis on the importance of cooperation between Canada and the U.S., as well as with other circumpolar countries to establish regulations that adequately protect the environment.[20]

Historian Jack Granatstein took the issue a step further by suggesting that the status of the Northwest Passage will become redundant if scientists are correct in estimating that within fifteen years the waters around the North Pole will be ice-free, thus opening a much shorter route across the Arctic Ocean. Although recent calculations put that event further into the future, he argues that circumpolar countries must devise "even tougher and more enforceable environmental standards," especially in the area surrounding the North Pole, to prevent the Arctic Ocean from becoming "a dumping ground for polluting merchant shippers and mineral and petroleum extraction companies." International law expert Donald Rothwell believes that individual states are presently unable to protect the Arctic environment and that an international legal regime for the Arctic is imperative to prevent pollution.[21]

Most, if not all, Canadian experts on Arctic sovereignty agree that Canada and the U.S. must work toward creating stricter regulations to protect the waters of the Northwest Passage against potential pollution. This may be more difficult than anticipated. When Canada attempted to make the voluntary NORDREG regulations mandatory in 2009, the U.S. issued a firm protest and the legislation was put on hold. Whether there were other reasons for deferral is still unclear.

The Northern Sea Route

While the Northern Sea Route is not located in the North American Arctic, the same issues arise with it as with the Northwest Passage.

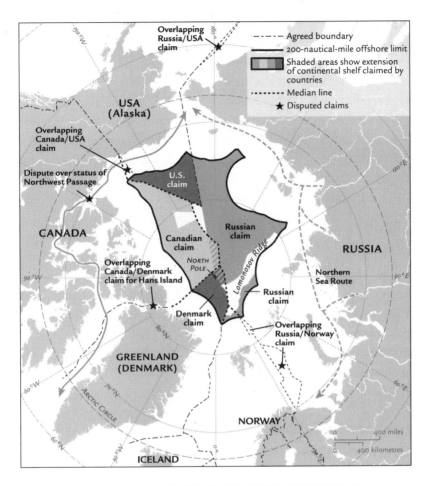

DISPUTED CLAIMS IN THE CIRCUMPOLAR ARCTIC, C2009

The significance lies in the different response made by the Russian Federation compared to that of Canada. Although portions of the Northern Sea Route could be considered international straits under UNCLOS, no state had challenged Russia's jurisdiction until release of the 2009 U.S. Arctic policy. This immediately prompted introduction of legislation before the Russian Parliament that defined the external borders of the Northern Sea Route and asserted its status as belonging to Russia's territorial waters. While transit by foreign ships will be permitted, the primary prerequisite is strict adherence to vessel specifications and environmental standards, including a ban on the discharge of any harmful substances. The legislation also provides Russian inspectors with the right to board foreign vessels and if necessary expel them for failing to comply with regulations. If in compliance with regulations, foreign ships will be allowed to traverse the route if accompanied by a Russian icebreaker and pilot ship.[22] To show that the process was fully operational, in the fall of 2009, Russia announced the successful transit of two German ships accompanied by one of its icebreakers through the Northern Sea Route, pointing out the considerable cost savings over southern routes.

At the same time, the Russian Federation enacted other measures to protect its interests in the Arctic. New laws now ensure that development of its offshore oil resources will be undertaken by state-run rather than foreign corporations. In support of the initiative, Russia's minister of industry and trade also announced the construction of three new shipyards to build icebreakers, LNG and oil supertankers, research vessels, offshore platforms and floating nuclear power plants. As reported by the deputy director of the Fridtjof Nansen Institute in Finland, oil supplies in western Siberia are declining and Russia will need new capacity within ten years.[23] Russia has also fully integrated protection of its sovereign rights with national defence plans, environmental protection and economic development. Moreover, it appears that the federation has enacted sufficient measures to enforce its claimed sovereign rights.

Maritime Boundary in the Beaufort Sea

Canada has consistently maintained that the maritime boundary in the Beaufort Sea should be an extension of the 141st meridian boundary between the Yukon and Alaska, based on the Anglo-Russian Treaty of 1825. The United States disagrees, maintaining that the maritime boundary should extend at a 90° angle to the coastline. As the proposed Canadian line is westward of the claimed U.S. line, the result is a disputed triangle in the Beaufort Sea that affects not only drilling rights but also enforcement of fisheries and anti-pollution regulations. The conflict initially surfaced in the 1970s when offshore drilling in the area was considered imminent. Ice conditions, however, thwarted potential development and the dispute lay dormant until climate change renewed plans to explore the area for potential oil and gas reserves.

In the summers of 2008 and 2009, Canadian and American scientists headed north in the Beaufort Sea to map the seabed and establish the underwater extension of their respective continental shelves. The two icebreakers carrying the scientists and their equipment, the aging CCGS *St. Laurent* and more powerful USCGC *Healy*, worked in tandem, one breaking a path through the ice with the other following to extract the first if caught in the ice. While both teams will share the data gathered, this does not guarantee they will agree on the interpretation of the findings. Nor will their findings resolve the dispute over the maritime boundary in the Beaufort Sea.[24]

Moreover, the disputed triangle covering approximately 21,500 square kilometres of ocean now poses an additional problem after the Alaska government announced its intention to ban commercial fisheries in the Beaufort and Chukchi Seas. While the proposed law is still under review by the U.S. Department of Commerce, it was expected to come into effect in the fall of 2009. Although Canadian fisheries policies are similar, the question again arises as to whether the United States or Canada has the right to regulate fisheries in the disputed triangle. Until a bilateral agreement is reached on the boundary line, close cooperation by the two countries will be required to manage resources in the triangle, whether fish, minerals or oil and gas.[25]

Hans Island

The only dispute over an Arctic land mass concerns an island located in the centre of Kennedy Channel in Nares Strait, equidistant between Ellesmere Island and Greenland. Hans Island is only 1.3 square kilometres in area and was never inhabited by Inuit for any extended period of time. The 1973 agreement negotiated by Denmark and Canada defining the maritime boundary between Greenland and the

Northwest Territories (now Nunavut) purposely excluded the island and adjacent waters from rights to seabed mining pending future resolution of its ownership. As a result, no exploratory licences have been issued on or around the island. In 2004, however, the island was visited by an ice-reinforced Danish frigate and a flag raised to signify the state's claim to ownership. The following summer, Canada's minister of defence also visited the island to stake a claim for his country.

At issue is the advantage of drilling for oil and gas on land versus offshore drilling platforms in the adjacent waters. While there are rumours and speculation in Greenland, to date there are no published scientific studies confirming the potential presence of hydrocarbons. It is noted, however, that Canada has issued exploratory drilling permits at the eastern entrance of Lancaster Sound. In a joint statement in September 2006, Denmark and Canada agreed to resolve the dispute based on scientific studies. A cooperative effort to map the seabed is ongoing to determine whether the island is an extension of Greenland's or Canada's continental shelf. In the interim, the two countries agreed to share the island for purposes of research. Then out of the blue Premier Hans Enoksen of the Greenland Home Rule Government surprised everyone at an international meeting in May 2008 by declaring that the island belonged to the Inughuit because they had discovered, occupied and named the island centuries before the arrival of Europeans.[26] While it has been confirmed that the Inughuit often stopped on the island on the way to hunt polar bears on Ellesmere Island, there is no archaeological evidence to suggest permanent settlement. With discovery claims no longer sufficient to maintain title to lands under customary law, it would be interesting to hear the outcome should an Inughuit claim be submitted to the International Court of Justice. Otherwise, the general consensus is that Canada and Denmark will work together to settle the dispute quickly and amicably.

Seabed Mining

The UN Convention on the Law of the Sea approved a formula for defining a country's rights to seabed mining within 60 nautical miles

Aerial view of Hans Island taken from the east with Ellesmere Island in the background. Although ownership of the island remains in dispute, both Canada and Denmark are awaiting further scientific data on the location of their continental shelves to determine the legitimacy of their respective claims. Courtesy photographer John England, University of Alberta

or 111 kilometres from the foot of its continental shelf with potential for an extension of the outer limits to a distance of 350 nautical miles or approximately 648 kilometres. Each country has a timeline of ten years since it ratified the treaty during which it may submit its evidence supporting extended rights to the UN Commission on Limits of the Continental Shelf. In 2007 Russia made worldwide headlines with the announcement that its scientists had deposited a Russian flag in a titanium capsule on the seabed at the North Pole. Russia claims the nearby Lomonosov Ridge on the basis that is an extension of Novaya Zemlya's continental shelf, and is in the process of submitting scientific evidence in support of its claim to the International Seabed Authority. Norway also is preparing a submission based on Spitzbergen's continental shelf. Meanwhile in March 2009 Denmark and Canada launched a joint scientific expedition to gain evidence in support of their claims in the region. The two countries have until 2013 to submit their evidence. Since the U.S, Russia, Denmark, Canada and Norway have all agreed to abide by existing international law, the general consensus is that potential disagreements will be settled by scientific evidence.

Ocean policy experts Scott Borgerson and Caitlyn Antrim came up with an interesting alternative in an article appearing in the *New York Times*, which suggested designating everything above 88° N latitude as a marine park to be managed by an international cooperative.[27] Although such a park is an interesting concept, supervision of it would be difficult if not impossible. Moreover, the suggestion that members of the "cooperative" would include the U.S. might be seen by some as an attempt to extend American influence over areas of the Arctic where the U.S. has no existing jurisdiction. Under the current law of the sea, only Canada, Denmark, Norway and Russia have any potential rights near the North Pole and then only for the purpose of seabed mining. Otherwise the waters are subject to full "freedom of the seas."

Maritime Boundary in the Bering Sea

As noted in the U.S. Arctic policy, there is a disputed maritime boundary between Russia and the U.S. in the Bering Sea, which also affects drilling rights for offshore oil and gas. An agreement settling the dispute was signed in 1990 and is awaiting ratification by the Russian Parliament before it comes into force. There is no indication that the agreement will be rejected.

Arctic Security

Although not a territorial dispute per se, the question of military rights to defend the Arctic has been an issue since World War II, when the U.S. assumed major responsibility for defence of the North American Arctic through bilateral agreements negotiated with Canada and later Denmark. The situation was very different during the Cold War, when Canada was under pressure to increase its military presence to protect its Arctic sovereignty. In 1987, for example, Perrin Beatty as minister of national defence argued in the white paper on defence that a fleet of nuclear submarines was essential to provide "adequate surveillance and presence" to protect Canadian claims in the North-west Passage and reduce dependence on the U.S. In his opinion, any nation "that contracts out the defence of its own territory is not *sovereign*, but a *protectorate*" (emphasis in original).[28] The plan came under severe criticism because of cost, with the result that in 1992 the Conservative government not only shelved the submarine plans but cut the defence budget by 35 percent. Whether or not the concept of Canada and Greenland as military protectorates is a reasonable interpretation, the U.S. has assumed major responsibility for defence of the North American Arctic. This is unlikely to change.

Times have changed since the end of the Cold War, as have the priorities attached to defence. Instead of chasing enemy nuclear submarines armed with nuclear ballistic missiles across the Arctic, the objective in recent years has been to develop effective surveillance measures—by air, underwater radar or satellite. Canada's new *Northern Strategy* lists the launching of Radarsat II as one of its initiatives to strengthen Arctic sovereignty, but the satellite is useless to monitor pollution or ship traffic unless equipped with Polar Epsilon technology, a step that will not likely occur until 2011 or later. Otherwise, the U.S. has ensured that the North American Arctic is well equipped with early warning systems to detect a possible attack by air, even though Russia is no longer the enemy. Potentially more dangerous than an air attack would be a terrorist attack by ship or submarine. Other concerns include piracy, illegal seabed mining and intrusion by a rogue submarine. U.S. nuclear subs still patrol the Arctic waters under the ice, surfacing occasionally for photo ops. Sharing technology, operational systems and reports with other Arctic nations might be the ultimate goal, but at present the United States has assumed the primary responsibility for security of the Arctic as part of its continental defence policy. The recent Arctic directive issued in January 2009 reaffirmed that U.S. interest in the region was military and that it extended across the entire North American Arctic. There is no indication that the U.S. would be prepared to relinquish that right.

Although there have been frequent suggestions that Canada should increase its naval presence in the Arctic, there appears to be no urgent need apart from adopting a more equitable share of the joint responsibility for Arctic defence. Denmark, on the other hand, has upgraded both naval and air forces, with most of its surveillance capacity deployed in patrolling Greenland waters for protection of its fisheries. At present, there is no apparent threat of an enemy attack.

Inuit/Eskimo Rights to Self-Government

The aboriginal right to self-government was not considered a sovereignty issue until Greenlanders made it so in their 2008 referendum for independence. Elsewhere, Inuit/Eskimos have not expressed interest in full independence. In Nunavut, where the territorial government is progressing toward further devolution of powers, Premier Eva Aariak announced in April 2009 that her government's priorities for the next five years would focus on addressing the basic needs of the local communities such as health, education and better housing, supported in part through local sustainable businesses. Only two priorities, but important ones, encompassed broader questions: protection of the environment and defence of Nunavut's interests globally.[29]

The Alaskan Eskimos do not have the same power inherent in Canada's Nunavut Territory, as they are a minority within the Native self-governing institutions of the state. Together with the Alaskan Indians, however, they have protected their interests against growth of the state's non-aboriginal majority. Barry Zellen summarizes the outcome in Canada and Alaska as retaining the "spirit of independence" within "sovereign duality," where "the modern state is no longer an opponent, but a powerful partner":

> As the age of land claims comes to an end, and the era of Aboriginal self-government begins, there is no doubt that the Natives of the North will continue to lead the way forward, interpolating between past and present, tribe and state, tradition and modernity, demonstrating their continued capacity to adapt and to learn, to negotiate and to bargain, to imagine and to implement new structures of governance—all the while showing the rest of

the world how to walk along the road of pragmatism and peace, finding practical solutions to achieve their dreams and hopes, and to restore their sovereignty, one step at a time.[30]

Greenlanders with their 80 percent majority have taken their objective to regain control over their lives a step further. If Self-Rule Government leads to full independence in 2021, as some hope, it will mark the most dramatic shift in Arctic sovereignty since Britain's transfer of the Arctic Islands to Canada. The world will be watching.

Challenges and Options

The effects of global warming on the North American Arctic have created new challenges for the circumpolar countries by providing easier access for ships of foreign countries. Otherwise, existing laws appear successful in encouraging bilateral resolution of disputes between Arctic countries. Since the UN Convention on the Law of the Sea acquired sufficient ratifications to bring the laws into force, there have been minor modifications but as yet no major changes that directly affect the Arctic. As of fall 2009, the U.S. was the only Arctic country that had failed to ratify the agreement. Under the Obama administration, it was expected that the Senate would consent to ratification, which would facilitate American participation in future discussions on any changes or amendments. Yet in spite of the 2009 U.S. Arctic policy's call for ratification, the issue does not appear to be a high priority.

An indication of the treaty's effectiveness was evident at the meeting of five Arctic countries, the U.S., Canada, Denmark, Norway and Russia, held at Ilulissat in November 2008. The result was a statement declaring unanimous agreement that existing international laws were sufficient to deal with outstanding conflicts over sovereign rights and jurisdiction. The greater danger lies in a potential challenge not covered by existing international laws or in rejection of the laws themselves by a dissident nation.

One might argue that the history of Arctic sovereignty appears to be coming full circle in terms of advances by the Inuit and other indigenous peoples toward regaining control over their lives and homelands. Yet as they acquire more authority, they too will be required to accept more responsibility to ensure a sustainable economy and protection of the local environment. It is hoped that their political leaders will have greater success than their former colonial masters.

On the other hand, it is the responsibility of each circumpolar country to ensure its overall Arctic policies are sufficient to protect its lands and waters from pollution and, if necessary, to work together to develop a multinational legal regime. This should be undertaken without interference from non-Arctic countries, but with full participation by northern indigenous peoples.

Greenlanders, should they decide to seek greater independence from Denmark, will require vigilance to ensure they do not suffer a *de facto* loss of economic sovereignty because of inordinate foreign investment or become little more than a military protectorate of the U.S. True independence cannot be achieved by renting their lands to foreign companies for the purpose of exploiting resources. As various leaders have rightly stated, full independence will be the decision of the Greenlanders but if they wish to preserve their majority in the new Self-Rule Government, they may need to reconsider immigration policies for new developments that require a sizable foreign workforce. In the interim, Denmark, Canada and the U.S. must ensure that Inuit/Eskimo leaders participate fully in policy discussions affecting their homelands. The former paternalistic approach of "looking out for their best interests" is no longer acceptable. The days of keeping the Inuit "on the land" and away from the affairs of government have long passed.

With the effects of global warming having such a major impact on the Arctic, the onus rests on all circumpolar countries to make a concerted effort to reduce toxic emissions from their own urban and industrial centres and promote cleaner energy alternatives. While it will not reverse the process any time soon, mitigation is critical to slow the process. Similarly, all levels of governments should invest in research and education on means to adapt to the changing climate.

Although economic stability ought to be a high priority for all circumpolar countries, achievement of that goal should not be at the expense of their respective northern hinterlands. In this context, the change in climate has created a major challenge both environmentally and economically. Aside from adverse effects on the environment, the rapidly melting ice promises freer access for exploration, production and transport in the development of potential offshore oil and gas reserves. Advanced technologies have refined drilling techniques and created new ice-resistant supply ships and supertankers to enable transport to and from southern ports, but research in environmental protection and cleanup, which is the responsibility of the sovereign state, still appears to be lagging. Nor has the melting ice reduced the fragility of the Arctic environment. Instead, the global recession has created a potential opportunity, if the Arctic countries agree, to defer further offshore oil and gas development until an international legal regime is in place to protect the Arctic from pollution.

Russia has taken steps to ensure that oil and gas production in its Arctic waters will remain a national enterprise, indirectly accepting responsibility for environmental protection. U.S. environmentalists have also recognized the dangers and lobbied against further drilling in the Beaufort Sea. Unexpectedly in April 2009, a ruling of a federal appeals court effectively cancelled Royal Dutch Shell's proposed drilling program in the Beaufort Sea, based on the opinion that it did not effectively protect the marine environment.[31] This ruling occurred in spite of the Obama administration's promise to reduce dependence on foreign oil. Conversely, Greenland has issued exploratory drilling permits in the waters of Davis Strait, with only one of the eight permits awarded to a Danish company. Similarly, Canada continued to issue drilling permits in the Beaufort Sea in June 2008, in spite of the World Wide Fund for Nature's urgent request to postpone the auction, citing environmental concerns.[32]

Two factors suggest a need to update environmental standards for offshore drilling in the North American Arctic: the increasing ferocity of polar storms and recent follow-up studies on the *Valdez* oil spill that showed pollution had lingered far longer than anticipated.

Corporate icebreakers towing the *Kulluk* oil rig from its icebound winter berth near Herschel Island, spring 1989. Potential problems associated with oil rigs in Canada's Arctic waters are not an issue to be dealt with sometime in the future. Company icebreakers and mobile drilling rigs are already hard at work. Courtesy photographer Richard Olsenius

Russia, Canada, the U.S. and Norway all have their own regulations to safeguard against pollution, but there are no international standards governing exploratory drilling in Arctic waters. Since economies can be managed more easily than environmental degradation, would it not be wise for all circumpolar countries to defer further offshore exploratory drilling in the Arctic until acceptable international standards and enforcement protocols are in place?

The development of identified Arctic oil and gas reserves in the remote Sverdrup Basin in the High Arctic also carries a high risk of pollution. The former Arctic Pilot Project, which proposed a pipeline across the uninhabited Melville Island to a deep-sea port on Lancaster Sound, has undergone new studies to determine the commercial feasibility with alternative means of sea transport. One option was added to the original concept that would require use of an ice-resistant tanker only as far as Nuuk on the west coast of Greenland, where a new port facility would be built to store the product before shipment to the eastern seaboard or Europe.[33] While of economic benefit to Greenland and potentially a source of employment for a few Inuit in Nunavut's High Arctic, this project appears unlikely to proceed anytime soon because of low natural gas prices and the abundance of new fields recently discovered in the U.S. and southern Canada. Considering the potential for pollution, there should be serious reconsideration whether these resources should ever be developed.

A major challenge faces the circumpolar countries to provide growth and stability for local Arctic economies without posing a threat to the environment. Yet global warming has opened up a number of other opportunities for both Greenland and Arctic Canada. Greenland's fishing industry, for instance, may benefit from the warmer waters to further enhance the sustainability of the island's economy without any negative effect on the environment. The proposed "clean energy" hotel at Ilulissat is another example, as is bottling of clean water from glacier ice. Some forms of mining might also pose fewer environmental risks if located in an area devoid of human and wildlife habitation and utilizing clean energy where possible. Climate change may have brought challenges, but it also offers an opportunity for creative initiatives with priorities attached to the environment rather than to the economy.

The recent economic downturn has added yet another factor to the challenges facing the circumpolar countries. The economic recession beginning in 2008 might slow development of Arctic resources, but it will also bring pressure by oil and gas companies and international shipping interests to reduce or forgo extensive environmental review, in hopes of earning a quick return on their investments. Similarly, some governments may welcome increased revenue from licences and royalties to reduce the debt accumulated as a result of their stimulus packages and may resist actions that might delay development.

There are alternatives. History has shown that the most effective and expedient means to protect the environment is through cooperation and negotiation of bilateral or multilateral agreements. The Arctic Council made significant advances with its Arctic Offshore Oil and Gas Guidelines and Arctic Marine Shipping Assessment, but these are only voluntary standards and must be replaced by mandatory requirements acceptable to all Arctic countries. Because marine pollution cannot be contained within maritime boundaries, legislated regulations are imperative for North America, if not for the entire Arctic. As an established forum, the Arctic Council has the opportunity to take a strong leadership position in advancing these objectives.

To enact new regulatory measures in the North American Arctic will require close cooperation and collaboration between the U.S., Canada and Greenland/Denmark, similar to that already institutionalized in the Barents Sea Agreement signed by Norway, Sweden, Finland and Russia. Although two separate agreements will create two distinct entities, each responsible for protection of approximately half the Arctic waters, closer coordination and consensus between the two entities should be inevitable, perhaps facilitated through the Environment Committee of the Arctic Council. A prerequisite policy statement is already in place for two of the three North American countries. Paragraph 2 of the Arctic Cooperation Agreement signed by Canada and the U.S. commits the two countries to cooperate in advancing "their shared interests in Arctic development and security" with the affirmation "that navigation and resource development in the Arctic must not adversely affect the unique environment of the region and the well-being of its inhabitants."[34] These two sentences provide sufficient basis for the two countries to move forward and begin planning the necessary regulations and infrastructure required to deal with any situation that might arise due to increased shipping and drilling in the Northwest Passage and other territorial waters. This is a "yesterday's agreement" that has huge potential for tomorrow.

Currently the Northern Strategy outlined by the Canadian government seems to be leading in the right direction, but implementation is sorely restricted by lack of available funds. The apparent interest expressed by the Prime Minister should be encouraged, but it is time Canadians demanded concrete action. As a first step, the government must initiate immediate plans to apportion a major share of the revenue from drilling licences and production royalties to the three territorial governments, in advance of granting them provincial status. To deny them this right places Canadian democracy in a backwater compared to the United States and Denmark. The Canadian government must also honour its obligations and provide the money owed for retraining Inuit to enable them to participate in administrative and other employment opportunities in Nunavut. Denying them their rights reinforces their colonial dependency. At the same time, more money must actually be spent in the Arctic rather than on feasibility studies conducted by southern agencies. If Canada's Arctic sovereignty is to be protected, it will require more transparency and direct action by the current party in power, as well as more cooperation and support by all political parties, all levels of government, all private and public institutions—and all Canadians.

Meanwhile, the former priority attached to developing new offshore oil and gas resources should be deferred until such time as the Canadian government has acquired the physical means to enforce anti-pollution regulations and closely monitor shipping in the Archipelago waters. Existing regulations may be sufficient once NORDREG is made mandatory, but at present Canada lacks manpower and patrol vessels to enforce them. With a little ingenuity and foresight, costs of such measures might be incorporated into a package which could be promoted as essential to protect national interests and future prosperity.

The American government, on the other hand, has an opportunity to play a more cooperative role as an Arctic nation, rather than unilaterally asserting its perceived rights as a major world power. Aside from ratifying UNCLOS, representatives of the U.S. government can play a constructive role in furthering the effectiveness of the Arctic Council by encouraging expansion of the organization's mandate beyond environmental and economic concerns.

Historically, the United States has resisted signing on to consensus agreements such as the Kyoto Protocol or UNCLOS. Now may be the time for Americans to find their moral compass and show real leadership in a world on the brink of instability.

The Copenhagen Conference on Climate Change in mid-December 2009 brought concerned citizens of the world to a standstill with the realization of how much materialism and self-interest had become entrenched in the minds of global leaders, as day by day it became all too apparent that national priorities had taken precedence over survival of the planet as we know it today. The drive to create wealth at the expense of others was never so evident as in the rift that developed between Inuit leaders. As reported in *Nunatsiaq News* (18 December 2009), Jimmy Stotts from Alaska, newly appointed chair of the International Inuit Circumpolar Council, argued that Inuit-owned energy and mining projects should be exempted from global agreements on emission cuts. This argument concurred with statements by Premier Kleist of Greenland, who claimed that his country needed to double its carbon dioxide emissions to ensure future independence from Denmark. On the opposing side, Canada's Sheila Watt-Cloutier argued vehemently for Inuit to stand their "moral ground," a view shared by Greenland's Aqqaluk Lynge, vice-chair of the ICC, who warned that Inuit would suffer dire consequences if they turned their back on traditional knowledge and sought independence by resorting to industrial projects that greatly increased toxic emissions.

Even the grim predictions by scientists at the U.K.'s renowned Hadley Research Centre made little impression on those who wished to profit from global warming. Using the best scenario of full agreement on emission cuts, the centre warned that the Arctic would continue to warm by a further 3°C before the temperature stabilized. As world leaders dithered about costs and who would pay, scientists also advised that delaying action would only require larger cuts to cool the planet and create even greater uncertainty about the final outcome. Canadian leaders put the country to shame by their refusal to place restrictions on oil sands development until foolproof means of cutting emissions are in place. How this will all play out over the next year is unclear, but the world is in desperate need of wise and dedicated leadership. As Sheila Watt-Cloutier has reminded us, "Climate change and Arctic sovereignty are two sides of the same coin."

It appeared that Canada might have some options to better secure its sovereign rights in the Arctic waters, when an interim report released in June 2008 by the Standing Committee on Oceans and Fisheries recommended the purchase of six new icebreakers for the Canadian Coast Guard to give Canada a year-round presence in the Arctic and enable adequate supervision of shipping operations. Chaired by Senator Bill Romkey, the Committee also recommended that more Inuit be hired by the coast guard and that compliance with NORDREG be made mandatory for all ships sailing in Canada's Arctic waters, as was currently the case on the Atlantic and Pacific coasts.[35]

In December 2009, however, a final report was released with a total of 14 revised recommendations. The government generally supported nine of these with detailed explanations, rejected two of them outright and only partially agreed with three others. On the question of icebreakers, their position was firm. There would be only one new icebreaker—a replacement for the aging *Louis St. Laurent*.[36]

As never before, the onus rests with the media as the key source for public information to ensure that their facts are accurate, the opinions expressed justified and their message supportive of transnational cooperation. The Arctic may be the homeland of indigenous peoples, but it is in each and every one's interest that it be protected.

NEW ISSUES and challenges will continue to confront new generations of political leaders, who in turn will shape new Arctic strategies and objectives in the twenty-first century. But now is the time for Canada and the United States, in cooperation with Greenland/Denmark and Inuit leaders, to work together toward a common goal of securing future stability of the North American Arctic. While the political future of Greenland appears more stable under the new Self-Rule Government, it is still a potential wild card. In the end, it will be up to political leaders of the Arctic countries to ensure that the circumpolar world does not fall victim to competitive corporatism or nationalism and related threats to Arctic sovereignty. This will also require a well-informed and discerning public to elect them.

Fifty million years ago, the Arctic enjoyed a subtropical climate long before humans roamed the earth. Around 5,000 years ago, the first Palaeo-Eskimos arrived on the shores of Alaska. Less than 150 years ago, the last change in sovereign authority took place with the British transfer of the Arctic Islands to Canada. The current climate change has created yet another tipping point in the history of Arctic sovereignty. Although a decade represents little more than a split second when measured against the age of the planet, a lot can happen within a "split second" and much adversity can be prevented.

Notes

· · · ·

CHAPTER ONE

1. Robert McGhee, *The Last Imaginary Place* (Toronto: Key Porter, 2005), 19.

2. Robert M. Bone, *The Geography of the Canadian North* (Toronto: University of Oxford Press, 1992), 17–27.

3. Arctic Monitoring and Assessment Programme, *Arctic Pollution Issues: A State of the Arctic Environment Report* (Oslo, Norway: AMAP, 1997), 5–9.

4. Ibid., 11–19.

5. Ibid., 126.

6. Michael Byers and Georg Nolte, eds., *United States Hegemony and the Foundations of International Law* (Cambridge, UK: Cambridge University Press, 2003).

7. Franklyn Griffiths, "Canadian Arctic Sovereignty: Time to Take Yes for an Answer on the Northwest Passage," *Northern Exposure: Peoples, Powers and Prospects for Canada's North* (Montreal: IRPP, 2009), 3.

8. Malcolm N. Shaw, *International Law*, fifth edition (Cambridge, UK: Cambridge University Press, 2003), 455–56.

9. Michael Byers, *Custom, Power and the Power of Rules: International Relations and Customary International Law* (Cambridge, UK: Cambridge University Press, 1999), 3. Numerous government reports have been written on the legality of Canadian claims under international law, including the basic primer prepared for the Research Branch of the Library of Parliament, "Foundation of Canada's Sovereignty over the Arctic Region" (Ottawa, May 1969). Other legal interpretations as they applied to Arctic regions include Gustav Smedal, *Acquisition of Sovereignty over Polar Areas* (Oslo: 1 Kommisjon Hos Jacob Dybwad, 1931); L.C. Green, "Canada and Arctic Sovereignty," *Canadian Bar Review*, 48 (1970); Ivan I. Head, "Canadian Claims to Territorial Sovereignty in the Arctic Regions," *McGill Law Review*, 9 (1962–63). For a historical summary, see Gordon W. Smith, "Sovereignty in the North: The Canadian Aspect of an International Problem." in R. St. J. Macdonald, ed., *The Arctic Frontier* (Toronto: University of Toronto Press, 1966).

10. Byers, *Custom, Power and the Power of Rules*, 3.

11. Shaw, *International Law*, 960.

12. Donat Pharand, *Canada's Arctic Waters in International Law* (Cambridge, UK: Cambridge University Press, 1988), 45.

13. In addition to Pharand's book, there are countless articles and book-length studies on the subject, such as D.M. McRae, "Arctic Waters and Canadian Sovereignty," *International Journal*, 38 (1983); Douglas M. Johnston, *Canada and the New International Law of the Sea* (Toronto: University of Toronto Press, 1985); Franklyn Griffiths, ed., *Politics of the Northwest Passage* (Montreal/Kingston: McGill-Queen's University Press, 1987) and Elizabeth Riddell-Dixon, *Canada and the International Seabed: Domestic Determinants and External Constraints* (Montreal/Kingston: McGill-Queen's University Press,1989).

14. William R. Morrison, "Canadian Sovereignty and the Inuit of the Central and Eastern Arctic," *Études/Inuit/Studies*, Vol. 10, 1–2: 246–47.

15. Broader applications appear in recent scholarly discourse, as in Robert Wright's *Virtual Sovereignty: Nationalism, Culture and the Canadian Question* (Toronto: Canadian Scholars Press, 2004).

16. Thomas Berger, *A Long and Terrible Shadow: White Values, Native Rights in the Americas, 1492–1992* (Vancouver: Douglas and McIntyre, 1991), 1–25; also by the same author, *Village Journey: The Report of the Alaska Native Review Commission* (New York: Hill & Wang, 1985), 138–39; and Olive P. Dickason, "Concepts of Sovereignty at the Time of First Contacts," in L.C. Green and Olive P. Dickason, *The Law of Nations and the New World* (Edmonton: University of Alberta Press, 1989), 221, 235. The latter book, which is divided into two equal sections written by each author, provides an in-depth description of the interpretation and evolution of international law as applied to North America during the Age of Discovery and colonial settlement.

17. Green, "Claims to Territory in Colonial America," in Green and Dickason, *The Law of Nations and the New World*, 18.

18. Dickason, "Concepts of Sovereignty," 234–36.

19. Green, "Claims to Territory," 7–17.

20. Morrison, "Canadian Sovereignty and the Inuit," 246.

21. Lassa Francis Lawrence Oppenheim, *International Law: A Treatise* (Oxford: Clarendon Press, 1905–6), 275; also para. 222, as quoted in a confidential memo from the Advisory Technical Board to the Department of the Interior, 13 October 1920. LAC, Department of the Interior records, RG 15, Vol. 1, file "Arctic Islands—memos, maps etc."

22. Constance Backhouse, *Colour Coded: A Legal History of Racism* (Toronto: University of Toronto Press, 1999), Chap. 2; Richard Diubaldo, "The Absurd Little Mouse: When Eskimos Became Indians," *Journal of Canadian Studies*, 6 (Summer 1981), 34–41.

23. Olive P. Dickason, "Conclusion: The Changing Face of Sovereignty," in Green and Dickason, 241.

24. Bo Johnson Theutenberg, "Mare Clausum et Mare Liberum," *Arctic* 37/4 (December 1984), 481–83. In the same volume, R. Chevallier, "The Greco-Roman Conception of the North from Pytheas to Tacitus," 341–46; and Grethe Authén Blom, "The Participation of the Kings in Early Norwegian Sailing to Bjarmeland, and Development of a Royal Policy Concerning the Northern Waters in the Middle Ages," 385–88. See also Green and Dickason, *Law of Nations*.

25. Theutenberg, "Mare Clausum et Mare Liberum," 484–86.

26. Ibid., 484.

27. Green, "Claims to Territory," in Green and Dickason, 12.

28. Theutenberg, "*Mare Clausum et Mare Liberum*," 484–91.

29. William Edward Hall, *Treatise on International Law* (Oxford: Clarendon Press, 1880). A second work of importance was *A Treatise on the Foreign Powers and Jurisdiction of the British Crown* (Oxford: Clarendon Press, 1894), published shortly before his death.

30. As an example of its lasting importance see Lassa Francis Lawrence Oppenheim, *International Law: A Treatise*, 7th ed., edited by H. Lauterpacht (London: Longman's, 1963).

31. Library and Archives Canada (LAC), Northern Affairs Records, RG 85 Vol. 584, file 571 pt 5, draft copy of W.F. King report dated 1904, p. 21, as cited in a "Confidential Memo re: the Arctic Islands" by Hensley Holmden in charge of the Map Division, to A.G. Doughty, Deputy Minister and Dominion Archivist, 26 April 1921.

32. Ibid., paras. 222, 275. Also see LAC, Department of the Interior records, RG 15, Vol. 1, file "Arctic Islands—memos, maps etc." Quotations are cited in a confidential memo from the Advisory Technical Board to the Deputy Minister of the Department of the Interior, 13 October 1920.

33. LAC, J.B. Harkin Papers, MG 30 E 169, Vol. 1, file "1919–Oct 1920," marked "strictly confidential," a draft report on regarding title to the Arctic islands, likely written for the Advisory Technical Board by John Harkin, p. 3A. As an authoritative source, Oppenheim's treatise and new interpretations of international law had been forwarded to the Department of the Interior by Under-Secretary of State Sir Joseph Pope.

34. LAC, Department of External Affairs records, RG 25 Part 1A, Vol. 2668, file 9058 E 40. Despatch from L. Harcourt, Secretary of State for the Colonies, to Canada's Governor-General, 10 May 1913: paragraph 6.

35. Aside from the manuscript records of John D. Craig (MG 30 B 59) and J.B. Harkin (MG 30 E 169), who were both involved in Arctic sovereignty discussions from 1919 to 1925, a number of government records contain a full complement of correspondence, memos and reports on Arctic sovereignty issues: the Department of the Interior (RG 15) and various branches (RG 85 and RG 22); External Affairs (RG 25); the Royal Canadian Mounted Police and predecessors (RG 18); Marine and Fisheries (RG 42), and to a lesser extent the Privy Council Office (RG 10). Other sources include manuscript collections of Sir Wilfrid Laurier, Clifford Sifton, Arthur Meighen and Loring Christie.

CHAPTER TWO

1. David Morrison and Georges-Hébert Germain, *Inuit: Glimpses of an Arctic Past* (Ottawa: Canadian Museum of Civilization, 1995), 38.

2. Andrew C. Revkin, "Studies Portray Tropical Arctic in Distant Past," *New York Times* (1 June 2006).

3. "Search for a Tropical Arctic," CBC-CGS video (1990).

4. "North Pole Was Once Tropical," *BBC News Archives* (7 September 2004), and "DNA Reveals Greenland's Lush Past," *BBC News Archives* (6 July 2007), http://news.bbc.co.uk/2/hi/sciencenature/.

5. Edward B. Daeschler, Neil H. Shubin and Farish A. Jenkins, Jr., *Nature*, 440 (6 April 2006), 757–63.

6. Revkin, *New York Times* (1 June 2006); "Turtle Fossil Shows How 'Super-Greenhouse Effect' Created Tropical Arctic," *London Telegraph* (1 February 2009),

http://www.telegraph.co.uk/earth/environment/climate change/; "Ancient Turtle Fossil Found on Axel Heiberg Island," *Nunatsiaq News* (13 February 2009): 17; Henk Brinkhuis et al., "Episodic Fresh Surface Waters in the Eocene Arctic Ocean," *Nature* (2 June 2006), 606–09; Appy Sluijs et al., "Subtropical Arctic Ocean Temperatures During the Palaeocene/Eocene Thermal Maximum," *Nature* 411 (1 June 2006), 610–13. See also Peter Clark, "Long Debate Ended Over Cause, Demise of Ice Ages—May Help Predict Future," http://oregonstate.edu/us/nes/209/aug/.

7. Natalia Rybczynski, Mary R. Dawson, Richard H. Tedford, "A Semi-aquatic Arctic Mammalian Carnivore from the Miocene Epoch and Origin of Pinnipedia," *Nature* 458 (23 April 2009), 1021–24.

8. Robert McGhee, *The Last Imaginary Place: A Human History of the Arctic World* (Toronto: Key Porter Books, 2005), 11–17, 442–43; also Robert McGhee, *Ancient People of the Arctic* (Vancouver, BC: UBC Press, 1996), 19.

9. McGhee, *Last Imaginary Place*, 11–19; and Robert McGhee, *Ancient Canada* (Ottawa: Canadian Museum of Civilization, 1997), 14–22.

10. Most of the information on the Palaeo-Eskimos is derived from McGhee's *Last Imaginary Place* and *Ancient People of the Arctic*; see also Robert McGhee, *Canadian Arctic Prehistory* (Ottawa: Canadian Museum of Civilization, 1990); Peter Schledermann, *Crossroads to Greenland: 3000 Years of Prehistory in the Eastern High Arctic* (Calgary: Arctic Institute of North America, 1990); and Maureau S. Maxwell, "Pre-Dorset and Dorset Prehistory of Canada" in David Damas, ed., *Handbook of North American Indians*, Volume 5: *Arctic* (Washington: Smithsonian Institution, 1984), 359–68.

11. Morrison and Germain, *Inuit*, 38; see also McGhee, *Last Imaginary Place*, 44.

12. McGhee, *Ancient People*, 104.

13. Ibid., 34–55; Jared Diamond, *Collapse: How Societies Choose to Fail or Succeed* (New York: Penguin Books, 2006), 255; Richard Vaughan, *The Arctic: A History* (Dover, NH: Alan Sutton, 1994), 7–8. See also *Inuit Kanatami: Inuit of Canada* (Ottawa: Inuit Tapiirit Kanatami, 2003); and McGhee, *Ancient People*, 41–105.

14. McGhee, *Canadian Arctic Prehistory*, 52–58.

15. Ibid., 63, also McGhee, *Ancient People*, 110–18; and McGhee, *Last Imaginary Place*, 122–23.

16. McGhee, *Ancient People*, 142–45.

17. McGhee, *Canadian Arctic Prehistory*, 71–72; McGhee, *Last Imaginary Place*, 52–3.

18. William W. Fitzhugh and Valérie Chaussonnet, *Anthropology of the Pacific Rim* (Washington: Smithsonian Institution, 1984), 33; and William W. Fitzhugh and Aron Crowell, *Crossroads of Continents: Cultures of Siberia and Alaska* (Washington: Smithsonian Institution, 1988), 121–19. For a concise synopsis of recent findings and conclusions, see McGhee, *Last Imaginary Place*, 116–17.

19. McGhee, *Last Imaginary Place*, 122–28.

20. Ibid.; Peter Schledermann, *Voices in Stone: A Personal Journey into the Arctic Past* (Calgary, AB: The Arctic Institute of North America, 1996), 111-16; Peter Schledermann and K.M. McCullough, "Western Elements in the Early Thule Culture of the Eastern High Arctic," *Arctic*, 33:4 (1980), 833–41; Robert McGhee, "When and Why Did the Inuit Move to the Eastern Arctic," *The Northern World* AD 900–1400: *The Dynamics of Climate, Economy, and Politics in Hemispheric Perspective*, Herbert Maschner and Robert McGhee (Utah: University of Utah Press, 2009), 4; and Jens Peder Hart Hansen, et al., eds., *The Greenland Mummies*, English ed. (Nuuk and Copenhagen: Christian Ejlers' Forlag, 1991), 15.

21. McGhee, *Last Imaginary Place*, 54–55.

22. Father Guy Mary-Rousselière, "Factors Affecting Human Occupation of the Land in the Pond Inlet Region from Prehistorical to Contemporary Times," *Eskimo*, 41:28 (Fall/Winter 1984–1985), 8–9.

23. Susan Cowan, ed., *We Don't Live in Snow Houses Now* (Ottawa: Canadian Arctic Producers, 1976), 15.

24. McGhee, *Ancient People*, 210–35; and McGhee, *Last Imaginary Place*, 53–55.

25. Mary-Rousselière, "Factors Affecting," 8–12.

26. Richard Vaughan, *Northwest Greenland: A History* (Orono, ME: University of Maine Press, 1991), 6–9.

27. McGhee, *Canadian Arctic Prehistory*, 101–17.

28. McGhee, *Last Imaginary Place*, 33 and 22–32; see also, J.R. Weber and E.F. Roots, Chap. 2 "Historical Background," *The Geology of North America, Vol. I: The Arctic Ocean Region* (Denver, CO: Geological Society of America, 1990), 5–6.

29. Louis Rey, "The Evangelization of the Arctic in the Middle Ages," *Arctic*, 37: 4 (December 1984), 324–26; Magnus Magnusson, *Vikings!* (London: Bodley Head, 1980), 182–247; Gisli Sigurðsson et al., *Vikings in the New World* (Reykjavik: Culture House, 2000), 1–16.

30. Population figures cited in Kirsten Seaver, *The Frozen Echo: Greenland and the Exploration of North America ca. A.D. 1000–1500* (Stanford, CA: Stanford University Press, 1996), 43; Magnusson, *Vikings*, 212–47. Much of the information about the early Norse settlements appearing on the following pages has been compiled from Finn Gad, *The History of Greenland: I Earliest Times to 1700* (London, UK: C. Hurst & Company, 1970); and Seaver, *Frozen Echo*. Additional details are found in Sigurdsson et al., *Vikings in the New World*, 31–2; McGhee, *Last Imaginary Place*, 74–101; Vaughan, *The Arctic*, 40–50; Schledermann, *Voices in Stone*, 124–30; Hansen et al., *Greenland Mummies*, 15–22; and Vilhjalmur Stefansson, *Greenland* (New York: Doubleday and Doran, 1942), 94–164. Also of interest but controversial are three chapters on Norse colonies in Jared Diamond, *Collapse: How Societies Choose to Fail or Succeed* (Toronto: Penguin, 2005), 211–77.

31. Quotation from Seaver, *Frozen Echo*, 42–43. For details on Viking ships see Seaver 66, 108, 131–38; and Finn Gad, *History of Greenland: I*, 79–81. For recent research by Pat Sutherland, see Heather Pringle, "Strands of Evidence," *Canadian Geographic*, 129:2 (April 2009), 45–56.

32. Schledermann, *Voices in Stone*, 124–30; Hansen et al., *Greenland Mummies*, 17–18; Vaughan, *The Arctic*, 42.

33. Cited in Hansen et al., *Greenland Mummies*, 18–19.

34. Magnusson, *Vikings*, 212–47.

35. Ibid. See also Stefansson, *Greenland*, 67–85. For evidence of Norse items found at Tuniit sites in northern Baffin Island, see Patricia D. Sutherland, "Strands of Culture Contact: Dorset-Norse Interactions in the Canadian Eastern Arctic," in Martin Appelt, Joel Berglund and Hans Christian Gullov, eds., *Identities and Cultural Contacts in the Arctic: Proceedings from a Conference at the Danish National Museum* (Copenhagen: Danish National Museum and Danish Polar Center, 2000).

36. The full story of Sutherland's research is found in the article by Pringle, "Strands of Evidence," 44–56.

37. Seaver, *Frozen Echo*, 88–9; Vaughan, *The Arctic*, 49–50; McGhee, *Last Imaginary Place*, 94–96.

38. Seaver, *Frozen Echo*, 247–53, 311; Vaughan, *The Arctic*, 40–41; Diamond, *Collapse*, 273–76; McGhee, *Last Imaginary Place*, 96–98.

39. Sigurdsson and Jóhannsson, *Vikings in the New World*, 18. The same story is referenced by Kirsten Seaver, *Frozen Echo*, 355, n48; and Helge Ingstad, *Land Under the Polar Star* (London: Jonathan Cape, 1966), 329–32.

40. Schledermann, *Voices in Stone*, 136.

41. Hans Egede Saabye, *Journal in Greenland, 1770–1778* (Hanover, NH: IPI Press, 2009), 49.

42. Magnusson, *Vikings*, 247, also 245–46; Hansen et al., *Greenland Mummies*, 15–22; McGhee, *Last Imaginary Place*, 95–98.

43. Paul Brown, "Melting Ice Cap Brings Diamond Hunters and Hopes of Independence to Greenland," *The Guardian* (4 October 2007).

CHAPTER THREE

1. From letter published in 1589 by Richard Hakluyt, quoted in Clive Holland, ed., *Farthest North: The Quest for the North Pole* (London: Robinson, 1994), 2.

2. Robert McGhee, *Canada Rediscovered* (Kingston/Montreal: McGill-Queen's University Press for Canadian Museum of Civilization, 1991), 76–79.

3. Ibid., 82–90. See also Saladin d'Anglure, "The Route to China: Northern Europe's Arctic Delusions," *Arctic*, 37:4 (December 1984), 446–52.

4. Ibid. Inscription on 1527 map cited p. 99.

5. Ibid., 100. Citing a report written by Pietro Pasqualigo, Venetian ambassador to Portugal.

6. For early exploration and colonization attempts by the French, see Marcel Trudel, *The Beginnings of New France, 1524–1663* (Toronto: McClelland & Stewart, 1973).

7. Robert McGhee, *The Last Imaginary Place* (Toronto: Key Porter, 2005), 139–40.

8. The section on the Frobisher voyages relies heavily on Robert McGhee, *The Arctic Voyages of Martin Frobisher: An Elizabethan Adventure* (Montreal/Kingston: McGill-Queen's University Press for Canadian Museum of Civilization, 2001); and McGhee, *Last Imaginary Place*, Chap. 8, and *Canada Rediscovered*, 156–66. Other important sources include W.A. Kenyon, *Tokens of Possession: The Northern Voyages of Martin Frobisher* (Toronto: University of Toronto Press for Royal Ontario Museum, 1975); and T.H.B. Symons, ed., *Meta Incognita: A Discourse of Discovery* (Ottawa: Canadian Museum of Civilization, 1999).

9. McGhee, *Arctic Voyages*, 16.

10. Ibid., 100, quoting from George Best, in Vilhjalmur Stefansson and Eloise McCaskill, eds., *The Three Voyages of Martin Frobisher* (London: Argonaut Press, 1938).

11. Canadian Museum of Civilization, "Voyages of Martin Frobisher: Cartography During and After the Voyages," at www.civilization.ca/hist/frobisher/frsub15e.

12. McGhee, *Arctic Voyages*, 186.

13. S.E. Morison, *The European Discovery of America: The Northern Voyages AD 500–1600* (New York: Oxford University Press, 1971); Clements Markham, *Life of John Davis, the Navigator* (London: George Philip & Son, 1889); and L.H. Neatby, *In Quest of the North-West Passage* (Toronto: Longmans Green, 1958).

14. William W. Fitzhugh and Aron Crowell, eds., *Cultures in Conflict: The European Impact on Native Cultural Institutions in Eastern North America*, A.D. 1000–1800 (Washington: Smithsonian Institution, 1985), 32.

15. Ibid., see article by Susan A. Kaplan, "European Goods and Socio-Economic Change in Early Labrador Society," 56–57.

16. Richard Vaughan, *The Arctic: A History*, rev. ed. (Gloucestershire, UK: History Press, 2008), 62, and McGhee, *Last Imaginary Place*, 141–45.

17. Information on explorations in the 17th and 18th centuries was compiled from Alan Cooke and Clive Holland, *The Exploration of Northern Canada: 500 to 1920, a Chronology* (Toronto: Arctic History Press, 1978); Vaughan, *The Arctic*; and Terence Wise, *Polar Exploration* (London: Almark Publications, 1973). See also Daniel Francis, *Discovery of the North: The Exploration of Canada's Arctic* (Edmonton: Hurtig Publishers, 1986).

18. Louis Bobé, *Hans Egede: Colonizer and Missionary of Greenland* (Copenhagen: Rosenkilde and Bagger,1953), 60–61.

19. In addition to the above references, a second book by Daniel Francis, *A History of World Whaling* (Markham, ON: Viking Books, 1990), provides a detailed description of the competition for control of whaling in the waters around Spitzbergen.

20. J.H. Verzijl et al., *International Law in Historical Perspective*, Vol. IV, 1968 (Netherlands: Martinus Nijhoff Publishers, 1968); R.P. Anand, *Origin and Development of the Law of the Sea* (Leiden, Netherlands: Brill Publishers, 1983), 105–7; and Hersch Lauterpacht, *The Grotian Tradition in International Law* (London: British Yearbook of International Law, 1946).

21. For decades, the definitive history of the Hudson's Bay Company was E.E. Rich, *History of the Hudson's Bay Company, 1670–1870*,Vols. 1, 2 (London: Hudson's Bay Record Society, 1958); a more recent history is Peter C. Newman, *Company of Adventurers*, Vols. 1, 2 (Toronto: Penguin Books, 1985, 1987).

22. Peter C. Newman, *Empire of the Bay: An Illustrated History of the Hudson's Bay Company* (Toronto: Madison Press,1989), 43–45.

23. James Pritchard, *In Search of Empire: The French in the Americas, 1670–1730* (New York: Cambridge University Press, 2007); William Eccles, *Canada Under Louis XIV 1663–1701* (New York: Oxford University Press, 1964).

24. As cited in Francis, *Discovery of the North*, 36.

25. Francis, *History of World Whaling*, 55.

26. Finn Gad, *History of Greenland: Volume 1, Earliest Times to 1700* (Montreal/Kingston: McGill-Queen's University Press, 1971), 308.

27. Richard Jordon, "Neo-Eskimo Prehistory of Greenland," David Dumas, ed., *Handbook of North American Indians, Volume 5, Arctic* (Washington, DC: Smithsonian Institution, 1984), 540–48.

28. Bobé, *Hans Egede*, 47.

29. Ibid., 89.

30. Ibid. Information on 1700s settlements in Greenland is extracted largely from Chaps. 9–18. See also Diamond Jenness, *Eskimo Administration: IV, Greenland* (Montreal: Arctic Institute of North America, 1967).

31. Terence Armstrong, George Rogers and Graham Rowley, eds., *The Circumpolar North* (London: Methuen, 1978), 170.

32. Jenness, *Administration: IV, Greenland*, 30–31.

33. For the section on the Russian Arctic and Alaska, see Terence Armstrong, *Russian Settlement in the North* (Cambridge: Cambridge University Press, 1965), 9–29; Lydia T. Black, "The Story of Russian America," in William W. Fitzhugh and Aron Crowell, eds., *Crossroads of Continents: Cultures of Siberia and Alaska* (Washington: Smithsonian Institution Press, 1988), 70–82; McGhee, *Last Imaginary Place*, 146–50; Vaughan, *The Arctic*, 96–115.

34. Dorothy Jean Ray, *Ethnohistory in the Arctic: The Bering Strait Eskimo* (Kingston: Limestone Press, 1983), 10–12.

35. Vaughan, *The Arctic*, 116.

CHAPTER FOUR

1. Henry W. Howgate, *Polar Colonization: Memorial to Congress* (Washington: private publication, 1878), 70. "Excerpts from the Writings of John Barrow" (undated), as read by the President of the Royal Geographical Society, 23 January 1865.

2. Diamond Jenness, *Eskimo Administration IV: Greenland* (Montreal: Arctic Institute of North America, 1967), 37–38; and Terence Armstrong et al., *The Circumpolar North* (London: Methuen, 1978), 172–75.

3. Lydia T. Black, *Russians in Alaska* (Fairbanks, AK: University of Alaska Press, 2002), 169–81; and Theodore J. Karamanski, *Fur Trade and Exploration: Opening the Far Northwest 1821–1852* (Vancouver: UBC Press, 1983), 28–30; Stephen Haycox, *Alaska: An American Colony* (Seattle: University of Washington Press, 2002), 106; Basil Dmytryshyn, *Imperial Russia: A Source Book 1700–1917* (Fort Worth, TX: Holt, Rinehart & Winston, 1990), 330.

4. James Raffan, *Emperor of the North: Sir George Simpson and the Remarkable Story of the Hudson's Bay Company* (Toronto: Harper Collins, 2007), 308–28; Peter C. Newman, *Caesars of the Wilderness*, Vol. 2 (Toronto: Viking, 1987), 204–73; and E.E. Rich, *History of the Hudson's Bay Company*, Vol. 2 (London: Hudson's Bay Company Record Society, 1958).

5. Daniel Francis, *A History of World Whaling* (Markham, ON: Viking Books, 1990), 76–77.

6. Robert Lloyd Webb, *On the Northwest: Commercial Whaling in the Pacific Northwest 1790–1967* (Vancouver: UBC Press, 1988), 115; see also John Bockstoce, *Whales, Ice, & Men: The History of Whaling in the Western Arctic* (Seattle: University of Washington Press, 1986), Chaps. 5, 9.

7. Daniel Francis, *Discovery of the North: The Exploration of Canada's Arctic* (Edmonton: Hurtig Publishers, 1986), 71.

8. Fergus Fleming, *Barrow's Boys: The Original Extreme Adventurers* (New York: Atlantic Monthly Press, 1998), 2.

9. Unless otherwise noted, most information concerning the Admiralty explorations is found in Fleming, *Barrow's Boys*.

10. Janice Cavell, *Tracing the Connected Narrative: Arctic Exploration in British Print Culture, 1818–1860* (Toronto: University of Toronto Press, 2008), 5. See also Ian S. Maclaren, "The Aesthetic Map of the North, 1845–1859," *Arctic*, 38:2 (June 1985), 89–193; and Robert McGhee, *The Last Imaginary Place* (Toronto: Key Porter, 2005), 232–33. For examples of the Admiralty's polar narratives see John Ross, *A Voyage of Discovery, Made under the Orders of the Admiralty, in His Majesty's Ships Isabella and Alexander, for the Purpose of Exploring Baffin's Bay and Inquiring into the Probability of a North West Passage, 1818* (London: John Murray, 1819); and William Edward Parry, *Journal of a Voyage for the Discovery of the*

North-West Passage from the Atlantic to the Pacific: Performed in the Years 1819–1820 (London: John Murray, 1821).

11. Fleming, *Barrow's Boys*, 62.

12. Parry, *Journal of a Voyage*, 275–88; and W. Gilles Ross, "Whaling, Inuit, and the Arctic Islands," in Morris Zaslow, ed., *A Century of Canada's Arctic Islands* (Ottawa: Royal Society of Canada, 1981), 33–43.

13. Fleming, *Barrow's Boys*, 154–76.

14. John Ross, *Narrative of a Second Voyage in Search of a North-west Passage, and the Arctic Regions During the Years 1829, 1820, 1831, 1832, 1833* (London: A.W. Webster, 1835), xiii.

15. Fleming, *Barrow's Boys*, 379.

16. George W. Corner, *Doctor Kane of the Arctic Seas* (Philadelphia, PA: Temple University Press, 1972), 76. See also Nancy Fogelson, *Arctic Exploration & International Relations* (Fairbanks, AK: University of Alaska Press, 1992), 11.

17. Michael F. Robinson, *The Coldest Crucible: Arctic Exploration and American Culture* (Chicago: University of Chicago Press, 2006), 28.

18. Corner, *Doctor Kane*, 85–101. The crew that first discovered Franklin's winter camp on Beechey Island belonged to the expedition led by whaling captain William Penny and sponsored by Lady Franklin.

CHAPTER FIVE

1. Quotation from William Henry Seward, *The Works of William H. Seward*, ed. George E. Baker (Boston, 1853–83), Vol. 3, 616; as cited in Walter LaFeber, *The New Empire: An Interpretation of American Expansionism 1860–1898*, rev. ed. (Ithaca, NY: Cornell University Press, 1998), 26–27.

2. Thomas R. Hietala, *Manifest Design: American Exceptionalism and Empire*. Rev. ed. (New York: Cornell University Press, 2003), 255n1.

3. For full details on various annexation movements from 1849 through to 1869, see Hugh L. Keenleyside, *Canada and the United States: Some Aspects of the History of the Republic and the Dominion* (New York: Alfred A. Knopf, 1929), 116–66. American views on annexation of Canada are discussed in LaFeber, *The New Empire*, 32–34.

4. Anders Stephanson, *Manifest Destiny: American Expansion and the Empire of the Right* (New York: Hill and Wang, 1996), xiv, 117. See also 4–5.

5. Ibid., 127.

6. Hietala, *Manifest Design*, 271.

7. LaFeber, *The New Empire*, 3.

8. Unless otherwise noted, the primary sources for activities of the Russian-American Company are Lydia T. Black, *Russians in Alaska* (Fairbanks, AK: University of Alaska Press, 2002), 168–268; and P.A. Tikhmenev, *A History of the Russian-American Company*, translated by R.A. Pierce and A.S. Donnelly (Seattle: University of Washington Press, 1978). See also Theodore J. Karamanski, *Fur Trade and Exploration, Opening the Far Northwest, 1821–1852* (Vancouver: UBC Press, 1983), 31–34; Stephen Haycox, *Alaska: An American Colony* (Seattle: University of Washington Press, 2002), 119; and Glynn Barratt, *Russian Shadows on the British Northwest Coast of North America, 1810–1890* (Vancouver: UBC Press, 1983), 5.

9. For the boundary description as set out by the 1825 Convention, see Lewis Green, *The Boundary Hunters* (Vancouver: UBC Press, 1982), 2–3.

10. Thomas A. Bailey, *A Diplomatic History of the American People*, 2nd ed. (New York: F.S. Crofts & Co., 1944), 396.

11. Dorothy Jean Ray, *Ethnology in the Arctic: The Bering Strait Eskimo* (Kingston: Limestone Press, 1985), 49.

12. Tikhmenev, *Russian-American Company*, 372–75.

13. Ibid., 446.

14. Black, *Russians in Alaska*, 255–60.

15. Ibid., 234–45; 344–46.

16. Ibid., 379–95.

17. Ray, *Ethnology in the Arctic*, 83–84.

18. Black, *Russians in Alaska*, 261–66.

19. Ibid., 262–68; also Glyndon G. Van Deusen, *William Henry Seward* (New York: Oxford University Press, 1967), 537.

20. Richard Vaughan, *The Arctic: A History* (Dover, NH: Alan Sutton Publishing, 1994).

21. Ibid., 182–83; Black, *Russians in Alaska*, 273–75; and William W. Fitzhugh and Aron Crowell, *Crossroads of Continents: Cultures of Siberia and Alaska* (Washington, DC: Smithsonian Institution Press, 1988).

22. Of the many books and articles on the purchase of Alaska, four in particular provide both a detailed description of events and insightful analysis: Bailey, *Diplomatic History*, 395–405; Van Deusen, *Seward*, 536–49; LaFeber, *The New Empire*, 24–31; and Haycox, *Alaska*, 148–56.

23. Samuel Eliot Morison, *The Oxford History of the American People* (New York: Oxford University Press, 1965), 726–27.

24. LaFeber, *The New Empire*, 26.

25. Van Deusen, *Seward*, 536–37; Bailey, *Diplomatic History*, 407.

26. Van Deusen, *Seward*, 540–41.

27. Ibid., 541–42; and Bailey, *Diplomatic History*, 398.

28. Hon. Charles Sumner, *Speech of Hon. Charles Sumner, of Massachusetts, on the Cession of Russian America to the United States* (Washington: Congressional Globe Office, 1867, reprinted by University of Michigan Library, Ann Arbor), 13–43.

29. LaFeber, *The New Empire*, 28.

30. The quotation from the *New York Herald* is cited in Bailey, *Diplomatic History*, 402.

31. Vaughan, *The Arctic*, 84.

32. Van Deusen, *Seward*, 544, 548.

33. *Speech of Hon. Charles Sumner*, 48.

34. Van Deusen, *Seward*, 546–47.

35. Ibid., 547–48.

36. General Records of the U.S. Government, 15 Statute 539.

37. Black, *Russians in Alaska*, 284–87.

38. Quotation from LaFeber, *The New Empire*, 28. See also Stephanson, *Manifest Destiny*, xiv, 59–63; Van Deusen, *Seward*, 531–35; Bailey, *Diplomatic History:* 392–405; and William R. Hunt, *Arctic Passage: The Turbulent History of the Land and the People of the Bering Strait, 1897–1975* (New York: Charles Scribner's Sons, 1975), 174.

39. Van Deusen, *Seward*, 549.

CHAPTER SIX

1. As cited in Peter C. Newman, *Caesars of the Wilderness*, Vol. 2 (Toronto: Viking Press, 1987), 365.

2. Among the countless books written on Confederation, those most often consulted include Richard Gwyn, *John A.—The Man Who Made Us: The Life and Times of John A. Macdonald, 1815–1867* (Toronto: Random House Canada, 2007); Donald Creighton, *John A. Macdonald*, Vol. 1, *The Young Politician*, and Vol. 2, *The Old Chieftain* (Toronto: Macmillan of Canada, 1952); W.L. Morton, *The Critical Years: The Union of British North America, 1857–1873* (Toronto: McClelland & Stewart, 1964) and Peter B. Waite, *The Life and Times of Confederation* (Toronto: University of Toronto Press, 1963).

3. Newman, *Caesars of the Wilderness*, Vol. 2, 365.

4. Hugh L. Keenleyside, *Canada and the United States: Some Aspects of the History of the Republic and the Dominion* (New York: Alfred A. Knopf, 1929), 126–37; Gwyn, *John A.*, 256.

5. Carl Berger, *The Sense of Power: Studies in the Ideas of Canadian Imperialism, 1867–1914* (Toronto: University of Toronto Press, 1970), 52–53; and Carl Berger, "The True North Strong and Free . . ." in Peter Russell, ed., *Nationalism in Canada* (Toronto: McGraw-Hill Ryerson, 1966), 5. See also Alexander Morris, *Nova Britannia*, pamphlet published in Montreal, 1858; and R.G. Haliburton, *The Men of the North and Their Place in History: A Lecture Delivered before the Montreal Literary Club, March 31, 1869* (Montreal, 1869).

6. Doug Owram, *Promise of Eden: The Canadian Expansionist Movement and the Idea of the West, 1856–1900* (Toronto: University of Toronto Press, 1980), 38–78; and Shelagh Grant, "Myths of the North in the Canadian Ethos," *The Northern Review*, 2/4 (Summer/Winter 1989), 24–25.

7. Sources for the annexation of Rupert's Land and the North-Western Territory to Canada include Gordon W. Smith, "Sovereignty in the North: The Canadian Aspect of an International Problem," in R. St. J. Macdonald, ed., *The Northern Frontier* (Toronto: University of Toronto Press, 1966), 194–204; James Raffan, *Emperor of the North: Sir George Simpson and the Remarkable Story of the Hudson's Bay Company* (Toronto: Harper Collins, 2007), 387–92; Newman, *Caesars of the Wilderness*, Vol. 2, 341–74. Sources for the role played by James Wickes Taylor also include the *Dictionary of Canadian Biography*, Vol. 12 (Toronto: University of Toronto Press, 2002), 1029–32; Gwyn, *John A.*, 432; and *James Wickes Taylor Correspondence 1859–1870* (Winnipeg: Manitoba Record Society, 1968).

8. Newman, *Caesars of the Wilderness*, Vol. 2, 367–68.

9. Ibid., 364; and Gwyn, *John A.*, 432.

10. Gwyn, *John A.*, 432.

11. Quotations cited in Gwyn, *John A.*, 432–34.

12. Ibid, 278.

13. Ibid., 431.

14. Newman, *Caesars of the Wilderness*, Vol. 2, 364.

15. For precise details regarding the imperial order-in-council that admitted Rupert's Land and the North-Western Territory into the Union, see *Constitutional Documents of Canada* (Toronto: Oxford University Press, 1930), 644.

16. Newman, *Caesars of the Wilderness*, Vol. 2, 372.

17. W. Gillies Ross, *Arctic Whalers Icy Seas* (Toronto: Irwin Publishers, 1985), 173; also Francis Leopold McClintock, *The Voyage of the "Fox" in the Arctic Seas, in Search of Sir John Franklin and His Companions* (London: John Murray, 1881), 13; and "Obituary Notice for Captain William Adams Sr" in the *Dundee Year Book, 1890* (Dundee, Scotland, 1891).

18. For sources on whaling in the eastern Arctic see Ross, *Arctic Whalers;* W. Gillies Ross, "Whaling, Inuit, and the Arctic Islands," in Kenneth S. Coates and William R. Morrison, eds., *Interpreting Canada's North* (Toronto: Copp Clark Pitman, 1989), 225–51; Philip Goldring, "Inuit Economic Responses to Euro-American contacts: Southeast Baffin Island," in Coates and Morrison, *Interpreting Canada's North,* 252–77; and W. Gillies Ross, *This Distant and Unsurveyed Country: A Woman's Winter at Baffin Island, 1857–58* (Montreal/Kingston: McGill-Queen's University Press, 1997).

19. John Bockstoce, *Whales, Ice, and Men: The History of Whaling in the Western Arctic* (Seattle: University of Washington Press, 1986), Chap. 8.

20. Robert McGhee, *The Last Imaginary Place: A Human History of the Arctic World* (Toronto: Key Porter, 2005), 149–50; Richard Vaughan, *The Arctic: A History,* rev. ed. (Gloucestershire, UK: History Press, 2008), 222–24; and Joan Lied, *Siberian Arctic: The Exploration and Development of the Kara Sea Route* (London: Methuen, 1960), 39.

21. Vaughan, *The Arctic,* 265–66; Terence Armstrong, *Russian Settlement in the North* (Cambridge: Cambridge University Press, 1985), 120.

22. Unless otherwise noted, most of the information in this section on Greenland was found in Finn Gad, "History of Colonial Greenland," David Dumas, ed., *Handbook of North American Indians,* Vol. 5, *Arctic* (Washington, DC: Smithsonian Institution, 1984), 564–70; and Finn Gad, *A History of Greenland,* Vol. 3, *1782–1808* (Montreal/Kingston: McGill-Queen's University Press, 1973), 1–70.

23. Diamond Jenness, *Eskimo Administration IV: Greenland* (Montreal: Arctic Institute of North America), 53–58; Austin A. Clark, *Iceland and Greenland.* War Background Studies 15 (Washington: Smithsonian Institution, 1943), 47–89; and Robert Petersen, "Colonialism as seen from a Former Colonized Area," *Arctic Anthropology,* 32:2 (1995), 118–26. Terence Armstrong, George Rogers and Graham Rowley, *The Circumpolar North* (London: Methuen, 1978), 171–75.

24. K. Secher and O. Johnsen, "Minerals in Greenland," in *Geology and Ore,* No. 12 (February 2008), 4–9.

25. Gad, "History of Colonial Greenland," 566.

26. As cited in Henry W. Howgate, *Polar Colonization: Memorial to Congress* (Washington: private publication, 1878), 68–69.

CHAPTER SEVEN

1. As cited in Gordon W. Smith, " Sovereignty in the North: The Canadian Aspect of an International Problem," in R. St. J. Macdonald, ed., *The Northern Frontier* (Toronto: University of Toronto Press, 1966), 203. Original source was the Public Record Office, Colonial Office Papers, Series No. 42, Vol. 759, p. 19 (29 January 1879).

2. LAC, RG 15, Vol. 1 file "Arctic Islands 1873–1880." Handwritten copy of Mintzer's letter of application addressed to Mr. George Crump, Acting British Consul in Philadelphia, 10 February 1874. Handwritten copies of all documents related to transfer of the Arctic islands to Canada are located in this file. According to the annotation on the top document, these were delivered with a map enclosed to the Department of Interior

by legal counsel O.M. Biggar on 24 October 1921, with note that they referred to sovereignty of the Arctic Islands. One document is clearly stamped as received on 27 October 1921 by the manuscript room in the Public Archives of Canada. Typed copies of the same documents, but without annotations, are also found in the J.D. Craig Papers, LAC, MG 30 B 57, Vol. 1, file "1874–1880" and in Northern Affairs Records, LAC, RG 85, Vol. 584, file 571 pt. 4.

3. RG 15, Vol. 1 file "Arctic Islands 1873–1880." Report from Hydrographer Jno. Evans, 20 April 1874, sent by Robert Hall, Secretary to the Admiralty, to Lord Carnarvon, Secretary of the Colonial Office, 21 April 1874.

4. W. Gillies Ross, "Whaling, Inuit, and the Arctic Islands," in Morris Zaslow, ed., *A Century of Canada's Arctic Islands 1880–1980* (Ottawa: Royal Society of Canada, 1981), 48–49.

5. RG 15, Vol. 1, file "Arctic Islands 1873–1880." Despatch marked "Secret" outlining the proposal from Lord Carnarvon to Lord Dufferin, 30 April 1874.

6. Ibid., Dufferin to Carnarvon, 4 November 1874 with report attached from the Committee of the Privy Council dated 10 October 1874, signed by the Clerk for the Privy Council, W.A. Himsworth. In Canada, the Privy Council was appointed by the governor-general for life on the advice of the prime minister but only those Privy Council members who were in the cabinet of the current government could act as a "Committee" to issue "orders-in-council." This practice allowed for restricting the number of individuals informed of the proposed transfer.

7. Ibid., Hydrographer's report of 2 December 1874, with covering letter from Robert Hall to Carnarvon.

8. Ibid., Dufferin to Carnarvon, 1 May 1875, with attached report from the Committee of the Privy Council, 30 April 1875.

9. Ibid., Hydrographer's report 23 January 1879, refers to the previous American claims. See also Geoffrey Hattersley-Smith, "The British Admiralty Expedition, 1875–1876," *Polar Record* 18 (1976), 117–26; and Clive Holland, ed., *Farthest North: A History of North Polar Exploration in Eyewitness Accounts* (London: Robinson Publishing, 1994), 75–85.

10. RG 15, Vol. 1, file "Arctic Islands 1873–1880." Blake to Carnarvon with attachment, 15 August 1876.

11. Ibid., see correspondence 22, 23 August, and 13 September 1876.

12. Ibid., Carnarvon to Dufferin, 1 November 1976.

13. Ibid., Secretary of the Admiralty to the Colonial Office, 8 October 1877, Carnarvon to Dufferin, two despatches dated 23 October 1877.

14. Ibid., Dufferin to Carnarvon 1 December 1877.

15. Henry W. Howgate, *Polar Colonization: Memorial to Congress* (Washington: private publication, 1878), 40–52. Author copy.

16. Ibid., 53–58.

17. Ibid., 59–78.

18. Morris Zaslow, *The Opening of the Canadian North, 1870–1914* (Toronto: McClelland and Stewart, 1971), 253, citing Canada, House of Commons *Debates* (1878), 2386–94.

19. Gordon W. Smith provides a concise and accurate version of the correspondence in "Transfer of Arctic Territories from Great Britain to Canada in 1880, and Some Related Matters, as Seen in Official Correspondence," *Arctic* 14:1 (March 1961), 57–58. He cites

sources from the Colonial Office Records, but copies of the same documents are also found in LAC, RG 15, Vol. 1, file "Arctic Islands 1873–1880."

20. RG 15, Vol. 1, file "Arctic Islands 1873–1880." Report of the Admiralty hydrographer Frederick J. Evans, 23 January 1879, with covering letter 28 January 1879 from Secretary of the Admiralty to Hicks-Beach; letter from Law Officers to Hicks-Beach, 3 April 1879, forwarded to the Marquis of Lorne, 18 April 1879; Marquis of Lorne to Hicks-Beach 5 November 1879, with an order-in-council from the Committee of the Privy Council, 4 November 1879.

21. Ibid., copy of the imperial order-in-council is attached to communiqué from the Privy Council Office to the Marquis of Lorne, 16 August 1880; copies also appear in the published report by Dr. W.F. King, *Report upon the Title of Canada to the Islands to the North of Mainland Canada* (Ottawa: Government Printing Bureau, 1905), 10; and in Smith, "Transfer," 62–63.

22. Alan Cooke, "A Gift Outright: Exploration after 1880," in Morris Zaslow, ed., *A Century of Canada's Arctic Islands* (Ottawa: Royal Society of Canada, 1981), 52.

23. LAC, RG 15, Vol. 1, file "Memos and Maps," Report for the Department of the Interior by Hensley R. Holmden of the map division, 14 November 1921. This report was based on his interpretation of the copies of documents and maps that had been forwarded from the Colonial Office. Versions of this statement appear in subsequent works, such as Smith, "Transfer," 64.

24. Three sets of the documents for the 1880 transfer are currently located in the LAC under three record groups, all annotated as having been received in October or November 1921. The set in RG 85, Vol. 584, file 571/pt. 4 received in the Archives in November 1921 are annotated as originally located in the secretary's office of the governor-general of Canada. The handwritten set in RG 15, Vol. 1, file "Arctic Islands 1873–1880," were annotated as having been delivered by legal counsel, O.M. Biggar, on 24 October 1921. The James Davidson Craig papers, MG30B57, Vol. 1, file "Despatches 1874–1880," also contain typed copies of the despatches, likely originating from either of the above. Hensley Holmden, the associate archivist in charge of the map division, wrote a lengthy report based on these documents dated 26 April 1921, in which he states that Dr. W.F. King did not have access to all the information when he wrote the 1904 report on sovereignty over the Arctic Islands. The timing suggests that these documents were not received by Canadian officials until later 1820 or early 1821.

25. "United States Arctic Colonization and Exploration in 1881," reprints of documents related to the Greely Expedition, *Kansas Review of Science and Industry* (August 1881), 212–14; also see Trevor H. Levere, *Science and the Canadian Arctic: A Century of Exploration, 1818–1918* (Cambridge: Cambridge University Press, 1993), 317.

26. Kenn Harper, "Henry Howgate: Part Two," *Nunatsiaq News* (26 October 2007).

27. Levere, *Science and the Canadian Arctic*, 304–37, quote on 310. I found no evidence that either Germany or the United States was aware that the Arctic Islands had been transferred to Canada.

28. Ibid., 316.

29. For details on the Greely expedition and rescue, see Levere, *Science and the Canadian Arctic*, 316–22; Leslie Neatby, *Conquest of the Frontier* (New York: H. Wolff, 1960), 167–230; John Caswell, *Arctic Frontiers* (Norman, OK: Oklahoma University Press, 1956); and Adolphus Greely, *Three Years of Arctic Service: An Account of the Lady Franklin*

Bay Expedition of 1881–1884 and the Attainment of the Farthest North (New York: Charles
Scribner's Sons, 1886).

30. Michael F. Robinson, *The Coldest Crucible: Arctic Exploration and American Culture* (Chicago:
University of Chicago Press, 2006), 162, also 89–100. See also Beau Riffenburgh, *The
Myth of the Explorer: The Press, Sensationalism, and Geographical Inquiry* (London: Belhaven
Press and Scott Polar Research Institute, 1992).

31. Stephan Stein, "The Greely Relief Expeditions and the New Navy," *International Journal
of Naval History*, 5:3 (December 2006). See also Donald W. Mitchell, *History of the Modern
American Navy from 1883 through Pearl Harbor* (New York: Alfred A. Knopf, 1946), Chaps.
1–8; and Walter LaFeber, *The New Empire: An Interpretation of American Expansionism
1860–1898*, rev. ed. (Ithaca, NY: Cornell University Press, 1998), 58–59.

32. LaFeber, *The New Empire*, 195.

33. Morris Zaslow, "Administering the Islands 1880–1940," in Zaslow, ed. *A Century*,
62; and Gordon Smith, "The Transfer," 65–67.

34. Levere, *Science and the Canadian Arctic*, 359–60; Zaslow, *Opening of the Canadian North*,
255–56.

35. The three debates cited here are found in Canada, House of Commons *Debates* (16 April
1888), 826; (27 June 1892), 4262–4623; and (28 May 1894), 3276–78. The report by
Lt.-Governor Schultz is in Canada, Department of the Interior *Annual Report for 1891*
(Ottawa: Queen's Printer, 1895), Pt. IV, 4.

36. Levere, *Science and the Canadian Arctic*, 344, 362–71, 375, 423.

37. William Wakeham, *Report of the Expedition to Hudson Bay and Cumberland Gulf in the
Steamship "Diana" under the Command of William Wakeham in the year 1897* (Ottawa: King's
Printer, 1898), 24, 75–78; also Zaslow, *Opening of the Canadian North*, 259–60.

38. Canada, Department of the Interior *Annual Report for 1894* (Ottawa: Queen's Printer
1895), Pt. IV, 4–5.

39. John Bockstoce, *Whales, Ice, and Men: The History of Whaling in the Western Arctic*
(Seattle: University of Washington Press, 1986), 256–89. *Thetis* was transferred to the
U.S. Revenue Cutter Service in 1899.

40. Canada, Department of the Interior *Annual Report for 1896* (Ottawa: Queen's
Printer, 1897), 41; and Canada, Sessional Papers (1897) No. 15, *Report of the Commissioner
of the North-West Mounted Police Force, 1896*. Appendix DD: 232–39.

41. D.J. Hall, *Clifford Sifton: Volume 1, The Young Napoleon, 1861–1900* (Vancouver: UBC Press,
1981), 168–69.

42. Ibid., 181.

43. Lewis Green, *The Boundary Hunters: Surveying the 141st Meridian and the Alaskan Panhandle*
(Vancouver: UBC Press, 1982), 67–68.

44. By far the best sources on the role of the NWMP are William R. Morrison,
Showing the Flag: The Mounted Police and Canadian Sovereignty in the North, 1894–1925
(Vancouver: UBC Press, 1985) and Samuel B. Steele, *Forty Years in Canada* (Toronto:
McClelland, Goodchild, and Stewart, 1915). Other important sources for the Klondike
Gold Rush and boundary dispute include Norman Penlington, *The Alaskan Boundary
Dispute: A Critical Reappraisal* (New York: McGraw-Hill, 1972); and Green, *The Boundary
Hunters*. For insight into the Canadian government's interaction with Britain and
the U.S., see Hugh Keenleyside, *Canada and the United States* (New York: Alfred Knopf,
1929); Robert Craig Brown and Ramsay Cook, *Canada 1896–1921: A Nation Transformed*

(Toronto: McClelland & Stewart, 1974); and Norman Penlington, *Canada and Imperialism 1896–1899* (Toronto: University of Toronto Press, 1965).

45. Stephen Haycox, *Alaska: An American Colony* (Seattle: University of Washington Press, 2006), 177–87.

46. Ibid., 201–16.

47. Hall, *Clifford Sifton: Volume 1*, 198–204; Green, *The Boundary Hunters*, 54–94; and Brown and Cook, *Canada 1896–1921*, 34–38.

CHAPTER EIGHT

1. Speech by Prime Minister Laurier at Massey Hall, Toronto, 20 May 1902.

2. Samuel Wittemore Boggs, *The Polar Regions: Geographical and Historical Data for Consideration in a Study of Claims to Sovereignty in the Arctic and Antarctic Regions*, dated September 1933, reprinted 1990 (Buffalo, NY: William S. Hein & Company, 1990), 46–47.

3. Robert Craig Brown and Ramsay Cook, *Canada 1896–1921: A Nation Transformed* (Toronto: McClelland & Stewart, 1974), 29.

4. Morris Zaslow, *The Opening of the Canadian North, 1870–1914* (Toronto: McClelland & Stewart, 1971), 262.

5. T.C. Fairley, ed., *Sverdrup's Arctic Adventures*, adapted from *New Land: Four Years in the Arctic Regions*, by Otto Sverdrup with added chapters by T.C. Fairley (London: Longmans Green and Company, 1959); see also Zaslow, *Opening of the Canadian North*, 260–61.

6. D.J. Hall, *Clifford Sifton, Volume 2, The Lonely Eminence 1901–1929* (Vancouver: UBC Press, 1985), 124–26.

7. Ibid., 114.

8. Norman Penlington, *Canada and Imperialism 1896–1899* (Toronto: University of Toronto Press, 1965), 262.

9. Shelagh D. Grant, "Myths of the North in the Canadian Ethos," *The Northern Review*, 3/4 (Summer/Winter 1989), 15–41; also by the same author, "Northern Identity: Barometer or Convector for National Unity?" in *"English Canada" Speaks Out*, J.L. Granatstein and Kenneth McNaught, eds. (Toronto: Doubleday Canada, 1991), 150–61.

10. Hall, *Sifton, Volume 2*, 111–24; and Brown and Cook, *Canada 1896–1921*, 46–48.

11. Ibid., Hall, 125.

12. The letter of appointment was witnessed by Lord Minto and a copy reproduced in Albert Peter Low, *Report on the Dominion Government Expedition to Hudson Bay and the Arctic Islands on Board the D.G.S. Neptune 1903–1904* (Ottawa: Government Printing Bureau, 1906), ix.

13. Cited in Zaslow, *Opening of the Canadian North*, 263.

14. Ibid.

15. Complete details of the Low expedition appear in his *Report on the Dominion Government Expedition*, 46–70.

16. American hopes for annexation still existed at the turn of the century, as evidenced in Grover Cleveland's election platform in 1896. For full details on the boundary dispute see Norman Penlington, *The Alaskan Boundary Dispute: A Critical Reappraisal* (New York: McGraw-Hill, 1972). For the Canadian version of events, see Charles Thonger, *Canada's Alaskan Dismemberment: An Analytical Examination of the Fallacies Underlying the Tribunal Award* (Niagara-on-the-Lake: private printing, 1904). For the American story,

see George Davidson, *The Alaska Boundary* (San Francisco: Alaska Packers Association, 1903). For Laurier's statement to Parliament see House of Commons *Debates*, 23 October 1903, p. 14817 as cited in John Hilliker, *Canada's Department of External Affairs, Volume 1—The Early Years, 1909–1946* (Montreal/Kingston: McGill-Queen's University Press, 1990), 25 and n 52.

17. William R. Morrison, *Showing the Flag: The Mounted Police and Canadian Sovereignty in the North, 1894–1925* (Vancouver: UBC Press, 1985), 92–94.

18. Hall, *Sifton, Vol.* 2, 126; Zaslow, *Opening of the Canadian North*, 261–62.

19. For full details of Bernier's involvement see Yolande Dorion-Robitaille, *Captain J.E. Bernier's Contribution to Canadian Sovereignty in the Arctic* (Ottawa: Indian and Northern Affairs, 1978).

20. W.F. King, *Report upon the Title of Canada to the Islands North of the Mainland of Canada* (Ottawa: Government Printing Bureau, 1905), 6–8. (Copy located in LAC, J.D. Craig Papers, MG 30 B 57, Vol. 1, file "Reports and Memos.")

21. Ibid., 24–26. The contents of the supplementary memo are also described in Zaslow, *Opening of the Canadian North*, 264–65.

22. LAC, RG 85 Vol. 584, file 571 pt. 5. "Confidential Memo re the Arctic Islands" to A.G. Doughty, Dominion Archivist, from Hensley Holmden, in charge of the Map Division, 26 April 1921.

23. Ibid., 33–38. Holmden describes the correspondence between the Colonial Office and Canada's Governor-General, and quotes the entire text of Lord Crewe's secret despatch dated 25 June 1908.

24. King, *Report*, 26; Zaslow, *Opening of the Canadian North*, 265.

25. LAC, MG 30 B 57, Vol. 1, file "correspondence." Memo to Bernier from the Deputy Minister of Marine and Fisheries, 23 June 1906.

26. Ibid., file "memos and reports 1904–1923." Summary of Reports of the Low and Bernier Expeditions, ND, but other material suggests c 1920.

27. Canada. Senate. *Debates.* 20 February 1907, 266–74.

28. LAC, RG 85 Vol. 584, file 571 pt. 5. "Confidential Memo re the Arctic Islands" to A.G. Doughty, Dominion Archivist, from Hensley Holmden, in charge of Map Division, 26 April 1921. Holmden refers to King report on p. 21.

29. Hilliker, *Canada's Department of External Affairs*, 30–43, 58.

30. Shelagh D. Grant, *Arctic Justice: On Trial for Murder, Pond Inlet 1923* (Montreal/Kingston: McGill-Queen's University Press, 2002), 39.

31. Hall, *Clifford Sifton, Vol. II*, 124–26, 224–35.

32. Nancy Fogelson, *Arctic Exploration and International Relations* (Fairbanks, AK: University of Alaska Press, 1992), 32–35; and Clive Holland, *Farthest North: A History of Northern Polar Exploration in Eyewitness Accounts* (London: Robinson, 1994), 169–79, 209–21.

33. Nancy Fogelson, "Robert E. Peary and American Exploration in the Arctic 1886–1910," *Fram: The Journal of Polar Studies* (1985, Part I), 131–40.

34. Fogelson, *Arctic Exploration*, 36–39.

35. Everett S. Allen, *Arctic Odyssey: The Life of Rear Admiral Donald B. MacMillan* (New York: Dodd, Mead and Company, 1962), 204–18, 314–29. Also see Fogelson, *Arctic Exploration*, 40–42; and a Canadian report, "Notes on Northern Expeditions," 9 December 1920, prepared by Dr. Klotz of the Dominion Observatory, found in LAC MG 30 B 57, Vol. 1, file "Memos and Reports," 7.

36. LAC, RG 25, Vol. 2668, file 9058 E 40. William Walker to G.J. Desbarats, DM of Naval Service, 7 May 1913; also despatch from L. Harcourt, Secretary of State for the Colonies, to Governor-General of Canada, 10 May 1913.

37. Richard Diubaldo, *Stefansson and the Canadian Arctic* (Montreal/Kingston: McGill-Queen's University Press, 1985). See also Gísli Pálsson, *Travelling Passions: The Hidden Life of Vilhjalmur Stefansson* (Winnipeg: University of Manitoba Press, 2003); William Hunt, *Stef: A Biography of Vilhjalmur Stefansson, Canadian Arctic Explorer* (Vancouver: UBC Press, 1986); Shelagh D. Grant, *Sovereignty or Security? Government Policy in the Canadian North, 1939–1950* (Vancouver: UBC Press, 1988).

38. Richard Vaughan, *The Arctic: A History*, rev. ed. (Gloucestershire, UK: History Press, 2008), 271–73, citing F.A. Faynberg, *Essays on the Ethnic History of the Foreign North* (Moscow: Nauka, 1971), 44–87.

39. Donald R. Rothwell, *The Polar Regions and the Development of International Law* (New York: Cambridge University Press, 1996), 324–27.

40. Ibid., 170, 344–45, quoting Mirovitskaya, Clark and Purver, "North Pacific Fur Seals" and Vaughan, *The Arctic*, 248.

41. Nancy Fogelson, "The Tip of the Iceberg: The United States and International Rivalry for the Arctic, 1900–25," *Diplomatic History*, 52:1 (Spring 1985), 135; and Fogelson, *Arctic Exploration*, 43, 79–98.

42. LAC, RG 85, Vol. 583, file 571 pt. 1. See the report by the Advisory Technical Board for the Minister of the Interior, 25 September 1920, p. 2.

43. LAC, MG 30 E 169, J.B. Harkin Papers, Vol. 1, file "Arctic Islands." For excerpts from Oppenheim's Treatise, see report titled "Arctic Islands—Sovereignty," 25 November 1920, p. 7. See also report on "Ellesmere Island" (ND) and correspondence related to Harkin's work for the Advisory Technical Board as the Commissioner of the Dominion Parks Branch of the Department of the Interior.

44. Ibid., Vol. 1, file "1919–October 1920." Minutes of a Special Meeting of the Advisory Technical Board, 1 October 1920 to hear Vilhjalmur Stefansson. Composition of the ATB and of the Sub-Committee on Arctic Sovereignty was found in a report in the William Walker files, RG 25, Vol. 2668, in reference to minutes of ATB meetings. Although a relatively junior member of the committee, Harkin as Commissioner of Dominion Parks was Stefansson's contact regarding protection of the muskox on Ellesmere Island, raising the question of Greenlanders hunting in Canadian territory.

45. LAC, Arthur Meighen Papers, MG 26 I, Vol. 13, Series 2, File 7 "Arctic Island Exploration." Stefansson to Meighen, 30 October 1920. There is no record of the prime minister actually meeting with Stefansson, but his report is on file.

46. LAC, RG 25, Vol. 2668, file 9058-F40, Report, Christie to Meighen, 28 October 1920.

47. LAC, RG 25, Vol. 2668, file 9057-40C, pt. 1, "Memorandum for the Rt. Hon. Mr. Meighen on Canada's claim to certain island within the Arctic Circle," from Pope, 25 November 1920.

48. LAC, RG 85, Vol. 583, file 571, pts. 1, 2, and 3. See related reports and correspondence. For specific proposals, see in part 3, "Confidential Memorandum" 11 February 1922; and memo from J.D. Craig to Harkin, 2 February 1922.

49. LAC, MG 30 B 57, Vol. 1, file "Correspondence." News clippings were included in correspondence from W.W. Cory, Deputy Minister of the Interior, to Sir Joseph Pope, Under-Secretary of State for External Affairs, 14 January 1920. See also memo from W.S. Edwards, Assistant Deputy of Justice, to J.D. Craig, 10 January 1921.

50. LAC, RG 85, Vol. 583, file 571 pts. 1–3, Memorandum from James Lougheed, Minister of the Interior; refer also to the taped account by former RCMP Corporal Finley McInnes concerning the rationale, preparation and his trip to the Arctic in 1922 to establish a new police detachment at Pond Inlet. Finley McInnes collection, University of Alberta Archives.

51. Full details of Inuit violence in the western Arctic, Grant, *Arctic Justice*. Also William R. Morrison, *Showing the Flag: The Mounted Police and Canadian Sovereignty in the North, 1894–1925* (Vancouver: UBC Press, 1985); and Sidney Harring, "The Rich Men of the Country: Canadian Law in the Land of the Copper Inuit, 1914–1930," in *Ottawa Law Review* (1989).

52. LAC, MG 30 B 57, Vol.1, file "Correspondence 1903–1922," memos and despatches dating from 14 January 1920 through to May 1921; also the telegram from the Secretary of State for the Colonies to the Governor-General of Canada, 9 June 1921.

53. Vaughan, *The Arctic*, 203. For a more complete story on Stefansson's attempts to gain the Canadian government's agreement to claim possession of Wrangel Island, see Diubaldo, *Stefansson and the Canadian Arctic*, 173–88.

54. LAC, RG 85, Vol. 602, files 2502 pt. 1, includes coded messages and expedition reports for 1922; in the same volume, file 2502 pt. 2, Deputy Minister of the Interior W.W. Cory to the Prime Minister, 5 July 1923. See also MG 30 B 68, Robert A. Logan Papers, Vol. 1, file "Report on Investigations on Aviation in the Arctic Archipelago," 1922; MG 30 B 129, William Harold Grant Papers, Vol. 1, file "Diary 9 July–October 1922"; and MG 30 B 57, John Davidson Craig Papers, Vol. 1, file "Diary of the 1922 Eastern Arctic Patrol."

55. A.E. Millward, ed., *South Baffin Island: An Account of Exploration, Investigation and Settlement during the Past Fifty Years* (Ottawa: Government Publishing Bureau for Department of the Interior and North West Territories and Yukon Branch, 1930), 7, 17.

56. LAC, RG 85, Vol. 347, file 100, "Application for Reclassification of the Northwest Territories and Yukon Branch." See also *Annual Report of the Department of the Interior* (Ottawa, 31 March 1922), Appendix A; also Diamond Jenness, *Eskimo Administration II. Canada* (Montreal: Arctic Institute of North America, 1964), 29.

57. For full details see Grant, *Arctic Justice*.

58. Hilliker, *Canada's Department of External Affairs*, 93–104.

59. Donald W. Mitchell, *History of the Modern American Navy: From 1883 through to Pearl Harbor* (New York: Alfred A. Knopf, 1946), 168, 290.

60. Fogelson, *Arctic Exploration*, 87–88; also 51 n 63.

61. LAC, RG 25, Vol. 85, file 4831, memo from the Deputy Minister of National Defence, G.J. Desbarats, to Minister of the Interior, W.W. Cory, with attached report by J.A. Wilson on meeting with Commander Byrd. See also Fogelson, *Arctic Exploration*, 93.

62. LAC, RG 25, Vol. 2669, file 9062-C40. Minutes of the First Meeting of the Inter-Departmental Committee, O.D. Skelton, chair, 24 April 1925.

63. Ibid., memo from Skelton to Cory, 25 April 1925.

64. Ibid., minutes of 13 May 1925 meeting, which included a report on Cory's meeting with Byrd and the reading of his subsequent letter. The subcommittee was composed of O.D. Skelton, G.J. Desbarets, James White and O.S. Finnie.

65. Ibid., minutes of the 26 May 1925 meeting, with draft of the statement sent to Washington attached.

66. LAC, RG 25, Vol. 2960, file 1/C47763. See copy of the despatch and covering letter from Lord Byng, 4 June 1925; also "Copy of the Code Telegram" to the British chargé d'affaires in Washington from the Governor-General, 12 June 1925.

67. Ibid., Frank Kellogg to H.G. Chilton, British chargé d'affaires in Washington, 15 June 1925; also related memos, telegrams and despatches in the file.

68. Fogelson, *Arctic Adventure*, 92, citing Navy Department and State Department records.

69. Ibid., 94–95, citing State Department Records.

70. LAC, RG 25 Vol. 2669, file 9062-C-40. See report of Commander George Mackenzie of the Eastern Arctic Patrol to the Northern Advisory Board, attached to the "Minutes," 19 October 1925.

71. Fogelson, *Arctic Exploration*, 95–96. Fogelson, in describing MacMillan's allegations that Byrd "knew perfectly well" that no permit had been issued, cites a conversation between U.S. Under Secretary of State Green and MacMillan. National Archives (NA) State Department Records, RG 59 031.11 m 221. There is no reference to whether Byrd denied or confirmed MacMillan's story.

72. LAC, RG 25, Vol. 2960, file 1/C47763. See code telegram from Byng to Chilton, 13 June 1925.

73. LAC, RG 85, Vol. 347, file 200-2, Report by External Affairs, "The Question of Ownership of the Sverdrup Islands," 23 October 1929: 10.

74. Sverdrup and Fairley, *Sverdrup's Arctic Adventures*, 288–95.

75. LAC, MG 30 B 68, Robert A. Logan Papers, Vol. 1, file "correspondence." Logan to Mackenzie King, 5 June 1925; O.D. Skelton to Logan, 9 June 1925; Desbarats as assistant deputy for national defence to Logan, 10 June 1925; Logan to O.S. Finnie, 24 June 1925; and Finnie to Logan, 29 June 1925.

76. Department of External Affairs, File no. 1176–1924 Part IV (May–August 1928), T 9105/81/377, Second Report on Territorial Waters, confidential. See also from same file, including Parts V and VI, memorandum, telegrams and meetings, including the minutes of the Canadian Committee on 28 March 1929. Pearson appears to have been secretary for the committee. Retrieved from the document collection in Alexander Stevenson Papers, Northwest Territories Archives (N-192-023).

77. Hilliker, *Canada's Department of External Affairs*, 129, 235–38.

78. Richard Vaughan, *Northwest Greenland: A History* (Orono, ME: University of Maine Press, 1991), 133.

79. For details about the Norwegian claims to northeast Greenland, see Vaughan, *The Arctic*, 130, 138–41, 264–65; also Knud Berlin, *Denmark's Right to Greenland: A Survey of the Past and Present Status of Greenland, Iceland and the Faroe Islands in Relation to Norway and Denmark* (London: Oxford University Press, 1932); and Gustav Smedal, *Acquisition of Sovereignty over Polar Areas* (Oslo: I Kommisjon Hos Jacob Dybwad, 1931).

80. Vaughan, *The Arctic*, 265.

81. Diubaldo, *Stefansson*, 186.

82. Vaughan, *The Arctic*, 206–9.

83. Jenness, *Eskimo Administration: II Canada*, 59–61.

84. Boggs, *The Polar Regions*, 116, also 112–23.

CHAPTER NINE

1. Adolph A. Berle, *Navigating the Rapids, 1918–1971* (New York: Harcourt, Brace Jovanovich, 1973), 427. Quotation is from a letter written to the U.S. Secretary of State, 9 September 1942.

2. Stetson Conn and Byron Fairchild, *United States Army in World War II—The Western Hemisphere*, Vol. 1: *The Framework of Hemisphere Defense* (Washington: Center of Military History, U.S. Army, 1989), ix, 3.

3. William S. Carlson, *Lifelines through the Arctic* (New York: Duell, Sloan and Pearse, 1962), 52–53; Richard Vaughan, *Northwest Greenland: A History* (Orono, ME: University of Maine Press, 1991), 134.

4. Unless otherwise noted, most details of U.S. wartime activities in northern Canada are found in Shelagh D. Grant, *Sovereignty or Security? Government Policy in the Canadian North, 1939–1950* (Vancouver: UBC Press, 1988). The literature on this subject is extensive. The most comprehensive source for U.S. military activities is Conn and Fairchild, *United States Army in World War II*, Vol. 1. Special reference to Chapter 1, "The Framework of Hemisphere Defense," Chap. 14, "The United States and Canada: Co-Partners in Defense," and Chap. 15, "The United States and Canada: Elements of Wartime Collaboration." Equally important is Vol. 2, Stetson Conn, Rose Engelman, and Byron Fairchild, *Guarding the United States and Its Outposts* (Washington, DC: U.S. Printing office for the Center of Military History, 2000), noting in particular Chap. 10, "Alaska in the War," and Chap. 17, "Greenland: Arctic Outpost." Also important are Wesley Frank Craven and James Lea Cate, eds., *The Army Air Forces in World War II*, Vols. 1, 6, 7 (Chicago: University of Chicago Press, 1948); C.P. Stacey, *Arms, Men & Governments: The War Policies of Canada* (Ottawa: Queen's Printer, 1970); S.W. Dziuban, *Military Relations Between the United States and Canada 1939–1945* (Washington, DC: Department of the U.S. Army, 1959).

5. LAC, RG 25, Vol. 2731, file 267 J-40/1. See telegrams, memos and notes, 9 April–20 May 1940.

6. For the story about competing interests in the cryolite mine, plans to occupy Greenland and the voyage of the *St. Roch*, see Shelagh D. Grant, "Why the *St. Roch*? Why the Northwest Passage? Why 1940? New Answers to Old Questions," *Arctic* 46: 1 (March 1993), 82–87. Related archival documents are found in LAC, Department of External Affairs, RG 25, Vol. 2731, file 267 J-4/1; and Department of National Defence, RG 24, Vol. 3919, file 1037-6-1/1.

7. Peter Neary, *Newfoundland in the North Atlantic World, 1929–1949* (Toronto: University of Toronto Press, 1989), 133–63; Oliver La Large, *The Eagle and the Egg* (Boston: Houghton Mifflin, 1949), 8–29. For the full story behind the Hyde Park Declaration, see Norman Hillmer and J.L. Granatstein, *For Better or For Worse: Canada and the United States into the Twenty-First Century* (Toronto: Thomson/Nelson, 2007), 148–51.

8. Craven and Cate, eds., *Army Air Forces*. Vol. 1, *Plans and Early Operations*, 115; Vol. 6, *Plans and Men*, Chap. 3, "Air Defense of the United States"; and Vol. 7, *Services Around the World*, 313.

9. See Walter Wood, "United States Arctic Exploration through 1939" in *United States Polar Exploration*, ed. Herman R. Friis and Shelby G. Bale Jr. (Athens, OH: University of Ohio Press, 1970); Carlson, *Lifelines through the Arctic*; Alexander Forbes, *Quest for a Northern Air Route* (Cambridge, MA: Harvard University Press, 1953); and Colonel Bernt Balchen, Major Corey Ford & Major Oliver La Farge, *War Below Zero: The Battle for Greenland* (Boston: Houghton Mifflin, 1944). Wilkins was Australian-born and received a knighthood from Britain, but eventually became an American citizen. Names of key

leaders were also cross-referenced in the Charles Hubbard Papers, National Archives (Washington), RG 401-17, Vol. 5, "Reports 1941–1950."

10. Craven and Cate, eds., "The AAF Weather Service," in *Army Air Forces*, Vol. 7, 311–28. See also "Thunder Over the North Atlantic," *Fortune*, 30:5 (November 1944), 156.

11. Richard Vaughan, *The Arctic: A History*, rev. ed. (Gloucestershire, UK: History Press, 2008), 236–37.

12. Conn et al., *Guarding the United States*, Chap. 17, "Greenland: Arctic Outpost." See also J.G. Elbo, "Cryolite and the Mine at Ivigtut, West Greenland," *Polar Record* 5:35 (1948): 185–88; Polly Burroughs, *The Great Ice Ship "Bear": Eighty-Nine Years in Polar Seas* (New York: Van Nostrand Reinhold, 1970); Samuel E. Morison, *Battle of the Atlantic, September 1939–May 1943*, Vol. 1 of *The History of the United States Naval Operations in World War II* (Boston: Atlantic, Little, Brown, 1948), 56–58; and Balchen et al., *War Below Zero*, 20.

13. Conn et al., *Guarding the United States*, Chap. 17: 444–54.

14. Carlson, *Lifelines*, 59–61; Alexander Forbes, *Quest for a Northern Air Route* (Cambridge: Harvard University Press, 1953), Chaps. 1, 2; and Alex Douglas, "The Nazi Weather Station in Labrador," *Canadian Geographic*, 101:6 (December–January 1981–82), 42.

15. Carlson, *Lifelines*, 61–62. Also National Archives (Washington), RG 401-100, William S. Carlson Papers, photo collection, Series 3, 8 and 11; and NA (Washington) RG 401-17, Charles J. Hubbard Papers, Vol. 5, file 3, "Report on Crystal Force Expedition with preliminary mention of Bluie West 8 and Bluie East 2."

16. Ibid.; also Craven and Cate, *Army Air Forces*, Vol. 7, 321–32; Morison, *History of United States Naval Operations*, 62; and "Thule Air Base," www.strategic-air-command.com/bases/Thule.

17. Carlson, *Lifelines*, 62–63; Craven and Cate, *Army Air Forces*, Vol. 7, 92–93; Canada, Department of External Affairs, *Documents on Canadian External Relations* (hereafter DCER), Vol. 9 (Ottawa: Supply and Services, 1976), document 1025, memo from N. Robertson to Prime Minister, and document 1026, containing extracts from Cabinet War Committee Minutes, both dated 28 May 1942; see also documents 1029–32, 12 June through 18 August 1942.

18. Carlson, *Lifelines*, 69–76; National Archives (Washington), RG 59, PJBD Series, Vol. 2, file "Goose Bay." La Guardia to Biggar, 16 June 1941; Forbes, *Quest*, 95; Craven and Cate, *Army Air Forces*, Vol. 1, 323, 348, 346.

19. Craven and Cate, *Army Air Forces*, Vol. 1, 349, 356, 638, and Vol. 7, 94; see also Forbes, *Quest*, 51–88.

20. Balchen et al., *War Below Zero*, 5, 25–26.

21. Ibid., 27–34.

22. Ibid., 23, 35–37.

23. LAC, RG 25, Vol. 2411, file 102-HX-40-C contains various reports of German activity from the Canadian consulate in Greenland, 1943 through December 1944; and Vaughan, *The Arctic*, 235–36.

24. Craven and Cate, *Army Air Forces*, Vol. 7, 99–104.

25. Major Oliver La Farge, "The Long Wait," in Balchen et al., *War Below Zero*, 41.

26. Carlson, *Lifelines*, 103.

27. Balchen et al., *War Below Zero*, 37.

28. Berle, *Navigating the Rapids*, 427.

29. DCER, Vol. 9, Documents 292, 293, 1025, 1026; Craven and Cate, *Army Air Forces*, Vol. 7, 93. See also LAC, RG 36/7, Vol. 14, file 28-6, "United States Defence Projects and Installations in Canada," 12 January 1944; NA, Washington. Charles Hubbard Papers, Vol. 5, file "Report on Crystal Force Expedition," and Forbes, *Quest*, 17–41.

30. J.L. Granatstein, *The Ottawa Men: The Civil Service Mandarins, 1935–1957* (Toronto: Oxford University Press, 1981), 2; Grant, *Sovereignty or Security?*, 22–23, 49–50.

31. DCER, Vol. 9, see documents 950, Norman Robertson to Prime Minister, 22 December 1941, and documents 951 and 952, memos by Hugh Keenleyside, 27 December 1941 and 14 April 1942; also LAC, MG 27 III 65, Escott Reid Papers, Vol. 9/10, "Oral History Review with Don Page," 21 July 1977. See also DCER 1022 through 1072 and NA (Washington), RG 59, PJBD Series, Vol. 10, correspondence files for 1942 and 1943 between John Hickerson of the State Department and Major General Guy Henry, senior U.S. Army member on the PJBC.

32. Conn et al., *Framework for Hemispheric Defense*. Chap. 1, 14–15; and Chap. 9, "The Garrisoning of Alaska, 1939–41"; also Stephen Haycox, *Alaska: An American Colony* (Seattle: University of Washington Press, 2006), 256–64; and Senator Ernest Gruening, "The Alaska Eskimos in World War II," in Muktutk Marsden, *Men of the Tundra: Alaskan Eskimos at War* (New York: October House, 1969).

33. K.S. Coates and W.R. Morrison, *The Alaska Highway in World War II: The American Army of Occupation in Canada's Northwest* (Toronto: University of Toronto Press, 1992); and Ken Coates, *North to Alaska: Fifty Years of the World's Most Remarkable Highway* (Toronto: McClelland & Stewart, 1992).

34. Conn et al., *Guarding the United States*, Chaps. 10, 11.

35. P.S. Barry, *The Canol Project: An Adventure of the U.S. War Department in Canada's Northwest* (Edmonton: private printing, 1985); Richard Finnie, *Canol* (San Francisco: Taylor and Taylor, 1945).

36. Craven and Cate, *Army Air Forces*, Vol. 7, 153, 161.

37. As an example of Canadian media accounts see "Baghdad on the Saskatchewan," *Vancouver Sun*, 30 April 1943; also *New York Times* (19 July 1943), "U.S. Army Tapping Canada's Oil," and Associated Press release in a teletype from Canadian Embassy in Washington, 21 June 1943 in LAC, RG 36/7, Vol. 13, file W-34-2-5.

38. The best summary is found in R.D. Cuff and J.L. Granatstein, *Ties that Bind: Canadian-American Relations from the Great War to the Cold War* (Toronto: Samuel Steven Hakkert, 1977), Chap. 5 "Getting on with the Americans: Canadian Perceptions of the United States, 1939–1945."

39. Craven and Cate, *Army Air Forces*, Vol. 1, 298.

40. NA (Washington), State Department Records, RG 59, Microfiche file M1221, R and A 549, "Changing Canadian American Relations" 5 March 1942, Situation Report no. 2 by the Office of Strategic Services for the British Empire Section of the State Department, 1; also R and A 738a, "Secret Survey of Canada," 2 September 1942, for the Office of Strategic Services of the State Department, 1–2, 84.

41. NA (Washington), State Department Records, RG 59, PJBD Series, Vol. 10, file "Correspondence January–March, 1943," Hickerson to Guy Henry, 3 March 1943; LAC, RG 36/7, Vol. 14, file 28-6, "United States Defence Projects and Installations in Canada," 12 January 1944.

42. University of Durham, England. Malcolm MacDonald Papers, 14/4/107–16, "Report on Tour of the American-Built Airfields in the Eastern Arctic," 29 August 1944; see also Arthur Pocock, *Red Flannels and Green Ice* (New York: Random House, 1949), 144–56.

43. Ibid.; also Pocock, *Red Flannels*, 114, 237–38; Nicolas Polunin, *Arctic Unfolding* (London: Hutchison, 1949), 70–73; Robert A. Bartlett, "Servicing the Arctic Bases," *National Geographic*, 85:5 (May 1946), 602; and NA (Washington), RG 401-17, Vol. 5, "Report on Crystal Force Expedition," and an added report by E. Goodale, October 1941–42.

44. Craven and Cate, *Army Air Forces*, Vol. 1, 292–93; Vol. 6, 636, 645–48; Vol. 7, 313–16.

45. NA (Washington), William Carlson Papers, RG 401-100, Vol. 11, file "History of the Arctic, Desert, and Tropic Information Centre," 1–3; and Paul H. Nesbitt, "A Brief History," 134–45; also Vol. 4, "Correspondence with Laurence Gould," Carlson to Gould (former ADTIC chief), 21 April 1945.

46. LAC, RG 2/7, Vol. 12, Cabinet War Committee Minutes for 3 December 1943; and United States, Senate, *Additional Report of the Special Committee Investigating the National Defense Program: The Canol Project* (Washington: Government Printing Office, 1944), 7.

47. J.W. Pickersgill, *Mackenzie King Record, Volume 1, 1939–1944* (Toronto: University of Toronto Press, 1960), 644.

48. LAC, King Papers, MG 26 J 4, Vol. 309, file 3282, "Exchange of Notes" 7 June 1944, related to the disposition of Canol; also Vol. 350, file 3788, including related memos, correspondence, minutes of meetings and copies of the "Exchange of Notes" dated 27 June 1944 and 31 March 1946; also LAC, RG 36/7, Vol. 14, file 28-6, memo dated 12 January 1944.

49. Coates, *North to Alaska*, Chaps. 4–6.

50. John Holmes, *The Shaping of Peace: Canada and the Search for World Order, 1943–1957* (Toronto: University of Toronto Press, 1979), 64–71.

51. Grant, *Sovereignty or Security?*, 132–33.

52. "Thunder over the North Atlantic," *Fortune*, 30:5 (November 1944), 153–206.

53. Quoted in Carlson, *Lifelines*, 191.

CHAPTER TEN

1. Text of speech given by Col. Bernt Balchen at the Explorer's Club in New York, 13 February 1954, Balchen Collection, Maxwell AFB, file 186.7053-93; as cited in Carroll V. Glines, *Bernt Balchen, Polar Aviator* (Washington: Smithsonian Institution Press, 1999), 244–45 and 297 n 53.

2. *Washington Post*, 6 July 1946, as cited in Glines, *Bernt Balchen*, 213.

3. Originally from the U.S. Department of Defense Plans for 1958, as cited in Robert T. Hayton, "Polar Problems and International Law," *American Journal of International Law* 52:4 (October 1958), 747.

4. Terence Armstrong, George Rogers and Graham Rowley, *The Circumpolar North* (London: Methuen & Co, 1978), 102, 136, 190, 281. The 1959 population and land mass figures for the Soviet North vary according to the interpretation of "north." Population figures used here are considerably less than found in the above source, but relate directly to the area north of 60° N latitude. See Terence Armstrong, *Russian Settlement in the North* (Cambridge, UK: Cambridge University Press, 1965), 188.

5. Armstrong et al., *The Circumpolar North*, 136–41.

6. Stephen Haycox, *Alaska: An American Colony* (Seattle: University of Washington Press, 2006), 266.

7. Ibid., 261–72; Diamond Jenness, *Eskimo Administration: 1. Alaska* (Montreal: Arctic Institute of North America, 1962), 41. See also Shelagh Grant, *Sovereignty or Security?* (Vancouver: UBC Press, 1988), 236.

8. Diamond Jenness, *Eskimo Administration*, Vol. 4, *Greenland* (Montreal: Arctic Institute of North America, 1967), 97–135.

9. H.C. Bach and Jergen Taagbolt, *Greenland and the Arctic Region: Resources and Security Policy*, translated by H. Johannsen (Copenhagen: Information Service of Danish Defence, 1979); also Lydus H. Buss, "U.S. Air Defense in the Northeast 1940–1957," Historical Reference Paper No. 1, Office of Information Services, U.S. Continental Air Defense Command (CONAD), 2 and 9, note.

10. "Defense of Greenland: Agreement between the United States and the Kingdom of Denmark, 27 April 1951," *American Foreign Policy 1950–1955, Basic Documents Volumes I and II*, Department of State Publication 6446, General Foreign Policy Series 117 (Washington: U.S. Government Printing Office, 1957).

11. Ibid., Articles 6, 7, 8.

12. Ibid., Articles 6, 7, 8.

13. Ibid., Article 11.

14. Bach and Taagbolt, *Greenland and the Arctic Region*, 10–12.

15. Norman Hillmer and J.L. Granatstein, *For Better or For Worse: Canada and the United States into the Twenty-First Century*, rev. ed. (Toronto: Thompson/Nelson Publishers, 2007), 178–80; and Joseph T. Jockel, *No Boundaries Upstairs: Canada, the United States and the Origins of North American Defence, 1945–1958* (Vancouver: UBC Press, 1987), 13–21.

16. NA (Washington), Charles J. Hubbard Papers, RG 410/17, box 5, file 1, "Arctops Project," Massachusetts Institute of Technology.

17. Ibid., file 8, "Report on Recommended U.S. Weather Bureau Arctic Operations for the Period of April 1946 to July 1, 1947, in compliance with Public Law 296," see section "Priorities and Military Cooperation," 19.

18. NA (Washington), Hubbard Papers, Box 5, file 8, "Report on Recommended U.S. Weather Bureau Arctic Operations for the Period of April 1946 to July 1, 1947." See "Introduction," Section 4, "Cooperation with Foreign Countries," and Section 5, "International Agreements."

19. LAC, RG 2/18, Vol. 74, file D-19-2, Cabinet Document no. 125, "Post War Defence Collaboration with the United States," 13 December 1945; and Canada, Department of External Affairs, *Documents on Canadian External Relations* (hereafter DCER), Vol. 12 (1946), document 956. "Appreciation" and "Basic Security Plan" as discussed in meetings 20–23 May 1946.

20. "Canada Another Belgium in U.S. Air Bases Proposal," *Financial Post* (29 June 1946) and *Financial Post*, "Ottawa Scotches U.S. Plan to Man Weather Bases in the Canadian Arctic" (29 June 1946). See also LAC, Privy Council Records, RG 2/18, Vol. 46, file A-25-1, Barclay to Heeney, 29 June 1946.

21. DCER, Vol. 12, 913, "Sovereignty in the Canadian Arctic in Relation to Joint Defence Undertakings," Section 27.

22. Ibid., and Document 921, Wrong to Heeney, 24 June 1946.

23. James Eayrs, *In Defence of Canada: Peacemaking and Deterrence* (Toronto: University of Toronto Press, 1972), 335.

24. John Holmes, *Shaping the Peace: Canada and the Search for World Order*, Vol. 1 (Toronto: University of Toronto Press, 1979), 172. See also article in the *Financial Post* under the headline "Ottawa Scotches U.S. Plan to Man Weather Bases in the Canadian Arctic."

25. John Holmes, *The Better Part of Valour: Essays on Canadian Diplomacy* (Toronto: McClelland & Stewart, Carleton Series, 1970), 13.

26. LAC, RG 2/18, Vol.74, file D-19-2. "List of Recent United States and Permanent Joint Board on Defence Proposals for Joint Defence Projects and Cooperation Measures," 30 June 1946.

27. NA (Washington), Charles Hubbard Papers, RG 401-17, Vol. 5, file 7, "1946 Report."

28. Ibid.; see also the history of the "Thule Air Base," on the SAC website: www.strategic-air-command.com/bases/Thule_AFB; and Richard Vaughan, *Northwest Greenland: A History* (Orono, ME: University of Maine Press, 1991), 134–35.

29. J. Tuzo Wilson, "Exercise Musk-Ox," *Polar Record* 5 (1947): 14–25; also correspondence, 10 June 1988, J. Tuzo Wilson to author. See also David Judd, "Canada's Northern Policy," *Polar Record*, 14 (May 1969): 595.

30. This view is supported by William R. Morrison in "Eagle Over the Arctic," in *Interpreting Canada's North*, Kenneth S. Coates and William R. Morrison, eds. (Toronto: Copp Clark Pitman, 1989), 180.

31. NA (Washington), RG 59, PJBD Series, Vol. 10, file "Correspondence—1946," memo on the subject of United States–Canadian relations, 28 August 1946; and "Problems of Canadian–United States Cooperation in the Arctic," office of the AC/s Intelligence, USAAF, 29 October 1946.

32. LAC, RG 2/18, Vol. 74, file D-19-2. Memo to the PJBD from Major-General Guy Henry, Senior Army Member, 9 September 1946, item #6; and NA (Washington), RG 59 PJBD Series, Vol. 2, file "Basic Papers," memorandum on "Joint Defense Discussions," 21 November 1946.

33. NA (Washington) RG 59, PJBD series, Vol. 2, file "Basic Papers," memo from Dean Acheson to President Truman, 1, 26 October; latter includes "Oral Message" handed to the prime minister. See also James Eayrs, *Peacemaking and Deterrence*, 340–54; Pickersgill and Forster, eds. *The Mackenzie King Record*, Vol. 3, 362–63, 394. For Truman's suggestion of "civilian cover" see Public Records Office, UK, CAB 122/629, memo by Group Captain Braithwaite, "United States Air Bases in Canada."

34. Hillmer and Granatstein, *For Better or For Worse*, 168.

35. Canada, House of Commons, *Debates*, 12 February 1947, 343–48. For other details of the negotiations and debate, see Grant, *Sovereignty or Security?*, 178–87.

36. Andrew Richter, *Avoiding Armageddon: Canadian Military Strategy and Nuclear Weapons, 1950–63* (Vancouver: UBC Press, 2002), 23.

37. LAC, RG 2/18, Vol. 57, file A-25-5, memo "Northern and Arctic Projects," 28 January 1948; John C. Reed, "United States Arctic Exploration since 1939," in Herman R. Friis and Shelby G. Bale Jr., eds., *United States Polar Exploration* (Athens, OH: University of Ohio Press, 1970), 23–24; NA (Washington), RG 59, PJBD Series, Vol. 5, file "Correspondence—1954," notes on Canadian agreements and undertakings, dated 15 October 1954; and NA (Washington), Charles Hubbard Papers, RG 400-017, Vol. 5, see personnel lists and operating schedules in reports 1947–50.

38. As cited in Nigel Bankes, "Forty Years of Canadian Sovereignty Assertion in the Arctic, 1947–87," *Arctic* 40:4 (December 1987), 287, referencing Hansard, 1947 (2), 990.

39. NA (Washington), Hubbard Papers, RG 400-017, Vol. 5, file 8, "Analysis of Possible Arctic Operations May 1946 to July 1, 1947" and file 9 "Arctic Activities—Summer 1947." See also "Eureka High Arctic Weather Station Celebrates 60 Years Operation," *EnviroZine: Environment Canada's Online Newsmagazine*, 72 (14 May 2007).

40. Hubbard Papers, Vol. 5, file 9, "Arctic Activities—Summer 1947."

41. "Establishment of Joint Canadian-United States Meteorological Stations in the Canadian Arctic, 1947–49," *Polar Record*, 5:40 (July 1950), 602–5. See also LAC, RG 2/18, Vol. 57, file A-25-5, and Vol. 74, file D-19-2, reports dated December 1947, 28 January, 23 April, and 10 July 1948 (including map); and NA (Washington), RG 59 PJBD series, Vol. 10, "Weather Stations."

42. NA (Washington), RG 59, PJBD series, Vol. 7, file "Weather Stations," memo by Gen. Guy Henry to the PJBD, 14 February 1947, and PJBD to Henry, 6 May 1947, and Henry to S.F. Rae, 19 May 1947. See also LAC, RG 2/18, Vol. 57, file A-25-5, memo "Northern and Arctic Projects," 28 January 1948.

43. LAC, RG 2/18, Vol. 57, file A-25-5, Cabinet Document no. 588, 16 January 1928. See also Graham W. Rowley, "The Role of the Advisory Committee on Northern Development in the Development of Policy and the Coordination of Federal Government Activities in Northern Canada," March 1990, unpublished manuscript provided to the author.

44. For problems encountered by the committee during the first two years, see Grant, *Sovereignty or Security?*, 223–30.

45. NA (Washington), RG 59, PJBD series, Vol. 2, file "Fort Churchill—2," memos regarding Operation Beetle dated 9 April 1947 and 2 September 1947.

46. Ibid., Vol. 3, file "1949 Correspondence," report 23 June 1950; and copy of "Ottawa Report," *Montreal Standard*, 24 June 1950.

47. Joseph K. Jockel, *No Boundaries Upstairs: Canada, the United States and the Origins of North American Air Defence, 1945–1958* (Vancouver: UBC Press, 1987), 44–47, 91.

48. Paul Nesbitt, "A Short History of the Arctic, Desert, and Tropic Information Center," 135–40, in *United States Polar Exploration*, Herman R. Friis and Shelby G. Bale Jr. (Athens, OH: University of Ohio Press, 1970), 140–45; see also NA (Washington), RG 59, PJBD series, Vol. 11, file "July–December 1948 Correspondence," memo from Magann to Snow, 29 November 1948.

49. John Reed, "Arctic Explorations," 22–23, and Nesbitt, "A Brief History," 135–40, both in Friis and Bale, *United States Polar Exploration;* also "The Arctic Research Laboratory at Point Barrow, Alaska," *Polar Record*, 5:36 (December 1948), 211–12.

50. NA (Washington), RG 59, PJBD series, Vol. 2, file "Fort Churchill—2," memos regarding expansion, from 22 August 1946 through to 16 February 1952. Note memos dated 3 February, 14 May and 2 September 1947.

51. Ibid., Vols. 2-3 for additional files on Fort Churchill files. See also *Handbook for Range Users, no. 95, Churchill Research Range* (Ottawa: Queen's Printer, 1967), 1-2-1.

52. William S. Carlson, *Lifelines through the Arctic* (New York: Duell, Sloan and Pearse, 1962), 192–224.

53. Canada, Department of Mines and Resources, "Factual Record Supporting Canadian Sovereignty in the Arctic," 28 June 1949: 203–7 (leather-bound mimeograph copy); also Major J.M. Berry, "Royal Canadian Army Service Corps in Northern Trials and Operations," *Arctic Circular*, 4:1 (January 1951), 3–10.

54. "United States Task Force 'Frigid' 1947," *Polar Record* 5:34 (December 1947), 78; "United States Navy Experimental Training Cruise in Alaskan Waters," *Polar Record* 5:40 (July 1950), 619–20; and "Exercise Firestep," *Arctic Circular* 4:4 (April/May 1951), 63.

55. "Exercise Sweetbriar and Exercise Sun Dog I," *Arctic Circular* 3:3 (September 1950), 32–33.

56. Glines, *Bernt Balchen*, 213–23.

57. Carlson, *Lifelines*, 225–38; Ivan Papanin, *Life on an Ice Floe* (London: Hutchison and Company, 1940).

58. Carlson, *Lifelines*, 225–67; Reed, "Explorations," 26–28; and "United States Air Force Rescue Activities in Alaska," *Polar Record*, 6:41 (January 1951), 115–16; and NA (Washington), RG 59, PJBD Series, Vol. 5, file "Correspondence—54," see note 5 regarding "Beaufort Sea Expedition."

59. "Establishment of Joint Canadian-United States Meteorological Stations in the Canadian Arctic, 1947–49," *Polar Record*, 5:40 (July 1950), 602–5; also NA (Washington), Charles Hubbard Papers, RG 400-017, Vol. 5, file 11, "Report on Airlift Operations Spring 1950," 35.

60. Hubbard Papers, Vol. 5, file 11, "Report on Airlift Operations Spring 1950," 35–47.

61. "Aircraft Accident at Alert," *Arctic Circular* 3:4 (October 1950), 47–48.

62. Glines, *Bernt Balchen*, 217–22.

63. Ibid., 222–26; also Bach and Taagbolt, *Greenland and the Arctic Region*, 67.

64. Glines, *Bernt Balchen*, 228–29.

65. For precise details on the history of construction and operation of the Thule Air Base, refer to the Strategic Air Command website, www.strategic-air-command.com/bases/ThuleAFB.htm.

66. Ibid.; Carlson, *Lifelines*, 196–203; "United States Air Force Fact Sheet," 1012th Air Base Group, Thule Air Base, Greenland; and personal observation during visit to the base with a Canadian Institute of International Affairs study group tour in June 1984.

67. Jens Brosted and Mads Faegteborg, "Civil Aspects of Military Installations in Greenland," *Information North*, publication of the Arctic Institute of North America, (Winter 1986): 14–15. The official announcement claimed that the Inuit had wanted to move because the noise had caused game animals to disappear. Recent Danish studies have shown that they had been exceedingly reluctant to move.

68. From firsthand account in 1961 by Gene McManus, "BMEWS—510 Full Days" (1996) at www.bwcinet.com/thule/2thule.htm.

69. Joseph T. Jockel, *Security to the North: Canada-U.S. Defense Relations in the 1990s* (East Lansing, MI: Michigan State University Press, 1991), 24–25.

70. Jockel, *No Boundaries Upstairs*, 60–71.

71. NA (Washington), RG 59, PJBD Series, Vol. 12, file "Corres 1952—Sept.–Dec.," memo dated 13 November 1952 to Raynor and Peterson of the State Department from W.L. Wright, American secretary to PJBD.

72. LAC, A.G.L. MacNaughton Papers, MG 30 E 133, PJBD Series V, Vol. 294, file "Sovereignty in the Arctic, Part II Appendix," contains full copy of the report.

73. For full coverage of the documentation for discussions and events leading up to the Inuit relocations in 1953 and later, see Shelagh D. Grant, "Inuit Relocations to the High Arctic, Errors Exposed," Vol. 1, unpublished submission to the Royal Commission on Aboriginal Peoples, June 1993, copy available for reference from DIAND and Trent University. Note particularly annotated "Chronology of Documents." For shortened

version, see "A Case of Compounded Error: the Inuit Resettlement Project, 1953, and the Government Response, 1990," *Northern Perspectives* 19:1 (Spring 1991).

74. DCER for 1952, no. 745, memo from Dana Wilgress, Assistant Under-Secretary to Secretary of State for External Affairs, L.B. Pearson, 31 December 1952; also LAC, MG 30 E 133, Series V, Vol. 294, file "ACND to 1953," memorandum for the ACND from secretary Chipman, 8 May 1953.

75. LAC, MG 30 E 133, Series V, Vol. 294, file "ACND to 1953," Minutes of the meeting held on 11 May 1953, with separate document outlining terms of reference for the secretariat.

76. LAC, RG 2, Vol. 1894, file C-20-5, cabinet document 250-53, 26 October 1953; for the Prime Minister's announcement in Parliament, see Canada, House of Commons, *Debates 1953*, 698.

77. NA (Washington), RG 59, PJBD Series, Vol. 12, file "Correspondence 1954," memo from Canadian chair, A.G.L. McNaughton, 19 August 1954, and from U.S. secretary to U.S. chair, 27 August 1954.

78. For explicit details of the location, date of construction and responsibility for costs and operation of all three radar lines (Pinetree, Mid-Canada and DEW Line), see Roy J. Fletcher, "Military Radar Defence Lines in Northern North America," *Polar Record*, 26:159 (1990), 265–76.

79. Jockel, *No Boundaries Upstairs*, 71–90; Eayrs, *Peacemaking and Deterrence*, 360–67; Bankes, "Forty Years of Canadian Sovereignty," 287; also Jockel, *Security to the North*, 24–25; Glines, *Bernt Balchen*, 131.

80. NA (Washington), RG 59, PJBD Series, Vol. 5, file "Military Cooperation Committee," memo from U. S. Air Force to the MCC, 29 March 1954.

81. Jockel, *No Boundaries Upstairs*, 4–5, 117–29.

82. Ibid., 3, 5.

83. Aside from the Strategic Air Command website noted above, details of the satellite outposts, scientific research and all Greenland icecap activities are found in Charles M. Daugherty, *City Under Ice: The Story of Camp Century* (New York: Macmillan Company, 1962); Walter Wager, *Camp Century: City Under the Ice* (Philadelphia: Chilton, 1963); U.S. Army, *The Story of Camp Century: The City Under Ice* (film, 1961). For brief accounts see Carlson, *Lifelines*, 196–215; and Vaughan, *Northwest Greenland*, 145–50.

84. Vaughan, *Northwest Greenland*, 145.

85. Carlson, *Lifelines*, 201–2.

86. Erik D. Weiss, "Cold War Under the Ice: The Army's Bid for a Long-Range Nuclear Role, 1959–1963," *Journal of Cold War Studies*, 3:3 (Fall 2001): 31–58.

87. Carlson, *Lifelines*, 192–95; for updated version relating to the DEW Line and its modernization with the BMEWS and new defence technology, see John Honderich, *Arctic Imperative: Is Canada Losing the North?* (Toronto: University of Toronto Press, 1987), 102–15.

88. Gordon W. Smith, "Canada's Arctic Archipelago: 100 years of Canadian Jurisdiction," report prepared for the Department of Indian Affairs and Northern Development (Ottawa: 1980), 18, as cited in Bankes, "Forty Years of Canadian Sovereignty," 287.

89. McManus, "BMEWS—510 Full Days" (September 1996), introduction and epilogue.

90. Commander William R. Anderson USN, *Nautilus 90 North* (Cleveland and New York: World Publishing Company, 1959).

91. Jockel, *Security to the North*, 161.

92. Information obtained by author during visit in 1984, and verified on Thule Air Base website, www.thuleab.dk/index/.

93. Handout provided at the Thule Air Base during visit by author, 1984.

94. Jockel, *Security to the North*, 24–25; Fletcher, "Military Radar Defence Lines," 270–75; also Glines, *Bernt Balchen*, 231.

95. The full story of the crash and subsequent investigations is available in the BBC Archives, with the best summary provided by Gordon Corera, "Mystery of the Lost U.S. Nuclear Bomb" (10 November 2008) on BBC NEWS/Europe website.

96. For in-depth details of the debate, see Jørgen Dragsdahl, "A Few Dilemmas Bypassed in Denmark and Greenland," for the Peace Research Institute in Frankfurt (August 2005), and Hans M. Kristensen, "Secrecy on a Sliding Scale: U.S. Nuclear Weapons Deployments and Danish Non-Nuclear Policy," *Bulletin of the Atomic Scientists* (November–December 1999).

97. Copy of the 2004 "Agreement to Amend and Supplement the 1951 Agreement on the Defense of Greenland" is found on the official Denmark website: http//denmark.usembassy.gov/1951-agreement.html.

98. "Department of the U.S. Air Force Fact Sheet," www.elmendorf.af.mil/library/factsheets.

CHAPTER ELEVEN

1. L.B. Pearson, "Canada Looks 'Down North'," *Foreign Affairs* 24 (Winter 1945–46), 638–47.

2. Shelagh Grant, "Myths of the North in the Canadian Ethos," *The Northern Review*, 3/4 (Summer/Winter, 1989), 15–41; see also Carl Berger, "The True North Strong and Free . . . ," in Peter Russell, ed., *Nationalism in Canada* (Toronto: McGraw-Hill Ryerson, 1966); and W.L. Morton, *The Canadian Identity*, 2nd ed. (Toronto: University of Toronto Press, 1972).

3. For views expressed on Canadian northern development at the time, see Maxwell Cohen, "The Arctic and the National Interest," *International Journal*, 26 (1970–71); Peter Russell, ed., *Nationalism in Canada* (Toronto: McGraw-Hill, 1965); R. St. J. Macdonald, ed., *The Arctic Frontier* (Toronto: University of Toronto Press, 1966); David Judd, "Canada's Northern Policy: Retrospect and Prospect," *Polar Record*, XIV/92 (May 1969), 593–602; Franklyn Griffiths, *A Northern Foreign Policy*, Wellesley Papers no. 7 (Toronto: Canadian Institute of International Affairs, 1975); and Science Council of Canada, *Northward Looking: A Strategy and Science Policy for Northern Development* (Ottawa, 1977). For oil and gas development, see Robert Page, *Northern Development: The Canadian Dilemma* (Toronto: McClelland & Stewart, 1986). For environmental and aboriginal issues, see Roderick Nash, *Wilderness and the American Mind*, 3rd ed. (New Haven, CT: Yale University Press, 1982); Robert McPherson, *New Owners in Their Own Lands: Minerals and Inuit Land Claims* (Calgary: University of Calgary Press, 2003); and Peter Burnet, "Environmental Politics and Inuit Self-Government," in Franklyn Griffiths, ed., *Politics of the Northwest Passage* (Kingston/Montreal: McGill-Queen's University Press, 1987), 181–99.

4. Elizabeth B. Elliot-Meisel, *Arctic Diplomacy: Canada and the United States in the Northwest Passage* (New York: Peter Lang Publishing, 1998), 124–28; and Ann Hollick, *U.S. Foreign Policy and the Law of the Sea* (Princeton: Princeton University Press, 1981), 19. Henceforth,

all references to miles when defining limits of marine jurisdiction should be read as nautical miles.

5. The works of Donat Pharand are the most widely accepted Canadian sources for issues related to Canadian sovereignty over Arctic waters: see *The Law of the Sea of the Arctic with Special Reference to Canada* (Ottawa: University of Ottawa Press, 1973); *Canada's Arctic Waters in International Law* (Cambridge, UK: Cambridge University Press, 1988); and for a concise version "Canada's Jurisdiction in the Arctic," in Morris Zaslow, ed., *A Century of Canada's Arctic Islands* (Ottawa: Royal Society of Canada, 1991). For a broader study of the Law of the Sea as it affected all circumpolar countries, see Donald R. Rothwell, *The Polar Regions and the Development of International Law* (Cambridge, UK: Cambridge University Press, 1996), 155–400. Equally informative for specific issues related to the Northwest Passage, see Griffiths, ed., *Politics of the Northwest Passage*.

6. R.M. Logan, *Canada, the United States and the Third Law of the Sea Conference* (Montreal: C.D. Howe Research Institute, 1974); Ivan Head, "Canadian Claims to Territorial Sovereignty in the Arctic Regions," *McGill University Law Journal*, Vol. 9 (1963); and L.C. Green, "Canada and Arctic Sovereignty," *The Canadian Bar Review*, Vol. 43 (December 1970).

7. J.L. Granatstein, "A Fit of Absence of Mind: Canada's National Interest in the North to 1968," in E.J. Dosman, ed. *The Arctic in Question* (Toronto: Oxford University Press, 1976); and E.J. Dosman, *The National Interest* (Toronto: McClelland & Stewart, 1975).

8. P.S. Barry, *The Canol Project: An Adventure of the U.S. War Department in Canada's Northwest* (Edmonton: private printing, 1985).

9. Joseph E. LaRocca, *Alaska Agonistes: The Age of Petroleum* (Chapel Hill, NC: Professional Press, 2003).

10. Stephen Haycox, *Alaska: An American Colony* (Seattle: University of Washington Press, 2006), 279–80.

11. A detailed description of early oil and gas exploration in the Arctic Islands is found in Gordon H. Jones, "Economic Development: Oil and Gas" in Zaslow, ed., *A Century of Canada's Arctic Islands*, 221–30.

12. Peter Dobell, "The Influence of the U.S. Congress on Canadian-American Relations," in Fox et al., eds. *Canada and the United States*, 314. The term "Ottawa Mandarins" was coined by Jack Granatstein in *The Ottawa Men: The Civil Service Mandarins, 1935–1957* (Toronto: Oxford University Press, 1981). See also Allan Gotlieb and Charles Dalfen, "National Jurisdiction and International Responsibility: New Canadian Approaches to International Law," *American Journal of International Law*, 67:1 (April 1973), 236.

13. Canada, House of Commons *Debates* (20 December 1968), 4221.

14. Robert Page, "Norman Wells: The Past and Future Boom," *Journal of Canadian Studies*, 16:2 (Summer 1981), 21; Canada, Standing Committee of Indian Affairs and Northern Development, *Minutes of Proceedings and Evidence* (25 March 1969) 514–15 and (22 April 1969) 668; and Dosman, *The National Interest*, 35.

15. P.J. Capelotti, USCGR, *Across the Top of the World: The U.S. Coast Guard's 1957 Northwest Passage Expedition* (Washington, DC: USCG Historian's Office, 2007).

16. Ken S. Coates, P. Whitney Lackenbauer, William R. Morrison, and Greg Poelzer, *Arctic Front: Defending Canada in the Far North* (Toronto: Thomas Allen Publishers, 2008), 83–107.

17. Ivan Head and Pierre Trudeau, *The Canadian Way: Shaping Canada's Foreign Policy, 1968–1984* (Toronto: McClelland & Stewart, 1995), 32–34; Rothwell, *The Polar Regions*

and Development of International Law, 191–93; Canada, House of Commons, *Debates* (1969), 26 February, 5978; 27 February, 6045, 28 February, 6057 and 7 March, 6336.

18. As quoted in E.J. Dosman, "The Northern Sovereignty Crisis 1968–1979," in Dosman, *The Arctic in Question,* 48.

19. Dosman, *The National Interest,* 47; Canada, House of Commons, *Debates* (15 May 1969) 8720-22, and (June 1969) 10424-27.

20. A.H.G. Storrs and T.C. Pullen, "ss *Manhattan* in Arctic Waters," *Canadian Geographical Journal,* LXXX (May 1970), 172–79.

21. Dosman, *The National Interest,* 48–51; and K.M. M'Gonigle and M.W. Zacher, "Canadian Foreign Policy and the Control of Marine Pollution," B. Johnson and M.W. Zacher, eds., *Canadian Foreign Policy and the Law of the Sea* (Vancouver: UBC Press, 1977); and Canada, Speech from the Throne, 23 October 1969: 3.

22. John Kirton and Don Munton, "The *Manhattan* Voyages and Their Aftermath," in Griffiths, *Politics of the Northwest Passage,* 80–81; and for a detailed, yet concise, account of events before and after introduction of the Arctic Waters Pollution Prevention Act, see Ivan Head and Pierre Trudeau, *The Canadian Way,* 25–64.

23. As cited in Head and Trudeau, *The Canadian Way,* 55.

24. Subject of an unpublished graduate paper by Shelagh D. Grant, "Of Oil and Ships and Sealing Wax: The Arctic Waters Pollution Prevention Act in Retrospect," for Professors John W. Holmes and John Kirton (International Affairs Graduate Studies, University of Toronto, 1982).

25. Ibid., 67–97; also Dosman, *The National Interest,* 58–59; Canada, House of Commons *Debates* (16 April 1970), 5973 and Senate, *Debates* (1969–70), 1175, 1201ff., 1241–43, 1249.

26. K.M. M'Gonigle, "Unilateralism and International Law: The Arctic Waters Pollution Prevention Act," *University of Toronto Faculty of Law Review,* 34 (Summer 1976): 189. For American opinions, see B.K. Carnahan, "The Canadian Arctic Waters Pollution Prevention Act," *Louisiana Law Review,* 31 (1971), 632–49; and Richard Bilder, "The Canadian Arctic Waters Pollution Prevention Act: New Stresses on the Law of the Sea," *Michigan Law Review,* 69:1 (October 1971), 1–12.

27. Kirton and Munton, "The *Manhattan* Voyages," 90–91.

28. Ibid., 93–96.

29. Canada, *Foreign Policy for Canadians* (Ottawa: Queen's Printer, 1980), 5.

30. Peter C. Dobell, *Canada's Search for New Roles* (Toronto: Oxford University Press, 1972), 72; also J. Alan Beesley, "The Right and Responsibilities of Arctic Coastal Straits: The Canadian View," *Journal of Maritime Law and Commerce,* 3:1 (October 1971): 1–12; M'Gonigle, "Unilateralism," 189. Pharand, *Canada's Arctic Waters in International Law,* 192–94, 229–34.

31. Pharand, *Canada's Arctic Waters in International Law,* 234–36.

32. Rothwell, *The Polar Regions and the Development of International Law,* 182–83.

33. Jones, "Economic Development: Oil and Gas," 224–28.

34. Philip Lauritzen, *Oil and Amulets: A People United at the Top of the World,* English ed. (St. John's, NL: Breakwater Books, 1983), 43; Haycox, *Alaska,* 273–87; Olive Patricia Dickason, *Canada's First Nations: A History of Founding Peoples from the Earliest Times* (Toronto: Oxford University Press, 1996), 393.

35. Lauritzen, *Oil and Amulets,* 41–46; see also Hugh Gregory Gallagher, *Etok: A Story of Eskimo Power* (St. Petersburg, FL: Vandamere Press, 1997).

36. Lauritzen, *Oil and Amulets*, 41.

37. Haycox, *Alaska*, 290–301; Thomas R. Berger, *Village Journey: The Report of the Alaska Native Review Commission* (New York: Hill and Wang, 1985), 20–42; Peter A. Coates, *The Trans-Alaska Pipeline Controversy: Technology, Conservation, and the Frontier* (Bethlehem, PA: Lehigh University Press, 1991), 175–216, 228; and L.J. Clifton and B.J. Gallaway, "History of the Trans-Alaska Pipeline System" (15 February 2001), http://tapeis.anl.gov/.

38. Coates, *Trans-Alaska Pipeline*, 230, Clifton and Gallaway, "History," 1-3-1/2.

39. Dickason, *Canada's First Nations*, 404–5; Billy Diamond, "Aboriginal Rights: The James Bay Experience," Menno Boldt and J. Anthony Long, eds., *The Quest for Justice: Aboriginal Peoples and Aboriginal Rights* (Toronto: University of Toronto Press, 1985), 265–85; Page, *Northern Development*, 71–72. For detailed information, see Boyce Richardson, *Strangers Devour the Land*, rev. ed. (White Junction, VT: Chelsea Green Publishers, 2008).

40. Mary May Simon, *Inuit: One Future—One Arctic* (Peterborough, ON: Cider Press, 1996), 46–49, 73–85; also www.nunavikgovernment.ca/en/archives/history.

41. Peter Ittinuar, "The Inuit Perspective on Aboriginal Rights," in Boldt and Long, eds., *Quest for Justice*, 48–53.

42. Peter Burnet, "Environmental Politics and Inuit Self Government," in Griffiths, ed., *Politics of the Northwest Passage*, 181–83; McPherson, *New Owners*, 57–70.

43. Mr. Justice Thomas R. Berger, *Northern Frontier, Northern Homeland: The Report of the Mackenzie Valley Pipeline Inquiry*, Vols. 1, 2 (Toronto: James Lorimer & Company for Ministry of Supply and Services, 1977). Quotations found in Vol. 1, Chap. 1.

44. Kenneth M. Lysyk, *Alaska Highway Pipeline Inquiry* (Ottawa: Ministry of Supply and Services, 1977), vi–xvi, 3.

45. Donat Pharand, "The Arctic Waters in Relation to Canada," R. St. J. Macdonald et al., *Canadian Perspectives on International Law and Organization* (Toronto: University of Toronto Press, 1974), 434.

46. David Johnston, "International Environmental Law: Recent Developments and Canadian Contributions," Macdonald et al., *Canadian Perspectives*, 581; also Gotlieb and Dalfen, "National Jurisdiction," 243–44.

47. J. Alan Beesley in SCEAND, *Minutes of Proceedings*, no. 4 (22 November 1973): 8; Robert Page, "Norman Wells," 22; and R.B. Byers, "Sovereignty and Canadian Foreign Policy: The Need for Enforcement Capability," in Dosman, ed., *The Arctic in Question*, 61.

48. Brian Buzan and Barbara Johnson, "Canada at the Third Law of the Sea Conference: Strategy, Tactics and Policy," in Barbara Johnson and Mark Zacher, eds., *Canadian Foreign Policy and the Law of the Sea* (Vancouver: UBC Press, 1977), 159–61.

49. Donat Pharand, "Canada's Jurisdiction," 115; see also Griffiths, *A Northern Foreign Policy*, 31; and Barbara Johnson and Mark Zacher, "An Overview of Canadian Ocean Policy," in Johnson and Zacher, eds., *Canadian Foreign Policy*, 374.

50. Donald McRae, "Law of the Sea," *Canadian Issues: Canada and the Sea* 3:1 (Association for Canadian Studies, Spring 1980), 164.

51. Lauritzen, *Oil and Amulets*; Simon, *Inuit*, 13–44; Peter Jull, "Inuit Politics and the Arctic Seas," Franklyn Griffiths ed., *Politics of the Northwest Passage*, 63–76; see also "A Short Biography of the Honorable Eben Hopson," Eben Hopson Museum, Barrow, Alaska: http://www.ebenhopson.com.

52. Eben Hopson, Sr., "Welcoming Address, First Inuit Circumplar Conference, Barrow, Alaska 12–19 June 1977," *Arctic Policy Review* (North Slope Borough, June–July 1983), 2.

53. Lauritzen, *Oil and Amulets*, 24–27.

54. Ibid., 28.

55. For circumstances leading up to Greenland's Home Rule Government, see Lauritzen, *Oil and Amulets*, 223-29; for subsequent activities and events see Philip Lauritzen, *Highlights of an Arctic Revolution: The First 120 Months of Greenlandic Home Rule* (Nuuk, Greenland: Atuakkiorfik, 1989).

56. Canadian Energy Research Institute, "The Economics of High Arctic Gas Development: Expanded Sensitivity Analysis," for the Department of Indian and Northern Affairs, January 2005; Jennifer Lewington, "Lessons of the Arctic Pilot Project," in Griffiths, ed., *Politics of the Northwest Passage*, 163–80; also Lauritzen, *Highlights of an Arctic Revolution*, 47.

57. Pharand, "Canada's Jurisdiction," 125–27; Coates et al., *Arctic Front*, 113–19; see also Philip J. Briggs, "The *Polar Sea* Voyage and the Northwest Passage Dispute," *Armed Forces and Society*, 16:3 (1990), 437–52.

58. Donald M. McRae, "Arctic Sovereignty: Loss or Dereliction," *Northern Perspectives* (Toronto: Canadian Arctic Resources Committee, 2000).

59. Carrie E. Donovan, "The Law of the Sea Treaty," Web Memo #470, The Heritage Foundation (2 April 2004), http://www.heritage.org.

60. M.J. Dunbar, "The History of Oceanographic Research in the Waters of the Canadian Arctic," Zaslow, ed., *A Century of Canada's Arctic Islands*, 148–50; and in the same volume, Gordon H. Jones, "Economic Development: Oil and Gas," 229–30.

61. John Livingston, *Arctic Oil: The Destruction of the North?* (Toronto: Canadian Broadcasting Corporation, 1981), 75; "Black Gold: The Beaufort Oil Rush," *Northern Perspectives* VII: 6 (1980), 1; and "Arctic Oil Spills: Prospects for Disaster," IX: 4/5(1981).

62. Thomas R. Berger, *Village Journey: The Report of the Alaska Native Review Commission* (New York: Hill and Wang, 1989); also Peter Jull, "Inuit Politics," 46–47.

63. Department of Indian and Northern Affairs press release, "Government of Canada, Government of Nunvut and Nunavut Tunngavik Incorporated set Path for Nunavut Devolution" (5 September 2008), http://www.ainc-inac.gc.ca/.

64. Nunatsiavut Government, "Our Land" and "Nunatsiavut Government," http://www.nunatsiavut.com/en/.

65. Nunavik Government, "History and Documents," http://nunavikgovernment.ca/en/; and Inuit Tapiriit Kanatami, "Nunavik Inuit Sign Offshore Claims Agreement" (1 December 2006), http://www.itk.ca/media-centre/media releases/nunavik.

66. Simon, *Inuit*, 16–27. As former president and long-standing member of the ICC, Mary Simon describes in detail the achievements of the organization since its inception.

67. Aqqaluk Lynge, *Inuit: The Story of the Inuit Circumpolar Conference* (Nuuk, Greenland: Atuakkiorfik, 1996), 96, 98.

68. Simon, *Inuit*, 29–44; see also Inuit Circumpolar Conference, *Principles and Elements of a Comprehensive Arctic Policy* (Montreal/Kingston: McGill-Queen's University Press, 1992).

69. Simon, *Inuit*, 38.

70. For general history, see various reports on the Arctic National Wildlife Refuge by the U.S. Fish and Wildlife Service, and "The Oil and Gas Resource Potential of the Arctic National Wildlife Refuge 1002 Area, Alaska," U.S. Geological Survey for the Department of the Interior, 1999.

71. Letter by Mayor Edward S. Itta, http://www.co.north-slope.ak.us/.

72. Oran R. Young, *Arctic Politics: Conflict and Cooperation in the Circumpolar North* (Hanover, NH: University Press of New England, 1992), 38–39.

73. Shelagh Grant, "Cooperation, Deference, and Avoidance: Historical Trends in the East West Dynamic of Circumpolar Relations," in Björnsson et al., eds., *North Meets North: Proceedings of the First Northern Research Forum* (Iceland: Stefansson Arctic Institute and the University of Akureyri, 2000), 52.

74. *Arctic Pollution Issues: A State of the Arctic Environment Report* (Oslo: Arctic Monitoring and Assessment Programme, 1997).

75. Mark Nuttall, *Protecting the Arctic: Indigenous Peoples and Cultural Survival* (Amsterdam: Harwood Academic Publishers, 1998), 69.

76. "Speech Notes for Sheila Watt-Cloutier for the Conference of Parties to the United Nations Framework Convention on Climate Change," *Silarjualiriniq: Inuit in Global Issues,* 17 (July–December 2003), 3.

77. Jane George, "U.S. Backtracks on Climate Change Proposals," *Nunatsiaq News* (6 February 2004): 15; "ICC Chair Testifies in Washington," *Nunatsiaq News* (12 March 2004), 20.

PART IV

1. Thomas R. Hietala, *Manifest Design: American Exceptionalism & Empire*, revised edition (Ithaca, NY: Cornell University Press, 2003), 272.

CHAPTER TWELVE

1. Oran R. Young, *Arctic Politics: Conflict and Cooperation in the Circumpolar North* (Hanover, NH: University Press of New England, 2003), 29.

2. Most of the information on climate change and the accelerated warming trend in the Arctic is derived from NASA Earth Observatory studies, news reports and feature articles available at http://earthobservatory.nasa.gov/ and the major reports by the UN-sponsored Intergovernmental Panel on Climate Change, http://www.ipcc.ch/. For an excellent visual summary of the meltdown of Arctic ice, see "Twilight of the Arctic ice," map insert for the *National Geographic* (May 2009). Additional references below indicate information gathered from other sources.

3. "Thaw Point: Global Warming and the Permafrost," *Economist* (1 August 2009), 70, Jia Wang et al., "Is the Dipole Anomaly a Major Driver to Record Lows in Arctic Summer Ice Sea Extent?" *Geophysical Research Letters,* 36 (6 March 2009); Arctic Climate Impact Assessment (ACIA) report, "Impacts of a Warming Arctic," first presented in November 2004 and finalized in 2005; see also "Unprecedented Melt Sinks Hope for Arctic Ice Recovery," *Ottawa Citizen* (11 August 2008); David Ljunggren, "Arctic Ice Shelf Size of 2,500 Football Fields Breaks Off," *National Post* (29 July 2008).

4. "2008 Was Earth's Coolest Year Since 2000," Goddard Institute for Space Studies News Release, NASA Earth Observatory (23 February 2009), http://www.earthobservatory. nasa.gov/Newsroom/view.php; and "Satellites Show Arctic Literally on Thin Ice," NASA (6 April 2009), http://www.nasa.gov/topics/earth/features/arctic_thinice_prt.html.

5. Randy Boswell, "Climate Change, Melting Arctic Clearly Linked: Study," *National Post* (1 August 2008); Bob Weber, "Trouble Bubbling in the Arctic," *Toronto Star* (7 September 2009), A3.

6. Azedeh Ansari, "Climate Change Forces Eskimos to Abandon Village," CNN News (24 April 2009), www.cnn.com/2009/TECH/science/04/24/climate.change.eskimos/; Jane George, "Climate Change May Force Relocation of Salluit," *Nunatsiaq News* (24 July 2009), 15.

7. "Unprecedented Melt"; Jane George, "Hungry Orcas Gorge on Nunavut's Marine Mammals," *Nunatsiaq News* (20 March 2009), 5.

8. Stefan Milkowski, "Alaska Climate Impact Commission Issues Findings," *Fairbanks Daily News-Miner* (18 March 2008); copy of the report available at www.housemajority.org.

9. Inuit Circumpolar Council, "A Circumpolar Inuit Declaration on Sovereignty in the Arctic" (April 2009), available for download at http://www.itk.ca/circumpolar-inuit-declaration-arctic-sovereignty. See also Nancy MacDonald, "A New Gold Rush: For Greenland, Global Warming Spells an Era of Booming Growth," *Maclean's* (7 September 2009), 24; "Not a Barren Country: Rights of Arctic Peoples," *Economist* (18 July 2009), 57.

10. Martin Mittelstaedt, "Climate Change Could Mean a Walk in the Arctic Woods," *Globe and Mail* (17 April 2009), A6; Jonathon Gatehouse, "Plan B for Global Warming," *Maclean's*, 122:15 (27 April 2009), 40–41; Jill Mahoney, "The Most Radical Ideas on Earth Might Just Save It," *Globe and Mail* (4 September 2009), A3.

11. "Summary for Policy Makers," *IPCC Fourth Assessment Report* (17 November 2007), www.ipcc.ch/; also "Science Panel Calls Global Warming 'Unequivocal'," *New York Times* (3 February 2007).

12. "United Nations Framework Convention on Climate Change: Changes in GHG Emissions from 1990 to 2004," http://unfccc.int/files/essential_background/.

13. Environment Canada, "Canada's 2006 Greenhouse Gas Inventory," updated report (4 April 2009); see also Natural Resources Canada, "Canada's Energy Outlook: The Reference Case 2006" (14 December 2006).

14. Environment Canada, "A Climate Change Plan for the Purposes of the Kyoto Protocol Implementation Act—2007" (6 September 2007); see also United Nations, Kyoto Protocol, Enforcement Branch of the Compliance Committee, re: CC-N008-1-6/Canada/EB, "Decision Not to Proceed Further," 15 June 2008.

15. Environment Canada, "Canada's 2007 Greenhouse Gas Inventory: A Summary of Trends," www.ec.gc.ca/pdb/ghg/inventory_report/2007/.

16. Environment Canada, "Greenhouse Gas Emissions—Countries" (9 February 2009).

17. John M. Broder, "Democrats Unveil Climate Bill," *New York Times* (1 April 2009); see also "New Day Dawns for U.S. Global Warming Policy," *Environment News Service* (30 March 2009).

18. "House Proposal Has Tougher Emission Caps than Obama," *New York Times* (1 April 2009), http://www.nytimes.com/2009/04/01/us/politics/01energycnd. References to dissenting U.S. organizations appear in Leslie Kaufman, "Dissenter on Warming Expands His Campaign," *New York Times* (10 April 2009), A13; and "Waiting for the Other Shoe to Drop: The Second Big Bill Before Congress Is Also in Difficulties," *The Economist* (12 September 2009), 34.

19. James Hogan with contributions by Richard Littlemore, *Climate Cover-up: The Crusade to Deny Global Warming* (Vancouver, BC: Douglas & McIntyre, 2009).

20. Shawn McCarthy, "Canada Can Meet Its Climate Goals, But the West Will Write the Cheques," *Globe and Mail* (29 October 2009), A1.

21. B. Hollebone and M.F. Fingas, "Oil Spills in the Arctic: A Review of Three Decades of Research at Environment Canada," in W.F. Davidson, K. Lee and A. Cogswell, eds., *Oil Spill Response: A Global Perspective*, NATO Science for Peace and Security Series C: Environmental Security (Dordrecht, Netherlands: Springer Netherlands, 2008), 5–6.

22. Barry Scott Zellen, *Breaking the Ice: From Land Claims to Tribal Sovereignty in the Arctic* (Lanham, MD: Lexington Books, 2008), 127–33, 329; for the significance of the bowhead whale in Inupiat culture, see Peter Matthiessen, "Alaska: Big Oil and the Inupiat-Americans," *New York Review of Books*, 54:18 (22 November 2007).

23. Zellen, *Breaking the Ice*, 208–32; also www.irc.inuvialuit.com/, "Inuvialuit Self-Government" and "2008 Distribution Payments," and "Inuvialuit Self-Government Newsletter," with update on negotiations, 3:1 (June 2008).

24. Thomas R. Berger, "The Nunavut Project: Conciliator's Final Report" (1 March 2006), i, xi, xii; see also press release, "NTI Launches Lawsuit Against Government of Canada for Breach of Contract" (6 December), NR 06-24 ENG NLCA litigation doc.

25. Stephen Fottrell, "Inuit Survival Battle Against U.S. Base," BBC *News Online* (27 May 2004); see also the Inuit Circumpolar Council Executive Resolution 03-03, "RE: Recognizing the Inughuit as a Distinct Indigenous People of Greenland and Their Right to Return to Their Traditional Lands" (27 June 2003).

26. Col. Lee-Volker Cox, "Thule Air Base: Mysterious and Fascinating," *Thule Times*, 11 (April–May 2008), 1–3; "No Apology from Denmark," *Sermitsiaq Newsletter* (24 August 2009); Malcolm Gladwell, *The Tipping Point: How Little Things Can Make a Big Difference* (New York: Little, Brown & Company, 2002).

27. Information provided to author (6 April 2009) by Aqqaluk Lynge, President of ICC (Greenland) and Vice-President of the ICC International, and confirmed in "Greenland Introduces Self-Rule," *Sermitsiaq Newsletter* (22 June 2009).

28. Mark Nuttall, "Self-Rule in Greenland: Towards the World's First Independent Inuit State?" *Indigenous Affairs*, 3–4 (2008), 62.

29. Paul Brown, "Melting Ice Cap Brings Diamond Hunters and Hopes of Independence to Greenland," *The Guardian* (4 October 2007).

30. Statement by Motzfeld cited by Mark Nuttall in "Self-Rule in Greenland," 70; Aqqaluk's remarks appear in "Melting Ice Cap," *Guardian* (4 October 2007).

31. "Divorce Up North? Greenland Creeps Toward Independence," *Economist* (29 November 2008), 55.

32. Nuttall, "Self-Rule," 65–68.

33. Rosing's remarks appear in "Melting Ice Cap," (4 October 2007); Aqqaluk's comments in person to the author (6 April 2009).

34. Update on changes in development objectives appears in *Sermitsiaq Newsletter* (29 July 2008).

35. "Indigenous Summit Stalls on Climate Change," *Nunatsiaq News* (1 May 2009), 11; and "ICC Unveils Arctic Sovereignty Statement," *Nunatsiaq News* (1 May 2009), 10.

36. "Nunavut's First Gold Mine Races to Completion," *Nunatsiaq News* (14 August 2009); Peregrine Unearths Four More Kimberlites," *Nunatsiaq News* (14 August 2009); Lisa George, "A Mine Is a Terrible Thing to Waste," *Nunatsiaq News* (3 July 2009).

37. Thomas Courchene, "Whose North Is It?" *Globe and Mail* (30 July 2009), A15.

38. Ken S. Coates et al., *Arctic Front*, see Chap. 5, "The Final Race," 136–37.

39. Hans Corell, "The North Is Not the Wild West," *Globe and Mail* (28 April 2008), A15.

40. Paul Wells, "The Cold Truth: Why Harper's Tough Talk on Arctic Sovereignty Is Empty" (7 September 2009), 17–18; "Danish Sovereignty Enforced with Military Exercise," *Sermitsiaq News* (7 September 2009).

CHAPTER THIRTEEN

1. Admiral Nils C. Wang of the Danish Royal Navy, speaking at the conference "On Thin Ice: Climate Change and Arctic Security in the Twenty-First Century," sponsored by the Danish Institute of Military Studies, 23 September 2009 at Copenhagen, reported in "How We Ensure a Safe Arctic Region," *Sermitsiaq News* (27 September 2009).

2. "EU Eyes Arctic Resources," *Sermitsiaq News* (27 November 2008); see also website of the European Parliament, "Resolution on Arctic Governance," 9 October 2008.

3. Commission of the European Communities, "Communication from the Commission to the European Parliament and the Council on the European Union and the Arctic Region" (Brussels: 20 November 2008), 2–3. Information and quotations in next two paragraphs are from the same document, 3–8, http://ec.europa.eu/external_relations/arctic_region/docs/com_08_763_en.pdf.

4. Ibid., 10.

5. Ibid., 12.

6. The White House, Presidential Directives NSPD-66 / HSPD-25, "Subject: The Arctic Region" (9 January 2009), 2–10. Quotations cited in following paragraphs are all found in this document. See http://www.fas.org.irp.offsdocz/nspd/nspd-66.htm.

7. Ibid., 3.

8. "Harper Government Launches Public Relations Campaign," *Globe and Mail* (16 May 2009), A1.

9. *Canada's Northern Strategy: Our North, Our Heritage, Our Future* (DIAND 2009). Aside from the glossy format, the document and the list of commitments are also available on the web, www.northernstrategy.ca/nsc-eng.asp; "Canada Unveils Arctic Strategy," *CBC News* (26 July 2009); and "Arctic Expert Questions Canada's Northern Strategy," *CBC News* (28 July 2009).

10. As examples, see "Ottawa Boosts Arctic Strategy," *Globe and Mail* (27 July 2009), A1; "Danish Military Plans Raise Fears of Arctic Conflict," *Globe and Mail* (27 July 2009), A5; Chris Windeyer, *Nunatsiaq News* (31 July 2009), 3; Colin Alexander, "Harper's Northern Strategy Fails Northern People," *Nunatsiaq News* (28 August 2009), 11.

11. Jeffrey Simpson, "It's an Arctic Policy Worth Building On," *Globe and Mail* (31 July 2009), A13.

12. Jim Bell, "Mackay Unveils New Arctic Surveillance Aircraft," *Nunatsiaq News* (28 July 2009), 15; "Harper of the Melting North: The Prime Minister Tries to Marry Defence and Welfare," *Economist* (29 August 2009), 34.

13. The original Russian document is found at www.scrf.gov.ru./documents/98.html. Further details from a Russian perspective are found on the Russian News and Information website; see "Russia's Security Council Turns to the Arctic," *Novosti* (30 March 2009, http://en.rian.ru/russia/20090330/. See also Michael Schwirtz, "Russia: Arctic Deployment Planned," *New York Times* (28 March 2009) and Dmitry Solovyov, "Russian Arctic Forces Boost to Secure Vast Mineral Reserves," Reuters, Moscow (28 March 2009).

14. "Russia's New Arctic Force to Focus on Border Protection," *Novosti* (30 March 2009).

15. For example, see "Russia Won't Bully Canada in the Arctic, Cannon Vows," *Globe and Mail* (30 March 2009); similar headlines appeared in newspapers from coast to coast. The interview by Russian Ambassador Mamedov was watched by the author on CBC Newsworld, 9.38 PM, ET, on the same evening.

16. Inuit Circumpolar Conference (now Council), *Principles and Elements for a Comprehensive Arctic Policy* (Montreal/Kingston: McGill-Queen's University Press, 1992); a detailed description of the document also found in Mary May Simon, *Inuit: One Future—One Arctic* (Peterborough, ON: Cider Press, 1992), 29–44.

17. Franklyn Griffiths, "Canadian Arctic Sovereignty: Time to Take Yes for an Answer on the Northwest Passage," *Northern Exposure: Peoples, Powers, and Prospects for Canada's North* (Montreal: Institute for Research on Public Policy, 2009); and in the same volume, Rob Huebert, "Canada and the Changing International Arctic: At the Crossroads of Cooperation and Conflict." See also Michael Byers, *Who Owns the Arctic?* (Vancouver: Douglas & McIntyre, 2009); Donat Pharand, "Canada's Arctic Sovereignty and the Northwest Passage," *Meridian* (Spring/Summer 2009), 1–5; François Côté and Robert Dufresne, "The Arctic: Canada's Legal Claims," Library of Parliament Information Services, PRB0-05E (October 2008); Donald McCrae, "Arctic Sovereignty? What Is at Stake?" *Behind the Headlines,* 64 (January 2007); Terry Fenge and Tony Penikett, "The Arctic Vacuum in Canada's Foreign Policy," *Policy Options* (April 2009), 65–70.

18. Donald R. Rothwell, *The Polar Regions and the Development of International Law* (Cambridge, UK: Cambridge University Press, 1996), 188–200.

19. Øystein Jensen, "Arctic Shipping Guidelines: Towards a Legal Regime for Navigation Safety and Environmental Protection," *Polar Record,* 44:229 (April 2008), 107–14.

20. For example see Rob Huebert, "Canada and the Changing International Arctic"; Coates et al., *Arctic Front,* 203; McCrae, "Arctic Sovereignty?"18; Griffiths, "Canadian Arctic Sovereignty," 19–20; and Michael Byers, *Who Owns the Arctic?*

21. J.L. Granatstein, "Does the Northwest Passage Matter?" *Globe and Mail* (12 January 2009); also Rothwell, *The Polar Regions,* 457.

22. "Russia Prepares Law on Northern Sea Route," *Barents Observer* (13 February 2009), www.barentsobserver.com/russia/.

23. "New Icebreakers, Platform and Tankers for Russia," *Focus on Russia* (2 February 2009), www.focusonrussia.com/English/; and "Arctic Resource Policies in Russia," seminar sponsored by the Finnish Institute of International Affairs (3 March 2009).

24. Paul Koring, "U.S. and Canada Allies in Science, Rivals for Riches," *Globe and Mail* (29 July 2009), A11.

25. Anna Mehler Paperny, "Fisheries Conservation Plan Stirs up the Waters," *Globe and Mail* (29 July 2009), A11.

26. Randy Boswell, "Hans Island Was Ours First, Greenland Says," *Ottawa Citizen* (18 December 2008).

27. Scott Borgerson and Caitlyn Antrim, "An Arctic Circle of Friends," *New York Times* (28 March 2009), A17.

28. Adam Lajeunesse, "Sovereignty, Security and the Canadian Nuclear Submarine Program," *Canadian Military Journal* (Winter 2007–8), 78–81.

29. "Aariak Tables GN's Five-year Vision Statement: Government Stresses Basic Needs," *Nunatsiaq News* (3 April 2009), 13.

30. Barry Scott Zellen, *Breaking the Ice: From Land Claims to Tribal Sovereignty in the Arctic* (Lanham, MD: Lexington Books, 2008), 329–30.

31. "Appeals Court Cancels Alaskan Offshore Drilling Program," *The Kingston Whig Standard* (19 April 2009).

32. "Ottawa Awards BP $1.3B in Exploration Permits in Beaufort Sea," CBC *Evening News* (9 June 2008).

33. Canadian Energy Research Institute, "The Economics of High Arctic Gas Development: Update" (January 2005), 1.

34. Canada, "Agreement between the Government of Canada and the Government of the United States on Arctic Cooperation," Canada Treaty Series, 1988/29.

35. "The Coast Guard in Canada's Arctic," (June 2008) and "Rising to the Arctic Challenge," (May 2009), interim reports tabled by the Standing Senate Committee on Fisheries and Oceans.

36. "Canada's Arctic Waters: Role of the Canadian Coast Guard," final report by Standing Senate Committee on Fisheries and Oceans (December 2009).

SELECTED BIBLIOGRAPHY

. . . .

IN ADDITION to references in the endnotes, the following is a
selection of relatively recent publications available in libraries or
bookstores and other sources that provide more in-depth analysis of the many issues touched on in this book. For information on
recent events, press releases and official documents, the best sources
are official government websites, along with those of the Arctic
Council, Inuit Tapiriit Kanatami and the Inuit Circumpolar Council.
Media archives are available online for the CBC, the BBC, Canada's
Globe and Mail and *National Post*, the *New York Times* and London's *Times*
and *Guardian*. Coverage of current local news is easily accessed on
the Web from Nunavut's *Nunatsiaq News*, Greenland's *Sermitsiaq News*
and a number of Alaskan newspapers. Two other sources of particular significance are the Canadian Library of Parliament, which
provides updated reports on the status and chronology of events
for Arctic sovereignty, and the *Canadian American Strategic Review*
(CASR), which offers detailed descriptions of current military status
and procurements of the circumpolar countries. For accurate and
updated scientific reports on climate change, see the 2004 report
of the UN-sponsored Intergovernmental Panel on Climate Change,
http://www.ipcc.ch/, and its four-part compendium published in
2009. An additional source for recent scientific data is the NASA
Earth Observatory website, http://earthobservatory.nasa.gov/arctic/.

The following is by no means a comprehensive list, but one that
provides a variety of interesting reading.

Interpreting History

Wade Davis, *The Wayfinders: Why Ancient Wisdom Matters in the Modern World* (Toronto: House of Anansi Press, 2009). A compelling argument why our present way of life falls short of human potential.

Margaret MacMillan, *The Uses and Abuses of History* (Toronto: Penguin Canada, 2008), offers important insights into how history should and should not be used to examine current situations—critical for anyone reading or writing history.

John Ralston Saul, *The Unconscious Civilization,* reprint (Toronto: Anansi Press, 2008). Winner of the Governor General's Award, this insightful book provides a compelling argument on how corporatism developed a stranglehold on many Western democracies—a must-read.

Ronald Wright, *An Illustrated Short History of Progress* (Toronto: Anansi Press, 2006). A stimulating discourse that relates the rise and fall of past civilizations with a look to the future.

Arctic History

Lydia T. Black, *Russians in Alaska, 1732–1867* (Fairbanks: University of Alaska Press, 2004). An exceptionally well-researched history of Russian settlements in Alaska and events leading up to purchase by the United States.

Shelagh D. Grant, *Arctic Justice: On Trial for Murder, Pond Inlet, 1923* (Montreal/Kingston: McGill-Queen's University Press, 2002). An unusual sequence of events illustrates the difficulties of administering justice in the Arctic Islands to ensure Canada was fulfilling the criteria required to secure its title to the Arctic Islands .

Stephen Haycox, *Alaska: An American Colony* (Seattle: University of Washington Press, 2002). A well-grounded and detailed history of Alaska from the Russian era to the 1990s.

Robert McGhee, *The Last Imaginary Place: A Human History of the Arctic World* (Toronto: Key Porter, 2005). An excellent history of the circumpolar world told in the context of an archaeologist's own work and travels throughout the Arctic—another must-read.

Michael F. Robinson, *The Coldest Crucible: Arctic Exploration and American Culture* (Chicago: University of Chicago Press, 2006). A critical insight into the effect of polar exploration on American culture.

Marjolaine Saint-Pierre, author, translated by William Barr, *Joseph-Elzéar Bernier 1852–1934: Champion of Canadian Arctic Sovereignty* (Montreal: Baraka Books, 2009). At last, a full-length biography of the first Canadian assigned the task of asserting Arctic sovereignty.

Kirsten A. Seaver, *The Frozen Echo: Greenland and the Exploration of North America ca A.D. 1000–1500* (Stanford, CA: Stanford University Press, 1996). This expansive study of early Norse settlement in Greenland offers some controversial conclusions.

Richard Vaughan, *The Arctic: A History,* rev. ed. (Gloucestershire, UK: History Press, 2008). An exceptional history of the circumpolar world filled with precise details, maps and illustrations not readily available elsewhere. Equally important is Vaughan's *Northwest Greenland: A History* (Orono, ME: University of Maine Press, 1991).

Glyn Williams, *Arctic Labyrinth: The Quest for the Northwest Passage* (Toronto: Viking Canada, 2009). This recent contribution to the history of Arctic exploration is comprehensive, well-illustrated and supported by exemplary research.

Arctic Sovereignty

Michael Byers, *Who Owns the Arctic? Understanding Sovereignty Disputes in the North* (Vancouver: Douglas & McIntyre, 2009), by the Canada Research Chair in Global Politics and International Law at the University of British Columbia. This book is written with candour and designed to dispel confusion surrounding current Arctic sovereignty issues.

Ken S. Coates, P. Whitney Lackenbauer, William R. Morrison and Greg Poelzer, *Arctic Front: Defending Canada in the Far North* (Toronto: Thomas Allen Publishers, 2008), written by three historians and a political scientist. This critical examination of the Canadian government's policies in the Arctic and Subarctic is well worth reading.

Arctic Anthropology and Archaeology

Hugh Brody, *The Other Side of Eden: Hunters, Farmers and the Shaping of the World* (New York: North Point Press, 2001). Fascinating analyses of Inuit and other hunting cultures compared to early European settlers.

Robert McGhee, *Ancient People of the Arctic* (Vancouver: UBC Press, 1997). A well-illustrated history of the migrations and culture of the Palaeo-Eskimos in the North American Arctic.

David Morrison and Georges-Hébert Germain, *Inuit: Glimpses of an Arctic Past* (Hull, QC: Canadian Museum of Civilization, 1995). This handsomely illustrated book focuses on the history of the Copper Inuit in the central Arctic.

Peter Schledermann, *Voices in Stone: A Personal Journey into the Arctic Past* (Calgary: University of Calgary Press, 1996), places Dorset and Thule archaeological findings within the narrative of his own experiences; an enjoyable read with interesting photographs.

Climate Change

Alun Anderson, *After the Ice: Life, Death and Geopolitics in the New Arctic* (New York: HarperCollins, 2009). With a background in biology and science journalism, Anderson examines the winners and losers in the rapidly changing Arctic by combining history of science, politics and business.

Al Gore, *Our Choice: A Plan to Solve the Climate Crisis* (Emmaus, PA: Rodale, 2009). This time without exaggeration, the latest work by former vice-president Gore focuses more on the means available to address the problem and is illustrated by an exceptional collection of photographs.

James Hoggan with contributions by Richard Littlemore, *Climate Cover-up: The Crusade to Deny Global Warming* (Vancouver: Douglas & McIntyre, 2009). An insider's view of how the energy industry fuelled a phony debate on climate change.

Henry Pollack, *A World Without Ice* (New York: Avery Publishers, 2009).
This compelling argument by a renowned scientist affirms the consensus
view that climate change is not only real but has a potential for catastrophic
consequences.

The North in Canadian Identity

Sherrill Grace, *Canada and the Idea of North* (Montreal/ Kingston:
McGill-Queen's University Press, 2002). An outstanding study of literature,
film and art, which reveals how Canadians have integrated the North
into their identity.

Renée Hulan, *Northern Experience and the Myths of Canadian Culture*
(McGill-Queen's University Press, 2003). In contrast to Grace's book,
Hulan offers a convincing and sometimes disquieting argument that
questions whether Canada is truly a northern nation and Canadians
a northern people. The two should be read together.

Canadian Politics and Government

Michael Byers, *Intent for a Nation: A Relentless Optimistic Manifesto for
Canada's Role in the World* (Vancouver: Douglas & McIntyre, 2007). Note
especially Chap. 6 "Climate Change," Chap. 7 "A True North Strong
and Free" and Chap. 8 "Canada-U.S. Military Relations."

Donald J. Savoie, *Governing from the Centre: The Concentration of Power in
Canadian Politics* (Toronto: University of Toronto Press, 1999). A critical
perspective which should be read in conjunction with the same author's
*Court Government and the Collapse of Accountability in Canada and the United
States* (Toronto: University of Toronto Press, 2008).

American Foreign Policy

Gail Osherenko and Oran R. Young, *The Age of the Arctic: Hot Conflicts and
Cold Realities* (Cambridge, UK: Cambridge University Press, 2005). An
American perspective on the many influences affecting military, economic,
social and political actions in the Arctic, calling for the creation of an
International Arctic Science Committee.

Walter LaFeber, *The American Age: United States Foreign Policy at Home and Abroad 1750 to the Present, volumes 1 and 2, 2nd edition* (New York: W.W. Norton & Co., 1994). This classic, now updated to the 1900s, is very readable and yet comprehensive, analytical and highlighted with political cartoons—an excellent introduction to the history of American foreign policy.

Stephen R. Weissman, *A Culture of Deference: Congress's Failure of Leadership in Foreign Policy* (New York: Basic Books, 1995). A disquieting insight into the influence of lobbyists and self-interest groups on Congressional decisions related to foreign affairs.

Canadian-American Relations
Elizabeth B. Elliot-Meisel, *Arctic Diplomacy: Canada and the Northwest Passage* (New York: Peter Lang, 1998). An unbiased interpretation of events, supported by impeccable research.

Nancy Fogelson, *Arctic Exploration & International Relations, 1920–1932* (Fairbanks: University of Alaska Press, 1992). A detailed study of Canadian and American competing interests in the Arctic and diplomatic initiatives during the first quarter of the 20th century.

Norman Hillmer and J.L. Granatstein, *For Better or Worse: Canada and the United States in the Twenty-First Century,* 2nd ed. (Toronto: Nelson Education Publishers, 2006). An excellent narrative of events and consequences of Canadian-American relations, particularly during World War II and the Cold War.

Arctic Security
Joseph T. Jockel, *Security to the North: Canada-U.S. Defense Relations in the 1990s* (East Lansing, MI: Michigan State University Press, 1991). An American perspective on Canada-U.S. military cooperation in the Arctic.

Andrew Richter, *Avoiding Armageddon: Canadian Military Strategy and Nuclear Weapons, 1950–63* (Vancouver: UBC Press, 2002). Historical review of the Cold War years from a Canadian viewpoint.

Senator Bill Rompkey, Chair, *Canada's Arctic Waters: Role of the Canadian Coast Guard*, Report of the Standing Senate Committee on Fisheries and Oceans (Ottawa: Government Publishing, December 2009). An extensive survey of Canada's coast guard capabilities and sovereignty-related issues, with recommendations that include temporarily arming the ice breakers until patrol ships are available to enforce Canadian regulations.

International Law

Antony Anghie, *Imperialism, Sovereignty and the Making of International Law* (Cambridge, UK: Cambridge University Press, 2005). A broad international perspective on the evolution of international law resulting from wars and imperialism.

Michael Byers, *Custom, Power and the Power of Rules* (Cambridge, UK: Cambridge University Press, 1999), argues that international law is primarily driven by world powers, most recently by the United States.

L.C. Green and Olive P. Dickason, *The Law of Nations and the New World* (Edmonton: University of Alberta Press, 1989). Best overall history on how European laws affected indigenous peoples of the New World.

Donald R. Rothwell, *The Polar Regions and the Development of International Law* (Cambridge, UK: Cambridge University Press, 1996). Valuable source for a factual history of events related to the Arctic and Antarctic regions, concluding with the impact of polar regions on the evolution of international law.

Matthew N. Shaw, *International Law*, 5th ed. (Cambridge, UK: Cambridge University Press, 2003). An encyclopaedic reference work covering anything one might wish to know about the history and current status of international law.

Inuit Culture and Aboriginal Rights

Erik Anderson, ed., *Canada's Relationship with Inuit: A History of Policy and Program Development* (Ottawa: Indian Affairs and Northern Development, 2009). A government publication which provides accurate details of various Inuit land claims agreements.

Natalia Loukacheva, *The Arctic Promise: Legal and Political Autonomy of Greenland and Nunavut* (Toronto: University of Toronto Press, 2007). A well-researched history of the Inuit struggle for recognition of their aboriginal rights to self-government in Canada and Greenland.

Robert MacPherson, *New Owners in Their Own Land: Minerals and Inuit Land Claims* (Calgary: University of Calgary Press, 2003). A detailed narrative of Inuit success in gaining ownership and co-management rights to lands with mineral potential.

Mark Nuttall, *Protecting the Arctic: Indigenous Peoples and Cultural Survival* (New York: Routledge, 1998). An in-depth study of the effect of the modern world on Inuit culture in Greenland.

Barry Scott Zellen, *Breaking the Ice: From Land Claims to Tribal Sovereignty in the Arctic* (Lanham, MD: Lexington Books, 2008). A detailed narrative of Inuit and northern Amerindians' struggle for control over their traditional lands and rights to self-government in Alaska and northern Canada.

INDEX

. . . .

MICHAEL CULLEN

SHELAGH D. GRANT is the author of the award-winning *Arctic Justice: On Trial for Murder, Pond Inlet, 1923; Sovereignty or Security? Government Policy in the Canadian North, 1936–50*; a history of Mittimatalik (Pond Inlet) translated into Inuktitut; and numerous scholarly articles on related topics. She is an adjunct professor in the Canadian Studies Program and a research associate of the Frost Centre at Trent University. She lives with her family in Peterborough, Ontario.